THE WYCLIFFE HANDBOOK OF PREACHING AND PREACHERS

THE WYCLIFFE HANDBOOK OF PREACHING AND PREACHERS

by

Warren W. Wiersbe

and

Lloyd M. Perry

MOODY PRESS

CHICAGO

© 1984 by
THE MOODY BIBLE INSTITUTE
OF CHICAGO

ISBN: 0-8024-0328-X

1 2 3 4 5 6 7 Printing/AH/Year 89 88 87 86 85 84

Printed in the United States of America

Acknowledgments

Over the years we have appreciated the encouragement and assistance given by many friends and colleagues as we have studied preachers and preaching, done some preaching ourselves, and taught courses in this field. We are only too happy to acknowledge their help, and we say *thank you* to:

David A. Simmons, a former student at Trinity Evangelical Divinity School, whose paper on "Sermonic Style" has been valuable to us in writing this book;

many other students and graduate assistants whose criticisms, suggestions, and even mistakes helped us sharpen our focus and raise our standards;

various professors and instructors, particularly Dr. Charles W. Koller and Dr. Faris D. Whitesell;

professional colleagues in the field of preaching and practical theology, particularly Dr. Richard A. Bodey who read the entire manuscript and helped us to improve it considerably;

patient parishioners who listened to us preach and helped us to realize that it is really worth it all;

our wives and families, our most encouraging listeners and our best critics!

Also, we gratefully acknowledge our indebtedness to two well-known volumes long out of date: *Lectures on the History of Preaching* by John A. Broadus (New York: Armstrong, 1893) and *The Art of Preaching in the Light of History* by Edwin Charles Dargan (New York: George H. Doran, 1922).

Warren W. Wiersbe
Lloyd M. Perry

Contents

Part 4
AN ILLUSTRATIONAL PERSPECTIVE

Introduction

One way of learning to preach is to study the preaching of others. Such a method might include a study of the history of preaching, reading published sermons, and listening to other preachers. Experts in public speaking in the secular field have advocated a similar approach in developing skill in oral communication.

Gerald Ray Jordan, in his book *You Can Preach,* says: "The fact that many preachers do not diligently study the history of preaching is a major reason for so many failures in the pulpit."[1]

Dr. Andrew Blackwood, in his book *The Preparation of Sermons,* said:

> Ideally every minister ought to know something about homiletics and more about the art of preaching, but he should think most of all about the sermon. He ought to look on himself not as a scientist with a massive knowledge or an artist with a gift of appreciation, but as a preacher with an ability to prepare all sorts of sermons. In order to do such work again and again he ought to study the sermons of other men and then form habits all his own.[2]

In *Sermons Preached Without Notes,* Charles Koller wrote: "This volume of sermons has a two-fold purpose. First, there is the obvious purpose of communicating Biblical Truth to bless the lives of the readers. Beyond this, it is hoped that ministers of the Gospel will find these sermons helpful from a structural point of view and for illustrative material."[3]

James Hoppin, in the *The Office and Work of the Christian Ministry,* said that the preacher, especially the young preacher, should strive to comprehend and combine the excellence of the different kinds of preaching of all times and ages and to enrich and elevate his own preaching by imitating what is good in them.

Robert Dabney encouraged his students to read sermons written by Samuel Davies,

1. Gerald Ray Jordan, *You Can Preach* (New York: Revell, 1951), 46.
2. Andrew W. Blackwood, *The Preparation of Sermons* (Nashville: Abingdon-Cokesbury, 1948), 20.
3. Charles Koller, *Sermons Preached Without Notes* (Grand Rapids: Baker, 1964), 7.

John Mason, and Robert South because he felt that those men were masters of sermonizing. Henry Graves felt that his students should read the sermons of Beecher, Brooks, Spurgeon, and Maclaren for the same reason.

Arthur Hoyt, in *The Work of Preaching,* recommended that the preacher select one or two men who in some way especially spoke to him. He should make those preachers his companions by reading all that he could about them and what they had written. Thus he would be encouraged to think their thoughts, speak their language, and receive the impression of their personalities. Hoyt felt those selected homiletical companions would become a source of profitable guidance for the preacher toward the improvement of his own presentation.[4]

Church Father Augustine wrote in *On Christian Doctrine* that speaking is best learned by studying Christian speakers and that good style in preaching is more caught that taught, which is accomplished by exposure to the great speakers. (Incidentally, this work by Augustine was the last significant homiletical work for seven hundred years.)

John Witherspoon, in his lectures on moral philosophy, eloquence, and divinity, said that the best form of training is a wise study and *imitation of great models*. This same advice was shared by Edward Tyrell Channing, who occupied the famous Boylsten Chair of Rhetoric at Harvard University.

Benefits of Studying Sermons

One benefit derived from sermon study is the development and enrichment of the preacher's own devotional life. Another is seeing how others have successfully communicated the gospel. Sermon study is helpful in providing guidance in formulating homiletical patterns. The sermonizer will also glean helpful insights into biblical interpretation. Subject matter and methodology can often be gained as profitably from good sermons as from other sources.

Many are opposed to reading sermons of others for fear that it will stifle their own creativity. Actually, there are few original thinkers. Most preachers select their subject matter from a variety of sources, including the work of others.

Let a sermonizer read all he can from every source available. By sharing the ideas of great preachers of the past, the preacher can provide additional blessings for his congregation. Most church members are not given to this kind of reading. An honest sermonizer will be perfectly willing to let his people know that he read some books in preparing his message and will have no hesitancy in giving due credit.

In studying the sermons of the past, the present-day sermonizer should realize that the historical context in which a sermon is written and presented has a significant bearing on its content and application. The same warning applies to the adaptation of sermon structures from the past. Listening habits have changed; the sermonizer must recognize that and adapt his sermonic structure accordingly.

Sermons are not preached in general, but for particular people with particular needs in particular places. Preparation for preaching must include not only basic homiletical skills, but a knowledge of and a concern for the elements in society that affect the listeners.

4. Arthur S. Hoyt, *The Work of Preaching* (New York: Macmillan, 1918), 61.

What is good preaching? The members of the congregation answer that question in terms of the sermon that meets their needs.

Preaching serves to fulfill the church's responsibility for communication. Its function is to explain the gospel to the church and share it with those outside the church. Preaching is inherent in the nature of the church and the church preaches to fulfill its mission. The proclamation (*kerygma*) and the teaching (*didachē*) are both a part of the preaching function of the church. Both are suitable, but under different conditions.

After salvation there is a need for indoctrination (Eph. 4:14), consecration (Rom. 12:1), inspiration (Neh. 8:10), comfort (1 Thess. 4:18), strengthening (Col. 1:11), conviction (Acts 4:20), and action (James 1:22).

The sermonizer desiring to study the sermons of others is faced with a dilemma. Many preachers over many years in many denominational groups have used many methods with many points of strength and weakness. The authors of this volume have taken both a telescopic and a microscopic look at preaching and preachers. Perhaps this survey will help solve that dilemma.

Part 1
A CHRONOLOGICAL PERSPECTIVE

1

A General Historical Survey of the Art of Preaching

The history of Christian preaching may be divided chronologically into nine periods. These divisions are indicated in the following chart.

Chronological Table of Preaching

Period	Dates
Apostolic	4 B.C.-A.D. 69
Patristic	70-430
Early Medieval	430-1095
Central Medieval	1095-1361
Reformatory	1361-1572
Early Modern	1572-1789
Late Modern	1789-1900
Contemporary	1900-present

APOSTOLIC PERIOD

The *apostolic period* included the preaching of Jesus and the apostles. Albert Bond, in *The Master Preacher,* his work on the homiletics of Jesus, suggested that the preaching of Jesus was characterized by simplicity, picturesqueness, versatility, practicality, optimism, a tone of authority, and above all else, the use of Scripture.

The preaching of the apostles was what we would call *occasional* preaching, because it consisted largely of messages addressed to specific, special occasions. It intermingled doctrine and ethics, and there was a noticeable absence of political and social concern. It had a wide diversity in content and form, yet it contained a prevailing unity.

Apostolic preaching included dialogical presentations in the synagogues and consisted of less variety than the preaching of Jesus.

There were challenges to follow the personal example of the messenger. The chronological pattern of apostolic preaching first involved the entrance into a new city or area of need. Then came a demonstration of the power of God in a sign miracle. The third stage of the pattern involved the proclamation of the Word of God. That was not always preceded by a sign miracle. Finally, a concentration of the believers and follow-up took place.

Kerr suggests that the preaching of the apostles may be classified in two ways: missionary, which involved the preaching of the gospel; and pastoral, which involved the building up of individuals in the faith.

Patristic Period

The preaching of the patristic age was influenced by the example and teaching of the apostles, the humble circumstances of the early believers, and the philosophy and wisdom of the age.

The first twelve chapters of the book of Acts describe the history of the Christian movement during the first fifteen years after Christ's death and resurrection. The Holy Spirit was given in accordance with the promise of Christ, providing power for witnessing in a hostile world, bringing the presence of Christ for fellowship and strength, and giving leadership from Christ in the initiation of important movements. At Pentecost, men from every part of the world were saved and doubtless went back to their own cities to establish Christian churches. Persecution, want, and internal bickering were only temporary hurdles to jump (Acts 3-6).

The martyrdom of Stephen marked a turning point in two respects: (1) it began the persecution that drove the Christians out of Jerusalem into all Judea and Samaria to be witnesses; and (2) it profoundly moved Saul the persecutor in the direction of personal conversion to Christ. The local witness was expanded by the preaching of Peter to a Gentile, the founding of the Gentile church at Antioch, and the martyrdom of James, son of Zebedee. The conversion of Saul, his preparation for service, and his ministry at Antioch provide the background for the second stage of Christian development.

Under the leadership of the Holy Spirit a new direction of witnessing began with the inauguration of the missionary tours of Paul and Barnabas.

The functioning New Testament church showed no signs of developing into an ecclesiastical hierarchy of spiritual despotism. It was a local autonomous body with two classes of officers and two ordinances. The two officers were those of pastor (sometimes called bishop, presbyter, elder, or shepherd) and deacon. Those leaders usually worked with their hands for their material needs. There was no artificial distinction between clergy and laity.

Despite its remarkable growth, Christianity was not a popular movement in the second century. Its character, so altogether different from anything known by the people of the Roman Empire, made it an object of suspicion and hate. That opposition to Christianity took three general forms: popular antagonism, intellectual assaults, and physical persecution.

The period from A.D. 70 to 430 has been designated as the *patristic period* for preaching. Within that broad expanse of time two clearly marked periods are discernible: 70 to 300 and 300 to 430.

The first was a time of great crisis. The fall of Jerusalem, the expansion of the Roman Empire, and the persecutions of the Christians profoundly influenced preaching during that period.

For about one hundred years following the death of Peter and Paul (c. 70 to 170), we find few remaining traces of the preaching. Near the end of the second century in the work of Origen, Clement of Alexandria, Irenaeus, and Hippolytus, there is clear evidence of an increase in the power of preaching.

Three sources supplied sermonic content for the preachers: apostolic tradition, the Bible, and the preacher's own personal contributions. The form of sermons of that period was the homily (unpretentious address) or simply a running commentary on Scripture.

Preaching of the early patristic period had less spiritual power and was more impersonal than that of the apostolic period, as time separated the minister from Christ. Such preaching was also quite unstable as preachers waxed hot and cold.

On the positive side, preaching was successful because of the *natural* power of the gospel. In addition, several external factors aided Christianity. The Roman world was at peace; communication lines were open; old Greco-Roman religions were disintegrating; preachers were faithful to their task of preaching; and because they were free from professionalism, their preaching was simple and direct. For 400 years the Christian church had no great preacher by rhetorical standards. The first great preacher was Chrysostom. Yet during those centuries, Christianity conquered the Mediterranean world by the faithful witness of the common believer.

The period from A.D. 300 to 430 saw a remarkable rise in the power of preaching. This is one of the five climactic periods in the history of Christian preaching.

Governmental help and blessing, social prestige, the people's love for oratory, education, and excellent schools played prominent roles in advancing preaching to new heights. Within Christianity, more form in sermons, a closed canon, more biblical preaching, a more orderly worship service, stability of doctrines, and the culture and training of preachers added luster to the pulpit. The great preachers during this period were Basil the Great, Gregory of Nazianzus, Gregory of Nyssa, Chrysostom, Hilary, Ambrose, and Augustine.

A more systematic form of address developed as the homily, which had been an informal kind of message, took on the characteristics of a more formalized kind of structure. The content of sermons took on more of the flavor of expressing public opinion rather than the direct proclamation of the Word of God. There were the apostolic Fathers Polycarp, Ignatius, and Clement of Rome, and the apologists Justin Martyr and Tertullian. Two groups of Ante-Nicene Fathers formed the Western group, including Irenaeus, Hippolytus, and Cyprian, and the Eastern group, including Clement of Alexandria and Origen. The general group of church Fathers included Athanasius, Basile, Gregory of Nazianzus, Gregory of Nyssa, Ambrose, Augustine, and Chrysostom.

Early Medieval Period

The *early medieval period* was one of decay as far as preaching was concerned. The years from A.D. 430 to 1095 saw the power of the pulpit all but destroyed as a long black night of ignorance settled over the so-called civilized world. Preaching suffered along with all religious and social institutions. Preachers became corrupt, and the liturgy strangled the power of the pulpit. The sacerdotal spirit grew until the preacher became the priest. Doctrinal controversies became common in the face of mounting corruption of doctrine. The Roman Empire was in the process of disintegration. During the seventh and eighth centuries allegorizing was rampant, and the faithful exposition of the Scriptures was almost nonexistent. Bede (the Venerable) was a great Bible preacher (also remembered for his translation work), taking the message to northern England.

Central Medieval Period

The *central medieval period* was one in which preaching was popular but extreme. The time from 1095 to 1361 has been called the scholastic age. Four forces helped to awaken Europe, the church, and preaching during those years: (1) scholasticism ushered in a new concern for learning; (2) the Crusades, under the leadership of men such as Peter the Hermit and Pope Urban II, brought Europe into touch with the culture and commerce of the Orient and thereby quickened the cultural pulse of Western civilization; (3) mysticism developed and brought a fresh breath of spiritual power to a decadent religion; and (4) during that time the missionary preaching orders developed. Driven by a genuine love for people, Francis of Assisi began a movement for taking Christianity to people in need. From his zeal sprang the Franciscans. About the same time Dominic, concerned for the welfare of the Catholic church, initiated a movement to convert heretics and confirm the weak in faith. Because those men did so much effective preaching, the latter part of that period is known as a revival period in the history of the Christian pulpit.

Reformatory Period

The period from 1361 to 1572 has been designated as the *reformatory period*. Usually the preachers of this period have been listed as pre-Reformers (1361 to 1500) and Reformers (1500 to 1572).

This Renaissance and late medieval period was one of decay in preaching after the high points of the twelfth and thirteenth centuries. Preachers were typically described as popular, scholastic, and mystical. But an increasing reformatory element was beginning to make itself felt, and that new element eventually led to the high standard of the sixteenth century. That new note in preaching was best seen in John Wycliffe, a powerful preacher who was known as the "Morning Star of the Reformation." Girolamo Savonarola, the Italian pre-Reformer, also deserves mention as one of the most eminent preachers in history. His natural gift of oratory made him very popular.

After a thousand years of being relegated to a secondary role behind the Mass, there was a genuine revival in preaching as it emerged as the most effective method for proclaiming God's good news. Martin Luther, John Calvin, Ulrich Zwingli, Hugh

Latimer, John Knox, and a great host of others broke the shackles that had bound preaching and liberated God's chosen means for telling the world about His Son and salvation. Those men were not merely preachers, but they were *biblical* preachers. The pulpit was central, and the sermon was in the language of the people; and the Bible was the supreme authority for the spoken messages. The Reformers recognized, practiced, and taught that preaching was the primary function of a minister of the Lord Jesus Christ.

The sermon would normally open with an invocation followed by an introduction that was intended to grab the interest and attention of the listeners. It often had very little to do with the sermon proper. Then came the reading of the text in Latin at which time the people would be given the outline. The argumentation and proof would follow. Beyond that would be the telling of anecdotes, stories, and fables. The sermon would then be concluded with a summary and short prayer.

Balthasar Hübmaier was a forceful preacher with a good sermonic arrangement. He is remembered as the father of the Anabaptist movement. Hugh Latimer was the father of the English pulpit and has been called the foremost preacher of the English Reformation. Zwingli was a great expository preacher. Martin Luther was a gifted preacher with a fresh, natural use of words. In his sermon construction he gave more attention and work to the body of the sermon than to the introduction or conclusion. John Calvin was one of the most outstanding preachers of all time. He was intellectual in his approach. His outstanding weakness, however, was his lack of the personal touch in his preaching.

EARLY MODERN PERIOD

The *early modern period* (1572-1789) has been known as the golden age of English preaching. In 1611 the King James Version of the Bible was published. It initiated its era of influence and dominance that has lasted until this day. The seventeenth century was great in literary output but poor in morality. The English preachers were motivated to great efforts to correct those abuses. Among the great preachers were Richard Baxter, John Bunyan, Jeremy Taylor, and John Donne. Joseph Hall has been referred to as the "Chrysostom of England." He made strong use of biographical material. Thomas Adams, the "Shakespeare of the Puritans," was an outstanding expositor. Jeremy Taylor was one of the great masters of English literature and has been called the "Poet of the Pulpit." The best known of the Puritan preachers was Richard Baxter. Historians have referred to him as the "English Demosthenes." John Howe was chaplain to Oliver Cromwell.

LATE MODERN PERIOD

The *late modern period* (1789-1900) was the time in which new countries appeared and new denominations were formed. Biblical criticism and liberalism made their mark on preaching. Several outstanding preachers came from this period. H. P. Liddon was an accomplished rhetorician and a master of sermon construction. R. S. Candlish was a master of argumentative preaching. Thomas Binney started the trend toward the kind of preaching now known as "life-situation preaching." Joseph Parker has been remembered as a great expositor. What he lacked in formal education was made up in natural eloquence. Charles Spurgeon had the Metropolitan Tabernacle of London as his preaching station for many years. His preaching was noted for its exposition, illustration, and evangelistic fervor. Alexander Maclaren achieved almost perfection of style in his sermons. He, together with F. W. Robertson and Spurgeon, is especially remembered for obtaining his sermon subjects from the text. Christmas Evans has been called the "Poet of the Pulpit." The sermons of William Jay were models of practical textual analysis. Thomas Chalmers was the greatest preacher Glasgow, Scotland, ever had.

CONTEMPORARY PERIOD

The *contemporary period,* including the twentieth century, holds names that are far more familiar to us.

The twentieth century was ushered in with emphasis on the social aspects of Christianity. Walter Raushenbusch was the prophet of the new order. Many perversions and corruptions came into the pulpit through a misunderstanding of what the gospel really was. Whereas preachers in the first century fully understood that the *kerygma* came first, then the *didachē,* men in the early days of the twentieth century did not.

One of the contemporary giants was G. Campbell Morgan, who wrote some seventy books and pastored the Westminster Chapel in London. He emphasized the importance of the conclusion in his preaching and is remembered as one who believed strongly in preaching for a verdict. Walter A. Maier preached to fifteen million people per week over one thousand radio stations on "The Lutheran Hour." He averaged a quotation of a verse of Scripture each minute during his preaching and spent an average of twenty hours in the preparation of each sermon.

F. B. Meyer was a popular Baptist preacher. Frank Gunsaulus was noted for his charming rhetoric. George W. Truett of Dallas, Texas, was certainly one of America's greatest preachers. Harry A. Ironside employed a sermonic method of explanation, illustration, and application. James S. Stewart is noted for his clear, energetic, and elegant style. Ralph Sockman has been referred to by some as America's greatest preacher. George A. Buttrick is a scholarly and largely biblical preacher. His applications to national and personal situations are especially good.

Donald Grey Barnhouse had tremendous insight into Scripture and also possessed a special ability in bringing the truth that he gleaned in Bible study to the layman in such a way that the Scripture would come alive. Theodore Parker Ferris was noted for his good use of illustrations. His preaching has been compared to that of Phillips Brooks. Harry Emerson Fosdick has been noted as one of the most distinguished preachers of the twentieth century. His sermons were mostly life-situation sermons.

William Franklin (Billy) Graham has probably preached to more people than any other man in history. He will probably be remembered as the greatest evangelistic preacher of all time. His sermons are especially noted for their biblical content. Oswald Hoffman is clear and direct in his preaching. C. Oscar Johnson was known as the preacher of the "merry heart." His sermons were preached in the language of the marketplace.

Robert G. Lee was known as the "silver-tongued orator" of the South. His sermons were preached with a high emotional emphasis and contained an extensive amount of figurative and descriptive language. Clarence E. Macartney possessed great powers of description. That is especially seen in his sermons on Bible characters. His preaching was essentially evangelistic and always biblical. Harold Ockenga makes powerful use of the expository method of sermonizing. His preaching is oriented toward the intellectual rather than the emotional. His outlines are clear and concise, possessing excellent organization.

Stephen Olford is a good expository and evangelistic preacher with a fondness for alliteration. His sermons contain apt personal and biblical illustrations. Paul Scherer possessed a great mastery of words and had the ability to analyze Scripture and to phrase truth in new, fresh language. Clovis G. Chappell is noted for his warm evangelical preaching. His sermons are often evangelistic and have a wholesome biblical emphasis. Gerald Kennedy has been listed as one of the top ten American preachers.

Norman Vincent Peale attempts to meet the personal religious problems of the people who attend his services. He insists that his sermons do not fit the conventional homiletical pattern because he limits them to personal problems and employs a style, terminology, and approach that are simple and free.

Whenever Christianity has made substantial progress, great preaching has led the way. There have been five great centuries of growth and development in the history of Christianity. Those same five periods are also the five centuries of great preaching: the first century with the apostles; the fourth century with Chrysostom and Augustine; the thirteenth century with Francis of Assisi and Dominic; the sixteenth century with Martin Luther and John Calvin; and the nineteenth century with Charles Spurgeon and Alexander Maclaren. However, preaching was weak and ineffective in many countries during the Dark Ages (fourteenth and fifteenth centuries) and in the seventeenth and eighteenth centuries. Historically, whenever preaching has declined, Christianity has become stagnant.

SELECTED READING FOR THE HISTORY OF PREACHING

THE BIBLICAL ROOTS OF PREACHING

Broadus. *The History of Preaching*, chap. 1.
Garvie. *The Preachers of the Church*, chaps. 1-2.
Handy. *Jesus the Preacher*, I.S.B.E., *Prophetic Literature*, 1:201.
Horne. *The Romance of Preaching*, chaps. 1-3.
Kerr. *Preaching in the Early Church*, chap. 1.
Pattison. *History of Christian Preaching*, chaps. 1-3.

PREACHING IN THE EARLY CHURCH (A.D. 70-430)

Broadus. *The History of Preaching*, chap. 2.
Garvie. *The Preachers of the Church*, chap. 3.
Horne. *The Romance of Preaching*, chap. 4.

Kerr. *Preaching in the Early Church*, chaps. 5-6.
Pattison. *History of Christian Preaching*, chap. 4.

MEDIEVAL AND RENAISSANCE PREACHING (430-1498)

Broadus. *The History of Preaching*, 93-113.
Garvie. *The Preachers of the Church*, chap. 4.
Pattison. *The History of Christian Preaching*, chaps. 5-6.
Petry. *No Uncertain Sound*, Introductory essay, 1-44.

REFORMATION PREACHING (SIXTEENTH CENTURY)

Broadus. *The History of Preaching*, 113-33; 186-96.
Garvie. *The Preachers of the Church*, 87-104.
Horne. *The Romance of Preaching*, chap. 5.
Pattison. *The History of Christian Preaching*, 114-62.

THE BEGINNING OF THE MODERN AGE (SEVENTEENTH AND EIGHTEENTH CENTURIES)

Broadus. *The History of Preaching*, 135-77; 197-223.
Horne. *The Romance of Preaching*, chap. 7.
Hoyt. *The Pulpit in American Life*, 1-4.
Pattison. *The History of Christian Preaching*, chapters 8-10.

NINETEENTH-CENTURY PREACHING

Hoyt. *The Pulpit and American Life*, 86-170.
Pattison. *The History of Christian Preaching*, chaps. 12-16.
Thompson. *Changing Emphases in American Preaching*.

TWENTIETH-CENTURY PREACHING

Garvie. *The Preachers of the Church*, part 2.
Horne. *The Romance of Preaching*, chap. 8.
Hoyt. *The Pulpit and American Life*, 171-280.

2

The Apostolic Period

(4 B.C.—A.D. 69)

In the New Testament the preacher is an individual with an inner call from the Holy Spirit and an external call from the church to preach. His vocation is addressing the popular mind and heart on religious truth, as that truth is set forth in the sacred Scriptures, for the spiritual profit of the hearer. No agency in religion is older than preaching. In biblical usage the terms referring to preaching mean "the proclamation of religious truth." Preaching belongs particularly to the New Testament, but it has antecedents in the Old Testament. *A System of Christian Rhetoric for the Use of Preachers and Other Speakers* by George W. Hervey provides an excellent coverage of both Old and New Testament preaching.

Christ not only instituted the great work that was to be the chief agency for the establishment of His kingdom on earth, but became an instructor of preachers. The essence of Christ's revolutionary impact lies in three words: principles, practice, and pattern.

If we would understand preaching today, we must examine its heritage. We need to be aware that the prophets, like Moses, appeared with a distinct commission. They were to remind the people of their sins, exhort them to repent, and instruct them in religious, moral, social, and personal duties.

The great prophetic period in Israel's history began with Samuel (the last judge and the first prophet) about 1050 B.C. In the centuries that followed other preachers such as Nathan, Elijah, Elisha, Joel, Micah, Isaiah, and Jeremiah warned, pleaded, rebuked, and encouraged their people, punctuating their messages with "Thus saith the Lord."

The Jewish sermon as exposition of Scripture did not develop clearly until the postexilic period but has been carried over into the Christian sermon from the beginning of the church. Only Judaism and Christianity make use of the freely spoken word as an essential part of corporate worship.

The synagogue setting in which sermons were presented was an oblong room, bare of images and paintings, with a desk on a low platform opposite the entrance. From that platform Scriptures were read and discourses delivered. Behind the platform stood the ark, or container of copies of the law. The overriding mood of the building and the service was simplicity.

Until approximately 200 B.C the Scripture lesson was chosen from the Pentateuch; after that time the words of the prophets also were used. Sermons were delivered every Sabbath and, on special occasions, on both Friday night and Saturday morning. Often younger rabbis led the activities of the assembly, and an elder sage would not appear until it was time for him to deliver the sermon.

Usually the prophets proclaimed their messages orally, either to individuals or to assemblies, and afterward committed them to writing. They were teachers and foretellers of future events. In their didactic utterances they taught the people righteousness and enforced the authority of the Almighty. The prophets, with the exception of Ezekiel, were laymen rather than clergymen. Weatherspoon discusses, in rather minute fashion, the nature of a prophet, showing that such a person was necessary as a forerunner of the New Testament apostles.

Three streams—ancient oratory, Hebrew prophecy, and the Christian gospel— comprise the sources of Christian preaching.[1] Ancient oratory and Hebrew prophecy flowed separately for hundreds of years, but by the third century A.D. those two merged with the Christian gospel to produce Christian preaching.

Among the Hebrew people, before the time of the great prophets, several examples of ancient oratory can be found. "The speech of Judah before Joseph, is unsurpassed in all literature as an example of the simplest, tenderest, truest pathos."[2]

The author of Job was well-acquainted with oratory. The farewell speech of Moses is found in the book of Deuteronomy. Other examples of Old Testament speeches may be found in Judges 9 and 1 Samuel 24-26.

The third stream of Christian preaching, the Christian gospel, is found in the ministries of John the Baptist, Jesus Christ, and the apostles.

THE PREACHING OF JOHN THE BAPTIST

John the Baptist had a unique ministry. He was to create a new Israel in preparation for the coming of the Messiah. His preaching was ethical, eschatological, and judgmental. He was fearless in his attacks on the sins of the people.

THE PREACHING OF JESUS

The preaching mission of Jesus was essentially one of proclaiming good tidings concerning the kingdom of God. To explain the kingdom was the purpose of His preaching. It was offered to all on the basis of simple faith, repentance, a sincere heart, and self-sacrifice. It provided a rewarding relationship with God. His preaching became a basis for later preaching. His dominate note was one of authority, and many of the external features of His preaching were akin to the general preaching of His time.

1. Edwin C. Dargan, *A History of Preaching*, 2 vols. (New York: George H. Doran, 1905), 1:14.
2. John A. Broadus, *Lectures on the History of Preaching* (New York: A. C. Armstrong and Son, 1902), 6.

We would do well to note the themes that are embodied in the preaching of Jesus. His sermons were largely doctrinal, and His ethical themes covered the areas of domestic, social, and civil life.

Jesus' preaching was on a high level. His eloquence drew its strength from the ascendancy of His moral nature. His teachings were grounded on principles rather than on precepts. His appeal was to the conscience, and there was no compromise in His message. His message was always consistent with what He had previously proclaimed.

The special characteristics of Jesus' preaching are worthy of note. Bond, in his work *The Master Preacher,* refers to Jesus' gentleness, simplicity, sincerity, originality, and variety. In *Homiletics,* Kidder says that the preaching of Jesus was noted for its instructiveness, directness, adaptability, and austerity.

Burrell lists seven characteristics of the homiletic method employed by Jesus, namely, simplicity, picturesqueness, versatility, use of Scripture, optimism, and a tone of authority. Robbins notes the fact that in our Lord's first sermon, its base and point of departure was a connected passage of Scripture; His method was the unfolding of the meaning of the passage; and the conclusion involved an application to the present, linking eternity with time. There is no better example of the importance of form in preaching or of its skillful use than in the preaching of Jesus.

Jesus secured attention in His preaching by the unexpected and occasional opportunities that would lend themselves to homiletical ends. We find at least four points of contact in Jesus' preaching: religious-social, the intellectual, the emotional, and the volitional.

His most frequent audience was made up of the common people. Those audiences were generally characterized by apathy, antipathy, and sympathy. His delivery was serious, direct, forceful, attractive, personal, impassioned, and conversational. He appears to have concentrated His presentations on a few and did not strive for great numbers. However, he did not neglect the masses. He stayed in contact with His audience. There was a recognition on His part that He needed some time away from the crowd for spiritual and physical renewal. He challenged His followers to consecration, demanding that they count the cost.

Jesus' preaching appealed to certain motives. He appealed to the universal desire of men for the knowledge of God and for friendship with God, to the universal desire of men for life, and to the universal desire of men for a leadership other than their own.

It must not be forgotten that the common people heard gladly because they understood His words. A high degree of instructiveness characterized his discourses. Adaptation was a striking feature of our Lord's preaching, and it was characterized by variety. Another characteristic of Christ's preaching was its directness of point.

Jesus was an illustrator of the truth. That can be seen especially in the Sermon on the Mount with its simple thoughts and illustrations from nature. In His preaching Jesus issued denunciation, apostrophe, condensation, and repetition. His use of questions should be noted especially. Forty-eight of His messages give us 168 questions. Fifty-eight of the questions were included in His messages of the Last Week.

Jesus' methods of presentation were interesting. He used parables combining story or mental pictures with the truth he desired to present. He made extensive use of visual aids. That is seen in His writing on the ground, references to the widow's mite, lilies of the field, birds of the air, and the Temple. He made use of dialogical preaching, using the question and answer method. Most of His presentations were informal.

Prayer was prominent in Jesus' ministry. There are sixteen references to His praying. Six prayers are recorded from the Last Week and six references are made to His retiring for prayer.

Jesus preached at various locations. He preached in the Temple, the synagogue, the market place, by the wayside, on the mountain, in private homes, and at public feasts.

It is noteworthy that our Lord's method of instruction coupled precepts and practice. The effect of practice on the disciples was to teach them humility and inspire them with an anxious desire for further qualifications. Our Lord adopted various modes to illustrate to His disciples the duty and style of character they needed to cultivate. A notable example of this was His taking a little child and setting him in the midst of them as the object of a discourse. The washing of the disciples' feet was another practical lesson designed to teach them true humility. In the transfiguration, a lesson of overwhelming sacredness and power was given to a select number of the disciples to assure them of the reality of things invisible and of the connection of Messiah's kingdom with the glory of God. By such means the twelve were gradually educated for their great mission.

The training of the first disciples as preachers involved a twofold design: (1) their moral and spiritual culture, inclusive of their indoctrination in Christian truth; and (2) their instruction in the mode of teaching others what they themselves had learned. Following the ascension of the risen Savior, the apostles became examples of what preachers ought to be and do. In the apostolic example we have the exact counterpart of the Savior's instructions, and by it we are clearly taught that a special call, a divine commission, and the baptism of the Holy Spirit are essential prerequisites to preaching the gospel with apostolic power. If any should imagine that the apostles would pause after the ascension of our Lord to compose elaborate discourses to be read under favorable circumstances to attentive or admiring audiences, careful attention to the scenes in which they acted will correct that error. The duty of being prepared and willing to preach the gospel in all places is equally taught by a consideration of the varied circumstances in which the apostles preached. Christ was the great theme of apostolic preaching. The purposes behind their preaching are clearly understood by noting the results of their preaching, namely the conversion of unbelievers (both Jews and Gentiles), the establishment and edification of churches, and the training of evangelists. Idolatry was overthrown as a result of this preaching.

In apostolic preaching the evangelical order was observed: the gospel came first, then the fruits of the gospel in the lives of those who had received it. Men were not asked to become righteous by their own exertion. Modern preaching needs to study the apostolic experience. If the experience of study in a great school at the feet of a great teacher could prepare men for preaching, surely those men would be well-equipped. Their teacher had left nothing undone in anchoring their souls and giving them under-standing.

THE PREACHING OF PETER

Peter's sermon at Pentecost was preceded by much prayer. There was a logical order in its content. It was personal and urgent and progressed from conviction to inquiry, faith, repentance, conversion, and consecration. There was an absence of subjective material and an emphasis on objective facts. It included much Old Testament material, thus giving authority to its message.

THE PREACHING OF PAUL

It would prove especially profitable to study the preaching of Paul because of the abundance of such material at our command and because of the prominence that Paul gave in his ministry to preaching. His sermons are reported only in brief outline, but they can be expanded. His speeches to the elders of Ephesus before Felix, Herod, and Agrippa are especially helpful because they reveal Paul to be a skillful rhetorician. His preaching was logical, and his style was that of a well-educated orator. He possessed a great imagination and made use of illustrations.

Paul was courageous and had great endurance and gave evidence of having what we term a "pastor's heart." He displayed an extensive knowledge of the Old Testament. As we study his preaching we cannot miss his love for Christ and his loyalty to the gospel. Also apparent was his strong zeal for witnessing.

The preaching of the biblical proclaimers had four characteristics: (1) it was a setting forth of the mighty acts of God in history, (2) it included the present confirmatory and illuminative miracle-signs, (3) there was a unique power and conviction in the words of the speaker through the Holy Spirit, and (4) there was an emphasis on the relevance of the message to the contemporary situation.

Although their sermons were in thumbnail-sketch form, analysis reveals an essential unity in their basic content identified as the *kerygma*.[3] It is said that Charles Dodd's approach marked the first known time that a single biblical concept had been related to all New Testament material.

The kerygma delineated by Dodd pointed to an irreducible core of New Testament preaching; the total New Testament is but its elaboration and clarification. There is some variation among scholarly interpretations, but basically the kerygma involves these points:

1. The age of fulfillment, or the coming of the kingdom of God, is at hand.
2. This coming of the kingdom has taken place through the ministry, death, and resurrection of Jesus.
3. By virtue of His resurrection, Jesus is exalted at the right hand of God.
4. The Holy Spirit in the church is the sign of Christ's present power and glory.
5. The messianic age will shortly reach its consummation at the Second Coming of Christ.
6. Forgiveness, the Holy Spirit, and salvation come with repentance.[4]

Obviously the New Testament contains records of speaking, described as preaching, other than the kerygmatic variety. Apostolic preachers dealt, as do preachers today, with matters that pressed for attention, and they sought to apply the gospel to them.

The New Testament is a book of preaching that sheds rewarding light on matters that

3. Charles H. Dodd, *The Apostolic Preaching and Its Developments: Three Lectures with an Appendix on Eschatology and History* (New York: Harper & Row, 1964), 27.
4. Claude H. Thompson, *Theology of the Kerygma* (Englewood Cliffs, N.J.: Prentice-Hall, 1962), 3-4.

are fundamental to preaching in every age. The New Testament has something to say to us about preaching; about its essential nature, its central and controlling message, its aims, and its evangelistic and interpretative task. New Testament preaching regarded the Scriptures as God's Word which had been spoken through prophets. The message also centrally and principally spoke of Christ.

New Testament preaching was occasional in the sense that it was not confined to conventional times and places but was alive to the occasion, having regard to the particular circumstances and using them tactfully and insightfully to obtain a favorable hearing. It was appropriate to the hearers in the sense that its supporting materials were chosen from the "commonplaces" of their knowledge and experience. It was personal in the twofold sense that it represented the personal belief of the preacher and was often openly autobiographical. It was directly and intensely evangelical. These men were doing one thing—preaching the gospel.

In the apostolic commission as stated by Matthew, the only imperative verb form is "make disciples." That central objective, however, gives imperativeness to all the rest. A primary place was therefore given to the historical foundation of faith, and an important place was given to the interpretation of the gospel in its theological and moral meaning. The preaching that built up the strong advancing church of the first century was prevailingly direct and positive. The preacher displayed a wide diversity along with a prevailing unity. Apostolic preaching involved the constant intermingling of theological and ethical interpretation. Particular problems of personal and group life were treated, showing carefully where Christian principles were involved in giving practical counsel for their solution. There is one other aspect of apostolic preaching to the churches that must be brought into the picture—the absence of any direct criticism of the character of government or rulers or social institutions. The purpose of the apostolic ministry to the churches was clearly to bring the whole life of believers under the rule of Christ.

In summary, the apostolic period of preaching was a time when the church became organized. The Old Testament Scriptures and the Person and work of Christ were emphasized. The homiletical structure was not rigid. Except for Paul's preaching in the synagogue, most of the preaching was done outside. The proclamation of the gospel in this period gave rise to persecution.

3

The Patristic Period

(A.D. 70—430)

With the passing of the apostles came the period known as the patristic age or the era of the church Fathers. The Fathers have been variously defined, but they were usually prominent bishops and other Christians who formulated doctrines and codified religious observances. Their work is noted mainly for sound judgement, intellectual enthusiasm, and a sense of balance. In fact, during the Reformation both Roman Catholics and Protestants used their writings as a "court of appeals."

INFLUENCE OF THE ROMAN EMPIRE

The Roman Empire served as the environment for early Christianity. Rome was mistress of the world at that time and held sway in commerce, trade, and empire. The boundaries were the Atlantic Ocean on the west, the Nile River on the south, the Euphrates River on the East, and the Danube River on the northeast. In 4 B.C. Augustus Caesar was ruling. He was defensive and peaceful and possessed practically complete rule.

Because of trade relations and the various conquering expeditions, the population of Rome was one of mixed races and nationalities; it included the Celts, Greeks, and Jews, together with many others. Within the Empire was an extremely large slave population, which was a contributing factor that led to the fall of the Roman political system.

The Roman Empire was bilingual. Latin language was used commonly by both the working folk and the soldiers as they traveled through the Empire. The Greek language belonged more to the cultured class and was used in the arts and sciences.

The religious situation was one of distress. The Greeks of the educated class within the Empire rebelled at the superstition and inadequacy of the mystery cult religions from the East. Roman religion itself had come down through the centuries in the form of mythology. Jupiter was supposed to be the father god, and the other gods were his descendants. That system grew to such an extent that the Romans eventually had gods for everything.

Philosophy played an important part in the religion of this great people. Stoicism, with its teaching that the best possible thing was to pass from the trials of this life and be united into the great soul world in eternity, served to influence many. The Epicureans told the people that they should get the most from this life because death would soon take them, and that would end all possibility of future enjoyment. The Pythagoreans attributed evil to matter and were very ascetic in their attitudes.

The Romans, in the midst of so many differing views of religion, were tolerant of all views and only insisted that the emperor should receive due recognition and worship.

In the midst of a national religion of emperor worship and of a philosophical religion that trained the conscience, there was still a need felt for a great regenerating force. It was thus that "when the fulness of time came, God sent forth His Son" (Gal. 4:4).

AIDS TO THE SPREAD OF CHRISTIANITY

The Roman rule at this time was one which bred dissatisfaction. The wealthy class had all possible privileges of life, while those of the common and low classes were oppressed by poverty. That unrest within the Empire opened a door of entrance for a comforting religion. The extended conquests of the Roman state aided Christianity in many ways. First, it showed the conquered people that the gods in whom they had been placing their trust were not able to protect them in their time of strife. The conquests of Alexander spread Hellenistic influence. Alexandria and the sustaining of Antioch served as centers of trade and culture and provided places where Christianity could touch the flow of human life. Citizenship in the Roman Empire opened the way for missionary enterprise. The building of good roads furthered the convenience of travel. The unity of rule gave the new religion a unified political system under which Christian missionaries could operate.

The influence of Greek language and culture served to give a foundation for intellectual and moral sympathy. It enlarged and enriched the minds of the people of that day. The Septuagint (Greek version of the Bible) was used by the Greeks and even by the Jews beyond the borders of Palestine. It was also circulated by trade and commerce. Therefore, the Greek language gave Christianity a way of transferring its message in written form.

The spread of Christianity was greatly indebted to the Jewish Dispersion (the Diaspora) for much of its success. Many of the Jews remained in Babylonia and Alexandria instead of returning with Ezra in 457 B.C. or with Nehemiah in 444 B.C. That kept the Jewish influence in a broader field, and because salvation came through the Jews, Christianity could reach out through the arms of that diffused race.

The Greeks contributed philosophy, science, and culture. The Romans gave the law and civil polity. Salvation, however, came through the Jews.

THE INFLUENCE OF MYSTERY CULTS ON CHRISTIANITY

There were various mystery cults that influenced Christianity. The worship of Cybele (mother of the gods) was brought to Rome two hundred years before Christ. Along with the worship of that goddess of fertility came a great number of priests and Temple workers whose duties consisted of carrying out the worship.

Another cult involved the worship of Attis (sometimes referred to as the son of Cybele). According to mythology he was supposed to have been put violently to death and then to have arisen from the dead.

The worship of Isis came from ancient Egypt. Her characteristic quality was similar to that possessed by Cybele in that she was supposed to be the goddess of the reproductive and regenerating force. The presence of a resurrection account was prominent among most of those mystery cults.

The last mystery cult that we shall mention was the worship of Mithra, or the Persian sun-god. The cult was supposed to supply a means of escape from the forces of evil and appealed to men of various occupations. It was the strongest competitor of Christianity.

Those religions were called mystery cults because their proponents had secrets of religion that could not be told to the common people. They afforded a means of "salvation" and followed the general plan of many religions; first mourning, then rejoicing. Some of the cults believed in a life after death.

There is much debate as to the actual effect of the mystery religions on Christianity. It is inaccurate to claim that there was no connection between them and the Roman Christianity. Both religions combined a belief in spiritual and natural worlds.

THE EASTERN CHURCH

The separation between the Eastern and Western churches began under Diocletian. That separation became more evident, however, when rival empires were established in both the East and West. The line of separation extended from the Adriatic Sea to the Baltic Sea and into Abyssinia. Everything to the east of that line was the Eastern church. It was predominately Greek with Constantinople as its central place of importance. The Western church was dependent on Rome. There were three patriarchates in A.D. 325; one at Rome, another at Alexandria, and a third at Antioch. Constantinople was added to the group in 381. Rome obtained preeminence in the West because there were three in the East among which the power had to be divided. For many years the churches of the East were controlled by the government. Rome, however, fought against 'state control and even tried to put the state under church control. The Western church used Latin in its masses, whereas the Eastern church used the vernacular.

Origen was the source of the theology for the Eastern church, and Tertullian, Cyprian, and Augustine governed the theology of the Western church. The Protestant church, of course, eventually grew out of the Western church.

The theology of the Eastern church was speculative, philosophical, oriental, and mystical, as opposed to the Western religion, which was legalistic. Eastern theology emphasized two areas: incarnation and life. The Council of Nicea discussed the relation of the life of Christ with the Trinity. The Eastern church was interested in the plan of salvation and came to the conclusion that salvation comes through Christ in us. It believed that that was merely a step to the resurrection life. It held that Christianity was a life.

Origen was interested in the preexistence of the human soul. He believed that a soul was placed in the child at birth. He was a universalist in regard to salvation. Both churches held to the place of the Holy Spirit in their doctrine. The Eastern church held that the Holy Spirit proceeds from the Father alone, and not the Son.

The prominence of the theory of transubstantiation is evident in the Western church at this time. The worship in the Eastern church had more symbolism and was more mystical.

THE CONVERSION OF CONSTANTINE

Prior to his spectacular conversion, Constantine had reverenced monotheism. Before his victory over Maxentius in October 312, he allegedly saw a large cross in the sky with the words on it: "In this sign conquer." Constantine took that as a personal message from God. He then proceeded with moral and civil reforms in the state. It was not until just prior to death that he accepted baptism for himself. He delayed the ceremony because he wanted to be sure that all of his sins were forgiven. Many times in his later life his Christianity failed to influence his actions.

Because the Empire had one emperor and one centralized government, Constantine believed that it should also have a unified religion. He proceeded cautiously with his plan. At first, the emperor did not control worship, discipline, or doctrine. It was not until 476 that Basilicus began to set what standards were to be taught for the church.

In 325 a council was held at government expense at Nicea to discuss and formulate a creed, later known as the Nicene Creed.

REASONS FOR THE ULTIMATE SUCCESS OF CHRISTIANITY

The first reason was that Christianity was endorsed by Constantine. That endorsement placed the state and church in a new relationship. The state served as a protectorate for the faith.

The growing disintegration of society aided the spread of Christianity. Old cultures and religions were broken down, which opened the way for Christianity. There were many slaves and a migrant population that welcomed the friendship obtained from the Christians. As a result, Christianity established its foothold in the larger cities.

The protective organization developed by the church was an important factor. There was a closely knit alliance between the believers. The Christian group was bound together somewhat like the Empire itself. It could claim loyalty from its followers and was therefore solid and secure.

The inclusiveness of Christianity was a dominant factor. It had a place for all races and peoples within its ranks. That can be contrasted with Judaism, which seldom went outside of its own race group. Christianity appealed to both the poor and the rich, the educated and the uneducated.

The fifth reason for success is found in the fact that Christianity was inflexible. It would not compromise in doctrine or teaching. Therefore, the break made with the social order served as a stimulus to arouse the people in time of persecution.

The sixth reason was that Christianity supplied the need that the Graeco-Roman world was asking of religion and philosophy. It assumed immortality and salvation from sin. Christianity had a definite connection with Judaism, and it is reported that much of the philosophy of that day was taken from the Hebrew Scriptures. There naturally would be a common basis of agreement in such a case.

The miracles of Christianity served not only as a means of curiosity but also attracted attention and supporters to the faith. The power to expel evil spirits also attracted the attention and support of the people.

The high standards of morality and the lack of the spirit of bitterness even in the face of persecution served as admirable qualities worthy of following.

The greatest reason for the success of Christianity, however, is found in the Person of Jesus Christ. Something definitely happened in the lives of the followers of Jesus. They kept in contact with Christ, were sure of His resurrection, and eagerly looked for His return. The uniqueness of Jesus and the power of His personality and life served as the great impulse that kept Christianity above the tide of whirling religions.

CHRISTIANITY AMONG THE LATINS

Mary, the mother of Jesus, was given the name, "Mother of God." The worship of Mary came as a result of the worship of the saints. She was viewed as a mediator and was particularly worshiped by the monks. It undoubtedly crept into Christianity partly because of the importance placed on women by the Christian religion.

The heroic age had passed, but the veneration of saints remained. Each town had its respective saint who was worshiped. The saints were those who were martyrs and apostles of the early Christian days. Many of the feast days were held in memory of those saints.

The feast of Easter should be included among the major feasts observed by the church at that time. It began with Palm Sunday and concluded on the eighth day, which was called White Sunday. It included morning and evening services with a special emphasis on Thursday, Friday, and Saturday. Special services were held every Wednesday and Friday, and there was a feast of New Year.

In the worship services we find considerable use of music. Such hymns as "Gloria in Excelsis," "Holy, Holy, Holy," and the "Te Deum" were used. Each church had its own liturgy.

Christian art and decoration came into more general use at this time. When the heathen became Christianized they brought their desire for trimmings, which were exemplified in their pagan temples, into the decoration of the Christian church. Christianity now became more of a religion for the rich. That undoubtedly had its favorable influences toward the advancement of art.

HOMILETICAL EMPHASES

The sources for a history of preaching in the post-apostolic era are very scanty. For the first time, in Ignatius's letter to Polycarp, we meet the word *homilia* as a description of the word spoken in the congregation. It refers to an address of admonition.

It is necessary to generalize about the preaching in a period when the practices were obviously quite diverse. On the whole, it was a time of preaching excellence, of rich and rapid growth in homiletical theory and skills, and in the expansion of the church. As early as A.D. 150, Justin Martyr mentioned preaching as part of the regular liturgical services. Tertullian provided a reference to a sermon of the martyred bishop of Smyrna, Polycarp, who had been instructed by the apostles and actually had talked with many who had seen Christ. Eusebius, in the fourth century, collected the sermons of Irenaeus.

If we were to read the writings and sermons of the church Fathers with the expectation of profound reasoning and clear analyses, we would be disappointed. We would question their biblical understanding and interpretation. Christianity was yet in its infancy, and each person to a certain extent was a product of the time in which he lived. The patristic sermons and writings do have intrinsic worth, however, for they are rich in thought, energetic, elegant, and some were even examples of sublime oratory. They also cast light on the history of doctrine. The sermon came to have a traditional place in the church service immediately following the reading of the psalms and lessons from the Scriptures. It was introduced by a short prayer for divine aid, as suggested by Augustine when he instructed the preacher to pray both for himself and for others before beginning to teach.

Apparently, it also was customary before the first sentence of the sermon for the preacher to salute his people with "Peace be unto you," and for them to respond, "And with your spirit." Records show that sometimes the sermon to the people of Antioch began, "Blessed be God who has comforted your sorrowful soul." Quite often the preacher concluded with the doxology.

The content of the messages was about fifty percent apostolic tradition. The remaining part combined Scripture (often the text was read) and the personal contributions of the preacher. The messages contained very little doctrine. There was, however, a firm conviction manifested regarding the power of the gospel to save from sin. Records show that sometimes several passages from the Psalms, epistles, and the gospels were brought together as the basis for the sermon. Generally, the expository method of preaching was used, with the preacher delivering a running commentary on his text. In the expository sermons it was common first to develop the meaning of a given passage and then to follow through with an appropriate lesson or application for the particular situation or occasion. In some cases, the moral lesson was held until the conclusion of the sermon and introduced there effectively through illustration and application. In the homilies of Chrysostom and Augustine were series of sermons, or connected discourses, on whole books of the Bible.

Generally, the discourses of the church Fathers were basically extemporaneous. The Greeks called them *homilies,* which is from a Greek word meaning "to converse in company."

At first there were no schools for the training of the clergy, but later one was established in Alexandria. By the end of the fourth century a Christian school was formed in Antioch and became a general center for professional Christian study.

As the preaching office began to be taken away from the majority of the clergy, primarily because of their poor background in skills needed for sermonizing, it was passed on to the bishops. Since the bishops could not preach in all the churches with reasonable regularity, the parish clergy had to do what they were trained to do, namely preside over the liturgy. As liturgy increased in usage, preaching as a separate proclamation of the kerygma diminished. The problem was not that the power of preaching had failed, but that the clergy was not equipped to exercise that power.

The fourth century was one of the high points in the history of preaching for several reasons. Attending church became a social function; therefore, attendance increased. The increased number of listeners served to motivate the preachers to do better work. Organization came into church work because of the attempted unity between Christianity and the Roman Empire. Consequently, the church was given more power. During this period the worship service became more elaborate. It is interesting to note that the preacher was seated in the service and the people were the ones standing.

It was not until Augustine's epoch-making little book *On Christian Teaching* (397-426) that a definite theory of preaching was formulated. That work, of which the fourth book was completed in 426, has the distinct honor of being the first treatise on the art or theory of preaching.

The beginnings of the Latin sermon are cloaked in obscurity. Greek, the language of the church during the early centuries, had at first been the language of preaching in the West. Hippolytus, the Roman church's greatest theologian at the beginning of the third century, still wrote and talked in Greek. From the time of Tertullian we must consider Latin rhetoric a factor in the development of preaching in the West.

In Augustine, the bishop of Hippo, we meet one of the greatest personalities in the history of Christian thought. Few others have spoken a word in a specific situation that has attained universal significance and retained its actuality for centuries. And here, for the first time, we see the Latin sermon shed the Greek yoke and assume an original form. That was one of the most significant crises in the annals of preaching.

The arrangement of the subject matter of the Latin sermon is strikingly simple; often it is wholly absent. Augustine avoided the elaborate, often somewhat extended introductions that the Greek preachers loved.

If we had nothing else from Augustine than his sermons, of which some three hundred and sixty remain that are reckoned genuine, we should recognize him as a richly-gifted preacher and feel ourselves powerfully attracted to and impressed with his genius, his mighty will, passionate heart, and earnest piety. The chief peculiarity of Augustine's style was his fondness for and his skill in producing pithy phrases.

Classical rhetoric and biblical principles of preaching for a time flowed parallel in the same channel and finally mingled. That had a double effect on homiletical theory: (1) it secured to the educated by actual culture, and to the uneducated by imitation and custom, the application of the common principles of rhetoric to preaching; (2) the exaggeration and sophistry that marked the oratory and rhetoric of the age put many church Fathers into a critical attitude toward the current trend of rhetorical teaching.

In regard to the working out of the biblical principles of public speech in the practice and teaching of the Fathers, there are four matters of importance to be remembered: (1) the influence of the noble content of the gospel message and the Bible morality on those who would set them before others must not be forgotten; (2) the actual use of the prophets and apostles as models of effective religious speech, especially as they were regarded as immediately inspired of God, must not be overlooked; (3) a most powerful influence in shaping homiletical theory was the very nature of preaching itself as being primarily an interpretation and application of Scripture; and (4) along with the authority of the Word, the authority of the teacher was also an important matter.

In the preaching, teaching, and enduring influences of Origen we begin to discover more distinct traces of a real art of preaching and of instruction in its principles. There is no formal treatise on preaching among his works, but scholars have collected passages from his writings that enable us to present his homiletical teachings in a somewhat orderly way.

Origen's example and teachings encourage a higher appreciation of the homily as a studied discourse. Before his time it had been only a loosely connected string of comments on the passage of Scripture.

The main element of Origen's homiletics was hermeneutical. He insisted that the preacher must get his message from the Word of God; and to that end, study and interpretation were necessary. Origen did not invent, but he did elaborate and practice what is known as the *allegorical method* of interpretation.

There were three modes in interpreting any given passage of Scripture: (1) the grammatical and historical, by which the exact meaning of the text was sought and set forth; (2) the moral or hortatory, whereby the ethical doctrine of the text was applied to the hearers; and (3) the allegorical, or spiritual, whereby some mystical or hidden sense beyond the literal meaning (and especially suited to minister to the spiritual life) was wrought out and applied to the purpose of edification. Later, the methods were increased to four by dividing the third one into the tropological (figurative) and the allegorical (spiritual). The Fathers of the Western church, notably Ambrose and Augustine, adopted allegorization with enthusiasm and practiced it with amazing ingenuity.

Four points summarize Origen's homiletical theory: (1) the preacher's character must be sound and devout; (2) he must get his message from Scripture by a careful study of all its possible meaning, literal and figurative; (3) he must faithfully apply that meaning to life; and (4) he must take thought for the form and method of his discourse, using but not abusing the accepted principles of the art of public speaking.

The world-famous preacher John Chrysostom, of Antioch and Constantinople, was carefully educated by Libanius, the finest teacher of rhetoric during the age. The Greek homily never rose to greater heights than it did in John, the patriarch of Constantinople, known subsequently to the world by the name Chrysostom ("golden mouth").

His sermons and homilies give constant evidence both of his native powers and of his excellent training and practice. He was an admirable pastor and a careful and untiring student of the Bible. His principle of interpretation was that of Antioch rather than of Alexandria. He paid attention to the literal and moral teaching of the Word and indulged in little or no allegorizing.

Evaluations of Chrysostom's rhetorical gifts vary. Some have classified him as a true Atticist who continued the noblest tradition in Greek prose. On the other hand, his style often bears the marks of too many illustrations and of an undisciplined vocabulary, placing him in clear opposition to the masters of Attic prose. His style was influenced by the metaphorical language of the Bible.

The great Latin Father Ambrose was the eloquent and celebrated bishop of Milan. He had the conventional rhetorical education and had been trained for the civil service. His practice was formed on that of the Greek preachers of the Alexandrian method of interpretation, and his allegorizing was excessive.

In summary, fifty percent of the content of the sermons in the patristic period consisted of apostolic tradition, thirty percent consisted of Scripture, and twenty percent of personal contribution by the preacher. The preaching was mainly extemporaneous. The homilies had no logical order or outline. They included exposition and application, but very little doctrine.

BIOGRAPHICAL SURVEY

THE APOSTOLIC FATHERS

Polycarp (68-160). Bishop of Smyrna. Only one of his writings remains: *The Letter to the Philippians.* He taught Irenaeus and studied under John the apostle.

Ignatius (30-110). Bishop of Antioch. He wanted to be a martyr: "Lead me to the beasts that I by them may be made a partaker of God." His writings were noted for their originality, freshness, and sparkling terse style.

Clement (50-100). Third bishop of Rome. His style was abrupt and vigorous. He was well educated but humble.

THE APOLOGISTS

Justin Martyr (120-190). He was a rhetorician and philosopher prior to his conversion. He had no strict rhetorical method.

Tertullian (170-240). The great Latin Father. He was a lawyer and was converted at about forty years of age. He had a strong imagination, a moving style, and a passionate delivery.

ANTE-NICENE FATHERS

Western Group

Irenaeus (120-195). A missionary in Gaul. He was a pupil of Polycarp. He is remembered as a great pastor.

Hippolytus (170-236). Both his style and structure were elegant.

Cyprian (200-255). Most eloquent of the early preachers. He was trained in public address before he became a preacher. He was converted at forty years of age.

Eastern Group

Clement of Alexandria (150-202). He was an outstanding theologian and is remembered for his work in exegesis. He was a poet who felt called to preach to the cultured.

Origen (180-253). Father of expository preaching. He was the most important preacher of the third century. He believed that the preacher should have a divine call. He made the text the real basis of his preaching. His writings give evidence of depth in Christian character.

GENERAL GROUP OF OTHER CHURCH FATHERS NOT CLASSIFIED ELSEWHERE

Athanasius (297-373). He took from Origen the idea of expository preaching but, unlike him, did not allegorize. He was more of an author and administrator than a preacher.

Basil the Great (330-379). He had the ability to reach both the rich and poor. He was noted for his ability in pastoral work.

Gregory of Nazianzus (330-390). He was a student of public address and a renowned poet. He was noted for his eloquence and imagination.

Gregory of Nyssa (330-394). He is remembered for his extreme allegorization. He had a strong desire for winning men to Christ.

Ambrose (340-397). Bishop of Milan. He was well trained in public address.

Augustine (354-430). Greatest Latin teacher. A teacher of public address and one who possessed genuine expository skill. His sermons were noted for their logic.

Chrysostom (347-407). The golden-mouthed orator. He was a good student and teacher of rhetoric who used Scripture extensively and employed many illustrations. His sermons normally were arranged in three parts: *introduction*; *exposition*— extensive quotations of Scripture with no application; and *application*. His work *On the Priesthood* was the first treatise on homiletics.

Ulfilas (311-381). A Bible translator and missionary to the Goths.

4

The Early Medieval Period

(430—1095)

The fall of Rome in 476 marked the end of classical civilization and the settling in of a period in the West called the Dark Ages. That period saw the decay of the former Roman Empire and the devastating effects of hopelessness and defeat that were prevalent.

The writings of Ambrose and Augustine's *The City of God* reflected the disillusionment with the decadent society around them in comparison with that truly eternal city of God. This was the age of the rise of barbarism and atrocities that prevailed until the first Crusade.

With the death of Theodosius in 395 and the subsequent division of the Empire between his two weak sons, the rift between the East and West became more apparent. There were brief episodes of unity, such as in the sixth century. But Rome's glory met its ultimate demise at the hands of Goths, Vandals, Huns, and Lombards, completing the destruction that internal decay had begun. Justinian stands as the one true light in the dark age. Although not a great intellect himself, he collected great minds around him from the civil government, the military, and the establishment. His generals achieved a brief glimpse of unity, and his great lawyer, Tribonian, completed the massive task of codifying the confused and voluminous laws of the Empire. Justinian also had the world-famous church of St. Sophia rebuilt during his reign.

In Germany turmoil was evident, but the defeat of the Huns at Chalons in 451 at least averted the menace of their conquest of eastern Europe. In Italy, first the Goths and later the Lombards laid foundations of real political power. In Spain the Goths built a kingdom that was the basis for future development. The Burgundian power along the Rhine was important at that time and would have a significant influence on later events.

Meanwhile, amid the ruins of early Rome arose a religious and political power that remains a significant factor today. The papacy became firmly established. The church developed a polity revolving around five great church rulers, called patriarchs, found in the cities of Jerusalem, Antioch, Alexandria, Constantinople, and Rome.

Leo I was the strong leader of the West who, in his time (440-461), not only asserted his claim to supremacy but also claimed Scripture for his defense. The words of Christ to Peter (Matt. 16:18) became the touchstone of papal authority. Gregory the Great (590-604) followed Leo and did much to confirm and perpetuate the papal authority.

During this period and for a long time afterward, the Greek language and literature were neglected. Gregory determined that all profane knowledge should be discouraged. It is easy to understand why the following centuries would come to be known as the Dark Ages.

Gregory introduced sundry innovations into Christian worship. He increased the ceremonies of the ordinary services, arranged elaborate chanting and singing, formed stations and smaller liturgies, and formed the sacramental service of the church almost in its present Roman Catholic form. Also about that time the notion of purgatory was invented, and Gregory spoke of purification by a fiery probation as a settled fact. Feast days were multiplied and so arranged as to coincide with the Lupercalia and other heathen festivals so that the idle and pleasure-lovers might not be losers by adopting Christianity in preference to paganism.

During the period from 451 to 1050 the Roman Catholic method of worship began to spread throughout the West. Variations in language, order, and liturgy were eliminated as much as possible. Worship was centered in the observance of the Mass, which had become more than a sacrament to bring grace to the ones partaking. It was now viewed as the "unbloody" sacrifice of Christ, the shedding of His blood and the breaking of His body. The symbolism had become completely literal. The wine was not yet withheld from the people. It was generally conceived that something happened to the bread in the Mass to change it into the body of Christ.

The Crusades were another factor that greatly aided in the rapid rise of the papacy. Various popes had hinted at the idea of recapturing Jerusalem from the Muslims long before it was carried out. Pope Silvester II (999-1003) had spoken of a grand crusade against the Turks; Gregory VII (1075-85) had actively planned an attack, but because of his struggle with Emperor Henry IV he was unable to secure the secular support necessary for such an undertaking. In 1095 the Greek emperor Alexius appealed to the West not to delay such an endeavor any longer, and the First Crusade began late that year. The Turks were threatening to take Constantinople. Pope Urban II (1088-99) called on secular powers to devote themselves to this divine crusade, promising forgiveness of sin to those dying in the effort. Europe was swept with the passion of slaughtering for the cross (the word *crusades* is a derivative from the Latin word for *cross*).

The Crusades, which went on periodically for 200 years, opened the eyes of many to a new world. New literature, new interests, and new ideas for economic and social reforms were brought back to Europe by those who had invaded the Eastern world. Commerce and trade were fostered, and new items for manufacture called for new industry.

A movement that made a distinct contribution to the rapid recovery of Roman Catholicism has been called *Scholasticism* and refers to the teaching of the schoolmen.

Some of the leading Scholastics were Johannes Scotus Erigena (c. 810-877), Anselm (1033-1109), Roscellinus (c. 1050-1125), Abelard (1079-1142), Alexander of Hales (c. 1245), Albertus Magnus (1206-80), Thomas Aquinas (1225-74), John Duns Scotus (1265-1308), and William of Occam (c. 1349).

Even beyond the contributions of monasticism, the Crusades, and Scholasticism, the spectacular rise of the Roman Catholic papacy to the height of power in the period from the eleventh to thirteenth centuries was the work of the strong popes. Had all the contributory factors existed, the Roman Catholic church could not have attained its position without the initiative and determination of the strong men who headed it. Two of those strong popes were Gregory I and Gregory VII.

Gregory I was born in Rome in 540. His parents were of the senatorial class and were Christians. When he was thirty-three years of age, he was made prefect of the city by Justin III. By 574 he devoted his wealth to the founding of monasteries and became a member of the monastery of St. Andrew in the Caelian hills. His own temperament, however, was too active for him to become a monk, so he was sent as papal ambassador to the courts of Constantinople by Pelagius II.

In 586 he was abbot of St. Andrew and in 590 was chosen as pope. It marked the first time that a monk had been chosen for the papal office. He died March 12, 604. Pope Gregory was a very versatile man, and we find that his work also carried him into missionary endeavor. In 596 he organized and sent forth a missionary group into England for the purpose of the conversion of those people. That group was headed by Augustine. Gregory also sent missionary workers among the Arian Lombards.

Hildebrand, who became Gregory VII, was called to be pope on April 22, 1073, while he was still an archdeacon. He seemingly accepted the office with reluctance, but when he became settled, he put real vigor and sagacity into the office.

He had a new theory of the relationship between church and state. If the clergy had the power to bind things in heaven, it also had the power to control the political things on earth. That power of the church was based on the idea of apostolic succession.

There were four major reforms Gregory aimed to achieve during his term as pope: (1) to free the papacy of all strings of foreign control; (2) to free the church from the lay dictation, which had reference particularly to the election of the bishops; (3) to secure reforms among the clergy itself that were connected with the celibacy of the clergy and aimed at the removal of the practice of simony; and (4) to make the papacy dominant over the secular sovereigns of Europe.

The church occupied an important place during the Middle Ages. The people made constant connections with the church, for nearly everyone belonged to it.

The individual was dominated by the church in that salvation depended on the administering of the sacraments, which could be done only by the church.

The ecclesiastical hierarchy constituted a feudal ecclesiastical system with the pope as the highest figure. The bishops and priests were his spiritual vassals. The functions of the priest, bishop, and archbishop were combined in the power of the pope.

The bishop was the only one who could anoint kings, consecrate churches, and ordain priests. He was also the only one who could conduct the sacrament of confirmation. His income was received from endowments and from his share of the local church contributions.

HOMILETICAL EMPHASES

This period contained much of interest to the history of preaching but contributed little to the growth of homiletics. It has been said that the seventh to the eleventh centuries might be considered the darkest in the history of preaching. Ignorance and other unfitness in the clergy, brutality and illiteracy among the people, and other hindrances worked against the preaching of this time. Preaching was not vigorous, nor was it able to overcome the trammels of liturgy. There was a growing concept of the preacher as priest rather than prophet. The preacher changed from a messenger of God into a petty mediator and dispenser of God's mercies and punishments. That led to a preaching of church discipline rather than repentance. In the disputes marked by the councils of Ephesus in 431, Chalcedon in 451, and Constantinople in 553, there was a protracted struggle over fine points of doctrine.

The sermon retained its character as an expository discourse, but the enforcement of church duties took up a large part of its content. The preachers of the Middle Ages took over Origen's method of allegorical interpretation from the ancient church and carried it a step further. Preachers of the time were expected to have seven or eight interpretations of any particular scriptural passage, often confusing and confounding even the simplest of texts. Preaching was far removed from daily life. Latin was still the accepted language for religious purposes, and the sermonizing was generally depressing. The sermons remained weak and were often mere copies of sermons from the past. They contained extravagant unscriptural laudations of Mary that placed her as nearly an equal of her divine Son.

Sermons were preached primarily in monastery chapels rather than in the parish churches, where worship was mainly liturgical. When the common people gathered in church, it was usually to witness ceremonies and to listen to chanting. Most of those who preached in the vernacular presented eulogies to the saints or accounts of current miracles rather than focusing on the Savior and the simple kerygma.

Preaching in the East dropped into its "conservative old age" from which came little, if any, change for centuries. Speculative thought became prominent, and the rhetorical art became more apparent than in the West. Superstition, angels, saints, images, rites, and Mariology grew out of proportion. Piety had degenerated into formalism. The dogmatic addresses almost wholly lacked the didactic element. The addresses dealt with the miraculous and were often incomprehensible. The whole idea of preaching seemed to bring astonishment and admiration.

Preaching in the West was neglected, and the quality and content of the sermon were no better than in the East. In the West the clergy were classified into three main groups. The first were the *parochial* preachers. Those were preachers and priests in the churches who addressed the people gathered on Sundays, saint's days, and festivals. The second group of preachers were the *cloistral* preachers. They lived in monasteries and were engaged in instructing and exhorting monks and nuns. The third group of preachers were the *missionary* preachers, who were engaged in preaching to the non-Christian lands. That effort received impetus from such men as Patrick and Columba and included some of the better preachers of the period. As a rule, however, the sermons were structureless, consisted of short homilies, and lacked style.

One bright spot in this dark period of preaching centered in the presentations of Isidore of Seville. He was a learned and notable prelate who formulated a condensed rhetoric that contained nothing distinctly homiletical. He emphasized that a speech should consist of four parts. The *exordium* should arouse the interest of the hearer. The *narration* should contain the explanation of what is being said. The *argumentation* should produce confidence by setting forth assertions. The *conclusion* should embrace the end of the whole oration. One writer said that if the work of Isidore was the bright spot of the period, we can just imagine how poor the rest must have been.

Isidore's most remarkable production was his twenty-volume treatise usually called the *Etymologies* (sometimes called the *Origins*) in which he briefly discusses all the learning of his time.

Nearly two hundred years after Isidore came the famous Rabanus Maurus (c. 776-856), archbishop of Mainz. He, too, was a learned and voluminous writer. His complete works occupy six volumes in Migne's *Latin Patrology*. The famous treatise *De Clericorum Institutione (On the Institution of the Clergy)* contains what he has to say on homiletical theory.

The treatise is a sort of textbook of clerical duties and matters pertaining to the clerical office. It treats the ranks of the clergy, tonsure, and vestments of the rites and ordinances, such as baptism, the Lord's Supper, extreme unction, and the Mass.

In the third book he took up preaching and described his purpose: "The third book sets forth how all things written in the divine books are to be investigated and learned, also those things in the studies and arts of the heathen which are useful to be studied by the ecclesiastic man."

After Rabanus to the end of this epoch, it appears that no other author dealt with the theory of preaching.

The Carolingian Renaissance (750-930) gave new life to the sermon. The goal was the Christian instruction of the people, and the content was always derived from the storehouse of the church Fathers. The objective was to translate the gospel, every time it was read, into the language of the people and to explain it with the addition of useful exhortations. All preaching in the church was to serve to enlighten the people; thus the pedagogical motif assumed a dominant position.

Two collections of homilies are the greatest monuments to the homiletical labors of the Carolingian Renaissance. Paul the Deacon, at Charlemagne's request, wrote a collection of homilies intended for use by the clerics as readings for the canonical office. Alcuin's compilation of homilies was designed to give the preachers source material for their exposition of the liturgical texts on Sundays.

The sermon had degenerated to a mechanical level and retained that status for the duration of the Middle Ages, even though it later developed into a rather unique artistic device.

In summary, the early medieval period was not a time when original thinking was prevalent. The sermons were devoid of good structure and exposition. The language used in preaching was Latin. The kinds of preaching that were prevalent were parochial, cloistral, and missionary. There were really no great preachers in this period, which led to its being called the "dark age of preaching."

BIOGRAPHICAL SURVEY

OUTSTANDING PREACHERS OF THE FOURTH TO SIXTH CENTURIES

Ulfilas (311-381).

Leo the Great (390-461). He was the first pope and a bold preacher. Noted more for his boldness than his greatness. He also possessed eloquence.

Gregory the Great (540-604). Wrote *Rule for Pastors* and is remembered for having been the first pope to send out missionaries. He was better as an administrator than a scholar and preacher.

Patrick (386-461). A Scottish missionary to Ireland, his call to preach came in the midst of a dream.

Columba (521-597).

Augustine of Canterbury (566-607).

OUTSTANDING PREACHERS OF THE SEVENTH—ELEVENTH CENTURIES

Venerable Bede (673-735). A great Bible preacher of his day. An extemporaneous preacher, his ministry was concentrated in northern England. He is remembered for translation and works in history.

Boniface (680-755). Remembered for boldness in preaching and missionary work.

Ansgar (801-865). A missionary to Denmark and Sweden.

Adalbert (950-997). A missionary to Poland and Russia.

Eastern Church

Christopher of Alexandria (d. 863). Remembered for the one homily he left as an example of literary excellence.

Photius of Constantinople (815-897). Patriarch of Constantinople.

Theophane Cerameus (d. 1052). Archbishop in Sicily; left 62 homilies as examples of simple style.

Theophylact (d. 1107). Noted scholar and teacher of one of the young emperors.

Western Church

Rabanus Maurus (776-856). A Benedictine; Archbishop of Mainz.

Peter (Damian) (1006-1072). An Italian Roman Catholic Reformer.

Anselm (1033-1109). Born in Italy; missionary to England; doctrinal preacher; Archbishop of Canterbury.

5

The Central Medieval Period

(1095—1361)

Attempts at monastic reforms within the church during this period failed. Corruption abounded, and a growing indifference to religion in general developed. The Waldensians, Albigensians, and Lollards made attempts to return to the simplicity of the early Christians and rediscover Christ, but they found strong persecution at every turn.

It is at this point that we find the *Investiture* controversy. When a bishop was elected, he was to receive a double investiture. His ring and staff, the symbols of his spiritual powers, were to be given by his spiritual superior. His regalia, symbolic of temporal authority, was to come from his secular superior. The emperor had often taken it upon himself to grant both. The Concordat of Worms in 1122 settled the controversy by adopting a compromise.

The papacy reached its zenith under Innocent III (1198-1216), when it virtually controlled Western Europe. The Fourth Lateran Council was really an international congress and was held in the pope's palace. It was attended by bishops, kings, and nobles. The pope was in the chair of control and claimed and exercised the right to depose monarchs and judge kings.

During this period there was a struggle for representative government. In 1215 King John of England was forced to sign the Magna Charta. No taxes were to be levied without the consent of the Great Council of Nobles.

In the area of science, astrology and astronomy were considered the most important. Leonard of Pisa in 1202 introduced arabic numbers to Western Europe. It was during those years that magnifying lenses, mariner's compasses, mechanical clocks, and gunpowder were developed. Marco Polo (1254-1324) reached China.

The field of literature saw Dante, the greatest and best known of the medieval poets, produce his *Divine Comedy*. The troubadours were the literary artists of the day, taking as subjects for their writing birds, flowers, women, and priests. Bernard of Clairvaux (1091-1153) was the writer of such hymns as "Jesus, the Very Thought of Thee," "O Sacred Head, Now Wounded" and "Jesus, Thou Joy of Loving Hearts."

Romanesque art was at its peak in the twelfth century, and its emphasis was on massive walls, rounded arches, small windows, and horizontal lines. Gothic architecture was in vogue from the twelfth to sixteenth centuries and was most prominent in the thirteenth. Gothic style stressed huge windows, thin walls, and vertical lines, and the buildings were higher.

This was the period of great cathedrals. The naves (main auditoriums) of those cathedrals often would be more than 100 feet in height. Cathedrals had Old Testament scenes in the north transept and New Testament scenes in the south. The last judgment was often portrayed in the west transept.

The twelfth century was marked by a rise in commerce from Venice. The Venetians controlled much of the salt, fur, grain, and slave trade that passed through the Mediterranean Sea during the thirteenth century. Italian ships also established trade routes to the Flemish coasts. A rise in the textile industry was experienced in England and Spain. Fairs were held annually, and goods were exchanged by barter. Land was the source of wealth, and its ownership was a symbol of power.

Jews were the bankers because canon law forbade Christians from taking interest on loans. Italians began to found banks and develop the use of checks. Many craft guilds also were formed during this period.

The clergy ranked at the top of the social ladder. The peasants lived in huts of interwoven lath stuffed with straw that had one room with a place for a fire in the center. There were no chimneys through the thatched roofs, no glass for window openings, and no beds on which to sleep.

Feudalism was at its height in the thirteenth century and lasted until the fourteenth century. It arose because the central government broke down, and there were no public powers to fulfill the functions of authorities. It was a time of disorder, raids, and brigandage. Heavy taxation drove the little landowners out of existence or into slavery. Feudalism was doomed to fail with the rise of towns. The serfs escaped to the city, where the demand for labor was minimal, especially after the Black Plague.

In the eleventh century an intellectual awakening began which culminated in the thirteenth. It had two phases: the founding of the universities and the development of Scholastic philosophy and theology. There were schools connected more or less directly with some of the cathedrals in the eleventh century, and they continued to flourish in the twelfth century. Students came from all over Europe to hear the lectures of eminent teachers. Because Latin was the common language of scholarship, there was no linguistic barrier. At those centers where a university arose, an organization had already been formed prior to the university. The first kind of organization was that of a guild of teachers. The students often organized themselves into "nations." The degrees of *master* or *doctor,* which for a long time meant the same thing, were certificates of competence to teach, a kind of teacher's license.

Even back in the period from Gregory VII to Innocent III when the papacy was very strong, there had been subversive movements. Perhaps the most violent was that of Peter of Bruys early in the twelfth century. It is not unfair to say that he was a fanatical revolutionist rather than a reformer. He rebelled against all ecclesiastical authority, would have no liturgical worship or ceremonial acts, denied the validity of infant baptism, and held that the church should own no buildings or property.

Like Peter of Bruys (but a little less extreme) was Henry of Lausanne, who was a kind of latter-day Donatist in holding that the sacraments were valid only if the ministering priest was morally pure and lived an ascetic life. He preached through western and southern France from 1101 until 1145. His followers were called Henricians.

Arnold of Brescia, a more picturesque character than either of those just mentioned and for a time more dangerous to the existing order, agreed with them in attacking the worldliness and wealth of the clergy.

The fifteenth century was a time of confusion. It began with the Great Schism and ended with the height of the Renaissance. The monastic orders suffered from decay and corruption as never before or after. The moral authority of the church was at low ebb. Its discipline over both clergy and laity was breaking down rapidly.

There was no communion or fellowship between the Eastern and Western churches at this time, although various attempts had been made toward such an end. The Western church turned to tradition as being authoritative. That included what Jesus and His disciples were supposed to have said, but had not written down. Tradition was made dogma at the Council of Trent in 1545-63. The Roman Church held that the word of the apostles had been under the guidance of the Holy Spirit; therefore, the church was still under divine control.

The idea of purgatory began at about the time of Augustine. People began to speculate as to just where the dead were. Some said that they were being purified in preparation for heaven. From that suggestion came the doctrine of mortal and venial sin; that is, the soul must go to purgatory until the debt for sin has been paid. It was possible to transfer penance to another, and consequently, the idea of prayers and masses for the dead emerged.

The Schoolmen included three parts in the doctrine of penance: contrition of the heart, confession, and satisfaction for the offender himself. The doctrine of indulgences resulted from the doctrine of penance.

The sale of indulgences was carried to such an extreme that people would lay up merits for the future to offset some of their evil practices. When those merits were needed as a means of retribution, all they had to do was to pay a portion of money to the priest, and supposedly the merits would offset the debits. The church was in such a state that only a reformation could hope to keep it alive.

HOMILETICAL EMPHASES

In the twelfth century the preaching in the East was of the conventional kind of decayed Greek preaching. Few preachers of the period are well known, and the sermons have nothing remarkable to offer.

The old form of the simple expository and hortatory discourse was retained. Attention was given to a more logical structure. An analytical method arose with Bernard from the West.

Oral teaching took place in the schools for clinical education. The teaching of homiletics was given a place, and numerous homiletical helps were provided. The style of the homilies was usually tame, unpretentious, and clear. Because of imitation and copying, style did not differ much between individuals.

Illustrations were frequently used, especially legends and anecdotes. Some sermons were noted for their play on words and their use of rhymed prose. This period has been referred to as the narrative period, because there was such a liberal use of narrative as opposed to argument, exposition, and doctrine. Actually, it would be difficult to declare any one method as being dominant during the century.

The use of Scripture was similar to its use in the preceding ages. The pericope often furnished the basis for the message. Sometimes no text was chosen as a basis for a message. Sayings from the church Fathers, or even passages from the liturgy, were often used as a basis. Many verses of Scripture were quoted in the sermons, but the verses were often misquoted and misapplied. Allegorical interpretation was even worse than in former times. Theoretically, the Bible was recognized as the source and foundation of preaching, but much extrabiblical material was used in its place.

The doctrinal and moral teachings were presented from a Roman Catholic standpoint. Great Christian doctrines were proclaimed but often misunderstood and obscured. The doctrine of the Trinity was emphasized but with little distinction between the members of the Godhead. Christ was represented as being truly divine but was often overshadowed by the emphasis on Mary and the saints. The atonement was overshadowed by the merit to be obtained by good works. The sinfulness of man and the need for repentance were emphasized, but the remedies were usually only outward penance and intellectual assent. The future life in heaven or hell was taught, but that teaching was also mingled with purgatory. And much attention was given to angels and the reality of Satan.

The preaching in the West brought a revived interest in the sermon. The clergy began to have a greater reward for preaching, and the people began to show a greater respect for preaching. There were at least three main reasons for this revival of preaching: the work of the heretics awakened the orthodox clergy, the Crusades stimulated preaching, and there was an increase in the usage of preaching in the language of the people.

The quality of preaching still left much to be desired. It lacked biblical content and could be characterized by excessive allegorizing. There was also a rise of scholastic preaching marked by minute analysis and the logical treatment of material.

The missionary element was distinctive and was mingled with an excessive use of legends. Allegorical interpretations of Scripture and the veneration of Mary were also very prominent. Sermon illustrations were drawn from a variety of sources, with humor and argument used freely.

The impulse given to preaching by the reforms of Hildebrand (c. 1050) and the first Crusade (c. 1095) first affected practice rather than theory. Within the flourishing epoch of medieval preaching, which reached its height in the twelfth and thirteenth centuries, we find that renewed attention is given to the art as well as the act of preaching.

One of the most important and famous writers of this age was Guibert of Nogent (1053-1124). His homiletical work appears in the preface to his commentary on the book of Genesis under the title *Liber Quo Ordine Sermo Fieri Debeat,* or *A Treatise on the Method by Which a Sermon Ought to Be Made*. It was by no means a formal treatise on rhetoric, sacred or secular, but rather a defense or explanation of the author's preferred method of interpreting Scripture.

We should also mention Alaine de Lille (Alanus ab Insulis), who was a Cistercian abbot and a voluminous author. His *Summary of the Art of Preaching* (*Summa de Arte Praedicatoria*) is a treatise that shows great acuteness of thought, ample learning, and considerable homiletical skill. It was the most important work in the theory of preaching since Augustine. It introduced the scholastic method and the more numerous treatises of the scholastic period.

Some of the preachers in this period, such as Peter the Hermit (Peter of Amiens), have been remembered across the centuries. Peter was a forceful preacher and surpassingly eloquent.

Bernard of Clairvaux, commonly called St. Bernard, lived in France from 1091 to 1153. He was a devoted monk and a fervently pious man. His sermons and other writings present treasures of devout sentiment.

About fifty years after the death of Bernard, two new monastic orders were founded: the mendicant orders of the Franciscans and the Dominicans. The latter order was founded for the express purpose of preaching.

Anthony of Padua, a Franciscan missionary to Africa, went to Italy, where he gained his extraordinary reputation as a preacher. He is reckoned by some as one of the most popular preachers who ever lived. We read of twenty thousand persons crowding at night around the stand where he was to preach next morning. At times, as many as thirty thousand were present when he preached. Much of his popularity was because of the superstitious belief that he had supernatural power and could work miracles. Anthony may have been the first preacher to make a careful division of his sermons into several main headings. He abounded in novel kinds of illustration.

Thomas Aquinas, the Neapolitan count and Dominican friar, is regarded as the greatest theologian of the Middle Ages and one of the greatest minds in the history of philosophy.

In the thirteenth century the most important name that emerges on the theory of preaching is that of the renowned "Seraphic Doctor," Bonaventura (1217-1274), theologian, mystic, cardinal, and saint. Among his numerous writings is *The Art of Preaching* (*Ars Concionandi*). That little work follows closely the *Christian Teaching* of Augustine. It discusses three main topics: division (the general outline of the whole discourse), distinction (the more minute and logical analysis of the proposition), and enlargement (dilatatio, filling out with illustrations, argument, appeal, etc.).

The next treatise of any importance is that of Humbert de Rommanis (d. 1277), a Dominican monk educated in Paris.

In summary, the central medieval period was one of the high points of preaching. Vast crowds listened to the proclamations. Preaching was noted for its popular element and was adapted to the needs of the poor and ignorant. The dramatic element was stressed in delivery. The sermons consisted of verse by verse running commentaries on the biblical text. Although Scripture was often misused, repentance and faith were urged.

BIOGRAPHICAL SURVEY

ITALIAN PREACHERS

Peter of Lombard
  Greatest teacher and representative of Scholasticism of his time
Arnold of Brescia
  1. Influenced by Abelard
  2. Attacked the corruptions of the church
  3. Possessed great eloquence
Joachim (Gioacchino)
  1. Head of Cistercian monastic order in Italy
  2. Exerted great personal influence

GERMAN PREACHERS

Honorius Scholasticus
  1. Collected sermons
  2. A noted theologian
Werner of Ellerbach
  1. Published a collection of sermons
  2. "Borrowed" from the Honorius collection
Conrad
  1. Published a collection of sermons in German
  2. Adapted his speech to the common people

ENGLISH PREACHERS

Ailred (Ethelred) of Revesby
  1. Highly esteemed by Henry II
  2. Effective missionary
Peter of Blois
  1. Proud and quarrelsome
  2. Preached in English
  3. Poor organizer

FRENCH PREACHERS

Urban II
  1. Open-air preacher
  2. Aroused the people for the Crusades
  3. Remembered for his eloquence

Peter the Hermit
  1. Crusade preacher under Urban II
  2. Good preacher but poor leader
Raoul the Ardent
  1. Concerned for the spiritual welfare of his hearers
  2. A great denouncer of sin
  3. Poor in style
Ivo of Chartres
  1. Intelligent and imaginative
  2. Great thinker
  3. Lacked character
Peter Abelard
  1. Brilliant lecturer
  2. Great thinker
  3. Poor in character
Bernard of Clairvaux
  1. Most prominent French preacher of twelfth century
  2. Monk, theologian, mystic, evangelist, and popular preacher
  3. Reformed the corrupt clergy
  4. Excellent preacher
Norbert
  1. Attacked the corrupt clergy
  2. Gifted as a preacher of peace and reconciler of disputes
Maurice of Sully
  1. Known as a good pastor and preacher
  2. Wrote a book on the art of preaching
Hugo of St. Victor
  1. Notable mystic
  2. Popular preacher

SCHOLASTIC PREACHERS

Jacques de Vitry
  1. Preached with the Crusaders
  2. Moved France with his preaching
  3. Had good variety
  4. Good use of illustration
Albert the Great
  1. Great teacher—influenced Aquinas
  2. Emphasized the Veneration of Mary
Thomas Aquinas
  1. Greatest representative of Scholastic theology
  2. A preacher of great acceptance and power

MISSIONARY PREACHERS

Dominic
  1. Remembered for his piety—founded Dominican order
  2. Preacher of great ability
Francis of Assisi
  1. Founder of Franciscan order
  2. Possessed saintly zeal
  3. His preaching was based on experience
Anthony of Padua
  1. Known for his faith and humility
  2. Open-air preacher
Berthold of Regensburg
  1. One of the most remarkable preachers of all time
  2. Personification of the good elements of both
  Scholasticism and mysticism
  3. Repentance was his major theme

MYSTICAL PREACHERS

John Fidanza (Bonaventura)
  1. Scholastic and mystical
  2. An eloquent preacher
Meister Eckhart
  1. Emphasized mystical union with God
  2. Defective on the cardinal doctrines

6

The Reformatory Period

(1361—1572)

The reformatory period in this chapter is composed of two distinct historical periods: (1) the Renaissance (1361-1499) and (2) the Reformation (1500-1572).

HISTORICAL BACKGROUND

THE RENAISSANCE

A change occurred in Europe near the beginning of the fifteenth century that produced a profound change in the thinking of men, in the values they cherished, in their artistic and cultural activities, and in their attitudes toward religion. That change is known as the Renaissance. Its earliest and most brilliant manifestations appeared in Italy. As a period of European history it may be conveniently dated from about 1400 to 1525.

The word *renaissance* means "rebirth"; or, by analogy, an awakening from a long, deep sleep.

Those things reborn included: classical scholarship; the Greek ideal of the free individual and the versatile personality; intellectual curiosity; a sense of the values to be found in the joy of this life and the beauty of this world (unconditioned by any theological considerations), and an approach to the problems of philosophy independent of theology. There was a consequent loss of interest in religion as represented by a church that was dogmatic and authoritarian on principle, which still resisted the demand for intellectual liberty.

Several important developments transpired during the Renaissance period. The first was the decline of papal power. It fell to its lowest point when Boniface VIII (1294-1303) was taken prisoner by Philip the Fair in 1303. Boniface died a mental invalid in 1303. His death was the tombstone of the papacy. One writer said, "He

41

entered as a fox, ruled as a lion, and died as a dog."

Other developments included the rise of new small nations, the rebirth of learning, and the rise of mysticism, scholasticism and nominalism. The Hundred Years War between England and France resulted in England's losing all continental possessions and eventually becoming a maritime power. The Black Death of 1348 destroyed half of the population of Europe. Gunpowder was introduced at the beginning of the fourteenth century and revolutionized warfare.

Benedict XI was Boniface's successor. He quietly disposed of many of Boniface's appointments. He was poisoned, however, before he really was able to carry out his changes effectively.

Clement V saw the handwriting on the wall and moved the papal chair from Rome to Avignon. Six popes who followed Clement also resided there. The papacy was further discredited at Avignon by vice and immorality.

The Great Schism took place between 1377 and 1414. Urban VI was the pope at Rome and Clement VII was the pope at Avignon. Indulgences doubled to support two popes. The church was scandalized and papal doctrine discredited. The Council of Pisa in 1409 deposed the two reigning popes and elected a third. The two deposed popes, however, refused to leave. That resulted in three popes. The Council of Constance in 1414 established itself above the pope and one pope was again elevated. The papacy could never again attain a higher prestige than it had displayed in the Fourth Lateran Council of 1215.

The church and state became divided as a result of the Renaissance. Culture asserted its independence of the church. Men no longer saw themselves in a divine perspective. *Humanism* became the philosophy of the day. The rebirth of learning meant a rebirth of critical scholarship.

One of the outstanding opponents of the papacy in the latter years of his life was the patriot and preacher, John Wycliffe (1320-84). Before 1376, Wycliffe withheld his attacks against the papacy, but the disreputable conditions surrounding the closing years of the Avignon papacy and the beginning of the papal schism in 1378 touched off his violent protests. Wycliffe urged that both of the popes be deposed. In his lectures at Oxford he advanced the idea that if any secular or ecclesiastical prince were not faithful to his task, his right to hold the office was forfeited. If bishop or even pope proved unworthy, civil rulers, as agents of God's will, had the right to despoil him of his temporal property.

No doubt encouraged by the protection given him by powerful English patriots, Wycliffe boldly continued his criticism of the papacy. Using the Bible (which he helped translate into English about 1382) as final authority, he vigorously attacked the Roman Catholic sacramental system, particularly the doctrine of transubstantiation. He also asserted that the New Testament made no distinction between the bishop and the presbyter (priest), and that consequently the Roman bishop had wrongfully usurped power that was not his. Wycliffe's views were greatly colored by his patriotism. He objected to papal extortion of English funds, papal appointments of foreigners to English benefices, and papal encouragement of mendicant monks in England who, said he, robbed the poor.

To give scriptural instruction, Wycliffe organized a group known as the *hollands* ("poor priests"), who wandered about two by two preaching and teaching. They were received joyfully by the people. Wycliffe was condemned by the pope in 1377, but was protected by political influence until his death in 1384.

English humanism also played a part in increasing antipapal sentiment. John Colet (1467-1519), dean of St. Paul's Cathedral in London, was an outstanding humanist. With William Grocyn and Thomas Linacre he formed a nucleus for the school of thought that despised the Scholastic methods and theology. Colet, a deeply spiritual and capable leader, was especially skilled in biblical interpretation. His eloquent voice constantly called for reform.

THE REFORMATION

The word *reformation* used to describe the revolution of the sixteenth century is, in a sense, a misnomer. The principal events did not center in reform but in schism.

During that period the Roman Catholic church in Western Europe was the most powerful institution of the Middle Ages. Only the church, through the Seven Sacraments, had the power to dispense divine grace.

Position in the hierarchy of church offices from pope to lowly parish priest constituted a class structure within the clergy. The church was democratic in that it offered opportunity for sons of the common people to acquire an education and rise to the highest positions.

Secular clergy were those who lived in the world among others, as opposed to the regular clergy who withdrew themselves to live according to the rule of the various monastic orders.

When the fullness of time had come, reform was in the minds of many and on the lips of a few. A pioneer was required to inaugurate a successful revolt against the Roman Catholic system. Martin Luther was that pioneer. Ulrich Zwingli and John Calvin were not far behind.

Luther's challenges to the doctrine and practice of the church set off the Protestant Reformation. The rising monarchies, nationalism, attitudes of the rising middle class, the criticism of the humanists, and secularism all contributed to the Protestant Reformation.

Luther became very much concerned with the problem of man's salvation. The church taught that salvation might be obtained by sacraments and good works. Luther came to believe that only justification by faith could save man.

Luther protested the sale of indulgences and made other criticisms of the church in the form of the Ninety-five Theses. According to custom, he posted these on the church door at Wittenberg in 1517 and stood ready to defend them in debate. He believed that the church was taking advantage of the fears of simple people.

Soon after Luther, the Frenchman John Calvin preached doctrines that in various nations of Western Europe gave rise to a second large group of dissenting (Reformed or Presbyterian) churches.

It was in 1519, less than two years after Luther posted his Ninety-five Theses, that Ulrich Zwingli underwent a religious conversion. While a priest at Einsedelen he joined the Reformation. He was later appointed to take charge of the central church of Zurich.

Zwingli's religion was practical, philosophical, and rational. Luther's religion was interested in dogma and more mystical. Zwinglianism was accepted by the city cantons of Switzerland, but so strongly opposed by the rural and forest cantons that war soon broke out. Zwingli was killed in 1531 at the end of the war. The restoration of peace left each Swiss canton free to choose either Roman Catholicism or the Reformed church.

In 1536 John Calvin assumed the leadership of the Reformed church in Geneva. Calvin, French in birth and schooling, was a well-trained scholar with a legal education. The writings of Erasmus and Luther converted Calvin to their ideas. In 1536 Calvin published the first edition of his great work, *The Institutes of the Christian Religion*. The book was noteworthy for its clarity and precise logic.

Calvinism was marked by three outstanding characteristics: (1) its emphasis on the sovereignty of God, which held that God *elected* some persons to be saved and others to be damned (predestination); (2) it called for more democratic church government; and (3) it prescribed a strict moral code drawn from the Bible, particularly the Old Testament. The code condemned worldly pleasures and regulated severely the conduct of all followers.

Calvin's outstanding disciple was John Knox from Scotland. Knox spent some years in Geneva and adopted Calvin's views. He preached his views in Scotland, where they were adopted in 1560 in what became the Presbyterian church.

Possibly no other late medieval development had such profound effects as the development of printing. It brought the relatively cheap and widespread dissemination of information and thus advanced all the pursuits of mankind. Europe learned how to make paper from the Muslims, and it came into general use by the end of the thirteenth century. John Gutenberg's great contribution to printing was the invention of movable type about the year 1446. He printed a Latin Bible about 1456.

The Anabaptists were called "the left wing" of the Reformation. They opposed both the papacy and the Reformers. They wanted a different kind of Reformation. They believed that the Reformers had not gone far enough in their attempts to bring about change.

Various kinds of revolt against the Roman Church occurred between 1517 and 1534. The Council of Trent (1545-63) represented the Roman Catholic reform. The Reformation period closed with the Thirty Years War (1618-48), which brought a measure of mutual toleration between the Roman Catholics and the Protestants.

HOMILETICAL EMPHASES

THE RENAISSANCE

Near the end of the thirteenth century the great age of preaching was already declining. The homiletics of the time did not show as much decline as did the preaching. The reason for that is that theory commonly follows practice. The theory of any epoch is likely to be based more on the theory of the preceding epoch than on contemporary practice. Even at best we find that the homiletics of the fourteenth and fifteenth centuries was marked by many faults of its own as well as those from the preceding age. The homiletics of this period cannot be regarded as the highest quality, but it is of much interest, both as an evolution from the past and as an impulse to the future of homiletical theory. The treatises are greater in number and more elaborate.

To the end of the thirteenth or the early part of the fourteenth century belongs a group of treatises of uncertain authorship. One of these is assigned to the famous theologian Thomas Aquinas, but it is almost certainly not his. Called *A Treatise on the Art of Preaching (Tractatus de Arte Praedicandi)*, the book discusses the nature, value, and effect of preaching; the mode of amplifying the discourse; and certain points the preacher must observe. A later supplement gives some examples of sermons of different kinds, and distinguishes three different modes of preaching: (1) the *laic* or popular mode, such as the old homily or running comment on Scripture; (2) the *thematic,* or topical form, which derives a statute or proposition from the text and logically unfolds it; and (3) the use of the text itself as the proposition that gives the division, and supporting it with illustrations, arguments, application. Thus we see that the threefold distinction so familiar to us—expository, topical, and textual—was already in use and clearly distinguished.

A Certain Treatise on Amplifying Sermons, an anonymous work belonging to the late thirteenth or early fourteenth century, was very brief—a sort of homiletical sketch showing how to expand a sermon. It gives eight ways of amplifying a discourse: (1) putting a proposition for a word—by definition, description, explanation; (2) dividing and analyzing, but not excessively; (3) reasoning, both direct and refutative; (4) citation of texts; (5) use of the degrees—positive, comparative, superlative; (6) use of figures of speech; (7) use of allegory and tropology; and (8) setting forth of causes and effects.

At about the beginning of the sixteenth century appeared two treatises that had fuller and more forceful treatments than the preceding ones. One of those works was a *Treatise on the Method of Learning and Teaching to the People Sacred Things, or the Method of Preaching*. The author called himself Hieronymus (Jerome) Dungersheim of Ochsenfurt and dedicated his work to Ernst, Archbishop of Magdeburg.

Another noteworthy homiletician was Ulrich Surgant, who said that he was a young priest in 1475. The first book of his treatise is dated 1502, whereas the second book mentions 1503 as the current year. His book bears the title *A Manual for Curates (Manuale Curatorum)*, and consists of two volumes. It is important both in itself and marked the transition to the homiletical work of the humanists of the next period.

Homiletics after Augustine was sadly lacking in originality and power. The treatment was lifeless and mechanical. One feature we cannot fail to commend, however, is its urgent insistence on fitness in character and culture in the preacher.

From the borders of Italy the revival of learning soon spread to Germany, where the Renaissance officially began in 1400. Twelve universities were founded between 1409 and 1506. Agricola was one of the outstanding teachers. Latin and Greek flourished at that time together with humanist immorality. Erasmus, the great Dutch humanist scholar, left England and went to Basel, where he found a place in which he could be alone to study. In 1516 he published a Greek New Testament and a Latin translation. It was through that work that he opened new Bible sources and thus aided the Renaissance.

In summary, the Renaissance was a period in which preaching suffered, for preaching was one of the weakest elements of Scholasticism. Preaching was popular, but it was also coarse and vulgar, dealing more with legends than with the Scriptures. When Scripture was used, it was often mishandled. The preaching was fanatic and extremist. There was a tendency to begin to adapt the preaching to the poor and ignorant, a fact that was soon to have far-reaching implications during the Reformation.

THE REFORMATION

The artistic and literary revival of the fourteenth and fifteenth centuries influenced the development of preaching in the next century. As a result, the sixteenth century and the Reformation years can be added to the fourth and thirteenth on the list of great periods of preaching.

In Europe in the fourteenth and fifteenth centuries, the Roman Catholic pulpit was in a state of decay. There was a Scholastic approach to preaching with wearisome divisions, tedious refinements, useless distinctions, and subtleties. The sermon applications and illustrations were taken mostly from fables or legends. The morals of Christianity, however, were usually clearly taught. The sermons were normally delivered with free speech and varying amounts of preparation. A manuscript was used on occasion.

In general the pulpit work tended to be empty, frigid, and without a moving effect. Plagiarism and slavish dependence on others were the order of the day. The interpretation of Scripture in the messages was allegorical, strained, and faulty. Doctrinal teaching was generally corrupt.

Because of the work of the Reformers, a new note was sounded in preaching in Europe in the sixteenth century. The age of the Reformation brought the sharpest turning point in the historical development of Christian preaching. That was evidenced in its contents, form, and spirit. This new era of preaching produced not only a revival in preaching but in biblical preaching. There was also a revival of controversial and doctrinal preaching. The special emphasis in doctrinal preaching was on grace.

Reformation preaching reflected the influence of the conflict with error. The Reformers gave a prominent place to Scripture in their messages. As a result, a new emphasis was placed on preaching as a vital element of Christian worship and life.

The contribution of humanism and the revival of learning to homiletical theory may be best exhibited by first considering the general influence of that great movement on homiletics, and then the definite contribution of two great humanists—John Reuchlin and Desiderius Erasmus.

In the most general aspects of the matter we may observe several lines of humanistic influence on the development of homiletics:

1. The general and widespread quickening of thought, which partly produced and fruitfully accompanied the revival of letters, inevitably worked its effects in the department of preaching and its theory.

2. The more accurate scholarship that came in with the movement, with its enthusiastic attention to the details of literary acquisition and expression, was a force of importance.

3. The improvement of literary taste must also be recognized as having important general influence in the improvement of homiletical theory.

Along with the other great classical writings, those that dealt especially with the principles of rhetoric came up for fresh and first-hand study. Aristotle, Cicero, Quintilian, and others were read anew and with greater zest. Chief among those who gave special attention to rhetorical and homiletical matters were Reuchlin and Erasmus.

Among John Reuchlin's many writings is one published in 1504 under the title *Liber congestorum de art praedicandi,* which means "a collection of rules, etc., on the art of preaching." It seems to be a brief and ill-arranged treatise, but it had the excellent effect of awakening a new interest in evangelical preaching. It owed much to Augustine, but went back to classical rhetoric for its leading principles. It urged preachers to have a proper conception of the dignity of their calling and to observe a suitable delivery and demeanor. The work treats briefly these homiletical topics: invention, introduction, reading of the Scripture divisions, proof, reformation, conclusion, commonplaces (i.e., usual subjects of discourse), memory (i.e., memorizing either the material or form of discourse for delivery).

Greatest among the humanists, and also most important for our present studies, was the famous scholar Desiderius Erasmus (1457-1536). He was a man of remarkable intellect, notable achievement, puzzling personality, and extensive, enduring influence. He was also a genial and witty talker, an admirable stylist, a sharp satirist, and on occasion a sane and judicious writer on moral and religious subjects, including rhetoric and homiletics.

Several general items can be noted in regard to Erasmus's rhetorical and homiletical work. His own Latin style was admirable, although it suffered from verbosity. He was deeply interested and thoroughly versed in general rhetoric. Those facts emerged from his book, *Copia,* published in 1511. It was a textbook on rhetoric intended to aid, as the title indicates, in the finding of both words and material. It was a very popular work, passing through nearly sixty editions during Erasmus's lifetime.

The most important work on the theory of preaching since Augustine (and indeed one of the most important of all times) is the long and labored treatise of Erasmus. It bears the title, *Ecclesiastes, sive Concionator Evangelicus* (i.e., gospel preacher), and was published at Basel during the last year of the author's life—the dedication being dated August 1535, shortly before his death in February 1536.

Erasmus treated the subject of preaching in four books. The first discussed the dignity of the preaching office and the virtues and character appropriate to the office. The second and third books consisted of doctrines and precepts on the art of preaching derived from rhetoricians, logicians, and theologians. The fourth book was devoted to the suggestion of particular subjects for pulpit treatment and the best ways of handling them.

In regard to the three kinds of rhetoric—judicial, deliberative, and epideictic (which he calls *fenus encomasticum*), Erasmus remarks that only the first applies to preaching. Deliberative, or persuasive rhetoric, however, gives many important hints to the preacher, especially in regard to the formulation and statement of propositions. Epideictic or laudatory rhetoric may be of help in the matter of praise and thanksgiving to God in sermons and in funeral or memorial addresses.

Another way of considering the rhetorical functions of the preacher comes to light in the accepted divisions of rhetoric: invention, arrangement, style, memory, and delivery. Erasmus compares invention to the bones; arrangement to the nerves; style to the flesh and skin; memory to vitality; and delivery to action or motion. Those are the essential items in preaching, and they underlie the other mode of presenting rhetorical theory according to the parts of the speech: exordium, narration, division, confirmation, confutation, and conclusion. In the discussion of those parts, the author treats introduction and narration together, distinguishes without separation positive and refutative argument, and omits the conclusion. The result is a presentation of the three very important topics of introduction, division, and argument.

Our survey would not be complete without some mention of the state of homiletical theory among the Roman Catholics of the period, although their contributions were minimal. In homiletics as well as in other spheres of reform, they owed much to both the humanists and Protestants. Besides Reuchlin and Erasmus, who never separated from the Roman church, there were many scholars of the time, especially those in Italy, who were warmer partisans of the ancient order. The work of those scholarly leaders was felt in every sphere of Catholic thought, including preaching. Prominent was Charles Borromeo, the famous archbishop of Milan, cardinal, and later saint. He took a deep personal interest in the improvement of preaching, and wrote a little book on pastoral duties in which he touched on the matter.

Some Catholic writers of the time deserve notice. Augustine Valerio, at the request of Cardinal Borromeo, published in 1575 a *Rhetoric Ecclesiastical*. He grouped and discussed the materials of preaching under the heads of things to be believed, hoped for, feared, avoided, and done. He insisted on maintaining a distinction between sacred and common rhetoric. In 1565 the Spanish court preacher Lorenzo Villavicentio published a treatise on preaching that seems (from the title and some indication of the treatment as given by Keppler in Werzer and Welte) to have been directly borrowed from the great Protestant homiletician Andrew Hyperius with such changes as the situation demanded. It had the same title as the work of Hyperius and adopted his classification of the kinds of preaching as distinguished from secular oratory.

In his *History of Spanish Literature* Ticknor mentions several works of homiletical interest. In 1589 Juan de Guzman published a formal treatise on rhetoric. In it he made an ingenious application of the rules of the Greek and Roman masters to the demands of modern sermonizing in Spanish.

Paton, the author of several works of little value, published in 1604 a crude treatise on *The Art of Spanish Eloquence,* which was founded on the rules of the ancients.

Among Catholic writers on homiletics of this period the most outstanding was the eminent Spanish preacher, bishop, and devotional writer Luiz of Granada (1504-1588). His *Rhetorica Ecclesiastical* or *Six Books on the Method of Preaching* was a work of real value for its contents, style, and place in the literature and history of homiletics.

Our survey of the development of homiletical theory from its beginning to the Reformation has shown that theory is both historically and naturally related to general rhetoric as the art or science of oratory. But it has also shown how impossible it is to consider preaching, with its artistic or theoretical expression, as merely one of the forms of public address.

Three great elements of preaching give it and its theoretical unfolding a distinction that marks off homiletics from general rhetoric. They are (1) the origin of preaching in the distinctively religious aims of the Hebrew prophets and Jesus and His apostles, (2) the historic unfolding of preaching as a fixed and characteristic element in the worship and work of the Christian religion, and (3) the unique relation of preaching to the Bible considered as the revelation of the mind and will of God for all time.

One of the immediate and lasting effects of the Reformation was that it induced and confirmed a greater respect for preaching as a divinely appointed means of instruction in Christian doctrine and conduct. The relative importance of preaching in relation to the other elements of worship was greatly enhanced. That heightened respect naturally produced a demand for a higher kind of pulpit work, which reacted powerfully and favorably on the art and labor of making sermons. It is true that the Reformation impulse was felt more in the content than in the form of sermons.

One of the most significant effects of the Reformation on preaching was that it brought in and established a better interpretation and application of Scripture in sermons.

The preacher's one great task was to set forth the doctrinal and moral teachings of the Word of God, therefore, the greater part of Reformation preaching was expository. Once more, after long centuries, people were reading the Scripture in their own language. Preachers studying the original Greek and Hebrew were carefully explaining to the people the connected teachings of passage after passage and book after book. The expository sermons of the Reformers are much more orderly than those of the Fathers.

The Reformation exemplified and expressed in its preaching a deeper interest in the spiritual life of the people, as regards both doctrine and conduct. The good of the hearers was its predominant aim, therefore, it had to be adapted in form and language to the hearers.

None of the outstanding leaders of the Reformation—Luther, Zwingli, Calvin, or Knox—left any treatise or definite instruction on the art of preaching. But all of them had something to say about the practice of preaching, and so their examples and instructions had much to do in helping others to formulate principles into theory.

It was a fundamental conception of Luther that preaching must have the central place in worship as being the true and living Word of God coming through the preacher. The main thought in Luther's esteem was the subject, or proposition, which should be biblical in substance and definite in the preacher's own mind.

Luther repeatedly taught that the aim of preaching is the spiritual good of the hearers. Therefore, it is essential that the preacher should be a well-trained and skillful speaker, and a master of the art of public address.

As to preparation and delivery, Luther's own practice varied, and his suggestions to others seem to have been in line with his own methods. Two things, however, stand out clearly: there must be careful preparation, and there must be freedom in delivery. A few of Luther's sermons were written out beforehand, many were spoken from more or less full notes, but all were spoken, not read.

Calvin's views and practice in regard to preaching are easily discovered and well known. As with all the great Reformers, he gave to preaching the central place in worship. He taught that it must be in spirit an exposition and application of the Word of God. His sermons were chiefly expository, and his exposition was acute, clear, reasoned, and sound. In form, his sermons are like the ancient homily, consisting of verse by verse commentary, but his logical and trained intellect gave both unity of theme and connection of thought to his discourses. His main object was to explain and convince, and his manner of speaking was eminently suited to this purpose. He does not seem to have written his sermons before or after delivery, but they were taken down and preserved by reporters. His delivery has been described as deliberate and forceful.

Both Ulrich Zwingli and Heinrich Bullinger agreed with the other Reformers in their estimate of preaching as the main element in worship and consisting chiefly of explanation and enforcement of Scripture.

Among the English Reformers the subject received some attention, for as early as 1613 we find an English translation of a Latin treatise on *The Art of Prophecying,* which of course was written earlier and showed a good grasp of homiletics. The book was written by William Perkins, and appears to have been the first homiletical treatise by an English author.

In general we may remark that while the Reformers laid more stress on the content and aim of preaching than on its form and method, they did not wholly neglect form and method either in their example or their teaching. They seemed to take it for granted that in requiring skill and training for a proper study and proclamation of the Word of God, they were demanding that the preacher should know how to use the accepted and tested principles of rhetoric as they were applicable to the preparation and delivery of sermons.

By far the most original and significant work by any early Protestant writer on homiletics is that of Andrew Hyperius (1511-1564). Andrew Gerard (Andreas Gerardus), better known as Hyperius from his birthplace, was born at Ypres in Flanders, May 16, 1511. His father was a lawyer of learning and distinction, whose name he inherited.

Hyperius was an all-round scholar. His lectures and works in exegetical, systematic, and practical theology were useful and justly noted. He wrote two homiletical books: (1) *De Formandis Concionibus Sacris* and *Topica Theologica.* The second was really an appendix to the first and contained, after the manner of the older homiletics, a list of subjects for preaching with suggestions for their suitable treatment. The earlier treatise, *On the Making of Sacred Discourses,* was and remains a work of the first importance in the development of homiletics. Writers such as Harnack did not hesitate to pronounce this work of Hyperius as the first really scientific treatise on the theory of preaching.

After Hyperius, Protestant homiletics fell into the slough of Scholasticism in the seventeenth century. Cold and minute analysis and refinement with little adaptation to life and need was the order of the day.

In England, as we have already seen, the theory of preaching received some notice at the hands of the Reformers, and there was at least one treatise devoted to the subject. It was written in Latin and early in the seventeenth century translated into English.

Let us note these characteristics of the Reformation preaching in general:

1. It was a *revival of preaching.*
2. It was a revival of *biblical preaching.* The greater part of Reformation preaching was expository. This expository preaching was based on a much more strict and reasonable exegesis than at any time since the days of Chrysostom.
3. The Reformation was a period of *freedom in preaching.* There was great variety evidenced in the sermons. Scripture was interpreted more correctly than it had been

for years. The introductions of the sermons had as their main aim the gaining of interest. A good portion of illustrative material was employed.

BIOGRAPHICAL SURVEY

RENAISSANCE PREACHERS (1361-1499)

Bernardino of Busti	d. c. 1500
Bernardino of Siena	1380-1444
Gabriel Biel	1420-1495
Jean Charlier	1363-1429
Conrad of Waldhausen	d. 1369
Vincent Ferrar	1357-1419
John Geiler	1445-1510
John Gritsch	d. 1430
Gerard Groot	1349-1384
John Huss	1373-1415
Jerome of Prague	1375-1416
John of Capistrano	1386-1456
John of Wesel	c. 1400-1481
Thomas a Kempis	1381-1471
Leonardo of Uttino	d. 1470
Mattias of Janow	d. 1394
John Militsch	d. 1374
Girolamo Savonarola	1452-1498
John Tauler	1290-1361
John Wycliffe	1324-1384

REFORMATION PREACHERS (1500-1572)

Reformation Preaching in Germany

John Brentz	1499-1570
John Bugenhagen	1485-1558
Martin Butzer	1491-1551
Capito Wolfgang	1478-1541
Veit Deitrich	1506-1549
Martin Luther	1483-1586
John Mathesius	1504-1565
George Morgenstern	end of 15th cent.
Pelbart	early 16th cent.
John Staupitz	1469-1524

Reformation Preaching in England

John Bradford	1510-1555
John Colet	1466-1519
Miles Coverdale	1488-1568
Thomas Cranmer	1489-1556

Bernard Gilpin	1517-1583
John Hooper	c. 1495-1555
John Jewel	1522-1571
Hugh Latimer	1490-1555
Matthew Parker	1504-1575
Nicholas Ridley	c. 1500-1555
John Rogers	c. 1500-1555
William Tyndale	1494-1536

Reformation Preaching in France

William Farel	1489-1565
Antoine Froment	1509-1581
Olivier Maillard	1500s
Michel Menot	d. 1518
Gerard Roussel	1480-1550
Pierre Viret	1511-1571

Reformation Preaching in Scotland

Patrick Hamilton	1504-1528
John Knox	1505-1572
John Willock	d. 1585
George Wishart	1513-1546

Reformation Preaching in Switzerland

Theodore Beza	d. 1605
Heinrich Bullinger	1504-1575
John Calvin	1509-1564
Berthold Haller	1492-?
Leo Jud	1482-1542
Ulrich Zwingli	1484-1531

Anabaptist Preaching

Balthasar Hübmaier	1480-1528
Menno Simons	1492-1559

Reformation Preaching in Northern Europe

Erasmus (Netherlands)	1456-1536
Olaf Petri (Sweden)	1497-1552
Laurent Petri (Sweden)	1499-1573
Hans Tausen (Denmark)	d. 1561

Reformation Preaching in Southern Europe

Augustino Cazalla (Spain)	1510-1559
Juan Gil (Spain)	d. 1556
Bernardino Ochino (Italy)	1487-1564

Miscellaneous European Reformation Preaching

Oswald Myconius (Basel)	1488-1552
Oecolampadius (Basel)	1482-1531
Paul Spretter (Prussia)	1484-1551

7

The Early Modern Period

(1572—1789)

Politics were dominated by religion during the Scottish Reformation, but in England religion had been secondary to political considerations. The barons and good burghers of the middle class in Scotland united under John Knox against the crown to bring about reform. In England the Reformation had been created from above by law of the ruler. It is little wonder that the Reformation in Scotland was more radical. In no other area except Geneva was the influence of Calvinism so strong.

In 1572 an attempt was made to establish episcopalian church government in Scotland. The battle against prelacy now took the place of the war against popery. Andrew Melville, the principal of Glasgow University, led the battle to restore the presbyterian system of church government, and in 1581 presbyteries were again set up on an experimental basis. In 1592, despite strong opposition from King James VI, Melville's cause was triumphant, and Presbyterianism was made the established form of religion in Scotland.

In 1570 Pope Pius V issued an edict excommunicating Elizabeth and freeing her subjects from allegiance to her. Elizabeth retaliated by an act aimed at the Jesuits who planned to recapture England for the papacy. A school had been set up at Douai on the French coast where men could be trained by the Jesuits to minister secretly to the followers of the pope in England. The pope then enlisted the aid of Philip of Spain to recover England for the Roman church. In 1588 Philip gathered a great fleet known as the Spanish Armada and sailed against England. His fleet was ignominiously defeated by the English fleet. This victory established England as the champion of Protestantism in Europe.

The defeat of Spain and the pope left the English rulers free to give attention to the problem of Puritanism. From 1567 to 1660 the Puritans were a dominant force in English domestic affairs.

The Puritans wanted to purify the Anglican church in accordance with the Bible, which they accepted as the infallible rule of faith and life. That desire led to their being nicknamed Puritans. Cambridge became the university center where the Puritans had their greatest influence.

After her danger from the pope ended, Elizabeth had an act passed against the Puritans in 1593. That act gave the authorities the right to imprison the Puritans for failure to attend the Anglican church.

Richard Hooker (c. 1554-1600), to meet the Puritan threat to the state church, wrote *Of the Laws of Ecclesiastical Polity,* a work primarily philosophical in nature. In it Hooker maintains that law, given by God and discovered by reason, is basic. Obedience to the ruler, ruling by consent of the people and according to law, is necessary because the ruler is head of both state and church.

Puritan theologians opposed his ideas because they believed that the people, under God, were the source of sovereignty in the church.

The emergence of Thomas Cartwright (1535-1603) as professor of theology at Cambridge about 1570 shifted the emphasis in the Puritan efforts from reform of liturgy to reform in theology and church government. Insistence on the final authority of the Scriptures led his followers to adopt a Calvinistic theology that would make the Thirty-nine Articles of the Anglican church even more Calvinistic. A number of the Puritans who did not follow the presbyterian pattern of Cartwright adopted the ideas of Henry Jacob (1563-1624). Jacob may be considered to be the founder of the Independents or Puritan Congregationalists. He was imprisoned for his view that each congregation was to be left free in the state church to choose its own pastor, determine its policies, and manage its own affairs. Independent or congregational Puritanism in England grew slowly from that humble beginning until under Oliver Cromwell it became more powerful than presbyterianism.

The earliest group of separatist congregationalists that established a church based on a covenant was led by Richard Fitz (c. 1570). Robert Browne (c. 1550-1633), who graduated from Cambridge in 1572 in the stirring days of Cartwright's proclamation of presbyterian ideas, gathered together a group under a church covenant in Norwich in 1581. From there he was forced to flee with his congregation to Holland, where he wrote three treatises elaborating the principles of separatist congregationalism. The separatists would have nothing to do with the state church.

When James VI of Scotland became James I of England in 1603, the Puritans hoped that the Calvinistic king, who liked episcopacy, would set up a presbyterian government in the Anglican church. To emphasize their hope, they presented him with the Millenary Petition (signed by nearly a thousand Puritan ministers) on his arrival in 1603 and asked that the Anglican church be completely "purified" in liturgy and polity. The ruler called the Hampton Court Conference in 1604. Permission to make a new English translation of the Scriptures was the net result of that meeting, and a group of learned divines began work on the Bible popularly known as the King James Version. It was completed in 1611 and in time replaced the Geneva Bible in the affections of English-speaking peoples.

Jansenism in the Roman Catholic church of France was the Continental counterpart of English Puritanism. Both found their main theological roots in Augustine's views. The Jansenist movement was a reaction from the Thomistic orthodoxy of the Council of Trent to a Bible-based Augustinianism that would revitalize personal life. Blaise Pascal (1623-1662) supported the Jansenists. Faith in mystical communion with God was his major emphasis.

One of the most influential movements in the period was the evangelical revival of the first half of the eighteenth century. In England it was known as the Wesleyan revival; in America, the Great Awakening. The Continent, with its pietistic movement and with historical connections between Augustus G. Spangenberg and John Wesley, deserves some share in the background of the Great Awakening, although the unwillingness of the pietists to organize for the perpetuation of their ideals prevented them from the possibility of spreading extensively like the Methodists.

Into that arid country flowed the refreshing streams of the Wesleyan revival. The leaders were John and Charles Wesley, bred in the parsonage of a high-church rector, and George Whitefield, son of a saloonkeeper. Both Wesleys spent a brief but important period in missionary service for the Church of England in Georgia. There they came into contact with the Moravian leader Spangenberg, from whom they learned the need for a personal experience of faith in Jesus Christ. Both returned to England, and in 1738 professed conversion and regeneration. Whitefield, too, had experienced a rebirth, and the three formed the triumvirate of the new Methodist movement.

Of the three, doubtless Whitefield was the ablest preacher; Charles Wesley was the great hymnwriter; while John Wesley was the methodical organizer who gave structure and endurance to the movement. It is noteworthy that Whitefield was a Calvinist, whereas the two Wesleys were Arminian. As a result, two kinds of Methodists were developed, although the great majority followed the Wesleyan kind. The exception was in Wales where the Methodists were organized into the Calvinistic Methodist church. These three Methodist leaders preached and sang throughout all of Britain, Wales, and Scotland, while Whitefield made extensive preaching tours in the American colonies. In some instances these men built upon the foundation others had laid. In Wales a layman, Howel Harris, had begun a Welsh revival two years before the Methodist leaders arrived to kindle fresh fire. In America Whitefield built upon the efforts of Frelinghuysen, the Tennents and Jonathan Edwards.

The first Great Awakening was the great revival of the early 18th century which swept across the colonies. The roots of this revival seem to have sprung from Europe. The warmhearted evangelistic movement there known as *pietism* had prepared the hearts of many of those emigrating to America. Several groups of Germans in Pennsylvania who had come under its influence were among the first to experience revival. By 1726 the preaching of Theodore J. Frelinghuysen, a deeply spiritual minister of the Dutch Reformed Church in New Jersey, became peculiarly effective in winning men to Christ and moving his hearers toward God. He inspired others during the next several years, one of the most important of whom was the Presbyterian minister, Gilbert Tennent, who became a zealous promoter of the revival.

By 1734, in what seems to have been a separate movement, Jonathan Edwards, Congregationalist pastor of Northampton, Massachusetts, found a deepened spiritual sensitiveness in his congregation and in the whole community. A great revival followed. It spread rapidly to every part of the colonies. Even John Wesley in England learned about it in 1738 and marveled.

Before the Great Awakening, Baptist progress was slow. By 1739, there were fewer than fifty Baptist churches in all America.

HOMILETICAL EMPHASES

In the wake of the Reformation, European preaching experienced its inevitable decline. Fortunately, it was neither so general nor so uniform as those of the past, because each nation experienced its own degree of decline. Two European countries— England and France—recovered rather rapidly from the decline and enjoyed the highest level of preaching ever. In the remainder of Europe there was none of the intellectual force, spiritual fervor, and popular success which the earlier and middle periods of the sixteenth century had witnessed in the pulpit.

This period has been called the golden age of preaching in England, for in this period preaching had a unique influence on the entire life of the nation. The evils of society were tremendous and the preaching of the Puritans alone could counteract such conditions. The sermons of the period often reflected the coarse and sharp polemic which the era enjoyed. This was the supreme age of literary giants, with William Shakespeare leading the playwrights and Milton leading the poets. John Bunyan has been made immortal by his allegory, Pilgrim's Progress.

Several church groups which developed at this time made their influence felt upon the country. Two leading parties, the Brownists (later Independents and Congregationalists) and the Anabaptists (later the Baptists), resulted from compromises under Elizabeth. The extreme Episcopal party had two elements: those who were really Romanists at heart, and those who opposed Rome but were strict sacramentalists and ritualists. There was another influential party generally called the Puritans, because they advocated that life, doctrine, and church polity should conform to the "pure Word of God." There were people in all segments of the church who considered themselves Puritans. Two great parties, the Anglicans and the Puritans, arose and alternated in ascendency and supremacy. Much of the turmoil ceased when, with the accession of William and Mary in 1688, the Act of Toleration was passed, establishing Episcopacy in England and Presbyterianism in Scotland.

Preaching in the Protestant pulpit was given to scriptural exposition and polemic against the church of Rome. The fierce sectarian struggles coupled with the tearing down of the Roman system, however, often led to private interpretations of Scripture and doctrine. The Puritans often descended into minute and exhaustive subdivisions of their text which must have been wearisome to their followers. Greek and Latin flowed profusely. The style of the age was often bombastic and overdone, highly imaginative, and fanciful. The services often lasted for hours at a time and the heavy content presented must have been formidable to endure.

On the positive side, it must be said that preaching did remain true to the Word of God and therefore was a chief source of strength and thought in days of literary and social greatness.

The seventeenth century was a century of vast change. Amid the crowded and rapidly shifting events arose the classic period of the British pulpit. Edwin C. Dargan, historian of preaching, comments:

> The British pulpit of the seventeenth century was a living factor of the age. It gave and received potent influence in the stirring events and movements of the time; and it cannot be understood or rightly valued apart from its intimate connection with the social, literary, and religious facts and forces which helped to make the seventeenth century in England, as in France, an illustrious epoch in the history of preaching.[1]

Dargan cites four reasons the age was so great in preaching: (1) loyalty to the Word of God, (2) consciousness of strength, (3) thoughtfulness, and (4) the use of language[2] It is important here that we allow Dargan to elaborate on his first point above:

> It was one of the Anglican divines of this period—William Chillingworth—who gave utterance to the famous dictum, "The Bible, and the Bible only, is the religion of Protestants." This principle was the very life-blood of the English preaching of the seventeenth century; its antecedents necessitated and its problems demanded an intelligent, strong, and confident appeal to the authority of God as revealed in His Word. That appeal was made with power and effect.[3]

· The conditions of thought and of preaching during the seventeenth century varied much with the different countries. There was not much worth noting in Spain. In Italy the elder Segneri introduced a new mode of preaching patterned on the branch models. Germany was desolated by the Thirty Years War, yet pietism arose with its new impulse in Christian life and preaching. Holland showed activity in theological thought, but not remarkable results in preaching. In England this was the turbulent era of the Stuarts and the Commonwealth, but also of the great classic preachers among churchmen, Puritans, and dissenters. In France the Edict of Nantes gave impulse to Protestant preaching, and that stimulated the Catholic pulpit, which reached its classic glory in the age of Louis XIV. Among all those peoples was development of theory as well as practice in the art of preaching.

In France several treatises on homiletics of exceptional value appeared during this period. The famous and beloved Protestant preacher Jean Claude produced an *Essay on the Composition of a Sermon,* which was first published after his death in 1688, and has since been much used and translated. Claude (1619-1687) was one of the greatest and best of the early French Protestants. His treatise was translated into English by Robert Robinson, the famous Cambridge preacher, and has been widely influential in both England and America.

Claude believed in an economy of divisions in the sermon—never more than four or five, and preferably two or three. They may come either from the text or from the subject suggested by the text. As for the division of the text itself, sometimes the order

1. Edwin C. Dargan, A *History of Preaching* (New York: George H. Doran, 1905), 2:137.
2. Ibid., 148.
3. Ibid.

of the words is clear and natural enough that no division is necessary; one needs only follow the order of the words.

Claude briefly treated exordium (introduction) and conclusion. "The principal use of an exordium is to prepare the hearer's mind for the particular matters you have to treat of, and insensibly to conduct him to them." Sensible suggestions are offered as to the brevity, clearness, and attractiveness of introductions. As for the conclusion he said: "The conclusion should be lively and animating, full of great and beautiful figures, aiming to move Christian affections." In his conclusion he made some general remarks on the need of variety, soberness, and other qualities of good preaching.

Among French Catholics in the earlier part of the century homiletical teachings were found in the writings of St. Vincent de Paul (c. 1580-1600) and St. Francis de Sales (1567-1622).

Almost at the end of the century the celebrated Archbishop of Cambrai, Frances Fenelon, wrote his famous and valuable *Dialogues on Eloquence*. He did not write out his sermons, but the accounts of his eloquence are full of recognition of his unusual powers in the pulpit. His little work on *Eloquence*, particularly referring to the eloquence of the pulpit, has a deserved fame and is still read and highly esteemed by students of the subject.

In Germany, although the times were distressing among all three of the leading branches of Christian opinion (Roman Catholic, Lutheran, and Reformed) there was a good deal of homiletical teaching and writing. Felix Bidenbach led the way in 1603, with a *Manual for Ministers*. During this period the term *homiletics* came more and more to designate the art of preaching.

In Holland, John Hoornbeek published in 1645 a *Treatise on the Method of Preaching*, which Van Oosterzee characterized as the first original work on homiletics published on Dutch soil.[4]

In these German and Dutch treatises two distinct homiletic tendencies are observable: (1) the scholastic aspect, which was mechanical, artificial, academic, tedious, and dry; and (2) the more scriptural and evangelical aspect, which showed greater reality and spiritual power. But even the latter did not free itself wholly from the dry method and empty spirit of the age. Nothing of significant value was added to the theory and practice of preaching from those writings. They merely continued the principles of the past and prepared for a reaction toward more wholesome and sound modes of treatment.

In England the first treatise on the art of preaching seems to have been that of William Perkins. Originally written in Latin, it was translated into English and published in 1613 by Thomas Tuke.

English homiletical literature in the seventeenth century followed the traditional rhetorical and sometimes Scholastic methods. However, the literature in general appears lacking in both originality and value. In the eighteenth century some teachings on homiletics appeared that are deserving of investigation. A treatise by Gaichies, *Maxims on the Eloquence of the Pulpit*, was published in 1710. In 1715 Gisbert's

---

4. J. J. Van Oosterzee, tran. Maurice J. Evans, *Practical Theology* (New York: Charles Scribner's Sons, n.d.), 146.

Christian Eloquence in Idea and in Practice appeared.

About 1793 Cardinal Maury published his *Principles of Eloquence of the Pulpit and of the Bar*. As the title suggests, it was a general treatise with applications to preaching.

The only French Protestant treatise of importance was *Lectures on Preaching,* a set of volumes by J. F. Ostervald,[5] the noted professor of theology at Neuchatel in Switzerland.

In Germany, the varieties of opinion and practice in preaching revealed themselves in the homiletical literature of the eighteenth century. Early in the century the influence of Spener, the eminent Pietist who repudiated the Scholasticism of the preceding epoch, was powerfully felt. He himself paid little attention to form in preaching.

More important and valuable than any of those works was that of J. L. Mosheim, the famous church historian and preacher. He lectured on homiletics at the University of Gottingen, and is called by Harnack "the father of modern spiritual eloquence." His lectures were published after his death (sometime between 1755 and 1763) by Windheim under the title, *Instruction on Preaching Edifyingly*.

Near the end of the century, F. V. Reinhard, lecturer and preacher at Wittenberg and later court preacher at Dresden, exerted a great homiletical influence from both chair and pulpit. Some of his principles were outlines in his confessions.

In Holland,[6] Cocceius and his followers revolted from the Scholastic method. Representing Cocceius is *Rhetorica Ecclesiastica* by F. H. Van der Honert. Also supporting Cocceius's views is an analytical table of subjects with *Hints on Preaching* by Van der Alphen. A still greater improvement is found in the work of F. A. Lampe (d. 1729), bearing the title *A Breviary of Homiletical Institutions*.

As near as can be determined, neither Spain nor Italy contributed anything of importance to homiletical development and discussion.

When we investigate English works on homiletics during the eighteenth century, it is interesting to find that one of the first was produced in New England. This little work came from the prolific pen of Cotton Mather, the famous Puritan preacher of Massachusetts. He was a preacher of power, a leader of influence, and a writer of learning.

Two of the most famous and influential English works were written by Scotsmen. George Campbell of Aberdeen published in 1775 his well-known *Lectures on Pulpit Eloquence*. His other work, *The Philosophy of Rhetoric,* enjoyed large circulation and use. The *Lectures on Pulpit Eloquence* are solid, judicious, and thoughtful. They encourage a scriptural and evangelical use of rhetorical principles.

The rationalistic branch of the Scottish church was represented by the famous Hugh Blair of Edinburgh. In his celebrated *Lectures on Rhetoric* several chapters are devoted to the eloquence of the pulpit. The style is elaborate, the sentiment classic, and the ideas and principles good and acceptable.

The greatest name among the English Puritans in the history of preaching is Richard Baxter (1615-1691), who through his treatise *The Reformed Pastor* (1656) influenced the free church clergy for centuries, even as his meditations on *The Saints' Everlasting Rest*

5. Daniel P. Kidder, *A Treatise on Homiletics* (New York: Methodist Book Concern, 1862), 458.
6. Van Oosterzee, *Practical Theology*, 147ff.

(1650) became one of the classic devotional books in English literature.[7]

George Whitefield became the greatest open-air preacher of all time. The descriptions of the masses who listened intently to his words are almost legendary. He is said to have spoken to a crowd of 30,000 at Bristol. On another occasion, Whitefield himself gave the number of listeners as 50,000.

Whitefield had a greater gift for preaching than did John Wesley. Although both of them usually spoke without written notes, Wesley was, nevertheless, the man with the pen and the ordered thoughts, whereas Whitefield possessed above all the gift of inspired rhetorical address. Both Whitefield and Wesley usually based their sermons on a short, freely chosen word of Scripture. That method subsequently became normal in all sermons in the English language.

A new era in English preaching appeared with John Tillotson (1634-1694). In his search for a more natural style he had predecessors in Bishop John Wilkens of Chester (1614-1672), who in his work *Ecclesiastes* or *The Gift of Preaching* (1946) demanded a less artificial method of preaching.

In summary, the early modern period has been remembered as the golden age of English preaching. Although Roman Catholics had a superiority in public address, the Protestant preachers paid more attention to textual analysis. The conversational approach was used with doctrine being emphasized more than application for practical living.

BIOGRAPHICAL SURVEY

The following entries are listed chronologically.

Thomas Hooker (1553-1600)
1. Gave little attention to rhetoric and gestures
2. Had good constructive influence on the development of English prose
3. Wrote *Laws of Ecclesiastical Polity*

Henry Smith (1550-1593)
1. Great orator, especially in the presentation of the Old Testament
2. Left many words of wisdom for preachers

Lancelot Andrews (1555-1624)
1. His sermons were noted for their puns
2. Kept true to the text
3. One of the translators of the King James Version
4. A high churchman, but an advocate of Protestantism
5. Was skilled in Oriental languages
6. Ninety-six of his sermons remain
7. His sermons were often overloaded with learning
8. A deeply spiritual person

7. Hugh Martin, ed., *The Reformed Pastor* (Naperville, Ill.: Allenson, 1956); *The Saints' Everlasting Rest* (Westwood, N.J.: Revell, 1962).

John Donne (1573-1631)
1. Entered the ministry at forty-two years of age
2. Noted for wit
3. Incorporated main divisions in his sermons
4. Noted for using short sentences
5. 156 of his sermons remain
6. Possessed poetic talent

Joseph Hall (1574-1656)
1. Witty, wise, and a master of word play
2. Spent the last year of his life in exile
3. A teacher of rhetoric
4. The "Chrysostom of England"
5. Used biographical sermons

Thomas Fuller (1608-1661)
1. More a writer than a preacher
2. Wrote *Church History of England*

Thomas Adams (1585-1630)
1. Excellent in exposition of scriptural text
2. The "Shakespeare of the Puritans"
3. Preached extensively on manners

David Dickson (1583-1662)
1. A serious Puritan preacher
2. Based his messages on passages of Scripture rather than an individual verse
3. Preaching was the noblest of professions to him

Samuel Rutherford (1600-1661)
1. A sharp controversialist
2. Banished from pastorate
3. Erred by being too positive, too determined

John Livingstone (1603-1661)
1. At twenty-seven years of age preached a sermon that won 500 people to Christ
2. Came from good Christian home training, and was deeply spiritual
3. Wandered abroad for many years and died in exile

Robert Leighton (1611-1684)
1. Pious and humble
2. Had a simple preaching style
3. Preached extemporaneously
4. Excelled in thought, language, and pronunciation

Thomas Goodwin (1600-1679)

1. Had his conversion experience after becoming a pastor
2. Resolved to preach only sound and wholesome words without affectations of wit and vanity of eloquence

John Owen (1616-1683)

1. Theologian and scholar
2. Dean of Christ Church College at Oxford
3. Remembered for his character and theology
4. Ready for college at age twelve
5. Slept an average of four hours each night
6. Good in pastoral work

Richard Baxter (1615-1691)

1. Had very little formal education
2. Best known of the Puritan preachers
3. Used many divisions in his sermons
4. Outstanding pastor
5. The "English Demosthenes"
6. His sources of greatness included earnestness, intellectual accomplishments, and his work as a pastor

John Bunyan (1628-1688)

1. Having had very little education, he could neither read nor write when married
2. Thousands flocked to hear him
3. A man of intense faith
4. Possessed a good imagination

Jeremy Taylor (1613-1679)

1. Remembered for eloquence of language and poetic style
2. Used many illustrations
3. Called the "Poet of the Pulpit"
4. Used many quotations and classical allusions
5. Given a doctorate at request of the king
6. One of four great English masters: (with Shakespeare, Milton, and Bacon)

John Howe (1630-1705)

1. Chaplain to Oliver Cromwell.
2. Endeavored to unite philosophy with religion; known as the "platonic Puritan"
3. A genuine biblical preacher
4. Exercised a lofty imagination

Isaac Barrow (1630-1677)

1. A very learned preacher
2. Preached very long sermons (three and a half hours)

3. Fellow of Trinity College at age nineteen
4. Well educated; spent five years in travel and interaction with great men
5. Held to Chrysostom's works as a pattern
6. Buried in Westminster Abbey

Edward Stillingfleet (1635-1699)
1. Chaplain to the king
2. His sermons were simple and to the point

John Tillotson (1630-1694)
1. Controversialist, but with a sweet and conciliating spirit
2. His sermons were clear in arrangement
3. His sermons were studied by all preachers as a correct pattern for homiletics

Robert South (1638-1716)
1. Most famous satirist in the annals of the British pulpit
2. Remembered as a politician rather than a preacher
3. Wrote sermons against extemporaneous prayer
4. The greatest defect in his preaching was a lack of tenderness

French Preachers of the Seventeenth Century
Claude (1619-1687)
1. Redeemed the sermon from the formal textual treatment of his Protestant predecessors, from the mere rhetorical display of the contemporary court preaching
2. His *Essay on the Composition of a Sermon* was one of the earliest Protestant treatises on the subject

Du Bosc (1623-1692)
1. Far more brilliant as an orator than Claude
2. Highly educated
3. Louis XIV called him the best speaker in his kingdom

Saurin (1677-1730)
1. The greatest of the French Protestant preachers of the seventeenth century
2. His preaching was extremely popular

Roman Catholic Preachers
Bossuet (1627-1704)
1. His sermons tended to be too lengthy
2. Too artistic in his rhetoric, too little an orator
3. Noted for his funeral orations
4. Moved the passions but mastered the will

Bourdaloue (1632-1704)
1. Called "the greatest preacher of his age"
2. The preacher to kings, the king of preachers
3. Less dogmatic, but more logical than Bossuet
4. His appeal was to truth and righteousness

Flechier (1632-1710)
1. Taught rhetoric
2. Smoothed bitterness of conflict between Catholics and Reformers
3. Funeral orations were his best sermons

Fenelon (1651-1717)
1. Noted for his deep spirituality
2. His sermons were carefully prepared
3. He preached from the heart and without notes

Massillon (1663-1742)
1. Beauty of style was his predominant characteristic
2. Used scarcely any gestures
3. The preacher most feared by Louis XIV
4. A true orator
5. Had a tender appeal in his delivery

8

The Late Modern Period

(1789—1900)

The vigors of revolution, reform, rights, and religion shaped England's people and history during the modern period. The influence of the international, national, and religious pressures was revealed from her pulpits and printing presses. "At no time and among no people does the Christian pulpit appear to greater advantage on the whole than in Great Britain during the nineteenth century."[1]

On the national scene, discontentment among the working classes, unemployment, low wages and high cost of living, discrimination, competition with foreign markets brought social changes (prison and child labor reforms, progress in education, and abolishment of slavery by 1833) along with revolutions, reforms, and riots. In 1802 the Society for the Suppression of Vice was formed and by 1830 British morals were transformed greatly through the work of the evangelicals. Urbanization and industrialization caused great cries for social and humanitarian improvements. Movements and men rose to the occasion with Thomas Arnold being the first prophet of the church's social policy.

Imperialism, science, technological advances (the telegraph in 1840, trans-Atlantic cable in 1866, and telephone and electricity in the 1870s) and struggle for power occupied England's energies. Socialism gained international scope with its favor for the laboring classes and the acclaim of leader Karl Marx.

National reforms affected every cause and neighborhood and church. Literature displayed a new social and scientific awareness. Journalism and literature were invaluable to the success of the Reformers. The writings of Tennyson, Browning,

---

1. Edwin Charles Dargan, *A History of Preaching* (New York: Hodder and Stoughton, 1905), 1:566 and 2:580.

Arnold, Dickens, Eliot, Darwin, Huxley, Scott, and Keats all spoke of social and political reform.

Religious life was divided between the Established church (Anglicans), the Dissenters (Nonconformists), the Catholics and the Jews. By 1828, Nonconformists grew from a 20 to 50 percent segment of church attenders.[2] Much of the social reform was born in the Nonconformist service and was extended through the missionary movements of men like Moffatt, Carey, Livingston, Hill, and Hudson Taylor. Constant divisions among Nonconformists gave birth to the formation of Primative Methodists in 1810, Bible Christians in 1815, Irvingites, Free Presbyterian Church of Scotland, Presbyterian Church of England, Plymouth Brethren, Disciples (Church of Christ), while the new Unitarian movement represented liberal trends. The Oxford or Tractarian movement grew out of the High Church party with John Newman, Keble, and Pusey in 1834. In 1842, about 500 ministers pulled out of Scotland's Established Church to form the Free Church of Scotland. Every English pulpit was influenced by scientific, critical, apologetic, social, and political questions. Class struggle, religious bitterness, division between Nonconformists and Anglicans all show the unrest and discontent of the people.

The working classes were indifferent and unconcerned about the church. In 1840, 75 to 90 percent of the urban class were unchurched. By the late 1880s more than 95 percent were unchurched.[3]

The 1870s stirred with the revivals of Finney, Moody and Sankey, and the rise in Bible conferences, the Keswick movement, and foreign missions. There were 285 meetings in London alone in 1875 that reached 2,500,000 people. Preaching was directed to the current social sins and promotion of practical holiness. The Salvation Army in 1877 and the YMCA reached to the "submerged tenth" and emphasized self-discipline and total abstinence. The emphasis of evangelicals was on personal salvation, the doctrine of the church as a company of believers, church autonomy, and the relationship of faith to life.

Outwardly, the scene was serene, but by the mid-nineteenth century undercurrents, which had been swirling for decades, surfaced through historical discussions on democracy and socialism, evolution and science, Christianity and agnosticism. The age of "revival faith" now became the age of uncertainty, as religion in the life of the common man declined. Though nearly everyone professed some Christian allegiance, church membership declined and biblical authority weakened from 1850 onward. Scientific thought and biblical criticism prompted the church to produce literature on exegesis, archaeology, criticism, apologetics, and devotional matter. The evangelicals found it difficult to hold the allegiance of the more cultured and intelligent. By 1870, the controversy over evolution was at its peak. Science was number one in popularity by 1899, replacing religion and stressing self-sufficiency.

The battle for the mind was fought from the pulpits, while historic Christianity sustained serious blows from men like Lyell, Engels, Darwin, and Spencer. The Victorian religion, once possessive of the elements of fear and death, hell and heaven,

2. Ernest A. Payne, *The Free Church Tradition in the Life of England* (London: S.C.M., 1959), 93.
3. Desmond Bowen, *The Idea of the Victorian Church* (Montreal: McGill U., 1968).

and a real devil, made a major shift from the intellect of the pulpit to the works of charity on the streets.

F. W. Robertson said: "By the change of times the pulpit lost its place. It does only part of that whole which used to be done by it alone . . . the pulpit is no more the pulpit of three centuries back."[4]

Four extensive religious movements affected England during this period.

MODERN FOREIGN MISSION MOVEMENT

The victory of England over France in 1763 sent explorers scurrying to find new land now controlled by England. Men such as David Brainerd in America were seeking out the Indians for Christ. It remained for William Carey, a young Baptist cobbler, to inaugurate and exemplify the modern foreign mission movement. A Baptist society for foreign missions was formed in 1792. Carey and others were sent to India. Inspired by Carey, English independents and the Church of England organized foreign missionary societies. Within the next 150 years almost every section of the inhabited world received missionaries from all segments of English Christianity.

RELIGIOUS REVIVALS AND CONTRASTING SKEPTICISM

Two parallel but contrasting trends occurred during the period. The Wesleyan revival in the previous period turned the hearts of the masses from infidelity and skepticism, but a strong core of antisupernaturalism was never touched in this or later revivals. The fires of revival diminished during the wars with the American colonies.

ECUMENICALISM

English Christianity as a whole has entered heartily into the ecumenicalism rooted in the burst of enthusiasm for world missions that followed the inception of the modern mission movement by William Carey.

English Baptist work, both home and foreign, grew rapidly under the inspiration of this example. Schools were founded and various social reforms were entered into in cooperation with other Christians. Preachers like Robert Hall (1764-1831), Charles Haddon Spurgeon (1834-92), Alexander Maclaren (1825-1910) and John H. Shakespeare (1857-1928) gave new respectability to the Baptist cause. In 1891 the division between General and Particular Baptists, which had existed from the beginning of English Baptist life was healed, principally through the work of John Clifford. In 1953 there were 202,361 Baptists in England proper, about 100,000 in Wales, 20,000 in Scotland, and 5,000 in Ireland.

HOMILETICAL EMPHASES

The eighteenth century has been called "the dark night of Protestantism." It was not

4. Ivor Bailey, "The Challenge of Change," *Expository Times* (October 1974):18-22.

all dark, however, because it was in this century that the great revival under Whitefield and Wesley occurred.

The evangelical view of Christianity was dominant in both the pulpit and the pew. The general trend of pulpit utterance was that of more adaptability to the people yet without loss of either intellectual vigor or strength of conviction.

The preaching contained better exegesis of Scripture, but there was less regard for its authority. A relatively large and prominent place was given to morals. Social reforms and evangelistic and missionary emphases found their place in the pulpit.

In general, the style was stately and solemn. The discourses remained aloof from life and lacked flexibility, familiarity, and humanness. Evangelical preaching made its appeal chiefly to the feelings. It was most commonly delivered without manuscript. The sermonic method for this period was topical rather than expository. On the whole the sermons of the leading preachers of this age showed strong thinking, profound earnestness, and a certain consciousness of power. The apologetic and polemic elements of preaching were well to the fore in English sermons toward the end of the nineteenth century. Sermons became more practical in aim and more popular in style. The age produced a low vitality in morals in the ministry, rationalism in the pulpit, and rather lifeless preaching even among the orthodox.

Some of the preachers of this century preached extemporaneously including Carson, Binney, Robertson, Maclaren, Liddon, and Dale. Others used few notes or short outlines including Hall, Parker, and Spurgeon. Several read their messages including Chalmers and Newman. Irving, Liddon, and Chalmers were known to write out their sermons in full and commit them to memory. The power of argument by Hall and oratory by Jay, Melville, and Spurgeon were accompanied by Spurgeon's wise use of humor and Maurice's use of application.

Almost all preachers were masters of illustrations, but several are most noteworthy through their use of imagination (Evans, Liddon), word pictures (Guthrie, Maclaren), use of adjectives (Candlish), and use of poetry (Spurgeon).

Nearly two-thirds of the preachers were students of Hebrew, Latin, and Greek. Many were avid readers and writers. Some were specially noted as men of prayer. Alexander Maclaren was singled out as a great public reader of Scripture.

Sermons were directed to the social concerns and needs of the day. By preaching the gospel for conversion and the sending of saved men back into the community, social problems would be alleviated. This emphasis was nourished through the rise of lay enterprises and involvement in open-air meetings, camp meetings, street preaching, home Bible studies, visitation, and week-day services (Maclaren and Parker were exceptional). Keswick's deeper life emphasis beginning in 1873, and the revivals under Moody and Sankey gave power to new church organizations for missionary, evangelistic, and social outreach. The China Inland Mission was born in 1866 with J. Hudson Taylor. The revival spirit diminished, however, by the turn of the century, and Moody directed his attention to education rather than more revival meetings.

In 1912, under the auspices of the Baptist Theological School at Rome, a treatise appeared in Italian by Professor N. H. Shaw under the title *The Pulpit,* or *Manual of Homiletics.* It was a clear and thoroughly modern presentation of the subject, showing both wide study and a firm grasp of the materials, acknowledging indebtedness to many writers, especially to Broadus's *A Treatise on the Preparation and Delivery of Sermons.*

In Switzerland and France, the production of treatises on homiletics was not as large as in some other countries, but the quality of the works produced is high and some of them have had extensive influence.[5] First in order and importance is *Homiletics*, or the *Theory of Preaching*, by Alexander Vinet. This book was published from the author's manuscripts after his death in 1847, with some additions from the notebooks of students. Vinet, an eminent scholar and literary critic, was professor at Lausanne from 1837-47. He was thoroughly Protestant, pious, and evangelical.

In the introduction Vinet defines the sermon as a "discourse incorporated with public worship, and designed, concurrently or alternatively, to conduct to Christian truth one who has not yet believed in it, and to explain and apply it so those who admit it." Further he says, "The object of pulpit eloquence, we are aware, as indeed that of all eloquence, is to determine the will; but this object is closely combined with that of instruction. Eloquence is but the form, the edge, so to speak, of instruction. The preacher is a teacher under the form of an orator."[6] Again, "Not only does teaching predominate in the eloquence of the pulpit; the preacher, we add, has a document as the basis of his eloquence. As we have before said, he speaks the Word of God."[7]

The eloquent and saintly Protestant preacher Adolphe Monod published a lecture on *The Delivery of Sermons,* which Broadus characterizes as "singularly good." The book grew out of the experiences of one of the greatest preachers of modern times and bore the stamp of his fine intellect and warm heart.

The art of preaching was not neglected among the Catholics of France. Sometime about 1870, Bishop Dupanloup issued a series of lectures under the title *The Ministry of Preaching*; and *Essay on Pastoral and Popular Oratory*. It was translated into English by Samuel J. Eales and published both in England and the United States.

Early in the century, Rudolf Stier tried to bring in a more biblical conception of the theory of preaching, and published a little book called *Keryktik*. This is from the Greek word *kerux*, meaning a "herald"; a word several times found in the New Testament for preacher. Franz Theremin put out a small volume called *Preaching a Virtue*, in which he stresses the moral and spiritual elements of the preacher's office, along with other good counsels on preaching. It was translated by Professor Shedd of Union Seminary and was well known in America a generation ago.

For a further list of significant works on preaching from this period see the bibliographic section in the appendix.

In summary, during the late modern period, preaching became secularized. The preachers sought to preach to people's needs, but were not committed to maintaining a high level of biblical content. As a result, preaching fell into a general decline. The age produced a low vitality in morals in the ministry, rationalism in the pulpit, and much lifeless preaching, even among the orthodox. English preachers did not give as much attention to expository preaching as the Continental Reformers had. Topical preaching was more common in England. The movements of modern thought in regard to both social and religious affairs were keenly felt. On the whole, there was a closer adherence to the evangelical tradition.

5. Alexander Vinet's *Homiletics*, trans. Skinner, 28.
6. Ibid., 29.
7. Ibid., 31.

BIOGRAPHICAL SURVEY

Thomas Binney (1798-1874) He was an evangelist; preached to problems of life and destiny.

R. S. Candlish (1806-1872) He was a master of argumentative preaching and a great expositor.

Alexander Carson (1776-1844) A great man of prayer. He preached in private homes, large barns, and in the open air. He possessed exegetical gifts and was a master of expository preaching with logical progression of thought.

Thomas Chalmers (1780-1847) The greatest preacher Glasgow ever heard and was foremost among founders of the Free Church of Scotland in 1843.

R. W. Dale (1829-1835) Educational style of preaching and reading of sermons. He stayed in one church for more than thirty-five years.

Christmas Evans (1766-1838) The "Poet of the Pulpit"; learned to read at age seventeen, and gave his first sermon one year later. He had the gifts of prayer and exhortation.

Thomas Guthrie (1803-1873) He was the greatest platform speaker of his time.

Robert Hall (1764-1831) He was humble and approachable, profound as a philosopher and pious as a saint.

Edward Irving (1792-1834) Charged with heresy in 1830; he died reciting Psalm 23 in Hebrew. A sect arose in 1832 called the "Irvingites."

William Jay (1769-1853) His sermons were models of practical textual analysis. He spent more than sixty years in the same pastorate and preached original textual sermons full of scriptural quotes.

H. P. Liddon (1829-1890) He opened St. Paul's Church in London to all. He was a great champion of orthodoxy whose elaborate sermons on difficult questions of religion were intelligible to any person.

F. D. Maurice (1805-1872) He was strong on application.

Alexander Maclaren (1826-1910) Exposition and illustration were his strengths. He had fresh, fertile illustrations of the textual analysis and was a powerful reader of Scripture. He spent nearly sixty hours of study for many of his sermons.

Henry Melville (1800-1871) A close follower of the text in his sermons.

J. H. Newman (1801-1890) Influenced the people by his logic and was an effective teacher and writer. He had direct preaching and good diction, with textual sermons.

Joseph Parker (1830-1902) Led a successful Thursday morning service. He was a supreme egotist, eccentric, theatrical, emotional, and sensational.

F. W. Robertson (1816-1853) He was a great two-point preacher and memorized all of the New Testament in English and much of it in Greek.

Charles Spurgeon (1834-1892) He consistently had audiences of more than 4500. He was converted in 1850 and preached his first sermon in 1851. One of his great themes was the "providence of God."

I. R. Watson (1781-1833) Helped formulate Methodist theology, trained preachers, and published *Theological Institutes*. He was an eloquent preacher, a naturally strong theologian, and a fervent, powerful champion of missions.

9

The Contemporary Period

(1900—Present)

HISTORICAL BACKGROUND

The twentieth century was characterized by optimism until the outbreak of World War I (1914-1918). The coming of the Second World War with its concentration camps was a further disappointment to the remaining optimists. Although the United States assumed new strength after the war was won by the Allies, pessimism still prevailed as the atomic bomb became the possession of the great and the envy of the small.

Between those two great wars, the world had experienced the Great Depression of the 1930s. Following World War II the "Cold War" developed as a battle of words, arms races, races for the moon, and any other way of gaining superiority over one's enemy. Nationalism gained prominence with many African nations undergoing revolutions for their own particular causes. The gap between the rich and the poor took on national proportions and international significance.

When historians are able to reflect on this century, they may call it an age of paradoxes. Despite the great material damage done by the world wars, reconstruction was remarkably rapid and complete. Spiritually and culturally, it is still a divided world inspite of all of the work of organizations and individuals to make it "one world."

The theory of evolution advanced by Darwin late in the nineteenth century came into prominence as an explanation of human origin. Existentialism was not only the philosophy, but also the world view of many living in the shadow of the pessimism that developed out of the two world wars and the Cold War. Technological and scientific advances unfolded at a faster pace. Mass communication made the world small enough by mid-century that nearly any geographical area could be contacted within a short period of time.

During the first forty years few religious leaders dared face the implications of the

71

scientific doctrine and the philosophy that grew out of it. One who did was Henry Drummond, a natural scientist at Edinburgh University, and for a time an associate of Dwight L. Moody. Drummond wrote *The Natural Law in the Spiritual World* and *The Ascent of Man*. He was the first conspicuous "Christian evolutionist." Another was Henry Ward Beecher, the most popular preacher in America, who contributed a pro-evolution article to the *North American Review* in 1880.

In philosophy, the teaching of Josiah Royce (1855-1916) at Harvard was noted for its emphasis on idealism, and his writings interpreted the religious insights of man in that light. Following him was William James (1842-1910), whose philosophy of pragmatism applied psychology to religion and life. The other outstanding name is that of Walter Rauschenbusch (1861-1918), whose preaching and later teaching at Rochester Divinity School in New York won a hearing for the social implication of the gospel. Religious experience was stressed as the prelude to action in the social crisis of the times, and the social aims of the gospel were transmitted in sermon and organization.

From that background the American way of life was profoundly motivated in the direction of idealism. The influence of Harvard with Royce, James, and others (including George Santayana) gave a boost to the philosophy of religion in the academic world and in the theological schools.

The influence of scientific thought, higher criticism of the Bible, materialism, and a popular psychology that ignored the Fall, led to a widespread spirit of religious liberalism at one time called the New Theology. In colleges and theological seminaries, in religious journals and in the pulpit it was not at all unusual to question the verbal inspiration of the Bible, the virgin birth, the deity of the Lord Jesus, His resurrection, and His substitutionary atonement.

Modern biblical scholarship produced not only a "new view of the Bible," but also new translations that are widely accepted and used even by those who do not accept the "new view." The English Revised Version (RV) of 1882-86 did not go far toward replacing the King James Version of 1611, while the American edition of the RV (American Standard Version, 1901) had even less popular appeal despite scholarly approval. Among many private translations the most notable were *A New Translation* by James Moffatt (1922-26) and the Smith-Goodspeed *New Testament, An American Translation* (1927-31). More recently the *Revised Standard Version* (1946-52) has won widespread acceptance. That is also true of the *New American Standard Bible* (1960-77), the *New English Bible* (1961-70), and the *New International Version* (1973-78).

Since the beginning of the modern Protestant ecumenical movement, which may be dated from 1910, there has been an almost continuous series of theological conferences involving representatives of a great number of religious bodies from around the world. A result of those ecumenical conferences, the present free circulation of theological literature across sectarian lines and the training of thousands of ministers in nondenominational seminaries (such as Yale, Union, and Chicago) has been the blurring of the theological lines between the denominations.

Church life suffered many changes during the twentieth century. In 1900 the average church was looked on as a place of worship and instruction. Sermons were preached morning and evening on Sunday in addition to a session of the Sunday school attended by old and young alike. On Wednesday evening many congregations had either a midweek service or a prayer meeting.

The twentieth century brought about removals and consolidations of church building locations. In the nineteenth century it was common practice to maintain a number of important places of worship in the business section of the town or city. It was assumed that the church people would go downtown to worship, just as they went downtown to transact business. Toward the end of the nineteenth century the removal of churches from the heart of the city to the suburbs began.

The period between 1905 and 1930 was an era of church construction. Places of worship, often of exceptional architectural merit, appeared throughout the country.

The fundamentalist-modernist controversy was a significant event of the first thirty years of the twentieth century. It was characterized by war cries and sometimes bitter words. Fundamentalists were dogmatic in preaching the doctrines of the Christian faith as given by God and declared in an inerrant Bible. Modernists were nebulous, insisting that one should search for truth and not accept necessarily what was written in the past. Five major doctrines were debated: the virgin birth of Christ; Christ's substitutionary atonement; Christ's bodily resurrection; Christ's second coming; and the infallibility of the Bible.

HOMILETICAL EMPHASES

Preaching has to be seen against the background of the age to estimate its worth and contribution. Rapid changes took place in the United States during 1918-44. The post-World War I era saturated minds with disturbing ideas and unsettled the social and religious outlooks of millions of people. The preacher found that those formerly eager to hear the gospel were turning to other voices. Preaching faced new competition. The word *crisis* was on everyone's lips.

The social crisis united many voices in the pulpits of the land, but there was variety in the needs faced and the solutions offered. The preacher of the divine message found that he had much to relate to human need and life situations.

Bishop Edwin Holt Hughes of the Methodist church pointed out that some preachers had ceased to be ministers and had become prohibitionists. The temptation to ride a hobby horse and attack one element of evil obsessed some preachers. But Hughes wisely counseled that in preaching the preacher should maintain a sense of proportion and weigh the biblical teaching as well as social and political motives.

Preaching in favor of civil rights was by no means unheard of prior to 1954. Evidence indicates, however, that apart from a few groups, especially the Unitarians, such sermons were rare. After 1954, the year the Supreme Court banned school segregation, many congregations heard an increasing number of sermons on race relations and civil rights.

To read through the sermons preached on race in the 1950s and 1960s is to be struck by a number of characteristics common to most of those messages: ridicule directed to the opposition; refutation of contrary arguments; firmness of conviction; urgency; and highly emotional and oratorical statements. Martin Luther King, Jr., one of the leaders of the civil rights revolution and himself a Baptist minister, made preaching a weapon to batter down the walls of segregation.

The fundamentalist-modernist controversy was noteworthy in the history of American theological disputes for being primarily a pulpit controversy. The controversy drew in many of the ablest religious leaders and spokesmen of the day. Fosdick, Macartney, Bryan, and possibly Riley would surely be listed in any "Who's Who" of rhetorical greats of the twenties. William Jennings Bryan became the unchallenged leader of the lay forces of fundamentalism. Harry Emerson Fosdick, "modernism's Moses," disclaimed polemical intent and simply championed the cause of "an intellectually hospitable, tolerant, liberty-loving church." In the struggle for that cause Fosdick was distinguished neither as an administrator nor as an ecclesiastical potentate, but he achieved leadership of the movement through the clarity and persuasiveness of his oral and written works.

The clash between modernists and fundamentalists was as evident in homiletic technique as it was in sermon content. Generally, oratory during the controversy ran the gamut from the fiery, impassioned exhibition of unrestrained fanaticism to the cool, reflective cadences of reasoned discourse. In composition, fundamentalists tended to be direct and concrete; with few notable exceptions, modernists tended toward abstractions and the theoretical. Fundamentalist orators generally exhibited their passion to defend the faith. Modernists were characteristically less heated and less urgent. For the fundamentalist, controversy seemed to be a vocation; for the modernist, participation in the controversy was more often an avocation.

About 1925 the preaching mission began to to take the place of the revival. G. Campbell Morgan was among the most famous missioners. He was an English Congregationalist who had served important congregations in his own country, and who had been one of Moody's most popular lecturers at the Northfield, Massachusetts summer assemblies.

The era of D. L. Moody saw the introduction of an organized mass evangelism that commanded the interest and support of church people. Leading citizens and public men backed this method of evangelism as they saw the accrued benefits in community and society.

Following Moody came evangelists who copied his new methods and sought to duplicate what he had begun. Not all were successful. Among the best were Reuben A. Torrey, J. Wilbur Chapman, Gipsy Smith, and Billy Sunday. Those men commanded a nationwide hearing as they went from city to city. Torrey and Chapman also visited Great Britain where they witnessed results not unlike those of Moody's day, although on a more limited scale.

Reuben Archer Torrey (1856-1928) was a contrast to Moody. Unlike Moody, Torrey was well educated and a graduate of both Yale University and Yale Divinity School. Following Torrey came J. Wilbur Chapman (1859-1918) who, with the song leader, Charles M. Alexander, led many evangelistic campaigns throughout America, Australia, and Great Britain. He had begun his ministry as a Reformed church pastor. Later, he went to the Bethany Presbyterian Church in Philadelphia, where he was associated with John Wanamaker, the merchant prince who had led in the building of the largest Sunday school in the nation. In 1903 Chapman was invited to be the leader of the Presbyterian church's committee on evangelism, and was granted a leave of absence from the pastorate to engage in evangelistic campaigns.

The life of George W. Truett followed the American pattern of success. He began as a farm boy and advanced to the highest denominational pulpit where he wielded influence over millions. The gospel was the heart of his message, and he delivered it with passion and power to both large and small congregations. He was a "plain" speaker in the sense that he used the language of the people and not the specialized talk of the intellectual. Sheer physical strength and moral conviction shone through his sermons. He belonged to that class of preachers who believe in the supremacy of preaching as a means of reaching men. To Truett, preaching was the embodying of a message, and he communicated freely and forcefully from the heart.

Harry Allan Ironside (1876-1951) was a pastoral preacher who was also the expositor-evangelist. Ironside came from the same tradition as C. I. Scofield, the lawyerlike expositor who was more noted for his specialized teaching ministry (his notes in the *Scofield Reference Bible,* first published in 1909) than for his preaching.

Donald Grey Barnhouse (1895-1960), pastor of Tenth Presbyterian Church in Philadelphia, was famed for his Sunday ministrations followed by four and five weeknight services in other parts of the country. Travel, study, writing, and lecturing occupied his days in an incredible amount of toil. A gifted teacher, his strength lay in Bible exposition. By means of radio broadcasts, telecasts, and the editorship of the monthly magazine known first as *Revelation* (later *Eternity*), he carried his message to Christians everywhere.

The sermonic work of the best-known of all Roman Catholic preachers flowed from a reservoir of study and research. Fulton J. Sheen's method was to work on the subject with notes and ideas culled from reading and reflection. An outline would be made so that illustrations and relevant material might be fitted in. He then would give his mind to the mastery of the outline with its subpoints.

Gerald Hamilton Kennedy (1907-1980), a Methodist, stands as a gracious example of a pastoral preacher in the grand tradition of Wesley. A pastor and professor, he is best known for his leadership at large as bishop of Portland, Oregon, and then of Los Angeles. He always maintained a close pastoral relation to people and congregations.

Oswald Carl Julius Hoffmann (1913-   ) is the successor to Walter A. Maier (1893-1950) on "The Lutheran Hour" radio program heard each Sunday. During the 1900s the Lutheran church (Missouri Synod) reached out by modern techniques to present the gospel to the public.

William Franklin (Billy) Graham (1918-   ), probably heard by more people than any other preacher in history, stands in the forefront of those who have made their contribution to world evangelization. A Southern Baptist, he has ministered largely to people of all denominations and to all levels of life.

An example of lay preaching is found in the life and career of Rufus Matthew Jones (1863-1948), known as the representative Quaker of his generation. He was a true intellectual and was erudite in his field of philosophy, a subject that he taught at Haverford College near Philadelphia. Throughout his influential life he gave himself to the discipline and cultivation of the spiritual life. As a Quaker he was closely identified with the Society of Friends and took his share of ministering in the meeting house, which was for him the local church and fellowship.

Since the time of Rufus Jones, the Friends have had no greater preacher-teacher than David Elton Trueblood (1900-   ), who represents the Quaker ministry in its excellence and devotion. Professor of philosophy and religion at Earlham College in Richmond, Indiana (1946-66), his teaching has influenced many. From the writing of *The Predicament of Modern Man* to *A Place to Stand,* more than thirty books have come from his pen. Through the circulation of those volumes he has become one of the most widely quoted interpreters of the Christian faith of this era.

Harry Emerson Fosdick's (1878-1969) rise to prominence took place in the liberalizing period of American preaching. A volume of sermons, *The Living of These Days* (1956) indicates the thrust of his time. With the advent of radio, Fosdick reached a generation made ready to hear by that new medium and made eager to listen by the ferment of social change. Fosdick took the social gospel of Gladden and Rauschen-busch, and with a critical interpretation of Scripture, made his sermons man-centered and problem-conscious.

Fosdick's many volumes of sermons have a strain of evangelical liberalism. He toiled daily to express truth and polish his vocabulary. His strength lay in the strong homiletical build-up of each sermon which climaxed in an appeal to action. According to Fosdick, preaching was never easy, but he believed in it as the effective communication of truth.

Closely akin to life-situation preaching is the preaching of those who bring the kind of understanding and sympathy to their congregations that is therapeutic and healing. Of that group, Norman Vincent Peale (1898-   ) is most prominent. He has had a long and enduring ministry in New York City.

As the era moved into the 1960s, the most striking feature in preaching was the phenomenal increase in Pentecostal preaching. Among Pentecostals a rigorism of practices was allied to spiritual claims that the baptism of the Holy Spirit was proved by glossolalia (speaking in ecstatic tongues).

During the period from 1940-50, conferences held in London, Stockholm, Toronto, Jerusalem, and Helsinki were attended by representatives of a worldwide Pentecostal fellowship numbering in the millions. The preachers were C. M. Ward, evangelist of The Assemblies of God; George Jeffreys, England; Oral Roberts, Tulsa, Oklahoma; and David J. du Plessis, South Africa. Those preachers had in common a simplistic style of speech, profusely illustrated from experience, striking claims of healing and charismatic revival, a strong emotional stress, and an evangelistic appeal for decisions.

The 1960s were days when the ministry at large became nebulous and uncertain in its search for meaning and in its diversities of message. The waning influence of neo-orthodoxy, the burial of the fundamentalist-modernist controversy, and the rise of the ecumenical movement brought other openings and emphases. Race relations threatened to disrupt communions, and many sermons addressed the social, political, educational, and economic issues of the day.

At this time, if estimates are correct, preaching again showed marked decline in influence. There were still centers of preaching where people listened eagerly. But a general impression spread across the nation that somehow preaching was no longer a strong influence.

The number of students for the ministry decreased, and many who offered themselves had no thought of the regular pastoral ministry, but inclined themselves to ministries in industrial, social, and political relations.

In summary, the twentieth-century period of preaching has been one that placed a premium on popular approaches to preaching. Much of the preaching has been of poor quality and not established on a scriptural foundation.

BIOGRAPHICAL SURVEY

Donald N. Baillie   Scottish Presbyterian   1887-1954
   Doctrinal

Sabine Baring-Gould   English Anglican   1834-1924

Donald G. Barnhouse   American Presbyterian   1895-1960
   Bible Teacher

Karl Barth   Swiss Reformed   1886-1968
   Doctrinal

Andrew Blackwood   American Presbyterian   1882-1968
   Teacher of Preachers

F. W. Boreham   Australian; Baptist   1871-1959

Emil Brunner   Swiss Reformed   1889-1966
   Doctrinal

Rudolf Bultmann   German Lutheran   1884-1976
   Doctrinal, but not evangelical

Harry Emerson Fosdick   American; Baptist   1878-1969
   Perhaps the most distinguished preacher;
   excelled in delivery and style

William (Billy) Graham   American; Baptist   1918-
   Bible preacher; evangelist; excellent illustrations and style

Carl F. H. Henry   American; Baptist   1913-

Oswald C. J. Hoffmann   American Lutheran   1913-

H. A. Ironside   Brethren   1876-1951
   Expository Bible preacher

E. Stanley Jones   American Methodist   1884-1973

J. D. Jones   Welsh Congregationalist   1865-1942

Gerald Kennedy   American Methodist   1907-1980
 Bishop of the Methodist church

Thomas Kepler   American Quaker   1897-1963

Charles Koller   American; Baptist   1896-
 Bible preacher; good with illustrations

D. Martyn Lloyd-Jones   Welsh Presbyterian   1895-1981

Halford E. Luccock   American Methodist or Congregationalist   1885-1961
 Homiletics professor; encouraged logical style,
 illustrations, and mastery of words

Clarence E. Macartney   American Presbyterian   1879-1957
 Best American conservative preacher of his day; doctrinal; imaginative; used illustrations; sermon methods included biographical and
 topical

J. Gresham Machen   American Presbyterian   1881-1937
 Doctrinal; theologian and New Testament professor

David A. MacLennan   American Presbyterian   1903-
 Teacher of homiletics

Walter A. Maier   American Lutheran   1893-1950
 Radio Bible preacher; evangelistic; had 15 million radio listeners;
 spent twenty hours of preparation per sermon (one hour for each
 minute)

Peter Marshall   American Presbyterian   1902-1949
 Manuscript preacher; possessed a mastery of words

G. Campbell Morgan   English Congregationalist   1863-1945
 Representative of the late modern age; a Bible preacher with good
 style; preached for a verdict

Reinhold Niebuhr   American United Church of Christ   1892-1970
 Doctrinal; widely published on theology

H. Richard Niebuhr   American United Church of Christ   1894-1962
 Doctrinal; made the gospel fit the world of existentialism

Morgan Phelps Noyes American Presbyterian 1891-1972

Harold John Ockenga American Congregationalist 1905-
 Doctrinal; textual

Stephen Olford American; Baptist 1918-
 Evangelistic and expository; good with illustrations and application

Garfield Bromley Oxnam American Methodist 1891-1963
 Used a text as a point of departure; a professor of social ethics

Norman Vincent Peale American Reformed 1898-
 Good with illustrations and style; limits sermons to personal
 problems

Harold Cooke Phillips American; Baptist 1892-1966
 Bible preacher

James Albert Pike American Episcopalian 1907-1969
 Lawyer; questionable theology

Liston Pope American Congregationalist 1909-1974

Alan Redpath Scottish Baptist 1907-
 Evangelistic

Paul Rees American Covenant 1900-

W. E. Sangster English Methodist 1900-1960

L. R. Scarborough American; Baptist 1870-1945
 Evangelistic; never lost his passion for souls

Paul E. Scherer American Lutheran 1892-1969
 Professor of homiletics; good on delivery

Fulton J. Sheen American Roman Catholic 1895-1979
 Professor of philosophy; radio and TV speaker

Joseph R. Sizoo American Reformed 1884-1966
 Professor, missionary; Army chaplain

William A. Sunday American Presbyterian 1863-1935
 Evangelistic

Arthur Teikmanis   American Reformed   1914-

Paul Tillich   American United Church of Christ   1886-1966
  Doctrinal; published many theological works

Reuben A. Torrey   American Presbyterian   1856-1928
  Evangelistic

Elton Trueblood   American Quaker   1900-
  Teacher

George W. Truett   American; Baptist   1867-1944
  One of American's greatest preachers; spent forty-one years in one
  church; wrote letters to the unsaved two mornings each week

Leslie D. Weatherhead   English Methodist   1893-1976
  Pastor of City Temple Church in London; good on illustrations from
  personal experiences; had a conversational delivery

10

American Preaching

Historical Background

The earliest colonists in America arrived in New Mexico in 1540 and in Florida in 1577, well antedating the settlements of Jamestown in 1607 and Plymouth in 1620. But it was at Plymouth, and soon afterward in the Massachusetts Bay Colony, that preaching in the American tradition began.

The religious controversies in Western Europe, and especially in England at the outset of colonization in New England, precipitated the exodus of Puritans and Nonconformists from England and Ireland, and later from Scotland and Western Europe. Colonization at the outset was almost exclusively English and primarily Protestant.

John Cotton (1584-1652), Puritan teaching elder and minister of the church in Boston from 1635 until 1652, is representative of the caliber of ministry in early New England.

In most cases in the early New England colonial village, the minister was the effective leader of the community. New settlements invariably built a church and obtained a clergyman. John Cotton wrote home to England that there was "nothing cheap in New England but milk and ministers."[1] The church, or the meeting house, was the hub of the village. The sermon was central in the service.

Things were quite different in Boston in 1640 from the way they had been in London, or Glasgow, or Leyden before immigration only a few months before. The minister was viewed as a messenger of God, a guide to help his people know God's will for their lives in the "New Canaan." He was expected to counsel concerning families, epidemics, and civil strife in addition to providing spiritual nurture.

In the early part of the eighteenth century new waves of Scottish-Irish immigration

1. Arthur Stephen Hoyt, *The Pulpit and American Life* (New York: Macmillan, 1921), 9.

began. Most of the people were radically Protestant, mainly Presbyterian, and all avidly supported a free church as opposed to a state church. That had its impact on preaching.

Shortly after Jonathan Edwards's experience at Northampton, George Whitefield (1714-1770), an itinerant Methodist evangelist from England, came to the colonies for his first tour, from August 1739 to January 1741. He was immediately accepted by the log-college preachers in the central colonies and quickly entered into the harvest of converts in the ongoing revival there. Dramatic results attended his first appearance, and while there was certainly opposition from the antirevivalists, he won the support of many educated and soberminded people, including Benjamin Franklin. Whitefield spent one month of his first tour in New England. With the help of Jonathan Edwards's literary efforts, he established a pattern of congregational revivalism that was used for the next several years.

Whitefield preached extemporaneously, moving freely about the pulpit and never using a manuscript. He acted out human interest stories and gave colonial America a real demonstration of drama in the pulpit.

Whitefield spent almost ten years in America, traveling from one end of the colonies to the other on seven different trips. During evangelizing tours he preached an average of forty sermons a week.

Among the churches, strongest support for the American Revolution came from Congregational, Presbyterian, and Baptist groups. The pacifists, Quakers, Mennonites, Moravians, and Dunkards declined to participate in the strife. The Dutch and German Reformed churches and the Lutheran churches, with no particular heritage for or against the British, generally favored the colonies. Roman Catholics and Jews were most often supportive of the colonial cause.

The Church of England in America was the greatest ecclesiastical casualty of the Revolution. It was stripped of its privileges, prestige, and support, and its congregations were depleted by defections to Methodism.

Congregationalists, Presbyterians, and Baptists, the three other denominations of British heritage, were tied together by common acceptance of Calvinistic confessions. All had been strongly identified with the colonial cause and survived the war with increased prestige.

The new nation opted for religious freedom as articulated in the Bill of Rights in 1791, which put all church groups on an equal footing.

The government would no longer recognize a state church or levy taxes for its support. All colonial laws penalizing Roman Catholics were removed, and freedom of worship was established for all Protestants.

Prior to the American Revolution there had been small settlements south of the Ohio River. But soon afterward there was a virtual stampede of courageous young men and women moving westward to look for economic opportunities. They headed west, leaving their churches, and often their religion, behind.

The frontier Baptist minister typically was a farmer-preacher who labored with his hands during the week and with his Bible and voice on Sunday. Usually, he had not been sent by any church or missionary society.

One notable phase of frontier religion was the development of the camp meeting as a unique way of adjusting to the religious needs of a shifting population. The idea was introduced at Logan County, Kentucky in 1797, by James McGready (1758-1817), a Presbyterian minister.

In the East, revolt against prevailing doctrinal orthodoxy led to an acceptance of Unitarianism, universalism, and Deism among some ministers and congregations. The doctrine of the Trinity was not the primary matter of contention. The issue was God's sovereignty versus the individual's freedom. The principal documents on the liberal side of the issue were William Ellery Channing's sermon at the ordination of Jared Sparks; Ralph Waldo Emerson's divinity school address; and Theodore Parker's South Boston sermon. Each address manifested an increasing "man-centeredness," and ultimately resulted in the founding of the American Unitarian Association. Of the sixteen pre-Revolutionary Congregational churches in Boston, fourteen were tending toward Unitarianism in the first decade of the nineteenth century. The movement continued to spread into smaller towns in the vicinity. In 1805 Henry Ware, an avowed Unitarian, was elected to the Hollis Professorship of Theology at Harvard. That marked the beginning of a trend that resulted in the founding of Andover Theological Seminary in 1808.

Both proslavery and abolitionist preachers mounted pulpits in America after 1830 to defend their positions on the basis of Scripture. The sinfulness of slaveholding was the central issue.

Mass evangelism among American Protestants reached its peak immediately prior to World War I, when there were at least 650 active evangelists and some 1,200 part-timers in the United States. But the war came and the number of converts of the evangelistic campaign trail inevitably diminished. After World War I, America's religious climate changed radically and evangelistic campaigns declined.

John R. Mott (1865-1955), leading American ambassador of missions and ecumenism for almost a half century, was rallying the Christian missionary forces at the turn of the twentieth century for a final campaign to "win the world for Christ in a single generation."

The social gospel emphasis, from approximately 1875 to 1915, was the church's response to social and economic inequities growing out of the industrial revolution and the accumulation of great fortunes. Baptist Walter Rauschenbusch (1861-1918), Congregationalist George Herron (1862-1925), Congregationalist Washington Gladden (1836-1918), and numerous other ministers worked through the churches and from their pulpits to bring about social reform and to establish a kind of society that should infuse Christian concern and a love-your-neighbor attitude into the business and labor world. The social gospel solidified into a movement when evangelicals of the late nineteenth century split into liberal and conservative forces. Liberals turned to social issues, while conservatives were concerned primarily with private issues.

The ecumenical movement as we now know it, however, was an outgrowth of the missionary activity of the latter part of the nineteenth century. It had its origin when overseas missionaries found it impossible to make denominationalism a real issue for new converts from non-Christian religion. The Federal Council of the Churches of Christ in America was established in 1908 by some thirty Protestant denominations. The World Missionary Conference followed in 1910 in Edinburgh. World War I intervened, but in 1927 the World Conference on Faith and Order met at Lausanne, Switzerland, and a decade after that the Conference on Church, Community, and State was held at Oxford, England. Those three movements: missionary, life and work, and faith and order led to the founding of the World Council of Churches on August 22, 1948, with representatives of 146 churches from forty-four countries.

In 1950 came the founding of the National Council of Churches of Christ in the United States as an interdenominational body representing twenty-nine churches. It replaced the Federal Council of Churches and seven other interdenominational agencies, which occasioned much sectarian, and even inflammatory, pulpit rhetoric.

The cultural disruption of the 1960s and the resulting decline in membership of the churches threatened the jobs of some pastors and denominational leaders. It was only natural that support for ecumenism should decline among those persons most threatened by church union.

The cutback in church programs during the 1960s closed some theological schools, caused mergers of others, and encouraged cooperative support for social-action programs and missions. It became fairly common for Roman Catholic priests to study in Protestant theological schools while Protestants studied in Roman Catholic schools. Indeed, some Roman Catholic schools have merged facilities with Protestant schools in expression of an inherent unity in Christian institutions.

In October 1929 the stock market crash initiated the Great Depression that lasted through the 1930s. The economic depression was associated with religious depression, as churches suffered along with the rest of the nation. Memberships dropped, budgets were slashed, benevolent and missionary enterprises were stranded, and professional church workers were discharged as churches closed for lack of money. However, newer and smaller religious groups prospered, ministering to the economically depressed classes who had no church home or were unable economically to sustain membership in a regular church.

The general revival of religion in the 1950s in America was marked by the dynamic, spirited preaching of Roman Catholic Fulton J. Sheen (1895-1979), the writings of Trappist mystic Thomas Merton (1915-1968), and the preaching of Billy Graham starting with his 1949 Los Angeles crusade.

The growing maturity of American Roman Catholics reflected a greater emphasis on intellectual pursuits, a stronger role of the laity in the church, and an increased sense of responsibility to society in general. Those concerns were reinforced by "caretaker" pontiff John XXIII and the Second Vatican Council (1962-65). Pope John's openness to the world rubbed off on the American Catholic church.

A revival of interest in the improvement of Catholic preaching began with the 1936 publication of Father Joseph Jungmann's *The Good News and the Proclamation of the Faith*. Immediately following World War II a number of priests pursued advanced studies in rhetoric at Northwestern, Ohio State, Wisconsin, and other schools. Like the church Fathers before them, they went back to the fountain of secular rhetoric to learn the basics of communication for application in proclamation of the Word of God. In 1958, to improve the preaching apostolate, the Catholic Homiletic Society was founded by Father Joseph M. Connors. A growing concern for the effective communication of God's Word from Catholic pulpits was evidenced by the establishment of the Word of

God Institute in Washington, D.C., which publishes preaching aids and holds conferences on preaching, the widespread use of experienced Protestant homileticians to teach in major Catholic seminaries, and a lively business in several varieties of homily services. This renewal received encouragement when Vatican Council II underscored the obligatory place of the homily in the regular liturgy of the church.

The Decree of Ministry and Life of Priests mandates that a series of courses in homiletics be included in the seminary curriculum so that priests, after finishing professional training, will be better prepared to preach.[2]

Pentecostals as a separate religious body appeared early in this century and for some three generations stood separate and apart from the rest of the Christian church structure. Today in the United States there are more than six million people in Pentecostal denominations, not counting charismatic groups that are widely dispersed in the non-Pentecostal denominations. There are some thirty million Pentecostals worldwide, most of them in Third World countries. Modern Pentecostals, both black and white, trace their beginnings to a small black church on Azusa Street in Los Angeles that was under the leadership of a black American preacher, William J. Seymour.[3]

HOMILETICAL EMPHASES

The earliest American theological seminary was founded at Andover, Massachusetts in 1808. That parent institution included a course on pulpit oratory. Among the earliest donors of the seminary was a wealthy New England merchant named William Bartlet, in whose honor the homiletics chair later was named. The first professor was Dr. Griffin. In 1811 Ebenezer Porter was appointed to the chair and its name was changed to that of Bartlet Professorship of Sacred Rhetoric. Porter served for twenty-three years and deserves high honor as the real beginner of homiletical instruction in theological seminaries in this century. In 1819 Porter published *The Young Preacher's Manual,* a collection of treatises on preaching, including with others of lesser value, Fenelon's *Dialogues,* Claude's Essay, Reybaz on *The Art of Preaching.* Porter used his manual for a number of years as a textbook, and supplemented it with lectures.

In 1834 Porter published his own volume on homiletics under the title *Lectures on Homiletics and Preaching and on Public Prayer, Together with Sermons and Letters.* The book went through a number of editions and is still historically important and contains good, sound teaching.

About 1830 Henry Ware, Jr., became professor of pulpit eloquence and pastoral care at Harvard. A few years later he published his little book *Hints on Extemporaneous Preaching.* It gave cogent reasons for the practice of free delivery after careful preparation.

In 1859 the Southern Baptist Theological Seminary was opened at Greenville, South Carolina, with John A. Broadus as professor of the preparation and delivery of sermons, in connection with his other chair of New Testament interpretation. His plan

2. *The Program of Priestly Formation of the National Conference of Catholic Bishops, United States of America,* 2d ed. (Washington, D.C.: Publications Office, 1976), 37.
3. James S. Tinney, "William J. Seymour, Father of Modern Day Pentecostalism," *Journal of the Interdenominational Theological Center* (Fall 1977): 34.

for homiletics, as quoted by his biographer A. T. Robertson, was as follows:

> Homiletics, or *Preparation and Delivery of Sermons*; Ripley's *Sacred Rhetoric*; Vinet's
> *Homiletics*; numerous lectures; ample exercises in formation of skeletons, criticism of
> printed sermons, general composition, and discussion; opportunities for students to preach,
> but no preaching merely for practice.[4]

In 1849 Henry J. Ripley, professor of sacred rhetoric and pastoral duties at the Newton Theological Institution near Boston, published his *Sacred Rhetoric*.

In 1853 Thomas H. Skinner, professor of sacred rhetoric and pastoral duties in Union Theological Seminary in New York, rendered a great service to the teaching of homiletics in this country by his translation of Vinet's *Homiletics*.

James W. Alexander taught homiletics at Princeton Theological Seminary. The results of his reading, experience, and thinking were published in 1860 in *Thoughts on Preaching*.

A valuable work, *A Treatise on Homiletics*, appeared in 1864. The author was Daniel P. Kidder, professor at Garrett Theological Institute in Evanston, Illinois, and later at Drew Theological Seminary.

The year 1867 witnessed the appearance of treatises on homiletics by two eminent and distinguished Presbyterians. The first was *Homiletics and Pastoral Preaching* by W. G. T. Shedd of Union Theological Seminary in New York. The other work was *Sacred Rhetoric* by R. L. Dabney, of the Union Theological Seminary of Virginia.

The chair of homiletics in the divinity school of Yale University was filled from 1861 to 1879 by J. M. Hoppin. He published in 1869 his well-known book on *The Office and Work of the Christian Ministry*.

Theological journals were published, some of which were designed especially as homiletical helps. The most outstanding among those was *The Homiletic Review*, which began in 1877 as the *Homiletic Monthly*.

Not a great deal has been done on the history of preaching by American writers. The subject has received attention in several of the books on homiletics, notably in that of Hoppin. Fleming James wrote an attractive little volume on *The Message and the Messengers*. In 1876 John A. Broadus published his *Lectures on the History of Preaching*, which were the lectures he gave at Newton Theological Institution. T. H. Patterson also wrote a later volume, *A History of Christian Preaching*, which is very readable and interesting in style. In addition to those, W. C. Wilkinson has addressed the subject with a fine discussion of some great preachers in his *Modern Masters of Pulpit Discourse*. A similar service was performed by Lewis O. Brastow in *Representative Modern Preachers* and *The Modern Pulpit*.

Some attention has been paid to psychology in relation to preaching. In 1901 a book by J. Spencer Kennard was published under the title *Psychic Power in Preaching*. Kennard was a well-known Baptist pastor and evangelist. In 1918 Charles S. Gardner, a professor of homiletics at Southern Baptist Theological Seminary at Louisville, published his *Psychology and Preaching*.

One of the most notable events in the field of homiletics was the establishment of the

4. A. T. Robertson, *The Life and Letters of John A. Broadus*, 168.

Yale Lectures on preaching in 1870. With few exceptions, that lectureship has been filled every year since its foundation by some prominent English or American preacher. George Wharton Pepper, a Philadelphia lawyer, had the distinction of being the only layman invited to give the lectures. His volume, *A Voice from the Crowd*, is useful, not only for its contents, but for an appendix that contains the full list of all the lectures since the foundation of the lectureship.

The Yale Lectures have not been specifically homiletical. Instead, they have dealt more with the pastoral and social work of the preacher, and with problems of thought and adjustment connected with his work. Only two of the series have been distinctly historical: those by W. M. Taylor on *The Scottish Pulpit,* and *Puritan Preaching in England* by John Brown. One lecturer, Charles Silvester Horne, used some of the greatest preachers in history as examples for his work. His lectures are found in his book *The Romance of Preaching*.

In 1871 John A. Broadus published his world-famous treatise *On the Preparation and Delivery of Sermons*. The story of its origin is related by the author himself in his *Life of James P. Boyce*. When the seminary reopened after the Civil War, student enrollment was very small. In the homiletics class was only one student, and he was blind. But the undaunted professor adhered to his resolution to make his subject worthwhile, and because the student could not take notes, Broadus gave his lectures to him in a conversational way, covering with thoughtful care the main subjects.

That was the origin of Broadus's book, which was published five years later and has become the leading textbook on homiletics. Broadus had to mortgage some property and borrow money for the making of the original book printing plates.

Since the appearance of Broadus's book, a great number of valuable, practical works on homiletics have been published in the United States. The two most important are the first series of Yale Lectures by Henry Ward Beecher and *Lectures on Preaching* by Phillips Brooks. Beecher discussed preaching in his characteristic way, and the result was a valuable and delightful book full of his own experiences, rich and suggestive on many points. Brooks's lectures constitute one of the most successful and perhaps the most widely read of the Yale series. It is famous for its definition of preaching as "the communication of truth through personality." Other notable volumes are: *Christian Rhetoric,* G. W. Hervey, c. 1870; *The Theory of Preaching,* Austin Phelps, 1890; and *The Ministry to the Congregation,* J. A. Kern, 1897.

T. Harwood Pattison produced several works on preaching, including *The Making of the Sermon. The Ideal Ministry,* a helpful volume by Herrick Johnson, was published in 1907. Arthur S. Hoyt was the author of two notable works: *The Work of Preaching* and *Vital Elements in Preaching*.

From two eminent New York pastors came lectures on preaching that have been published in book form. One is by David James Burrell who presented a series of lectures at the Union Theological Seminary of Virginia on *The Sermon*. The other book is a similar series of lectures given by S. Parkes Cadman at several different institutions before being published under the title *Ambassadors of God*.

The American sermon generally was built on a logical plan, cast into the form of an argument, with direct and practical lessons drawn from the demonstrated truth. Although it was generally biblical in tone, it did not confine itself to the interpretation of

Scripture and the setting forth of the Word of God. It addressed the head more than the heart.

BIOGRAPHICAL SURVEY

John Cotton (1585-1652)
  a. Pastor of one church for twenty years in Boston, Massachusetts
  b. Extemporaneous and expository preacher
  c. Strong in persuasive ability
  d. Unequalled in influence in the affairs of the Massachussetts Bay Colony

John Davenport (1597-1670)
  a. One of the founders of the New Haven Colony
  b. Came to the United States in June 1637

John Eliot (1605-1690)
  a. Translated the Bible into the dialect of the Algonquin Indians
  b. Abandoned a life of scholarship to be a missionary to Indians and called "apostle to the Indians"
  d. Served as pastor of the First Church in Roxbury, Massachusetts
  e. A persuasive preacher and a faithful pastor

Thomas Hooker (1586-1647)
  a. Had tremendous political and religious influence
  b. Founder of the colony at Hartford, Connecticut in 1636
  c. An evangelical and lively defender of the faith
  d. A prolific writer

Cotton Mather (1663-1728)
  a. Lamented failure of New England theocracy
  b. Preached on great social, political, and personal issues of the day
  c. Oldest son of Increase Mather
  d. Served as pastor of Second Church in Boston
  e. Eloquent preacher and possessed exceptional diligence

Increase Mather (1639-1723)
  a. President of Harvard College and a pastor in Boston
  b. Lamented era of decreasing conversions
  c. Preached sixty-two years in Boston
  d. Served as a pastor of Second Church in Boston
  e. Memorized his sermons and preached without notes
  f. He studied sixteen hours a day

UNITARIAN MOVEMENT

William Ellery Channing (1780-1842)
  a. Emphasized the present-day necessity of Christian living
  b. Brought about a high social and moral standard
  c. Protested the marked difference between clergy and laity
  d. Had beautiful style
  e. Defective doctrinally

f. Was pastor of Federal Street Congregational Church in Boston
g. The fatherhood of God and brotherhood of man were his main themes

Theodore Parker (1810-1860)

a. Tended toward exaggeration
b. More combative than Channing
c. Broke away from Unitarianism
d. Was a graduate in 1836 of Harvard Divinity School and had a command of twenty languages
e. Served as pastor of Twenty-eighth Congregational Church in Boston

CONTEMPORARY CONGREGATIONALISTS

Henry Ward Beecher (1813-1887)

a. Preacher, lecturer, writer, editor, agitator, and reformer
b. A master of illustrations
c. A fearless preacher
d. Held rigidly to biblical text in his preaching
e. Was liberal in theology, and vague on redemption

Lyman Beecher (1775-1853)

a. Preached against social sins
b. Resolved to drive out Unitarianism
c. Had a magnetic personality
d. Constructed a careful outline for all his sermons
e. Was persuasive, forceful, racy, pungent, imaginative, and doctrinal

Horace Bushnell (1802-1876)

a. Mediator between the old school of theology and new views
b. Had great civic and intellectual influence
c. Strove to translate the language of the pulpit into vernacular and restore reality to accepted theology
d. Preaching was biblical, logical, and orderly
e. Introductions were explanatory, connecting text with theme
f. Conclusions were practical as well as didactic
g. Used a manuscript when preaching

Timothy Dwight (1752-1817)

a. Had a firm faith in evangelical doctrines
b. Converted Lyman Beecher
c. Was maintained the life of orthodoxy in spite of contemporary Unitarianism
d. President of Yale and an "apostle to the educated"
e. Had a strong resonant voice and preached with vigor

Jonathan Edwards (1703-1758)

a. President of Princeton Theological Seminary
b. Wrote out his sermons and read them
c. Was argumentative, logical, and doctrinal
d. Was topical in his preaching
e. Was an intellectual genius and of saintly character

    f. Was a theologian of exceptional influence

    g. Each of his sermons was prepared with laborious care and was a literary masterpiece

Nathaniel Emmons (1745-1841)

    a. Held one pastorate for fifty-four years

    b. Topical preacher

    c. An outspoken opponent of secret societies

    d. Made little use of eloquence, calling it "rhetorical bluster"

    e. Depended on logic and built up his arguments proposition by proposition

    f. Kept hearers in keen anticipation and intellectual excitement

Charles G. Finney (1792-1875)

    a. A converted lawyer

    b. Believed intensely that preachers needed the baptism of the Holy Spirit

    c. Represented the most sane and intelligent kind of evangelist

    d. Supposedly argued more people into the kingdom than any other man

    e. Style was simple, clear, and powerful

Washington Gladden (1836-1918)

    a. Held tenaciously to Bible doctrine

    b. Introductions were flowery, but not offensive, and were laden with scriptural illustrations

    c. Possessed a keen imagination

    d. Primarily sought social reform

    e. Sermons were loosely organized

    f. Made much use of rhetorical questions

    g. Style combined vigor with grace

    h. Served as pastor of the First Congregational Church in Columbus, Ohio

Frank Wakely Gunsaulus (1856-1921)

    a. Possessed the charm of rhetoric: the power of appeal

    b. Gave Yale Lectures on preaching in 1882 and 1911

    c. His influence in Chicago has been placed on a level with that of Phillips Brooks in Boston and Henry Ward Beecher in Brooklyn.

    d. Had a rich, powerful, and vibrant voice, in addition to a lavish command of the English language

Newell Dwight Hillis (1858-1929)

    a. Remembered for his pleas for the richness of the Christian life

    b. In 1889 became pastor of Plymouth Congregational Church in Brooklyn, New York

Samuel Hopkins (1721-1804)

    a. Pastor in Great Barrington, Massachusetts for twenty-five years, and at Newport, Rhode Island for thirty-three years

    b. As a theologian he was biblical, Calvinistic, comprehensive, and scholarly

Richard (Russell) S. Storrs (1821-1900)

    a. Graduated from Amherst College

    b. Began as a lawyer

c. Served as pastor of one church for fifty-four years
d. Became one of the most noted pulpit orators in America
e. Had a remarkable command of the English language
f. A fundamentalist

BAPTISTS

Russell H. Conwell (1843-1925)
a. Built Tremont Temple on funds attained from preaching "Acres of Diamonds"; and instrumental in work of Temple
b. Expert with illustrations
c. Topical preacher
d. Had a rare persuasiveness and a phenomenal memory

Charles R. Brown (1855-1947)
a. Wrote *The Art of Preaching*
b. His preaching was noted for its simplicity of style
c. He employed the expository method
d. Was interested more in practice than theory

Henry Emerson Fosdick (1878-1969)
a. Pastor of Riverside Baptist Church.
b. Probably the greatest pulpit orator of his day
c. He exercised great freedom in the pulpit, and was especially noted for eye contact
d. He was noted for life-situation preaching

George C. Lorimer (1838-1904)
a. Was a converted actor
b. Memorized his sermons
c. Sermons included more poetry and literature than Bible
d. Sermons were topical and divisions were clear
e. Good imagination
f. Born in Scotland
g. Pastor of the Tremont Temple Baptist Church in Boston

F. B. Meyer (1847-1929)
a. Served as pastor of the Tremont Temple Baptist Church in Boston
b. Was an expository preacher
c. Noted for his evangelistic preaching
d. A crusader against public vices
e. His style had a suggestion of the ornate
f. Wrote seventy books that reached a circulation of five million before his death

Ezekiel Gilman Robinson (1815-1894)
a. Yale lecturer on preaching
b. President of Brown University and Rochester Seminary
c. Scholarly preacher; logical and verile
d. Main concern in life was education
e. Was liberal in his theology
f. Edited the *Christian Review* from 1859-64

Francis Wayland (1796-1865)
a. Supported higher education
b. A great champion of missions
c. Style excelled in clearness
d. Served as pastor of First Baptist Church in Boston, and First Baptist Church in Providence, Rhode Island
e. Had masterly analysis of subject
f. One of the most famous of American preachers
g. Was a crusader for higher education and missions

Roger Williams (1607-1683)
a. Encountered much opposition
b. Views of religious liberty ahead of his time
c. Excelled in languages, including Greek, French, and Dutch
d. An outstanding preacher

SOUTHERN BAPTISTS

John A. Broadus (1827-1895)
a. Recognized as a prince of the pulpit
b. His manner was calm and deliberate
c. His style was easy and conversational
d. Wrote *On the Preparation and Delivery of Sermons,* a classic in the field of homiletics
e. Compiled his lectures into the *History of Preaching,* (1876), an early work in the field of homiletics
f. Stressed expository preaching

Benajah Harvey Carroll (1843-1914)
a. Founder of Southwestern Baptist Seminary
b. For sixty years read 300 pages each day
c. Remembered for biblical preaching and his integrity
d. Sermons topical and textual
e. His sermon structure was good, and his outlines were clear and easy to follow
f. Possessed massive intellect and photographic memory
g. One of the greatest biblical preachers of modern times
h. Had a contagious evangelistic fervor

Richard Fuller (1804-1876)
a. A converted lawyer
b. Seems to have been influenced by Saurin
c. Was known for his eloquence
d. Sermons were published posthumously in 1877

Robert G. Lee (1896-1978)
a. Topical preacher
b. Memorized his sermons
c. Noted for his outstanding use of adjectives and adverbs
d. Most famous sermon: "Pay Day Someday"

e. Made 300 calls per year as a pastor

H. C. Mabie (1847-1918)

a. Evangelical
b. One of the truly great Baptist leaders
c. Excellent preacher; especially effective with young people and youth groups

George W. Truett (1867-1944)

a. One of America's outstanding preachers
b. Remembered for his pastoral prayers
c. Accidentally shot a deacon on a hunting trip; decided to leave the ministry, but was persuaded by his wife to stay
d. Served as pastor of the First Baptist Church in Dallas, Texas

EPISCOPALIANS

Phillips Brooks (1835-1889)

a. Preacher of extraordinary brilliance
b. Read his sermons
c. Prepared for the pulpit very carefully
d. Endeavored to bring theology down to life
e. Preached positively, to the conscience
f. Messages were Christ-centered

METHODISTS

Francis Cook (1747-1814)

a. Second greatest Methodist, surpassed only by John Wesley
b. He was the first Methodist bishop in the United States
c. At the age of seventy he volunteered for missionary service, and died among the West Indians

Bishop Matthew Simpson (1811-1894)

a. Often called to the White House by President Abraham Lincoln
b. Excellent preacher—aimed not to teach, but to persuade
c. Contributor to the Yale Lectures
d. Greatest Methodist preacher of his day
e. Served as Pastor of New York Avenue Presbyterian Church in Washington, D.C.
f. Stately in speech and manner
g. Preached both textually and topically
h. Was the President of Garrett Bible Institute in 1859
i. Was first trained as a physician, but practiced only for a short time

Ralph Sockman (1889-1970)

a. Served as pastor of Madison Avenue Methodist Episcopal Church
b. One of the greatest preachers of the contemporary world
c. Gave the Lyman Beecher Lectures in 1947-48
d. Was the preacher of the National Radio Pulpit, whose audience numbered in the millions

Archibald Alexander (1772-1851)
  a. First professor of theology at Princeton Seminary
  b. Separated rhetoric of pulpit and classroom
  c. Served as pastor of the noted Pine Street Church in Philadelphia
  d. Used brief notes, but rarely consulted them
  e. Planned his sermons with care
  f. Spoke in a lively conversational tone

Donald G. Barnhouse (1895-1962)
  a. Served as pastor of Tenth Church in Philadelphia
  b. Remembered for preaching through whole books of the Bible
  c. Produced a massive work on Romans that was the accumulation of expository messages representing a systematic theology put into the framework of the book

Arthur John Gossip (1873-1954)
  a. Topical preacher
  b. Good with the use of illustrations
  c. Was an expert in word choice

John Hall (1829-1899)
  a. Sermons were carefully prepared, but delivered without the benefit of a manuscript
  b. Gave Yale Divinity School Lectures (1875) "God's Word Through Preaching"
  c. Was chancellor of New York University
  d. Was an effective pastoral worker
  e. Pastored Fifth Presbyterian Church in New York

John Henry Jowett (1864-1923)
  a. Born and educated in England
  b. Served as pastor of Fifth Avenue Presbyterian Church in New York
  c. Detested sensationalism, flashy oratory, and emotionalism

Clarence Macartney (1879-1957)
  a. Topical preacher, but his source material was biblical
  b. Noted for his use of imagination in preaching
  c. A well-read man, he was noted for his biographical preaching

John Mitchell Mason (1770-1829)
  a. Ranks among the greatest of American pulpit orators
  b. Served as pastor of Scottish Presbyterian Church in New York City
  c. Had an extraordinary command of the English language
  d. Often turned his congregation into a great Bible Class, and expounded the Scriptures verse by verse
  e. Spoke extemporaneously with a strong, rich baritone voice, and used an ordinary conversational tone

Arthur Toppin Pierson (1837-1911)
  a. Moved thousands to salvation, Bible study, prayer life, and missionary service
  b. Strong on missions
  c. Remembered for his books on Bible study and preaching

    d. Was a Bible expositor

    e. Wrote *Evangelistic Work in Principle and Practice* (1887), *The Divine Art of Preaching* (1892), and *Seed Thoughts for Public Speakers* (1900)

T. DeWitt Talmage (1832-1901)

    a. A master of sensational rhetoric

    b. Often mistook an assertion for proof or an illustration for an argument

    c. A scene painter rather than an artist; good storyteller, although sometimes careless with facts

    d. Had an unconventional manner, and his sermons were badly organized

    e. Sermons published in 3,500 papers

LUTHERAN

Walter A. Maier (1893-1950)

    a. Fifteen million radio listeners

    b. Spent twenty hours of preparation on each sermon

    c. Remembered for his apt use of statistics in sermons

    d. Had a very fertile imagination

    e. Was gifted with an exceptionally keen mind

PLYMOUTH BRETHREN

Theodore Ledyard Cuyler (1822-1909)

    a. Graduated from Princeton Seminary

    b. Theologically conservative

    c. Early leader in a revival in New York

    d. Published twenty-two books of devotional nature; two volumes of sermons and 4000 articles

William E. Hatcher (1834-1912)

    a. Was staunchly baptistic

    b. Conservative in theology

    c. Sympathetic with the common people

Harry A. Ironside (1876-1951)

    a. Served as pastor of Moody Memorial Church in Chicago

    b. Called "archbishop of fundamentalism"

    c. Method of preaching was: (1) explain (2) illustrate (3) apply

    d. Was an avid reader, which compensated for his lack of education

William Morehead (1836-1914)

    a. Wrote biblical textbooks

    b. Taught forty years at Xenia Seminary

    c. A contributor to the *Scofield Reference Bible*

Part 2
A RHETORICAL PERSPECTIVE

11

Classical Rhetoric and the Science of Homiletics

Classical rhetoric reached its zenith in the works of Aristotle, Cicero, and Quintilian. Those men agreed that oratory had five parts.

When enlarged and developed, those five parts form the essence of public speaking theory. The first of those parts is *invention*, which is the origination or discovery of ideas or concepts used in the writing of a speech. The second part is *arrangement*, which is the organization of discovered material into a logical or topical progression. Consideration should be given to the comparative importance of the material. *Style* refers to the process of phrasing in oral language the ideas invented and arranged. The fourth part is *memory*, which involves the retention of ideas or thoughts in such a way that they can be reproduced. The fifth part is *delivery*, which covers the presentation of ideas that have been invented, arranged, phrased, and memorized. Delivery is concerned with both the audible and visible codes of speech.

The following outline constitutes an attempt to group some of the traditional items included in the science of homiletics under the five divisions of classical rhetoric.

References to a selected list of sixty-eight American homiletics trade and textbooks written between 1834 and 1954 are given so that the reader may find specific material dealing with the item. (See Appendixes 1 and 2 for more information.)

INVENTION

I. Invention in the Science of Homiletics

    A. Text
       1. Sources of texts
       2. Kinds of texts

3. Reasons for using texts
4. Objections to use of texts
5. Abuses of texts
6. Characteristics of texts
7. Rules for interpreting texts
8. Sources of error in interpreting texts
9. Rules for choosing texts

Broadus, John Albert. *A Treatise on the Preparation and Delivery of Sermons*. New York: A. C. Armstrong, 1889.
Fisk, Franklin Woodbury. *A Manual of Preaching*. New York: A. C. Armstrong, 1895.
Phelps, Austin. *The Theory of Preaching*. New York: Charles Scribner, 1930.

B. Subject
1. Characteristics of the subject
2. Sources of the subject
3. Selecting the subject
4. Treatment of the subject
5. Classification of subject
6. Originality of subject

Booth, Henry M. *The Man and His Message*. New York: Revell, 1899.
Brastow, Lewis Orsmond. *The Work of the Preacher: A Study of Homiletic Principles and Methods*. New York: Pilgrim, 1914.
Breed, David Riddle. *Preparing to Preach*. New York: George H. Doran, 1911.
Porter, Ebenezer. *Lectures on Homiletics and Preaching and on Public Prayer*. New York: Flagg, Gould, and Newman, 1834.
Shedd, William Greenough Thayer. *Homiletics and Pastoral Theology*. New York: Charles Scribner, 1867.
Stidger, William LeRoy. *Preaching Out of the Overflow*. Nashville: Cokesbury, 1929.

C. Theme
1. Identification of the theme
   a. by form
   b. by nature
   c. by purpose
   d. by place
2. Necessity of the theme
3. Advantages of the theme
4. Characteristics of the theme
5. Sources of the theme

Baughman, Harry Fridley. *Preaching from the Propers*. Philadelphia: Muhlenberg, 1949.

Brastow, Lewis Orsmond. *The Work of the Preacher: A Study of Homiletic Principles and Methods*.

Fry, Jacob. *Elementary Homiletics*. Reading, Penn.: Henry H. Bieber, 1893.

Graves, Henry C. *Lectures on Homiletics*. Philadelphia: American Baptist Publication Society, 1906.

Hoyt, Arthur Stephen. *The Work of Preaching*. New York: Macmillan, 1905.

Ray, Jefferson Davis. *Expository Preaching*. Grand Rapids: Zondervan, 1940.

D. Classification of the Sermon
  1. Biographical sermon

Caldwell, Frank Hill. *Preaching Angles*. Nashville: Abingdon, 1954.

  2. Book sermon

Caldwell, Frank Hill. *Preaching Angles*. 1954.

Jordan, Gerald Ray. *You Can Preach*. Westwood, N.J.: Revell, 1951.

Littorin, Frank T. *How to Preach the Word with Variety*. Grand Rapids: Baker, 1953.

Patton, Carl S. *The Preparation and Delivery of Sermons*. New York: Willett, Clark and Co., 1938.

  3. Doctrinal sermon

Brastow, Lewis Orsmond. *The Work of the Preacher: A Study of Homiletic Principles and Methods*.

Skinner, Thomas Harvey. *Aids to Revealing and Hearing*. New York: J. S. Taylor, 1839.

  4. Drama and art sermon

Stidger, William LeRoy. *Preaching Out of the Overflow*.

  5. Ethical sermon

Brastow, Lewis Orsmond. *The Work of the Preacher: A Study of Homiletic Principles and Methods*.

Porter, Ebenezer. *Lectures on Homiletics and Preaching and on Public Prayer*.

  6. Evangelistic sermon

Brastow, Lewis Orsmond. *The Work of the Preacher: A Study of Homiletic Principles and Methods*.

Weatherspoon, Jesse Burton. *Sent Forth to Preach*. New York: Harper and
    Brothers, 1954.

7. Expository sermon

Alexander, James Waddell. *Thoughts on Preaching Being Contributions to
    Homiletics*. New York: Charles Scribner, 1861.
Baughman, Harry Fridley. *Preaching from the Propers*.
Brown, Charles Reynolds. *The Art of Preaching*. New York: Macmillan, 1922.
Whitesell, Faris Daniel. *The Art of Biblical Preaching*. New York: Charles
    Scribner's Sons, 1950.

8. Historical sermon

Burrell, David James. *The Sermon: Its Construction and Its Delivery*. New
    York: Revell, 1913.
Dabney, Robert Lewis. *Sacred Rhetoric: Lectures on Preaching*. New York:
    Amson D. F. Randolph, 1870.

9. Life-situation sermon

Blackwood, Andrew Watterson. *The Preparation of Sermons*. Nashville:
    Abingdon-Cokesbury, 1948.
Caldwell, Frank Hill. *Preaching Angles*.
Luccock, Halford Edward. *In the Minister's Workshop*. Nashville: Abing-
    don-Cokesbury, 1944.

10. Music sermon

Caldwell, Frank Hill. *Preaching Angles*.
Stidger William LeRoy. *Preaching Out of the Overflow*.

11. Parable sermon

Jordan, Gerald Ray. *You Can Preach*.
Robbins, Howard Chandler. *Preaching the Gospel*. New York: Harper and
    Brothers, 1940.

12. Prophetic sermon

Robbins, Howard Chandler. *Preaching the Gospel*. 1940.

13. Symphonic sermon

Stidger, William LeRoy. *Preaching Out of the Overflow*.

Jordan, Gerald Ray. *You Can Preach.*
Caldwell, Frank Hill. *Preaching Angles.*

14. Textual sermon

Caldwell, Frank Hill. *Preaching Angles.*
Shedd, William Greenough Thayer. *Homiletics and Pastoral Theology.* New
    York: Charles Scribner, 1867.

15. Topical sermon

Blackwood, Andrew Watterson. *The Preparation of Sermons.*
Kidder, Daniel Parrish. *A Treatise on Homiletics.* New York: Carlton and
    Porter, 1864.

E. Functional Elements of the Sermon
   1. Amplification

Kern, John Adam. *The Ministry to the Congregation.* New York: Jennings and
Graham, 1897.

2. Application

Bowie, Walter Russell. *Preaching.* Nashville: Abingdon, 1954.
Breed, David Riddle. *Preparing to Preach.*
Broadus, John Albert. *A Treatise on the Preparation and Delivery of Sermons.*

3. Argumentation

Broadus, John Albert. *A Treatise on the Preparation and Delivery of Sermons.*
Kern, John Adam. *The Ministry to the Congregation.*

4. Description

Kern, John Adam. *The Ministry to the Congregation.*

5. Development

Brastow, Lewis Orsmond. *The Work of the Preacher: A Study of Homiletic
Principles and Methods.*
Fisk, Franklin Woodbury. *A Manual of Preaching.* New York: A. C.
Armstrong, 1895.
Hoppin, James Mason. *The Office and Work of the Christian Ministry.* New
York: Sheldon, 1869.
Phelps, Austin. *The Theory of Preaching.*

6. Disposition

Anderson, Galusha. *Notes on Homiletics*. Boston: Rockwell & Churchill, 1872.
Kidder, Daniel Parrish. *A Treatise on Homiletics*.

7. Exhortation

Kern, John Adam. *The Ministry to the Congregation*.

8. Explanation

Hoppin, James Mason. *The Office and Work of the Christian Ministry*.
Hoyt, Arthur Stephen. *The Work of Preaching: A Book for the Classroom and Study*.
Jones, Bob, Jr. *How to Improve Your Preaching*. New York: Revell, 1945.
Kidder, Daniel Parrish. *A Treatise on Homiletics*.
Phelps, Austin. *The Theory of Preaching*.

9. Explication

Anderson, Galusha. *Notes on Homiletics*.
Dabney, Robert Lewis. *Sacred Rhetoric: Lectures on Preaching*.
Porter, Ebenezer. *Lectures on Homiletics and Preaching and on Public Prayer*.

10. *Exposition*

Fisk, Franklin Woodbury. *A Manual of Preaching*.
Kern, John Adam. *The Ministry to the Congregation*.
Kidder, Daniel Parrish. *A Treatise on Homiletics*.
Ripley, Henry Jones. *Sacred Rhetoric: or Composition of Sermons*. Boston: Gould, Kendall, and Lincoln, 1849.

11. Illustration

Breed, David Riddle. *Preparing to Preach*.
Fisk, Franklin Woodbury. *A Manual of Preaching*.
Garrison, Webb Black. *The Preacher and His Audience*. Westwood, N.J.: Revell, 1954.
Kern, John Adam. *The Ministry to the Congregation*.

12. Instruction

Breed, David Riddle. *Preparing to Preach*.
Kidder, Daniel Parrish. *A Treatise on Homiletics*.

   F. How to Search the Scriptures Homiletically
      1. Study of the context
      2. Survey for the sermon ideas

Schenck, Ferdinand Schureman. *Modern Practical Theology.* New York: Funk and Wagnalls, 1903.

   G. Methods of Preparation
      1. General preparation
         a. General sources for material
         b. Processes of general preparation

Hoyt, Arthur Stephen. *The Work of Preaching: A Book for the Classroom and Study.*
Johnson, Herrick. *The Ideal Ministry.* New York: Revell, 1908.
Shedd, William Greenough Thayer. *Homiletics and Pastoral Theology.*

      2. Specific preparation
         a. Specific preparation for particular occasions
         b. Specific preparation for delivery

Kidder, Daniel Parrish. *A Treatise on Homiletics.*
Kirkpatrick, Robert White. *Creative Delivery of Sermons.* New York: Macmillan, 1947.
Shedd, William Greenough Thayer. *Homiletics and Pastoral Theology.*

   H. The Influence of the Setting on the Sermon
      1. Auditorium
      2. Congregation

Gardner, Charles Spurgeon. *Psychology and Preaching.* New York: Macmillan, 1918.
Shedd, William Greenough Thayer. *Homiletics and Pastoral Theology.*

      3. Occasion

Baxter, Batsell Barrett. *Speaking for the Master.* New York: Macmillan, 1954.
Breed, David Riddle. *Preparing to Preach.*
Kern, John Adam. *The Ministry to the Congregation.*

      4. Church Music

Hoppin, James Mason. *The Office and Work of the Christian Ministry.*

5. Prayer

Kern, John Adam. *The Ministry to the Congregation.*
Porter, Ebenezer. *Lectures on Homiletics and Preaching and on Public Prayer.*

6. Public reading of Scriptures

Kern, John Adam. *The Ministry to the Congregation.*
Ray, Jefferson Davis. *Expository Preaching.*

7. General worship

Hoppin, James Mason. *The Office and Work of the Christian Ministry.*
Noyes, Morgan Phelps. *Preaching the Word of God.* New York: Scribner's, 1943.
Schenck, Ferdinand Schureman. *Modern Practical Theology.*
Shedd, William Greenough Thayer. *Homiletics and Pastoral Theology.*

ARRANGEMENT

II. Arrangement in the Science of Homiletics

  A. Importance of Sermonic Arrangement
  B. Characteristics of Good Sermonic Arrangement
  C. Types of Sermonic Arrangement
  D. Introduction of the Sermon
      1. Necessity of an introduction
      2. Characteristics of an introduction
      3. Forms of introduction
      4. Purposes of an introduction
      5. Sources and materials of an introduction
      6. Preparation of an introduction
      7. Presentation of an introduction

  Phelps, Austin. *The Theory of Preaching.*

  E. Proposition of the Sermon
      1. Importance of proposition
      2. Definitions of a proposition
      3. Types of proposition
      4. Presentation of proposition
      5. Characteristics of proposition

  Kern, John Adam. *The Ministry to the Congregation.*

Davis, Ozora Stearns. *Principles of Preaching*. Chicago: U. of Chicago, 1924.

Phelps, Austin. *The Theory of Preaching*.

Porter, Ebenezer. *Lectures on Homiletics and Preaching and on Public Prayer*.

F. Body of the Sermon
   1. Kinds of styles of divisions
   2. Characteristics of divisions
   3. Rules governing the formulation of the sermon body
   4. Reasons for failure in the formulation of the sermon body
   5. Advantages to having evident divisions
   6. Relation between divisions and discussion
   7. Subdivisions of the sermon

Broadus, John Albert. *A Treatise on the Preparation and Delivery of Sermons*.

Burrell, David James. *The Sermon: Its Construction and Delivery*.

Kidder, Daniel Parrish. *A Treatise on Homiletics*.

Porter, Ebenezer. *Lectures on Homiletics and Preaching and on Public Prayer*.

G. Conclusion of the Sermon
   1. Purposes of the conclusion
   2. Importance of the conclusion
   3. Species of conclusion
   4. Characteristics of the conclusion
   5. Suggestions for formulating a conclusion
   6. Presentation of a conclusion

Brastow, Lewis Orsmond. *The Work of the Preacher: A Study of Homiletic Principles and Methods*.

Kidder, Daniel Parrish. *A Treatise on Homiletics*.

Porter, Ebenezer. *Lectures on Homiletics and Preaching and on Public Prayer*.

Shedd, William Greenough Thayer. *Homiletics and Pastoral Theology*.

H. Transitions of the Sermon

Broadus, John Albert. *A Treatise on the Preparation and Delivery of Sermons*.

Davis, Ozora Stearns. *Principles of Preaching*.

Hoyt, Arthur Stephen. *The Work of Preaching: A Book for Classroom and Study*

Ripley, Henry Jones. *Sacred Rhetoric*.

III. Style and the Science of Homiletics

    A. Nature of Style
       1. Definitions of style
       2. Style fitting for a public discourse

       Brastow, Lewis Orsmond. *The Work of the Preacher: A Study of Homiletic Principles and Method.*
       Hoppin, James Mason. *The Office and Work of the Christian Ministry.*
       Patton, Carl S. *The Preparation and Delivery of Sermons.*
       Porter, Ebenezer. *Lectures on Homiletics and Preaching and on Public Prayer.*

    B. Improvement of Style

       Phelps, Austin. *The Theory of Preaching.*
       Pittenger, William. *Oratory, Sacred and Secular.* New York: R. Wells, 1868.
       Whitesell, Faris Daniel. *The Art of Biblical Preaching.*

    C. Qualities of Style

       Broadus, John Albert. *A Treatise on the Preparation and Delivery of Sermons.*
       Burrell, David James. *The Sermon: Its Construction and Delivery.*
       Fisk, Franklin Woodbury. *A Manual of Preaching.*
       Skinner, Thomas Harvey. *Aids to Revealing and Hearing.*

IV. Memory and the Science of Homiletics

    A. Advantages of Memorizing
    B. Methods of Memorizing

V. Delivery and the Science of Homiletics

       Gardner, Charles Spurgeon. *Psychology and Preaching.*
       Kennedy, Gerald Hamilton. *His Word Through Preaching.* New York: Harper and Brothers, 1947.

    A. Psychological Factors

       Gardner, Charles Spurgeon. *Psychology and Preaching.*
       Garrison, Webb Black. *The Preacher and His Audience.*
       Kirkpatrick, Robert White. *Creative Delivery of Sermons.*

B. Visual Factors

Garrison, Webb Black. *The Preacher and His Audience.*

C. Auditory Factors

Broadus, John Albert. *A Treatise on the Preparation and Delivery of Sermons.*
Dabney, Robert Lewis. *Sacred Rhetoric.*
Phelps, Austin. *The Theory of Preaching.*
Skinner, Thomas Harvey. *Aids to Revealing and Hearing.*

D. Physical Factors

Broadus, John Albert. *A Treatise on the Preparation and Delivery of Sermons.*
Gardner, Charles Spurgeon. *Psychology and Preaching.*
Phelps, Austin. *The Theory of Preaching.*

E. Delivery from an Outline

Blackwood, Andrew Watterson. *The Preparation of Sermons.*
Jordan, Gerald Ray. *You Can Preach.*

F. Extemporaneous Delivery

Alexander, James Waddell. *Thoughts on Preaching.*
Breed, David Riddle. *Preparing to Preach.*
Kern, John Adam. *The Ministry to the Congregation.*
Shedd, William Greenough Thayer. *Homiletics and Pastoral Theology.*

1. Advantages of the extemporaneous method
2. Possible handicaps to acquiring an extemporaneous delivery
3. Injurious tendencies that sometimes result from using the extemporaneous method
4. Positive suggestions for developing extemporaneous delivery

G. Reading from Manuscript
   1. Advantages of reading from manuscript
   2. Disadvantages of reading from manuscript
   3. Demands for effectiveness from manuscript

Broadus, John Albert. *A Treatise on the Preparation and Delivery of Sermons.*
Hoyt, Arthur Stephen. *The Work of Preaching.*

H. Recitation from Memory
    1. Advantages of reciting from memory
    2. Disadvantages of reciting from memory

Broadus, John Albert. *A Treatise on the Preparation and Delivery of Sermons.*
Hoyt, Arthur Stephen. *The Work of Preaching.*

12

Classical Rhetoric and Homiletical Style

According to Franklin W. Fisk, *homiletics* is defined as rhetoric applied to sacred discourse. It is simply a body of principles or rules gathered by searching analyses of the best sermons in every age of the church.[1] Ferdinand S. Schenck said that "homiletics is the science of which preaching is the art."[2]

The word *sermon* is derived from a Latin word meaning "a speech." Thus, a sermon is an oral address directed to the popular mind and based on religious truth as contained in the Christian Scriptures.[3]

Edwin Charles Dargan, author of the classic work *The Art of Preaching in the Light of Its History,* would largely agree with those definitions. He says, "Homiletical theory, both in its origin and in its development, is the application of accepted principles of public speaking to the particular ends and demands of the Christian gospel."[4] The term *rhetoric* refers to those principles of public speaking. For rhetoric is really nothing more (at least in the classical sense) than the study of how to use those principles of public speaking in such a way that the hearer's thought and conduct are influenced in a direction desired by the speaker's.

THE PATRISTIC PERIOD (A.D. 70-430)

To understand the treatment of sermonic style of this early period one must be aware not only of the classical influence on sacred delivery, but also of the prevalence of sophistic rhetorical abuse.

During the first five centuries of the Christian era rhetoric held the chief place in

1. *A Manual of Preaching: Lectures on Homiletics* (New York: A. C. Armstrong and Son, 1895), 1.
2. *Modern Practical Theology* (New York: Funk and Wagnalls, 1903), 15.
3. Austin Phelps, *The Theory of Preaching* (New York: Richard R. Smith, 1930), 1.
4. Edwin Charles Dargan, (New York: George H. Doran, 1922), 28.

111

formal education. Therefore, at the time when Christianity ceased to be persecuted and became a care of government, a great educational system centered on the rhetorical method had come to be thoroughly wrought and established.[5] Thus the preaching and homiletics of patristic times received its classical influence.

Some of the classical rhetorical writings (e.g., those of Aristotle, Cicero, Quintilian, Longinus, Demetrius, Dionysius, etc.) passed down from before the time of Christ, or shortly thereafter, represented a high development of the best in rhetoric. The second through the fourth centuries A.D., however, were marked by exaggeration, bombast, unreality, and sophistry, which marred the oratory and public speaking of the patristic age. That caused many of the church Fathers to be critical toward much of the rhetorical teaching.

They assumed a corrective attitude toward current rhetorical theory as it applied to preaching. Theory did not so much need to be learned (it was already taught in the schools) as it needed to be applied to Christian uses.

The five most famous pulpit orators of the patristic age were all rhetorically trained. They were Basil, Gregory of Nazianzus, and Chrysostom in the East; Ambrose and Augustine in the West.

Origen (A.D. 180-253) did not disdain rhetoric itself, but rather the misuse of it. Regarding style, he said, "But a lucid discourse, the splendor of eloquence, and the art of arguing are with propriety admitted to the service of the Word of God."[6]

In his *Letter to Donatus*, Cyprian (200-258) spoke of the relations of secular and sacred speech:

> In the courts, in platform addresses let voluble ambition boast a wealth of eloquence. But when it is speech concerning the Lord God, then pure sincerity of speech rests for persuasives to faith, not upon the powers of eloquence, but upon things (i.e., reality). In fine, use not eloquent but forcible words, not those polished to attract a popular audience by artificial speech, but simple enough to proclaim with plain truth the divine love.[7]

Cyprian did not seem to disparage attention to good style itself, but rather to a sophistic distortion of style.

Hilary of Poitiers (315-357), a champion of orthodoxy against Arianism, believed style was important. James Murphy said of him that he "condemns Arian verbal display, yet prays for a good style in his own sermons. Honor, he says, is given to the Word of God by one who speaks with beauty of expression."[8]

The church Fathers were much more concerned about clarity of speech than mere verbal showiness. Basil of Caesarea (330-379) said, "Our writers do not waste their time in polishing periods . . . we prefer clarity of expression to mere euphony."[9]

The only authors of the patristic age who made direct contributions to the literature of

5. Ibid., 41.
6. Ibid., 47.
7. Ibid., 49.
8. James Murphy, "Saint Augustine and the Debate About a Christian Rhetoric," *Quarterly Journal of Speech* (December 1960): 404.
9. Ibid., 403.

homiletics were Chrysostom (his *De Sacerdotio* or *On the Priesthood*) and Augustine (his *De Doctrina Christiana*), the former representing the Greek church and the latter representing the Latin church.

According to Chrysostom's *On the Priesthood* (fourth century) the good preacher must work at cultivating speech skills. However, it is only fair to say that he also believed that the preacher should discard ambition for oratorical display and applause, and seek first of all the spiritual edification of his hearers.[10] With that understanding, style is properly studied by the preacher. Chrysostom goes on to say. "For since speaking comes not by *nature but by learning*, although one may attain to perfection in it, he who does not cultivate the faculty with constant zeal and practice would at last turn out destitute of it."[11]

Augustine in his *De Doctrina Christiana* made it clear that he believed the life of the minister had a greater persuasive influence than any sublimity of eloquence. He pointed out that there are those who speak the "truth" with eloquence but whose lives are an abomination, for they live not as they preach.[12] He said:

> But a man who has merely an empty flow of eloquence ought the more to be guarded against as he is the more pleasing to those in his audience in those matters which have no expedience, and, as his audience hears him speak with fluency, it judges likewise that he speaks with truth.[13]

In speaking of sublime eloquence, Augustine said, "Of what value is a golden key, if it will not open what we wish?—and what is the harm of a wooden one, if it will accomplish this purpose?—since all we need is to obtain access to what concealed."[14]

One thing that stood out preeminently in Augustine's teaching was his conviction that a skillful employment of accepted rhetorical principles is wise as far as they are serviceable to the preacher of the gospel.

Relative to homiletics, Augustine's treatise occupies the position of Aristotle's *Rhetoric* toward the art of speaking in general.

In book four of *De Doctrina Christiana* Augustine says that wisdom is more valuable than eloquence, but both are needed. He goes on to show how the sacred writers employed both.[15] He related, however, that a mastery of rhetorical rules as such is not necessary to good speaking; we can learn by hearing and following eloquent speakers.

De Doctrina Christiana had a great influence on subsequent theories of preaching. It was copied or quoted by Rabanus Maurus in the ninth century, Alain de Lille in the twelfth, Humbert de Romanis in the thirteenth, and Robert Basevorn in the fourteenth.[16]

After Augustine, no real treatises on preaching appeared for centuries.

10. Dargan, 53.
11. Ibid., 54.
12. Patrick O. Marsh, *Persuasive Speaking* (New York: Harper & Row, 1967), 577.
13. Murphy, 408.
14. Ebenezer Porter, *Lectures on Homiletics and Preaching, and Public Prayer Together with Sermons and Lectures* (New York: Flagg, Gould, and Newman, 1934), 179-80.
15. Dargan, 60-61.
16. Murphy, 400.

The Early Medieval Period (430-1095)

On the whole, homiletics after Augustine was sadly lacking in originality or freshness.

Gregory the Great's *Pastoral Rule* came in the sixth century, but had little value for homiletics. According to Murphy, "The *De Doctrina Christiana* provided the basic statement of a Christian homiletic until the emergence of the highly-formalized 'thematic' of the 'university style' sermon about the beginning of the thirteenth century."[17] Rabanus Maurus (d. 856), the archbishop of Mainz, is famous for his treatise *De Clericorum Institutione* (*On the Institution of the Clergy*), but in the area of homiletics it is really only a recapitulation of Augustine's teaching.

There are a number of medieval tractates on preaching. Some of them treat style, but seldom is the treatment original, and sometimes the definition of style is severely limited.

The Central Medieval Period (1095-1300)

In the late twelfth century, Alan of Lille wrote *Summary of the Art of Preaching*. His work was significant in that he introduced the *Scholastic method* into preaching. That method endeavored to reduce theology to a rigid and formal system and to employ as its chief agency the dialectics of Aristotle. The method was characterized by formalizing minute divisions and subdivisions of subject matter and ideas. This marked formality in procedure and narrow adherence to traditional teachings and doctrines probably did much to stifle true creativity, not only in theology, but also in the development of a sermonic style.

Excesses of style were rightly criticized. William of Auvergne wrote: "A simple sermon, unpolished, unadorned, moves and edifies the more." He despised the preacher "who, with ornate words, casts naked truth into the shadow."[18] Alan of Lille said:

> Preaching ought not to contain scurrilous or puerile words, or rhythmic melodies, or metric consonances. These contribute, rather to soothing the ear than to instructing the mind. Such preaching is theatrical; and therefore should be unanimously condemned. . . . Yet though preaching should not shine with purple verbal trappings, neither should it be depressed by bloodless words. Rather a middle course should be pursued.[19]

The most important name in the theory of preaching in the thirteenth century was Bonaventura. He was a theologian, mystic, cardinal, and saint. He wrote the *Art of Preaching*, a work that closely followed the *Christian Teaching* of Augustine.[20]

Also in the thirteenth century, Humbert de Romanis, a French and Dominican monk, wrote *On the Education of Preachers*. As it relates to the style of preaching, his criticism of his contemporaries was enlightening. He said, "There are those who are

17. Ibid., 407.
18. Harry Caplan, *Of Eloquence: Studies in Ancient and Medieval Rhetoric* (Ithaca, N.Y.: Cornell U., 1970), 82.
19. Ibid., 82.
20. Dargan, 84.

more studious for ornaments of language than for the views to be expressed; like those who care more for the beauty of the dish in which they serve food than for the food itself."[21]

Excessive attention to style at the expense of truth is a recurring phenomenon in the history of homiletics. The criticism by the thirteenth-century Dominican could be appropriately offered as well in the seventeenth through nineteenth centuries.

It was not until the revival of some of the classical works on style that a better and more enlightened theory of preaching style was developed.

The Renaissance and Late Medieval Period (1300-1500)

In this period extravagant ornamentation in sacred oratory is again criticized. Auksi said, "The doctrinal innovations of the mendicant friars, their homilies laced with secular tales, amusing poems, and rhetorical embellishments, and their forced unnaturally close exegesis wrung from plain Scripture—these Wyclif calls ungodly accretions."[22] The truth was that much of the preaching of the fourteenth and fifteenth centuries was in a sad state not only because of forced biblical interpretation, but because of the extreme use of racy speech to attract the masses. Allegory was often used when it distorted the true meaning of Scripture.

Ulrich Surgant wrote *A Manual for Curates* in 1475. As a priest he discussed the fourfold interpretation, including allegory.

A powerful and direct influence on homiletics in the fifteenth century was the revived study of classical rhetoric. Some classical works were rediscovered. Scholars went back to the firsthand study of Aristotle, Cicero, and Quintilian.

The Council of Trent gave active and decisive attention to reforming preaching and sought to correct some of the more flagrant abuses both in practice and theory.

The Reformatory Period (1500-1572)

This period represents some of the best and most powerful preaching of all time. Ulrich Zwingli, Martin Luther, Hugh Latimer, John Calvin, and John Knox were all powerful and very effective preachers.

Martin Luther seems to have been familiar with the classical conception of rhetoric and style. In one of his *Housepostils* quoted by Nebe, Luther declared: "Dialectic is the body, rhetoric is the dress with which the body is adorned."[23] In his *Table Talk* Luther said that the preacher should be master of the art of public address. In several places he declared that the preacher should be master of both logic and rhetoric. He went on to say that when the preacher preaches touching an article of faith and declares it, "he must adorn it with similitudes; and . . . earnestly reprove all the disobedient."[24]

The *Encyclopedia Britannica* has this to say about style in the sixteenth century:

> Elocution, or style, became the centre of rhetorical theory, and in Ramist (Petrus Ramus) hands it was almost solely concerned with figures of speech. Actually, a strong emphasis

21. Ibid., 85.
22. Peter Auksi, "Wyclif's Sermons and the Plain Style," *Archives* 66 (1975): 8.
23. Dargan, 128.
24. Ibid., 127-28.

upon the figures of speech had been evolving since the late Middle Ages. When responsibly taught, as linguistic postures, gesture; of the mind in confrontation with external reality, the figures served a useful purpose; and in Renaissance education they were widely employed . . . in the interpretation or analysis of discourse. Less responsibly taught, the figures became merely an ornamentation, like the metaphor in Aristotle.[25]

Dargan said that classical rhetoric was not belittled by the Reformers.

While the reformers laid more stress on the *content* and *aim* of preaching than on its *form* and *method*, they did not wholly neglect these either in their example or their teaching. They seemed to take it for granted that in requiring skill and training for a proper study and proclamation of the Word of God they were demanding that the preacher should both know and know how to use the accepted and tested principles of rhetoric as these were applicable to the preparation and delivery of sermons.[26]

The emphasis on style in the Reformatory period was not limited to the Protestant Reformers. In 1576, for example, Luis of Granada, (1505-1588) a Dominican friar in Spain, released his work *Rhetorica Ecclesiastica*.

He said: "The tasks of a preacher are chiefly three: invention, style and delivery"[27] Under style, he emphasized four essentials: (1) purity and correctness of language; (2) perspicuity; (3) adornment, including a good discussion of tropes and figures; (4) the avoidance of faults of language and expression.[28]

The most original and significant work by any early Protestant writer on homiletics is that of Andrew Hyperius (1511-1565). His *On the Making of Sacred Discourses* was an important work in the development of homiletics.

William Perkins, a Puritan, urged the use of the "plain" style. In his *The Art of Prophesying* (1592), he established the principle that Puritan preachers should not parade their human wisdom and learning if they were to reach the common people. He further said, "It is also a point of Art to conceal Art."[29] Thomas Hooker, another Puritan, warned against the evil consequences of a too ornate sermon style.[30] The plain style of the Puritans was not necessarily austere, bland, and uninteresting. The Puritan preacher was often the most highly educated man in his parish. He often knew the classics as well as the Latin, Greek, and Hebrew languages. He was aware of the best literature of the day. The English Bible had a tremendous influence on his style because he literally immersed himself in the Scriptures. His preaching was often powerful because he put a high premium on clarity of speech.

He even unconsciously used some of the best stylistic devices of the best literature of his day. The best style is that which in a sense is unconscious and does not call attention to itself. Turnbull said:

25. *Encyclopedia Britannica*. 15th ed. (Chicago: William Benton, 1974).
26. Dargan, 132.
27. Joseph Conners, "Homiletic Theory in the Sixteenth Century," *American Ecclesiastical Review* (May 1958): 316-32.
28. Dargan, 119.
29. Ralph G. Turnbull, *The Preacher's Heritage, Task and Resources* (Grand Rapids: Baker, 1968), 116.
30. Ibid., 117.

> There is no question about the influence of the King James Version of the Bible. . . . There the "simple and pure verity" of style was set out in that monument of Elizabethan English. The cadences and beauty of word and phrase, the simple sentence, the rugged Anglo-Saxon, the surge and thunder of idea and thought gripped the mind and molded the spirit. The Puritan preacher was steeped in the English Bible. The English language was then at its flowering and best.[31]

Some of the best sermonic style is learned through immersion in the English Scriptures.

E. W. Bullinger's *Figures of Speech Used in the Bible*[32] demonstrated that the Bible is full of various figures of speech. Writers on style frequently show that figures are instrumental in promoting energy (power) of style.

A neo-Scholasticism unfortunately pervaded much of Protestant homiletics. After Hyperius, especially in the seventeenth century, a cold and minute analysis and refinement with little adaptation to life and need was the order of the time. On the whole, the English treatises on homiletics during the eighteenth century were disappointing in number and quality.

There seems to have been little advance in thinking and theory during the fifteenth and sixteenth centuries.[33] Most of the rhetorical works of this early modern age had no great value or originality, but rather followed the traditional rhetorical methods. In German and Dutch treatises of the period one distinct tendency was the scholastic method, which was mechanical, artificial, academic, tedious, and dry.[34]

THE EARLY MODERN PERIOD (1572-1789)

There was a reaction to neo-scholasticism and a repudiation of its overtedious use of the classical rhetorical art. Joachim Lange, a German and a follower of Spener, the eminent Pietist, utterly disparaged the Scholasticism of the sixteenth century. Lange wrote *Sacred Oratory Purged from the Vanity of Homiletical Art,* a treatise published in 1707. According to Dargan, "The pious author criticized very sharply the extremes of the preceding period, but naturally tended too far the other way in not giving sufficient attention to rhetorical art in the composition of sermons."[35] One of the main divisions of the "rhetoric" Lange spurned was style.

Augustine Valiero (1531-1606) was a well-known Roman Catholic writer. His book on homiletics went through eight editions in his lifetime and was adopted as a Catholic seminary textbook. The third section of his work was on style. He spoke of the use of tropes and figures, but preferred the functional view of style over the ornamental. He took the three levels of style of Augustine, but combined them with the functional use of tropes and figures.[36] He gave examples of the figures that were to be used in the *fine* or *subtle,* in the *temperate* style, and in the *vehement* style of speaking.[37] He divided rhetoric as did Aristotle, but dealt with only the first three divisions of the fivefold

31. Turnbull, 118.
32. E. W. Bullinger, *Figures of Speech Used in the Bible* (Grand Rapids; Baker, 1968).
33. Dargan, 143, 178.
34. Ibid., 156.
35. Ibid., 165.
36. Conners, 323.
37. Mudd, 260.

division of classical rhetoric: invention, arrangement, and style.[38]

Three Protestant clerics of this period formed a moderate school of sorts regarding treatment of sermonic style: Hugh Blair, *Lectures on Rhetoric* (1783); George Campbell, *Philosophy of Rhetoric* (1776); Richard Whateley, *Elements of Rhetoric* (1861); and Campbell's *Lectures on Pulpit Eloquence* (1870). Those writers all devoted considerable time to style.

Campbell, for example said, "Thus it appears, that beside *purity,* which is a quality entirely grammatical, the five simple and original qualities of style . . . are *perspicuity, vivacity, elegance, animation,* and *music.*"[39]

It would seem that homiletical writers on style who have kept clarity and perspicuity to the forefront have almost always given us a more sensible view of style than those who have belabored the use of figures and tropes.

John Ward (1679-1758) believed that "the style . . . should always be adapted to the nature of the subject, which rhetoricians have reduced to three ranks or degrees; the low or plain style, the middle or temperate, and the lofty or sublime."[40] His work, *A System of Oratory,* was largely devoted to style.

Another Catholic writer who was also famous among Protestants of the day was Gisbert of France, who wrote *Christian Eloquence in Idea and Practice* (1715). He opposed the extravagant and artificial style of preaching.[41]

In England, Philip Doddridge (1702-1751) was one of the wisest and most pious divines. He taught that style should be pure, intelligible and clear, strong and nervous, calm and composed, orthodox, grave and solemn, plain and unaffected, interspersed with figures, free and easy, lively, various, and harmonious.[42]

THE LATE MODERN PERIOD (1789-1900)

There seems to have been at least five stylistic trends in this period. First, a classical emphasis on style in America; second, a strong belittling of the classical viewpoint on style; third, a trend toward emphasizing gestures rather than words; fourth, a restatement of the difference between secular and sacred oratory and a new look at the proper purpose of style in sermons, and last, a renewed emphasis on the importance of style for the preacher.

In America after the colonial period, the classical emphasis was combined with a religious intellectualism that dominated much of church life. Turnbull says:

> The learned Unitarian preacher was noted for his cadenced prose and careful wording. His style was different from the passionate exhortation of the Puritan, and certainly far removed from the frontier missionary-evangelist. . . . Unitarian preaching lacked the homely touch. Wisdom and education were commonplace ideas and religious intellectualism dominated the church life. . . . Rhetoric and speech were taught in the emerging colleges as a required

38. Conners, 319.
39. *Philosophy of Rhetoric,* condensed by Glenville Kleiser (New York: Funk and Wagnalls, 1912), 69.
40. Lester Thonssen, *Selected Readings in Rhetoric and Public Speaking* (New York: H. W. Wilson, 1942), 214.
41. Dargan, 164.
42. Ibid., 175.

subject. Debates were common in class and public . . . . During this classical period of education in the United States, the preacher was one to benefit by these trends.[43]

John Quincy Adams, John Witherspoon, and Edward Channing all had their part in the above emphasis.

Later in the nineteenth century traditional techniques of style were deemphasized by new interests, and then a Delsartean view held sway for a time. According to the *Encyclopedia Britannica*:

> Eventually all traditional techniques of style were devalued by interest in experiments; in Switzerland, cultural historian Jacob Burckhardt described antiquities' interest in rhetoric as a "monstrous aberration." In America, the Delsarteans, who stressed gesture rather than words, spread an antirhetorical approach to imagination, the passions, sensory experience, and delivery. Thus well into the 20th century, "elocution" in popular speech meant florid delivery and "rhetoric" because of its principle concern with oratory meant purple prose.[44]

Ebenezer Porter and Alexander Vinet reemphasized the proper purpose of style in sermon delivery. Having served as a professor of sacred rhetoric at Andover Seminary, Porter deserves credit as the real originator of homiletical instruction in theological seminaries in this country. In 1834 he published *Lectures on Homiletics and Preaching and on Public Prayer, Together With Sermons and Letters*. A historically important work, it insists that "style should be simple, serious, earnest." The usual qualities of style are discussed.[45] Porter also says:

> Would you know the difference . . . between the pulpit declaimer, and the pulpit orator? It is this: the former preaches for himself; the latter for God. . . . The style of declamation may indeed, be perspicuous. But its perspicuity differs as much from that of fervid eloquence, as the transparency of ice differs from the glowing transparency of melted glass, issuing from the furnace.[46]

In France, Alexander Vinet published *Homiletics* in 1847. In it he says:

> Neither an anathema on art, nor art for art's sake, but art for God's sake, is what we insist upon. It results, as it seems to us, from what we have said, that good style is necessary, and that good style does not come of itself.[47]

John A. Broadus reemphasized the importance of speaking style for the preacher. First published in 1871, his *On the Preparation and Delivery of Sermons* reached nearly twenty editions before it was revised, and became perhaps the leading homiletics text. Broadus, considering sermonic style in detail, says:

43. Turnbull, *A History of Preaching* (Grand Rapids: Baker, 1974), 3:802.
44. *Encyclopedia Britannica*, 15:802.
45. Dargan, 217.
46. Porter, 182.
47. Dargan, 188.

Style is not a thing of mere ornament. Style is the glitter and polish of the warrior's sword, but is also its keen edge. It can render mediocrity acceptable and even attractive, can make power more powerful still. It can make error seductive; and truth may lie unnoticed for want of its aid. Shall religious teachers neglect so powerful a means of usefulness? True, Paul says, "My speech and my preaching were not with persuasive words of man's wisdom." He refused to deal in the would-be philosophy and the sensational and meretricious rhetoric which were so popular in that rapidly growing commercial city; but his style is a model of passionate energy, and rises, upon occasion, into an inartificial and exquisite beauty. Yet style is in this country much neglected.[48]

Other important homiletical works of this period include Daniel P. Kidder's *A Treatise on Homiletics* (1864), which included a discussion of style, and J. M. Hoppin's *Homiletics* (1869), which dealt with the rhetorical principles of preaching in a very competent and instructive way, and devoted a considerable number of its pages to style. Lloyd Perry's 1954 doctoral dissertation on homiletics is helpful in discerning trends in the treatment of sermonic style between 1834 and 1954.[49] It devotes twenty pages to the nature, qualities, and improvement of sermonic style. Forty-five of the sixty-eight writers surveyed are concerned with items dealing with style.

Three writers devote more than seventy-five pages to a discussion of sermonic style, namely Hoppin, *Homiletics* (1869); Broadus, *On the Preparation and Delivery of Sermons* (1871); and Garrison *The Preacher and His Audience* (1954). There are no extended periods of time from 1834 to 1954 in which the subject of style was omitted from the homiletical text and trade books.[50]

THE CONTEMPORARY PERIOD (1900 TO PRESENT)

Twentieth-century writers in homiletics are certainly not agreed on the relative value of the cultivation of sermonic style. Some have ignored it, others have cried out in desperation against our ignorance of it, and still others have remained suspicious of it.

Spencer's book, *Psychic Power in Preaching* (1901), was important because he was a pioneer in the investigation of how the power of a preacher's personality affects his sermonic style. Spencer was a well-known Baptist pastor and evangelist.[51] His work in this area was significant because it came at a time when rhetoric and style were deemphasized in secular public address. The prevalent tendency was to attach greater significance to the matter presented than to the manner of presentation. Highly regarded homileticians such as Beecher and Greer stated in their Yale Lectures on preaching that style was not absolutely necessary to accomplish the task of persuading men.[52]

---

48. John A. Broadus, *On the Preparation and Delivery of Sermons* (New York: A. C. Armstrong, 1894), 322.
49. Lloyd Perry, "Trends and Emphases in the Philosophy, Materials, and Methodology of American Protestant Homiletical Education As Established by a Study of Selected Trade and Textbooks Published Between 1834 and 1954." Ph.D. diss., Northwestern U., 1954 (Ann Arbor, Mich.: University Microfilms, 1962), 234-58.
50. Ibid., 236.
51. Dargan, 227-28.
52. Lloyd M. Perry, "Sermonic Style in Contemporary Terms,"in *Baker's Dictionary of Practical Theology,* ed. Ralph Turnbull (Grand Rapids: Baker, 1967), 74.

In secular quarters extremely negative views toward rhetoric prevailed until the 1930s, when attention to the importance of studying how language was used was stimulated by logical positivism. That philosophical movement insisted that all statements must be verifiable by observation or experiment.[53]

Even during the 1920s authorities in sacred rhetoric were calling for a more effective sermonic style. In his 1922 Yale Lectures, William Pierson Merrill said:

> There are too many men in the pulpit who know a good deal, and think well enough, but have never gained the mastery of effective and simple language, through much companionship with the best writers, through deliberate and painstaking cultivation of a homely, forceful use of words. A preacher without skill in words is like a knight with no knowledge of sword play.[54]

Lutheran homiletics professor M. Reu published *Homiletics: A Manual of the Theory and Practice of Preaching* in 1924. His book has been translated from German into English by Albert Steinhaeuser, and it devotes more than seventy pages to style. Reu stated, "That the preacher should spare no pains to perfect his style, is made plain by President John Quincy Adams." Adams is then shown by Reu to argue that the man of God who has cultivated his style is far better equipped to minister and reach lost souls than the "cold and languid speaker" or the "unlettered fanatic" or even the "pious minister of Christ, who by neglect or contempt of the oratorical art, has contracted a whining, monotonous sing-song of delivery, to exercise the patience of his flock."[55]

Charles Jefferson was not at all vague in his view of the importance of style when he said, "Next to the baptism of the Holy Spirit the most indispensable gift for every American preacher is a mastery of the English tongue. No time should be begrudged that is spent in perfecting the preacher's style."[56]

In the 1940s there was a struggle to clarify the purpose and place of style for the preacher by those who recognized the value of good style but also recognized its abuses. Halford E. Luccock published *In the Minister's Workshop* in 1944. In it he said, "The minister, as long as he is true to his calling has no ambition to become a 'stylist.' He does not disdain art, he is committed to it by his allegiance as a bearer of the Word of God. But his literary creed is not art for art's sake but art for Christ's sake."[57] Luccock goes on to say that the preacher is himself "an ambassador of God. His words, in turn, must be ambassadors of his own soul and hence functional in their importance rather than decorative."[58]

A. J. Gossip points out the importance of using good stylistic principles to adapt language to the present day:

> Nothing can stop a spiritual revival by and by, except one thing—that the men who ought to lead it, you, who will be there in the pulpits, may not be zealous and apt and big enough for

53. *Encyclopedia Britannica*, 15:802.
54. Edgar DeWitt Jones, *The Royalty of the Pulpit* (New York: Harper and Brothers, 1951), 328.
55. M. Reu, *Homiletics: A Manual of the Theory and Practice of Preaching* (reprint; Grand Rapids: Baker, 1967), 236-37.
56. *Baker's Dictionary of Practical Theology* (Grand Rapids: Baker, 1967), 74.
57. Halford E. Luccock, *In the Minister's Workshop* (Nashville: Abingdon-Cokesbury, 1944), 182.
58. Ibid.

such great times as are certainly coming, may not know our Lord well enough, or may not have the heart for such a glorious adventure, or may not have acquired the art of translating the gospel into the speech of our own time, may be lumbering half a generation in the rear, still muttering ancient worn out shibboleths![59]

True conviction produces emotion in the soul, and true emotion produces eloquence in the educated preacher, an energy of style that overpowers the will and captivates it for higher ends.

The prominent German preacher-theologian Helmut Thielicke wrote:

> This is the point, it seems to me, where the secret distrust of Christian preaching is smoldering. Behind all the obvious and superficial criticism—such as that the sermon is boring, remote from life, irrelevant—there is, I am convinced, this ultimate reservation, namely, that the man who bores himself is not really living in what he—so boringly—hands out. "Where your treasure is, there will your heart be also"—in this case the treasure of the heart seems not to be identical with what it is commending to others.[60]

John R. Brokhoff would agree. In a 1977 article entitled "What Great Preachers Have in Common," he said, "Preaching in America is not going to improve until the preachers once again believe in preaching, both in its content and its method."[61]

BIBLIOGRAPHY

Auksi, Peter. "Wycliff's Sermons and the Plain Style." *Archives* 66 (1975): 5-23.

Blackwood, Andrew W. *Expositors Preaching for Today*. Grand Rapids: Baker, 1943.

——————. "Preaching in a Time of Reconstruction." *Pulpit*. 1945.

Broadus, John A. *A Treatise on the Preparation and Delivery of Sermons*. New York: George H. Doran, 1898.

Brokhoff, John R. "What Great Preachers Have in Common." *The New Pulpit Digest*, May-July 1977; 29-34.

Bullinger, W. E. *Figures of Speech Used in the Bible*. Grand Rapids: Baker, 1968.

Campbell, George. *The Philosophy of Rhetoric*. New York: Funk and Wagnalls, 1912.

Caplan, Harry. *Of Eloquence: Studies in Ancient and Medieval Rhetoric*. Ithaca, N.Y.: Cornell U., 1970.

Conners, Joseph. "Homiletic Theory in the Sixteenth Century." *American Ecclesiastical Review,* May 1958, 316-32.

Dargan, Edwin Charles. *The Art of Preaching in the Light of Its History*. New York: George H. Doran, 1922.

Encyclopedia Britannica, 15th ed. Chicago: William Benton, 1974.

Hoppin, James M. *Homiletics*. New York: Dodd, Mead, 1881.

Jones, Edgar Dewitt. *The Royalty of the Pulpit*. New York: Harper and Brothers, 1951.

Luccock, Halford E. *In the Minister's Workshop*. Nashville: Abingdon-Cokesbury, 1944.

59. A. W. Blackwood, "Preaching in a Time of Reconstruction," *Pulpit* (1945).
60. John W. Doberstein, trans. *The Trouble with the Church* (New York: Harper & Row, 1965), 9-10.
61. *The New Pulpit Digest,* May-July 1977, 31.

Marsh, Patrick O. *Persuasive Speaking*. New York: Harper & Row, 1967.

Mudd, Charles S. "The Rhetorica Ecclesiastica of Agostini Valiero." *Southern Speech Journal* (Summer 1956): 255-61.

Murphy, James J. "Saint Augustine and the Debate About A Christian Rhetoric." *Quarterly Journal of Speech*. (December 1960): 400-410.

Perry, Lloyd M. *Biblical Preaching for Today's World*. Chicago: Moody, 1973.

—————————. "Sermonic Style in Contemporary Terms." *Baker's Dictionary of Practical Theology*. Grand Rapids: Baker, 1967.

—————————. "Trends and Emphases in the Philosophy, Materials, and Methodology of American Protestant Homiletical Education As Established By a Study of Selected Trade and Textbooks Published Between 1834 and 1954." Ph.D. diss. Northwestern U., 1954. (Ann Arbor, Mich.: University Microfilms, Inc., 1962).

Phelps, Austin. *The Theory of Preaching*. New York: Richard R. Smith, 1930.

Porter, Ebenezer. *Lectures on Homiletics and Preaching, and on Public Prayer; Together with Sermons and Letters*. New York: Flagg, Gould, and Newman, 1834.

Reu, M. *Homiletics: A Manual of the Theory and Practice of Preaching*. Grand Rapids: Baker, 1967.

Schenck, Ferdinand S. *Modern Practical Theology*. New York: Funk and Wagnalls, 1903.

Thielicke, Helmut. *The Trouble With The Church*. John W. Doberstein, trans. and ed. New York: Harper & Row, 1965.

Thonssen, Lester. *Selected Readings in Rhetoric and Public Speaking*. New York: H. W. Wilson, 1942.

Turnbull, Ralph G. *A History of Preaching: Volume III*. Grand Rapids: Baker, 1974.

—————————. *The Preacher's Heritage Task and Resources*. Grand Rapids: Baker, 1968.

13

Rhetoric: The Classical Chameleon

Rhetoric has changed through the years. Its change can be likened to the purported change that takes place in the chameleon. The dictionary defines the chameleon as any of a group of lizards remarkable for their changes of skin color according to the mood of the animal or surrounding conditions. This change of color based on the environment is the characteristic that prompts us to refer to rhetoric as a "classical chameleon." Although the basic nature of rhetoric remains the same, its outward manifestation changes through the years, depending on the conditions that surround it. Rhetoric deals with principles and may refer to both written or spoken composition. The communication of ideas is included in the broad concept. As it is directed toward a popular audience, the purpose of rhetoric is projection rather than exploration.

The complexion of rhetoric keeps changing. In this chapter we will trace this changing process through the three main chronological periods. The primary emphasis in this chronological development will be on the personalities involved.

The first century set the stage for the three main periods that followed. Quintilian, Tacitus, and Seneca were the rhetoricians in this introductory period.

Cicero (d. 43 B.C.) was famous as a speaker because he was not afraid to speak out on the issues of the day. *Forensic* and *ceremonial* speaking had flourished because of the freedom of speech that was prevalent. Following the death of Cicero ceremonial speaking took the leadership because it could be separated from the content of the speech. Each speaker sought to gain the acclaim of the listeners by the employment of frills in speaking rather than through the employment of a content based on live issues.

Seneca (56 B.C.—A.D. 39) was a recorder of the first century. The nature of speech in his day can be noted in his title *Controversiae and Suasoriae*. The *suasoriae* were deliberative speeches on old or imaginative themes. They were facsimilies of real speeches.

Tacitus (c. A.D. 55-120) wrote *Dialogue on Oratory*. It was from that work and from the work of others that we can note the emphasis we now refer to as declamation. Both Cicero and Quintilian had advised students (the people) to prepare and deliver speeches for the purpose of training. During the first century the nature of declamation changed. The people were those already skilled in speech, and the purpose was exhibition.

Quintilian (c. A.D. 35-100) wrote his *Institutes of Oratory* in A.D. 95. It dealt with the training of the orator, and stressed the need for the orator to have sound moral and intellectual qualities. The orator was to be accomplished in all fields and was to avoid showiness in his presentation. Such emphases stood in contrast to the requirements for sophistic oratory. The first-century coloring of the classical chameleon was soon to change.

THE SECOND SOPHISTIC PERIOD

The *Second Sophistic period* (A.D. 100-650) was characterized by its emphasis on declamation. The origin of the name for this period can be appreciated only when we note some of the characteristics of sophistry as it appeared some five hundred years before this time. Sophistry was characterized by virtuosity, dilation, pattern, and the elaboration of style. Sophistic oratory was largely an oratory of themes, and was characterized by the use of stock examples, successful phrases, and whole descriptions selected to please the audience. The Sophist emphasized the memory of words rather than material.

Early sophistic oratory was noted for its emphasis on plausibility rather than probability. The first was a psychological concept whose purpose was the convincing of the listener. The logical concept of probability was not emphasized. Sophistry had been primarily a school of theoretical and practical skepticism. One of its outstanding errors lay in its complete indifference to truth. It had an aversion to sincere research. It was more anxious to persuade than to disseminate knowledge. Those characteristics of sophistry as practiced by the ancients were repeated during this period. It was for that reason that the period came to be known as the Second Sophistic.

The primary interest of this period was style. The many devices available to the public speaker were used for the exhibition of skill. The teaching of speaking was done by means of declamations. These declamations were based on fanciful themes. There was a general dearth of the higher educational interests.

Rhetoric was conceived as the art of giving effectiveness to the speaker. That diverted the emphasis that should have been placed on truth. The sophistic approach to rhetorical training did not necessarily imply that the technical training was deficient, but it did imply that the true motive for speaking was wrong. Education was thus impaired. The movement had departed from Aristotle's classical emphasis on rhetoric as the energizing of knowledge or the bringing of truth to bear upon men. The deterioration of rhetoric continued in the Second Sophistic period until it became only an art of display, devoid of any other motives. Rhetoric in this period was a historic demonstration of what rhetoric becomes when it is removed from the urgency of subject matter. The coloring of the classical chameleon thus changed radically. The gaudiness of the coloring almost hid the true nature of that which lay behind it.

There were twelve rhetoricians in this period. They can be classified into two groups: three of major importance, and nine of lesser importance. We will consider the contributions and emphases of the following ones of lesser importance first:

- *Hermogenes* (c. A.D. 170). *Elementary Exercises* and *De Rhetorica*.
- *Philostratus* (c. A.D. 238). *Lives of the Sophists*.
- *Ausonius* (c. A.D. 310-393). *Declamatio*. This was a collection of trivial verses. It was said that Ausonius could write a verse on anything. His style was decorative. His very poetical fame condemned the rhetorical taste of his age.
- *Fortunatianus* (fourth century) *The Art of Rhetoric*.
- *Capella* (c. A.D. 425). *The Marriage of Philology and Mercury*. Capella divided the school subjects into seven liberal arts: grammatica, dialectica, rhetorica, geometria, arithmetica, astronomia, and harmonia. The first three were called the *trivium,* and the last four were called the *quadrivium*.
- *Sidonius* (c. A.D. 475). Known for his letters and poems. He was obsessed with style in rhetorical education. A complacent reactionary of rhetoric's decadent past, he was a Christian bishop. He felt that the orator's achievement was not in the persuasion of his fellow men, but in his own virtuosity. He followed the sophistic tradition of declamation.
- *Boethius* (A.D. 475-525). *Topics, De Divivione, Categorical, and Hypothetical Syllogisms*. Boethius translated the whole of Aristotle's *Organon*.
- *Cassiodorus* (A.D. 485-575) wrote *Institutiones*. He was a monk, and by his influence he carried forward the idea of the seven arts.
- *Lucian* (c. A.D. 125). Was a professor of public speaking and a sophistic practitioner, but became a biting satirist of the Sophists after the age of forty. He provided a complete indictment of sophistry in reaction to the rhetoric of his day.

Among the more important men of the age, we find *Julius Victor* (c. A.D. 350), who wrote *The Art of Rhetoric*. It dealt with forensic rhetoric and was the most classical work on rhetoric during the period. It treated the five canons, and contained an additional chapter that dealt with letterwriting called *dictamen*. The function of an orator was to be able to make use of the science of speech that was credible and persuasive.

Augustine (A.D. 354-430) wrote *De Doctrina Christiana*. He is remembered as the Bishop of Hippo. He attacked the Sophists by completely ignoring the sophistic approach within his work. His work went back to the ancient idea of moving men by the truth. It gave to the work of Cicero a new emphasis for the urgent task of preaching the Word of God. Although he had been raised a Sophist, he tried to devote his energies to the reestablishment of the theories of ancient classical rhetoric. Augustine felt that Christian preaching was best learned from Christian preachers. *De Doctrina Christiana* was the first work in homiletics, and it insisted on an emotional appeal.

Isidore of Seville (A.D. 560-636) wrote the *Etymologiarum* (a survey of learning). For many years he was the chief purveyor of the seven liberal arts. Insight into the rhetoric of his day comes only by implication from his work, which is an important link in the history of rhetoric. He was the bishop of Seville, Spain, whose work was an aggregation of summaries. Rhetoric is portrayed as the lore of speaking well on political questions to persuade men of what is just and good. His work actually presented more of an interpretation than a history. Isidore was not an original thinker, but rather a compiler of knowledge, and a carrier of the old tradition. His entire work was reprinted ten times during the fifteenth and sixteenth centuries.

Before leaving the Second Sophistic period, we should mention the schools of Gaul. They became an important factor in the fifth and sixth centuries. The textbooks for those schools included *Grammatica* and *Dialectica,* written by Donatus and Priscian. Grammatica was the lore of interpreting poets, storytelling, and the theory of writing and speaking correctly. Those two textbooks were the most common Latin grammars of the Middle Ages and were the authoritative ones for that period. The *Logic of Aristotle* was also a standard text. The *Catechism of Fortunatianus* and the work of Julius Victor were also studied. The dominant member of the trivium during much of the fourth and fifth centuries was the rhetoric of ancient antiquity. During the Middle Ages the seven liberal arts of medieval education blended poetry and rhetoric so compactly that poetry became almost entirely absorbed by rhetoric. Rhetoric became so debased that it involved almost nothing more than a consideration of style and delivery. Sophistry became the prevailing tendency. The coloring of the classical chameleon was not destined to return to its original state until the seventeenth century.

CAROLINGIAN PERIOD

The *Carolingian* or *Middle period* (A.D. 650 to 1000) was so named after Charlemagne. During that time, rhetoric was overshadowed by another member of the trivium—*grammatica* (the was the lore of speaking correctly). Most of the writers of this time were also teachers. Charlemagne's concern was to secure a clergy that would first be educated and then to educate others. Most of the teaching was through the channel of the monasteries.

The teaching of rhetoric, even when it kept to the Roman method, was likely to lean to the declamation handed down by the Schools of Gaul.

Elocutio, the counsels of style, was widely used. Rhetoric was characterized by style during this period.

Alcuin (A.D. 735-804) wrote *Disputatio de Rhetorica* and *De Virtutibus.* He sought through his work on rhetoric to place at the disposal of the student the tools of oratorical powers. If he were living today, he would be called a minister of education. He turned to Cicero's *De Inventione* and Victor's *Ars Rhetorica* for his material. Eighty percent of his references were taken from Cicero's *De Inventione.* Special mention might well be made of the treatment of the virtues at the end of his work. He placed an emphasis on the concept of ethos.

Rabanus Marus (A.D. 776-856) wrote *De Clericorum Institutione.* He held that rhetoric was not outside the training for the church. He saw the larger and more vital conception of rhetoric.

Notker Labeo (c. A.D. 940-1022) wrote *De Arte Rhetorica.* Labeo was a Benedictine monk. He was the central figure in the brief revival of learning that flourished in St. Gall during the late tenth and early eleventh centuries. He sought to understand contemporary rhetoric along certain lines that have since proved themselves acceptable. He gave evidence of being well read in the rhetoric of his past. He defined rhetoric as: "A body of useful knowledge gleaned from the practice of speakers who were eloquent by nature." He almost completely separated logic and rhetoric . It was his intention to reassociate rhetoric with life in the present. During this period the classical chameleon began to lose some of its gaudiness of color and turn toward a more basic hue; some traces of its more permanent color began to show.

At the time of the fall of Rome, the trivium was dominated by rhetoric. In the Carolingian period, grammatica was stressed. In the high Middle Ages, dialectica was emphasized. The shift to logic probably began in the eleventh century. Part of the reason was because of Aristotle's *Organon,* which was available in Latin. Rhetoric had no educational vitality. John of Salisbury gave full scope to grammatica, then proceeded to dialectic, but merely mentioned rhetoric. Logic was the vital study that taxed and developed men's minds; grammatica was eloquence; dialectica was logical coherence; and rhetoric was ornament.

SCHOLASTIC PERIOD

The *Scholastic period* (A.D. 1000-1400) included such names as Hugh of St. Victor, John of Salisbury, Alain de Lille, Vincent of Beauvais, and Brunetto Latini. The period was characterized by an emphasis on dialectic.

Hugh of St. Victor (A.D. 1096-1141) wrote *Lore of Teaching.* It was a concise philosophical survey of education. His primary concern was the subject matter to be studied. The trivium was actually twofold with rhetoric theoretically subordinated.

John of Salisbury (A.D. 1120-1180) wrote *Metalogicus.* This was a more extensive, reasoned medieval survey of the trivium. It devoted most of its pages to logic. Rhetoric was dropped from the trivium completely. *Book I* argued that grammatica was not useless, for without it eloquence would fall short and the way toward the other expressions of philosophy would not be open. *Book II* stated that dialectic was the art of effective debate. John of Salisbury was preoccupied with logic and shunned rhetoric. No other medieval writer gave Quintilian's *Teaching of Rhetoric* more attention. John knew of the importance of traditional rhetoric, but left it out because of contemporary conditions. In his day, rhetoric lacked what he called "initial relations."

Several surveys were written during the thirteenth century. *Alain de Lille* wrote *Anticlaudianus,* an allegorical survey. It presented the idea that the function of education is the redemption of mankind. He defined and summarized the scope of each of the seven arts. Each had its function except rhetoric. Rhetoric was not operative as composition, only as style.

Vincent of Beauvais (A.D. 1210-1264) wrote *Speculum Doctrinale,* which was a compendium of all knowledge. Its arrangement and material followed the pattern of Isidore.

Brunetto Latini (A.D. 1220-1294) wrote *Tresor,* which gave more space to rhetoric than did Vincent's work. Latini was preoccupied with style, which was conceived as decorative dilation. Rhetoric in those surveys lacked a distinct function; its ancient function of composition. The only large field for the exercise of rhetoric, with emphasis on invention, was preaching. The rhetoric of the period was that of *De Inventione* and *Ad Herennium,* and the sophistry was that of Sidonius.

Because preaching was the only large field for the exercise of rhetoric with emphasis on invention, we need to survey the medieval tractates in preaching. Harry Caplan, one of the best authorities on the subject, states that the greatest emphasis was on an invention that almost exclusively dealt with material topics. The material topics were classified into several headings with the major topics usually ten in number and including: God, the devil, the heavenly city, hell, the world, the soul, the body, sin, penitence, and virtue. The topics of figures of scriptural interpretation were usually four in number. The topics of figures and amplification were also listed. These were ways of developing and expanding points. Special audiences were given special consideration. Humbert of Romans listed one hundred different types of audiences and had one hundred chapters explaining what to say to those audiences.

Those tractates on preaching developed the topic of emotions under the heading of invention. Persuasion was only slightly developed. The analysis of the audience is under invention. Arrangement or disposition was treated more lightly than invention, and by only a few writers. Style was dealt with by a few writers and treated less extensively than invention. Word memory was mentioned even less. Thought memory impinged on invention.

During the Scholastic period the classical chameleon was so overshadowed, that at times it suffered almost a complete blackout. Its color not only was changed, but almost obliterated. It was not until the breaking of the dawn of the Renaissance that the light from the surroundings of rhetoric so shone on it that its original coloring was restored. In the Second Sophistic period, declamation had taken precedence. In the Carolingian period, grammar received the greatest emphasis. In the Scholastic period, dialectic came to the forefront. The classical chameleon passed through all of those environmental changes, but never lost its original color. In the seventh century we once again see rhetoric making its appearance with its true ancient color.

14

Background and Development of American Rhetoric

Rhetoric may be defined as the faculty of discovering all the possible means of persuasion on a subject. It is the art that influences human behavior. Rhetoric deals with principles involved in the communication of ideas both written and spoken. Those ideas are directed toward a popular audience. Its purpose, therefore, is projection rather than exploration. Rhetoric is referred to as *sacred* rhetoric when it is applied to preaching. *Homiletics* is the technical term sometimes used for rhetoric applied to the preaching field.

CLASSICAL BACKGROUND

It has been said that Aristotle's *Rhetoric* was the basis for modern homiletical theory. That work was a treatise on the speaking art and the philosophy of discourse. From many points of view it offered as sound a rationale for the art of speaking as any other work on the subject. Aristotle's contribution rested on four basic postulates. The first was that rhetoric dealt with speaking as a useful art. Speaking was an instrument having functional value in the social order. Second, rhetoric was considered an interrelated art relying heavily on ethics, politics, psychology, and law. Aristotle's third postulate stated that rhetoric could be taught. He believed that the random performances of speakers could be improved through the study and application of systematized principles. Fourth, Aristotle believed that a sound projection of rhetorical theory was based on the avoidance of both excess and deficiency. In other words, the quality of a speech was directly related to its quantitative proportions. There must be neither too much nor too little of narrative argument or introductory detail.

Plato condemned rhetoric because of what he considered to be its separation from truth and its questionable influence on public life.

Cicero based his theory of rhetoric on the assumption that rhetoric and philosophy are closely related. That interrelation accounts in some measure for the relative scarcity of great orators.

One of the most ambitious projects ever undertaken by a rhetorician was the formulation of *Institutes of Oratory* by Quintilian. *Institutes of Oratory* traced the development and prescribed the pedagogical treatment of the prospective speaker from birth to retirement in old age. In twelve books Quintilian developed the complete course of training needful to develop a man skilled in speaking. The *Institutes* represented the most comprehensive analysis of oratorical training in print. It was the conviction of Quintilian that the orator must be a good man and that such a good man cannot exist without virtuous inclinations. It was also his conviction that no man would ever be thoroughly accomplished in eloquence who had not gained a deep insight into the impulses of human nature.

INTERNATIONAL BACKGROUND

Three leaders of rhetoric had their beginnings in England. John Hoskins (1566-1638) was a member of the House of Commons and learned in the arts, language, and politics. His rhetoric dealt basically with delivery and style. Leonard Cox wrote the first rhetoric text in English. His work, *The Arts or Crafts of Rhetoryke,* emphasized that rhetoric, necessary for all persons, was too little taught. He stressed four factors in rhetoric: invention, disposition, judgment, and eloquence. It was his opinion that invention was the most difficult of the four.

Richard Whateley (1787-1863) was an English logician and theologian. His rhetoric voiced a sharp protest against the elocutionary methods that relied on elaborate systems of notations to govern voice and bodily action. In turn, he proposed a method for the development of the natural manner in delivery. Archbishop Whateley endeavored in each case to convince the logical faculty of the mind. His Christianity appeared as a thing of the intellect rather than of the heart. His rhetoric was a forceful restatement of Aristotelian doctrines with primary emphasis on logical proof. His was the first strong protest against the elocutionary movement that had flourished for nearly sixty years.

Other contributions to the international background included Fenelon of France and his *Dialogues on Eloquence* (1685). In it he presented the rules and principles of speech. Philip Melanchthon (1497-1560) was one of the ablest teachers of his time. He has been referred to as "the scribe of the Reformation" and wrote *The Element of Rhetoric.* Erasmus (1466-1536) was famous in the field of scholarship, and has been referred to by many critics as the first real man of letters in Europe after the fall of the Roman Empire. He wrote several works on homiletics and published editions of the works of Aristotle and Demosthenes. George Campbell (1719-1796) was a Scottish theologian and is remembered chiefly for his *Dissertation on Miracles.* He also published a *Philosophy of Rhetoric* (1776), which may well have been the most important contribution to the field of rhetoric since Quintilian's *Institutes of Oratory.*

Hugh Blair (1710-1800) was a minister of the high church and professor of rhetoric and belles lettres at the University of Edinburgh. His lectures were published in 1783 and adopted at Yale as a text in 1785 and also at Harvard in 1788. Those lectures were not profound, but they were built on the classical tradition.

EARLY AMERICAN RHETORICIANS

John Witherspoon was president of Princeton and a professor of rhetoric and oratory. He was the first American to teach a systematic rhetorical theory in college while practicing it in the pulpit. His lectures on eloquence were delivered between 1768 and 1794 and formally published in 1800. Witherspoon disagreed with Aristotle's argument that public speaking should aim at persuasion. He stressed the need for purpose in speaking, and his emphasis in delivery was on conversational style. Like Cicero, he emphasized that a speech should be adapted to the audience.

The works of Thomas Wilson were based on Latin rhetorical theory. Invention was the subject of his first book, and disposition the subject of his second. Wilson was eclectic in his approach; his discussion of style and memory was taken from *Ad Herrenium*. In addition, he took much of his material from Quintilian, Erasmus, and Cox.

John Quincy Adams was the first professor of rhetoric and oratory at Harvard, where he taught from 1806-1808. He delivered a series of about forty lectures to the juniors and seniors. The materials and topics for the lectures were specified by the university's board of overseers. The lectures presented the principles and precepts of ancient rhetoric, and also prescribed the special rules required to form an accomplished pulpit orator. His lectures were classical in content and flavor. They went through only one printing, and we have no record that they were used in any other school.

AMERICAN RHETORIC IN 1850

Until 1850 American rhetoric was largely under the control of English teachings and works. Now American rhetoric came of age, and three works appeared within a decade. The first of those was W. G. T. Shedd's commentary and translation of Francis Thermin's *Eloquence a Virtue*. He presented his work to provide a philosophical background for American rhetoric. It was an attempt to provide an ethical critique for public address. Shedd believed that one of the distinguishing characteristics of rhetoric is its striving after an end. It was his belief that eloquence always aimed at an outward change either in the sentiments or conduct of individual men.

Henry Day formulated a doctrine of invention aimed at supplanting that of the ancients. He noticed the harm that had been done to rhetoric in the past by having so much emphasis placed on its style. M. B. Hope published the *Princeton Textbook in Rhetoric* in 1859. He was professor of rhetoric at Princeton and wrote his *Rhetoric* to replace Whateley's. Hope said that rhetoric was the art of enabling men to produce at will conviction and persuasion. He advocated the extemporaneous method of delivery. His discussion of rhetoric was divided into four parts: conviction, persuasion, style, and elocution.

ADDITIONAL DEVELOPMENTS IN AMERICAN RHETORIC

Samuel P. Newman, professor of rhetoric at Bowdoin College from 1822 to 1839, wrote *The Principles and Rules of Style, Inferred from Examples of Writing, to Which is Added a Historical Dissertation on English Style*. That work stressed written communication to the exclusion of oral communication. It was not at all concerned with persuasion in an active sense.

Edward T. Channing held the Boylston Chair of Oratory from 1819 to 1851 at Harvard. His lectures were published for the first time in 1856. He felt that there was little place for oratory in a democracy. He was more interested in literature than in oratory.

Ebenezer Porter held the Bartlet professorship at Andover from 1813 to 1831. His lectures were almost strictly in the fields of delivery and style. He mentioned Aristotle, Quintilian, and Cicero as the greatest of the ancients. Campbell was noted as the greatest of the moderns.

Henry Ware was the minister of a Boston church, and published a book in extemporaneous preaching in 1824. Written from a practical viewpoint, the book emphasized the rule for extemporaneous preaching and the importance of audience response.

Gilbert Austin wrote *Chironomia,* which dealt with rhetorical delivery. This book included a large amount of material on voice and bodily action. It is detailed and comprehensive in its treatment of gestures.

James Rush (1786-1869) wrote *The Philosophy of the Human Voice.* This was the most important contribution by an American to the field of speech prior to the twentieth century. It was the first great analytical inquiry into the physiology of vocal delivery.

Part 3
A BIOGRAPHICAL PERSPECTIVE

INTRODUCTION

The persons listed in this section (deceased only) are included because they had a direct relationship to preaching. Not all of them were "great" preachers, but all of them made a significant contribution to the field. The inclusion of a name does not mean that we endorse everything the person preached, wrote, or stood for.

The men who gave the Yale Lectures on preaching are identified with the title of their books, if their series were published. We have also given the titles of the best biographies of some of the key preachers as well as autobiographies.

For more detailed information on these men, consult *A History of Preaching* by Edwin C. Dargan and Ralph G. Turnbull (3 vols., Grand Rapids: Baker, 1954); *A History of Preaching in Britain and America*, by F. R. Webber (3 vols., Milwaukee: Northwestern, 1957), the standard encyclopedias; and *The New International Dictionary of the Christian Church*, edited by J. D. Douglas (Grand Rapids: Zondervan, rev. ed. 1978).

15

Capsule Biographies of Preachers

A

Abbott, Lyman (1835-1922). American Congregationalist; editor and reformer; succeeded Henry Ward Beecher at Plymouth Congregational Church in Brooklyn, New York; gave Yale Lectures (1904), *The Christian Ministry*

Abelard, Peter (1079-1142). French philosopher and theologian; a doctrinal preacher; accused of heresy by Bernard of Clairvaux

Abernathy, John (1680-1740). Irish Presbyterian minister and author

Adams, Thomas (1580-1653). English Puritan; "The Shakespeare of the Puritans"; rector of St. Bennet's at London, England

Adalbert (956-997). Missionary to Poland; opposed by Boniface

Aelfrio (d. 1006). Archbishop of Canterbury from 996 to 1006; scholar and writer

Albert the Great (1193-1280). "Albertus Magnus"; German Dominican preacher and teacher; mastered Aristotle; taught Thomas Aquinas

Alesius, Alexander (1500-1565). Scottish Reformer; first to lecture on Hebrew Scriptures at Cambridge

Alexander, Archibald (1772-1851). American Presbyterian; first president and professor of theology at Princeton; excelled in sermon delivery; trained more than 1800 ministerial candidates; a prolific writer

Alexander, James W. (1804-1859). American Presbyterian; eldest son of Archibald Alexander; pastored Fifth Avenue Presbyterian Church in New York City (1851-59); a prolific writer

Allon, Henry (1818-1892). English Congregationalist; for forty-eight years pastor of Union Chapel in Islington, London; emphasized congregational singing; a forceful preacher with messages "wise and eloquent"

Ambrose (340-397). Bishop of Milan; known for his delivery; trained in public address

Ambrose, Issac (1604-1663). English Presbyterian preacher and writer; author of *Looking Unto Jesus*, a popular work

Andrew of Crete (660-740). Archbishop of Crete; hymnwriter

Andrewes, Lancelot (1555-1626). One of translators of the King James Version of the Bible; known for his biblical and doctrinal preaching; used vivid language and illustrations

Angier, John (1605-1677). Studied under John Cotton at Cambridge; for forty-five years rector at Denton, Lancashire; his Puritan convictions aroused opposition; kept "private days" for the strengthening of his spiritual life

Anskar, or Ansgar (801-865). "Apostle to the north"; evangelized Denmark, Sweden, and Germany; first archbishop of Hamburg

Anselm of Canterbury (1033-1109). Born in Italy; missionary to England; Archbishop of Canterbury; doctrinal preacher

Anthony of Padua (1195-1231). Born in Lisbon, Portugal; known for his preaching skill and theological knowledge; used allegory; practiced open-air preaching; emphasized repentance; had excellent sermonic arrangement and delivery

Aquinas, Thomas (1225-1274). Born in Italy; taught in Paris; *Summa Theologica* was his masterpiece; reconciled Aristotle with Scripture; a doctrinal preacher who used allegory

Arndt, Johann Wilhelm (1555-1621). German Lutheran; first of the Pietists; had a mystical approach; first of the pietists; "the Wesley of his time"; *True Christianity* was his most famous book

Arnobius (c. 248-327). North African apologist and teacher of rhetoric

Arnold of Brescia (c. 1100-1155). Italian Augustinian reformer; advocated separation of church and state; preached eloquently against the sins of the clergy; led a revolt in Rome and martyred there

Arnold, Thomas (1795-1842). British Anglican; Master of Rugby; believed in a strong state church

Arthur, William (1819-1901). Wesleyan Methodist; born in Ireland; pastored Wesley's Chapel in London, and two churches in France; principal of Methodist College in Belfast, Ireland; emphasized foreign missions in his preaching

Asbury, Francis (1745-1816). First Methodist bishop appointed in America by Wesley; born in England, came to the United States in 1771; traveled extensively (nearly 300,000 miles during his ministry); the Methodist church experienced phenomenal growth under his leadership

Athanasius (c. 296-373). Doctrinal and expository preacher; opposed Arianism; skilled theologian; avoided allegory

Augustine of Hippo (354-430). Greatest of the Latin Fathers; known for excellence in delivery, style, and use of illustrations; doctrinal preacher; author of *The City of God*, *Confession*, and other works

Augustine of Canterbury (c. 566-607). Missionary to England; first Archbishop of Canterbury

B

Bacon, Leonard (1802-1881). American Congregationalist; preacher and educator; antislavery editor

Baille, Donald M. (1887-1954). Scottish Presbyterian theologian, writer, and ecumenical leader

Baille, John (1886-1960). Scottish Presbyterian theologian; brother of Donald M. Baille

Baring-Gould, Sabine (1834-1924). Church of England; British classical scholar and hymnwriter; wrote "Onward, Christian Soldiers"

Barletta, Gabriel (1470). Italian Dominican monk; known as an extraordinary preacher

Barnes, Albert (1798-1870). American Presbyterian; minister and writer; author of the famous *Barnes Notes* on the Old and New Testaments

Barnhouse, Donald Grey (1895-1960). American Presbyterian; pastor and conference speaker; thirty-three years pastor of Tenth Presbyterian Church in Philadelphia; founder of *Eternity* magazine; radio speaker on the "The Bible Study Hour"

Barrow, Issac (1630-1677). Church of England; British minister and mathematical scholar; preached lengthy sermons

Barth, Karl (1886-1968). Swiss theologian and writer; his *Commentary on Romans* (1919) heralded the neo-orthodox movement

Basil the Great (c. 329-379). Bishop of Caesarea and archbishop of Cappadocia; founded the first hospital for lepers; good administrator and preacher; ascetic life hastened his death; reached both the rich and poor

Baxter, Richard (1615-1691). Popular Puritan preacher and author; doctrinal and evangelistic; wrote *The Saints' Everlasting Rest, The Reformed Pastor, A Call to the Unconverted,* and nearly one hundred other books

Bede, the Venerable (c. 673-735). English monk and historian; wrote *Ecclesiastical History of the English Nation*; a popular Bible preacher who used the expository style; made use of allegory

Beecher, Henry Ward (1813-1887). American Congregationalist; son of Lyman Beecher; served for forty years as the pastor of Plymouth Congregational Church in Brooklyn, New York; a popular preacher known for his imagination and forceful delivery; used textual sermons; founded the Yale Lectures on preaching in honor of his father, and gave the lectures during 1872-74

Beecher, Lyman (1775-1863). American Congregationalist and Presbyterian minister; president of Lane Seminary in Cincinnati, Ohio; a doctrinal preacher

Behrends, Adolphus J. F. (1839-1900). American Baptist and Congregationalist; born in Holland; gave the Yale Lectures (1890), *The Philosophy of Preaching*

Bengel, Johann Albrecht (1687-1752). German Lutheran; theologian, Greek scholar, and writer; his *Gnomen of the New Testament* is still in use

Bernard of Clairvaux (c. 1090-1153). French Cistercian monk and mystic; popular preacher; hymnwriter of "Jesus, Thou Joy of Loving Hearts," "Jesus the Very Thought of Thee," and "O Sacred Head Now Wounded"

Bernardino of Siena (1380-1444). Italian Franciscan friar; founded 300 monasteries; open-air preacher

Berridge, John (1716-1793). British Methodist; itinerant open-air preacher; allied with George Whitefield and Calvinistic Methodism

Bersier, Eugene (1831-1889). French Reformed pastor

Berthold of Regensburg (c. 1210-1272). German Franciscan; "The Chrysostom of the Middle Ages"; open-air preacher; evangelistic

Beza, Theodore (1519-1605). Born in Burgundy; Greek scholar; Calvin's successor in Geneva; an eloquent preacher

Biederwolf, William Edward (1867-1939). American Presbyterian; author, evangelist, and conference speaker; director of Winona Lake (Ind.) Bible Conference; author

Biel, Gabriel (c. 1425-1495). German philosopher; helped to found University of Tübingen; "the last of the Schoolmen"

Bilney, Thomas (1495-1531). British minister; outstanding Cambridge preacher; led Hugh Latimer to faith in Jesus Christ; martyred as a heretic

Binney, Thomas (1798-1874). British Congregationalist; served for forty years as pastor of King's Weigh House Chapel in London; life-situation preacher

Binning, Hugh (1627-1653). Scottish preacher who ministered with distinction for only three years in Glasgow; abandoned the traditional homiletics of his day and presented the Word of God simply, with clear divisions

Black, Hugh (1868-1953). Scottish Presbyterian; brother to James Black, associate of Alexander Whyte in Edinburgh; taught at Union Seminary in New York City (1906-1938); published several volumes of sermons

Black, James (1879-1949). Scottish Presbyterian; preacher and teacher; wrote *The Mystery of Preaching*

Blackader, John (1623-1686). Scottish Presbyterian; had an effective ministry at Troqueer, near Dumfries; drew large congregations; ejected by the government, he became an itinerant field preacher; arrested, and died in prison

Blackwood, Andrew (1882-1966). American Presbyterian; taught homiletics at Princeton Seminary (1930-1950); author of many books on preaching and pastoral work

Blair, Hugh (1718-1800). Scottish Presbyterian; teacher of rhetoric, church moderator, and pastor of High Church in Edinburgh (1758); 1758; published four volumes of sermons and lectures on rhetoric

Bonar, Andrew (1810-1892). Scottish Presbyterian; compassionate pastor and soulwinner; wrote *The Memoirs and Remains of Robert Murray McCheyne* and other books of devotional nature

Bonar, Horatius (1808-1889). Scottish Presbyterian preacher and hymnwriter; brother of Andrew; wrote over 600 hymns

Bonaventura, Giovanni (1217-1274). Italian mystic; directed Franciscan order; used allegorical preaching, called "The Seraphic Doctor"

Bonhoeffer, Dietrich (1906-1945). German Lutheran; arrested for a plot to kill Adolf Hitler; hanged April 9, 1945; author of *The Cost of Discipleship*, *Letters and Papers from Prison*, *Creation and Fall*, and other works on Christian ethics and the church

Boniface (Winifred) (680-755). Born in Britain; apostle to Germany

Booth, William (1829-1912). British Methodist; founder ("General") of the Salvation Army; traveled about 5 million miles and preached nearly 60,000 sermons

Boreham, Frank W. (1871-1959). British Baptist; ministered in New Zealand, Tasmania, and Australia; author of more than fifty books of sermons and essays; the last student at Spurgeon's College to be chosen by Spurgeon himself

Bossuet, Jacques Benigne (1627-1704). French Roman Catholic bishop of Meant; writer; known for his funeral orations

Boston, Thomas (1677-1732). Scottish Presbyterian; minister and theological writer; *Human Nature in its Fourfold State* was his most popular book

Bourdaloue, Louis (1632-1704). French Jesuit orator; preacher to kings; known for style and logic; "the prince of French preachers"

Bowie, Walter Russell (1882-1968). American Episcopal; pastored in Richmond, Virginia and New York City; professor of practical theology at Union Seminary; professor of homiletics at Virginia Protestant Episcopal Seminary; gave the Yale Lectures (1935), *The Renewing Gospel*

Bradford, John (1510-1555). British reformer; his sermon outlines usually contained three questions; martyred

Brainerd, David (1718-1747). American missionary to Indians; his *Journal,* edited by Jonathan Edwards, is a devotional classic

Bray, William ("Billy") (1794-1868). Welsh Methodist evangelist and founder of chapels

Breese, Samuel (1772-1812). Welsh schoolmaster who became a Baptist preacher; vivid power of description; "one of the most popular and powerful preachers of the day"

Brenz, Johann (1499-1570). German Reformer; influenced by Martin Luther

Bridaine, Jacques (1701-1767). French Roman Catholic; one of the greatest evangelistic preachers of his day; used colloquial language to reach the masses

Broadus, John Albert (1827-1895). American Southern Baptist; author of *On The Preparation and Delivery of Sermons*, classic homiletics text; gave the Yale Lectures (1889); "a prince of the pulpit"

Brock, William (1807-1875). British Baptist; pastored Bloomsbury Chapel, London for twenty-four years; a brilliant scholar; opposed slavery; helped found the London Association of Baptist Churches

Brooks, Phillips (1835-1893). American Episcopal; bishop of Massachusetts when he died; gave the Yale Lectures (1877), *Lectures on Preaching*; published several volumes of sermons

Brooks, Thomas (1608-1680). British Congregationalist; preacher in London

Brown, Charles R. (1862-1950). American Congregationalist; dean at Yale Divinity School; doctrinal and expository preacher; gave the Yale Lectures (1906), *The Social Message of the Modern Pulpit* and (1923), *The Art of Preaching*

Brown, Hugh S. (1823-1886). British Baptist; pastored Myrtle Street Baptist Church at Liverpool, England for thirty-seven years; a forceful preacher who defended the fundamentals of the faith

Brown, John ("of Haddington") (1722-1787). Scottish minister; self-educated; pastored in Haddington for thirty-six years;

Brown, J. Baldwin (1820-1884). English Nonconformist; pastored several London churches in 1846, became pastor of Claylands Chapel in London where he served until his death; had great gifts but was not interested in crowds; considered liberal because he opposed the harsh Calvinism of his day

Bruce, Alexander B. (1831-1899). Scottish theologian, teacher, writer; *The Training of the Twelve* is one of his most enduring works

Bruce, Robert (1554-1631). Scottish preacher; banished twice from his church in Edinburgh for opposing the king; "no man since the days of the apostles had ever preached with such power"

Brunner, Emil (1889-1966). Swiss theologian and author who emphasized the importance of preaching

Bucer, Martin (1491-1551). German Reformer; assisted in the English Reformation

Bugenhagen, Johann (1485-1558). German Reformer, preacher, and professor; assisted Martin Luther in his Bible translation

Bulkeley, Peter (1583-1659). Puritan New England preacher who pastored in Concord, Massachusetts; opposed John Cotton's severe Calvinism; preached Christ-centered sermons

Bullinger, Johann Heinrich (1504-1575). Swiss Reformer; assisted Zwingli; succeeded Zwingli as pastor of the Great Minister Church in Zurich

Bultmann, Rudolf (1884-1976). German theologian who emphasized "demythologizing the New Testament"

Bunyan, John (1628-1688). British Puritan; wrote *Pilgrim's Progress* and many other works; his preaching drew large congregations; he was self-taught; imprisoned twelve years for preaching without a license; strong in allegory and evangelistic appeal

Burchard, Samuel D. (1812-1891). American Presbyterian; from 1839 served forty years as pastor of Houston Street Presbyterian Church in New York City; was declared dead after an operation, but survived to live thirty-eight more years; his statement that the Democratic Party was for "Rum, Romanism, and Rebellion" helped put Grover Cleveland into office

Burnet, Gilbert (1643-1715). Church of Scotland minister and historian; Bishop of Salisbury; a man of great learning

Burton, Nathanael J. (1824-1887). American Congregationalist; pastored in New Haven and Hartford, Connecticut; succeeded Horace Bushnell at North Church, Hartford, in 1870; had a strong dislike for publicity; gave the Yale Lectures (1884), *In Pulpit and Parish*

Bushnell, Horace (1802-1876). American Congregationalist; imaginative in his preaching; *Christian Nurture,* his most famous book, strongly influenced religious education

Butler, Joseph (1692-1752). Anglican scholar and bishop of Durham; wrote *Analogy of Religion* and sermons on the Christian virtues

C

Cadman, Samuel Parkes (1864-1936). British Congregationalist minister; served in America most of his life; one of the early radio preachers

Caesarius of Arles (c. 470-542). Bishop of Arles (in France); encouraged monastic preaching

Caird, John (1820-1898). Church of Scotland theologian and educator

Cairns, John (1818-1892). Church of Scotland minister; served for thirty years as pastor of Golden Square Church at Berwick-on-Tweed

Calderwood, David (1575-1650). Scottish Presbyterian; minister and church historian

Calvin, John (1509-1564). French Reformer; ministered in Geneva; preacher, administrator, commentator; preached 3000 sermons in fifteen years; used expository style

Cameron, Richard (c. 1648-1680). Scottish Covenanter preacher; martyred

Campbell, Alexander (1788-1866). One of the founders of the Disciples of Christ and Church of Christ; able preacher and debater

Campbell, Reginald John (1867-1956). British Congregationalist who finally became Anglican; pastored City Temple in London; preached what he called "new theology," and created a controversy that finally led to his resignation; P. T. Forsyth called his theology "fireworks in a fog"

Candlish, Robert S. (1806-1873). Scottish Presbyterian; leader of Free Church; educator; expository and doctrinal preacher of depth and power

Cant, Andrew (1590-1663). Scottish Covenanter; described as a "super-excellent preacher"; his Aberdeen congregations were often so large that he had to preach in the great square

Caraccioli, Robert (1517-1586). Italian Reformer; left his home and family to follow Protestant faith; lived in Geneva, Switzerland

Cargill, Donald Daniel (c. 1619-1681). Scottish Covenanter minister; martyred

Carroll, Benajah Harvey (1843-1914). American; Baptist; first president of Southwestern Baptist Seminary; author; a commanding teacher and preacher

Carson, Alexander (1776-1844). Born in Scotland; ministered for forty-one years at Tubbermore, Ireland; a popular author

Carstared, William (1649-1715). Church of Scotland preacher and educator

Carswell, John (1550-1570). A monk of Iona; rector of Kilmartin at Argyllshire; influential minister and scholar

Cartwright, Peter (1785-1872). American Methodist; circuit-riding preacher and evangelist; established many churches on the American frontier

Cavert, Samuel, M. (1888-1976). American ecumenical leader; secretary of the Federal Council of Churches; editor of the *Pulpit Digest*

Cazalla, Augustino (1510-1559). Spanish Reformer; martyred

Cecil, Richard (1748-1810). Church of England; eloquent minister who belonged to the Evangelical group; ministered in several London churches; his sermons were about forty minutes in length, brief for that day; original in his style and sermon structure

Chaderton, Laurence (1546-1640). English Puritan; helped translate the King James Version; pastored St. Clement's Church at Cambridge

Chadwick, Samuel (1860-1932). British Methodist of the "holiness" school; principal of Cliff College; emphasized the preacher's devotional life; prolific writer with a clear and appealing style

Chalmers, Thomas (1780-1847). Church of Scotland; considered by many to be the greatest nineteenth-century preacher; evangelistic, doctrinal, expository; emphasized "regeneration not reformation"; helped found a Free church in Scotland

Chambers, Oswald (1874-1917). British Nonconformist preacher and devotional writer; YMCA chaplain to British troops in Egypt during World War I; *My Utmost for*

His Highest is a devotional classic; used alliterative outlines to convey truth

Channing, William Ellery (1780-1842). American Unitarian eloquent and persuasive preacher; liberal in his theology

Chapman, John Wilbur (1859-1918). American Presbyterian evangelist; associated with D. L. Moody; his musician was Charles Alexander

Chappell, Clovis Gillham (1882-1972). American Methodist; eloquent evangelical Methodist preacher; published many books of popular sermons; specialized in biblical character studies

Charles, Thomas ("of Bala") (1755-1814). Welsh Methodist; Calvanistic preacher and Sunday school promoter

Charlier, Jean (also Jean of Gerson) (1363-1429). French Roman Catholic theologian and reformer

Charnock, Stephen (1628-1680). Puritan Presbyterian; author of *The Existence and Attributes of God*

Chauncy, Charles (1705-1787). American Congregationalist; pastored First Church in Boston (1727-87); outspoken critic of Jonathan Edwards and the revival movement; emphasized the intellect rather than the emotions

Chillingworth, William (1602-1644). Church of England; apologist; ministered for only six years

Chrysostom, John (347-407). "John the golden-mouthed"; an eloquent preacher; Bishop of Constantinople; teacher of rhetoric; evangelistic, his biblical preaching was noted for its good use of illustrations; used three-part sermons; his book *On the Priesthood* is the first known treatise on homiletics

Clarke, Adam (1762-1832). English Methodist; author of the famous *Commentary* that bears his name; personally selected by Wesley; his sermons did not follow a homiletical pattern but he always achieved his aim; self-taught, he learned Greek, Latin, Hebrew, and many modern languages; during one three-year ministry, he walked 7,000 miles

Claude, Jean (1619-1687). French Protestant; eloquent preacher; wrote *On The Composition of a Sermon,* which greatly influenced Charles Simeon's approach to preaching

Clement (of Alexandria) (c. 150-220). First "Christian scholar"; directed theological school at Alexandria; debated the Gnostics; doctrinal preacher; known for careful exegesis

Clement (of Rome) (c. 30-100). Most important of the apostolic Fathers; his preaching known for biblical content; his style was abrupt, vigorous

Clifton, Richard (1545-1616). One of the first Puritan pastors of the Scrooby Manor group; succeeded John Robinson when Robinson went to Holland; described as "a grave old man with a white beard"

Clow, William M. (1853-1930). Church of Scotland; preacher, and teacher of preachers

Coffin, Henry Sloane (1887-1954). American Presbyterian; served as pastor of Madison Avenue Presbyterian Church in New York City; president and professor of homiletics, Union Theological Seminary in New York; gave the Yale Lectures (1918),

In a Day of Social Rebuilding; combined preaching and pastoral ministry; an ecumenical leader

Coke, Thomas (1747-1814). First bishop of Methodist Episcopal church; ordained Francis Asbury as first bishop of Methodist church in the United States; an itinerant minister in America

Colet, John (c. 1467-1519). Dean of St. Paul's; classical scholar and friend of Erasmus; expounded Paul's epistles

Columba (521-597). Irish-Celtic scholar and able expositor; evangelized Scotland, France, Italy, and Switzerland

Conwell, Russell H. (1843-1925). American lawyer, preacher, lecturer; founded Temple University in Philadelphia; famous for his "Acres of Diamonds" lecture; forceful use of illustrations

Cooke, Henry (1788-1868). Irish Presbyterian; opposed liberalism and known as "the champion of orthodoxy"; pastored May Street Church in Belfast, Ireland for almost forty years; his emphasis was on doctrine and exposition

Cotton, John (1584-1652). Puritan scholar; pastored First Congregational Church in Boston, Massachusetts; a voluminous writer

Coverdale, Miles (1488-1568). Church of England; bishop of Exeter; translator of the first complete English Bible; assisted William Tyndale

Craddock, Walter (1606-1659). English Puritan; minister of St. Mary's at Cardiff; emphasized justification by faith

Craig, John (1512-1600). Scottish Reformer; minister at St. Giles' in Edinburgh; court preacher to Emperor Maximillian II

Cranmer, Thomas (1489-1556). Archbishop of Canterbury from 1533 to death; revised Anglican liturgy; martyred

Crosby, Howard (1826-1891). American Presbyterian; gave the Yale Lectures (1880), *The Christian Preacher*

Cumming, John (1807-1881). Scottish minister with popular appeal; preached on prophecy and other controversial themes

Cuyler, Theodore (1822-1909). American Presbyterian; served for thirty years as pastor of Lafayette Avenue Presbyterian Church in Brooklyn, New York; a revival leader; friend of D. L. Moody and Charles Spurgeon; temperance leader.

Cyprian (200-258). Bishop of Carthage; eloquent preacher; educated in public speaking; used allegory; emphasized salvation

Cyril (of Alexandria) (376-444). Patriarch of Alexandria; an allegorical preacher

Cyril (of Jerusalem) (315-386). Bishop of Jerusalem

Cyril (826-869). Missionary to the Slavs with his brother, Methodius; preached in the vernacular

D

Daille, Jean (Dallaeus) (1594-1670). French Protestant; eloquent preacher; known for sermons on Philippians and Colossians

Dale, Robert W. (1829-1895). British Congregational preacher; pastored Carr's Lane Chapel in Birmingham for thirty-six years; known for his doctrinal preaching;

involved in political issues; gave the Yale Lectures (1878), *Nine Lectures on Preaching*

Damian, Peter (1007-1072). Benedictine Roman Catholic reformer whose work strengthened papal power

Danforth, Samuel (1626-1674). Pastor in Roxbury, Connecticut for twenty-four years; assisted John Eliot; used forty to fifty Scripture texts in each sermon; also used illustrations from science and nature

Dargan, Edwin Charles (1852-1930). American Southern Baptist; professor of homiletics and biblical theology at Southern Baptist Seminary; author of the classic *History of Preaching* (2 vols.); an effective preacher as well as scholar and teacher

Davenport, John (1597-1670). English Anglican preacher who became Congregationalist; came to United States and helped found New Haven, Connecticut; known for his sensational revivalistic preaching

Davidson, John (1549-1603). Scottish preacher who attracted large crowds; persecuted for his evangelical faith; blunt and fearless in his preaching, he was feared by his enemies

Davidson, Andrew Bruce (1831-1902). Scottish Old Testament scholar and writer; although a world-famous scholar, he preferred to preach in smaller rural churches rather than in influential pulpits; considered to be "the father of higher criticism in Scotland"; never pastored a church

Davies, Samuel (1724-1761). Succeeded Jonathan Edwards as president of the College of New Jersey (Princeton University); pastored many years in Hanover County, Virginia; his sermons were known for their logic and imagination

Davies, Thomas R. (1790-1859). Welsh Baptist; ministered to both Baptists and Methodists; preached an average of five times a week during forty-seven years of ministry; at his request, he was buried in Christmas Evans's grave

Dawson, William J. (1854-1928). Wesleyan preacher and poet; preached ethical sermons, and then realized the need to preach the gospel and win the lost; became a Congregationalist and pastored the Highbury Quadrant Church in London for thirteen years; resigned in 1905 to carry on preaching missions; greatly influenced by Gipsy Smith

Dietrich, Viet (1506-1549). German Lutheran; secretary to Martin Luther; teacher and author

Delitzsch, Franz (1813-1890). German Lutheran; Old Testament scholar and Bible commentator

Denney, James (1856-1917). Scottish theologian, preacher, and author; stressed doctrine and believed that it must be preached

DeVitry, Jacques (1180-1240). French Roman Catholic who preached in favor of the Crusades

Dibelius, Martin (1883-1947). German; New Testament scholar; doctrinal preacher; helped to found the form criticism school of study

Dibelius, Otto (1880-1967). Bishop of the German Evangelical church; opposed Nazi dictatorship; both pastor and professor; emphasized "a theology of the cross"

Dickson, David (1583-1663). Scottish expositor; fearless in defending the faith, he was opposed by the established church; he believed in clear, positive preaching

Didon, Henri Gabriel (1840-1900). French Dominican educator and preacher; known for his impassioned eloquence

Dixon, Amzi Clarence (1854-1925). American; Baptist; served pastorates at both Moody Memorial Church in Chicago and Metropolitan Tabernacle in London; helped edit *The Fundamentals*

Doddridge, Phillip (1702-1751). English Nonconformist minister and teacher; trained ministers; author of classic *The Rise and Progress of Religion in the Soul*

Dominic (1170-1221). Founder of Dominican order of preachers; excelled in open-air preaching, persuasion, and use of illustrations

Donne, John (1573-1631). English scholar and preacher; dean of St. Paul's; a mystical poet; heavy emphasis on doctrinal preaching

Doyle, James W. (1786-1834). Irish Roman Catholic; bishop of Kildare and Leighlin at age 33; deeply interested in education; a forceful preacher who defended his Roman Catholic doctrine against all challengers

DuBosc, Pierre (1623-1692). French Reformed preacher who emphasized faith and holy living; favorite court preacher of Louis XIV

DuMoulin, Pierre (1568-1658). French Protestant preacher and writer

Durham, James (1622-1658). Scottish popular preacher and writer; influenced by David Dickson to become a pastor; succeeded Dickson as professor of theology at Glasgow University; a serious preacher who used short sentences and plain conversational style

Dwight, Timothy (1752-1817). American Congregationalist; president of Yale University; a theologian and known for his doctrinal preaching

Dykes, J. Oswald (1835-1912). Scottish Free church preacher; assistant to Robert Candlish at Free St. George's in Edinburgh; served for nineteen years as pastor of Regent Square Church in London, then principal of Westminster Presbyterian College at Cambridge; a popular preacher and author; his sermons were textual and expository

E

Eckhart, Meister (c. 1260-1327). German mystical preacher and writer; Dominican

Edwards, Jonathan (1703-1758). American Congregationalist; a brilliant theologian and a prolific writer; he read his sermons from a manuscript, yet preached with great power; one of the instruments in the Great Awakening; a friend of George Whitefield

Elias, John (1774-1841). Welsh Calvinistic Methodist; "the greatest of the Welsh preachers"; known for his powerful delivery

Eliot, John (1604-1690). American; began as Anglican and became Nonconformist; a missionary to Indians; helped publish *The Bay Psalm Book*

Emmons, Nathaniel (1745-1840). American Congregationalist; theologian; pastored at Franklin, Massachusetts for fifty-four years; a zealous patriot

England, John (1786-1842). Irish Roman Catholic; bishop of Charleston, South Carolina; one of the most eloquent preachers Ireland ever produced; ordained when only 22 years of age; champion of the orphan and outcast and crusader for liberty; preached before the United States House of Representatives

Ephraim (the Syrian) (c. 300-373). Poetic preacher and writer; weak theologian; a deacon, but never ordained as a priest

Erasmus, Desiderius (c. 1466-1536). Dutch humanist scholar and writer; helped prepare the way for the Reformation; published an edition of Greek New Testament

Erskine, Ebenezer (1680-1754). Converted to evangelical truth and experience after he was ordained; his new zeal attracted many people; dismissed from the Established church, he founded Scottish Secession church, then led Seceders out of the Established church to found a new Associate Presbytery; preached more from the Old Testament than the New Testament; often preached the messianic prophecies; free in his exegesis and very complex in his outlines

Erskine, Henry (1624-1696). Scottish preacher; father of Ralph and Ebenezer Erskine; ejected from his church for his evangelical faith; held open-air meetings; held in high respect, even by the unbelievers who opposed him

Erskine, John (1720-1803). Leader of the evangelical party in the Church of Scotland; strong missionary preacher who ministered in and around Glasgow; opposed the war with America; friends with George Whitefield and the Wesleys; preached from minimal notes

Erskine, Ralph (1685-1752). Church of Scotland; younger brother of Ebenezer; in spite of his scholarship, a plain and forceful preacher; his preaching awakened John Brown of Haddington; excelled in his closing appeals; followed traditional complex, homiletical style outline

Ethelred (of Revesby) (1109-1166). English missionary to Galloway Picts; historian

Evans, Christmas (1766-1838). Popular Welsh Baptist preacher; born on Christmas Day; imaginative in his preaching; "the Golden-mouthed Chrysostom of Wales"; "the Poet of the Pulpit"

Evans, Evan Herber (1835-1896). Welsh Congregationalist; pastored Salem Church in Carnarvon for thirty years; principal of the Congregational College at Bala-Bangor; often preached on the inspiration and inerrancy of the Bible; an eloquent speaker

Evans, William (1870-1950). American Presbyterian; director of Bible course for Moody Bible Institute; popular preacher, lecturer, and author; dean at Bible Institute of Los Angeles; author

F

Fairbairn, Andrew M. (1838-1912). British Congregationalist; principal of Mansfield College at Oxford for twenty-three years; writer and theologian; gave the Yale Lectures (1892), *The Place of Christ in Modern Theology*

Farel, Guillaume (1489-1565). French Reformation leader; a fiery preacher; influenced John Calvin to remain in Geneva as a minister

Farmer, Herbert Henry (1892-1981). British Presbyterian theologian and writer; gave the Yale Lectures (1946), *God and Man*

Farrar, Frederic W. (1831-1903). Dean of Canterbury; author of popular books on Bible themes; questioned the doctrine of eternal punishment

Faunce, William H. Perry (1859-1930). American; Baptist minister and educator;

president of Brown University; gave the Yale Lectures (1908), *The Educational Ideals of the Ministry*

Fenelon, Francois (1651-1715). French Jesuit leader; had a mystical emphasis on the inwardness of the spiritual life; counselor to Madame Guyon

Ferguson, David (1525-1598). Scottish Reformer; known for his wit, yet was serious in his preaching

Finney, Charles G. (1792-1875). American Presbyterian; trained as a lawyer; known for his doctrinal preaching, emphasized sanctification; widely blessed as an evangelist; president of Oberlin College (1851-66)

Flavel, John (c. 1630-1691) English Puritan Congregationalist; ministered in London and Devon; popular writer

Flechier, Valentin Esprit (1632-1710). Bishop of Nimes, France; known especially for his funeral orations

Fletcher, John (1729-1785). Known as "Fletcher of Mandeley" (in Shropshire); early Methodist preacher and educator; tried to mediate the Methodist Arminians and Calvinists

Forrest, Henry (1500-1553). Scottish Benedictine friar who embraced the evangelical faith; was burned at the stake

Forrester, David (1588-1663). Scottish preacher who opposed legalism and Romanism in the church; persecuted for his faith but not imprisoned

Forret, Thomas (1490-1540). Scottish Roman Catholic preacher; converted to the evangelical faith by reading Augustine; preached the gospel plainly to the common people; memorized three chapters of the Latin Bible daily; burned at the stake for preaching heresy

Forsyth, Peter Taylor (1848-1921). British Congregationalist; emphasized the grace of God and the cross; gave the Yale Lectures (1907), *Positive Preaching and the Modern Mind*; principal of Hackney College in London; prolific writer

Fosdick, Harry Emerson (1878-1969). American Baptist; perhaps the most distinguished preacher of his day; liberal in his theology; at center of fundamentalist-modernist controversy (from 1922 on); problem-centered preaching; taught at Union Seminary in New York City; pastored Riverside Church in New York (1925-1946); gave the Yale Lectures (1924), *The Modern Use of the Bible*

Foster, John (1770-1843). English Baptist; denied eternal punishment; left the ministry to become a writer

Fox, George (1624-1691). Founder of the Society of Friends (Quakers); popular preacher in Great Britain and the United States; campaigned to improve prisons and education

Francis of Assisi (1182-1226). Founder of the preaching order of Franciscans; popular orator; emphasized brotherly love and repentance

Francke, August Herman (1663-1727). Pietistic German Lutheran; preacher and theologian; doctrinal, but mystical; founder of orphan house at Halle, which influenced George Müller in his ministry in England

Fraser, James (1639-1699). "James Fraser of Brae"; Scottish preacher with evangelical convictions who was imprisoned for his faith; author of several devotional books based on doctrine; held in high regard by Alexander Whyte who wrote *James Fraser of Brae: An Appreciation*

Freeman, James (1759-1835). American Unitarian; founded the first Unitarian church in America in 1785

Frelinghuysen, Theodorus Jacobus (c. 1691-1748). American Dutch Reformed; a forceful preacher who helped spearhead the Great Awakening; possessed a unique blending of Reformed theology and Pietism

Froment, Antoine (1509-1584). French Reformed; associate of William Farel

Fulbert de Chartres (c. 960-1028). French Roman Catholic bishop

Fulgentius of Ruspe (468-533). Bishop of Ruspe (North Africa); apologist; wrote against Arians and Pelagians

Fuller, Andrew (1754-1815). English Baptist; helped to found the Baptist Foreign Missionary Society that supported William Carey (1792); expository preacher with doctrinal content

Fuller, Charles E. (1887-1968). American Presbyterian; early radio preacher; heard on "The Old Fashioned Revival Hour" for many years; founder of Fuller Theological Seminary

Fuller, Richard (1804-1876). American; Baptist; a converted lawyer; became president of Southern Baptist Convention; a "born orator"; for twenty-four years was pastor Seventh Baptist Church in Baltimore

Fuller Thomas (1608-1661). Church of England; preacher and historian; used humor in his preaching

G

Gaebelein, Arno C. (1861-1945). American Methodist; born in Germany; ministered to the Jews; his emphases were on Bible exposition and prophecy; author of many Bible commentaries; founded and edited *Our Hope*

Galloway, Charles B. (1849-1909). American Methodist; pastored churches in the South; became a bishop in 1886; trustee of both University of Mississippi and Vanderbilt University; a popular orator

Garvie, Alfred Ernest (1861-1945). Congregational Church of Scotland; principal of New College in London; a scholarly preacher who especially influenced students; *The Christian Preacher* (1920) gave his views of preaching

Geikie John Cunningham (1824-1906). English Presbyterian; later became member of the Church of England; author of books on various Bible themes

Geiler, John (1445-1510). German Roman Catholic; mystic and scholar; "the prince of the pulpit"

Gerson, Jean Charlier de (1363-1429). French Roman Catholic; administrator and influential preacher; tried to reform University of Notre Dame;

Gil, Juan (d. 1556). Spanish Roman Catholic converted to Reformed doctrine; popular preacher; condemned by the Inquisition as a "Lutheran"

Gill, John (1697-1771). English Baptist; pastored for over fifty years at Horsleydown, Southwark, in the church that eventually became Spurgeon's Metropolitan Tabernacle; wrote many books of which *A Body of Divinity* was known especially

Gillespie, George (1613-1648). Scottish Presbyterian; member of the Westminster Assembly; pastored important churches in Edinburgh; "one of Edinburgh's most distinguished preachers"

Gilpin, Bernard (1517-1583). English Anglican; ministered to the masses as a popular preacher; "apostle of the north"; dealt with social and educational issues

Gladden, Washington (1836-1918). Original name, Solomon Washington; American Congregationalist; had imaginative style, but loose organization; emphasized a social gospel; gave the Yale Lectures (1887), *Tools and the Man*

Goodman, Christopher (1520-1603). English Reformer; fled to Geneva, Switzerland where he shared the ministry of the English Church with John Knox; became rector in Chester

Goodwin, Thomas (1600-1680). English Congregationalist; doctrinal preacher and expositor, and prolific writer; a favorite of Alexander Whyte

Gordon, Adoniram Judson (1836-1895). American; Baptist; popular preacher and writer; pastored Clarendon Street Baptist Church in Boston from 1868; a missionary leader; founded Gordon College

Gordon, Charles William (1860-1937). Canadian Presbyterian; known as "Ralph Connor, the Sky-Pilot"; missionary pastor in the frontier; prolific author and popular preacher; served pastorates in Winnipeg, Manitoba; enjoyed an effective ministry as itinerant speaker in Canada, the United States, New Zealand, and Australia

Gordon, George Angier (1853-1929). Scottish Congregationalist; pastor of Old South Church in Boston for more than forty years; liberal in his theology; gave the Yale Lectures (1903), *Ultimate Conceptions of Faith*

Gore, Charles (1853-1932). Anglican bishop with high church leanings; rather liberal in his theology; doctrinal preaching

Gossip, Arthur John (1873-1954). Scottish Presbyterian; known for his style, illustrations, and imagination; preached well-known sermon after his wife died suddenly, "But When Life Tumbles In, What Then?"

Gray, Andrew (1633-1656). Converted through the witness of a beggar; ordained at age 21, and became pastor of Outer High Church in Glasgow; was fervent in the pulpit, drew large crowds; had only three years of ministry

Gray, James Martin (1851-1935). American Reformed Episcopal; dean and later president of Moody Bible Institute in Chicago; popular author and conference speaker

Greer, David H. (1844-1919). American Episcopal; known especially for his ministry as rector of St. Bartholomew's in New York, and as bishop of the New York diocese; supervised construction of the cathedral of St. John the Divine in New York; gave the Yale Lectures (1895), *The Preacher and His Place*

Gregory (the Great) (540-604). One of the four great "Doctors of the Roman Catholic Church"; served as pope from 590-604; wrote *Rules for Pastors*

Gregory of Nyssa (c. 330-394). Apologist; popular preacher with powerful delivery; used allegory; taught rhetoric

Gregory of Nazianzus (c. 330-389). Oratorical style; opposed Arianism; imaginative teacher and preacher

Grindal, Edmund (1519-1583). Anglican who tried to upgrade the preaching of his time

Groot, Gerard (1340-1384). Dutch Roman Catholic; was a deacon, not priest; large crowds came to hear him; founder of Brethren of the Common Life

Gunsaulus, Frank Wakeley (1856-1921). American Congregationalist; popular preacher and civic leader in Chicago; gave the Yale Lectures (1911), *The Minister and the Spiritual Life*

Guthrie, James (1612-1661). Scottish Presbyterian; martyred; before he was hanged, he cried, "The Covenants! The Covenants shall yet be Scotland's reviving!"

Guthrie, Thomas (1803-1873). Free Church of Scotland; the greatest platform speaker of his time; memorized his sermons; known for arrangement and delivery

Guthrie, William (1620-1665). Scottish Covenanter; wrote the popular book *The Christian's Great Interest*

H

Haldeman, Isaac M. (1845-1933). American; Baptist; pastored First Baptist Church in New York for over fifty years; fundamental leader; exponent of premillennial doctrine and known for prophetic preaching

Hall, Christopher N. (1816-1902). British Congregationalist; pastored Surrey Chapel founded by Rowland Hill; strong evangelistic preaching; author of the famous tract *Come to Jesus*

Hall, John (1829-1898). American Presbyterian; pastored Fifth Avenue Presbyterian Church in New York; evangelical and Calvinistic; believed in pastoral ministry, and systematically visited his people in their homes; gave the Yale Lectures (1875), *God's Word Through Preaching*

Hall, Joseph (1574-1656). Anglican; bishop of Norwich; "the Chrysostom of England"; popular pulpit orator and biblical preacher

Hall, Robert (1764-1831). British Baptist; began preaching at age 15; liberal in his early years, but later became more orthodox; doctrinal; had eloquent delivery and good application

Hallesby, Ole Kristian (1879-1961). Norwegian Lutheran; preacher and devotional writer; missionary executive

Halyburton, Thomas (1674-1712). Scottish Presbyterian; one of Scotland's greatest theologians

Hamilton, James Wallace (1900-1968). American Methodist; popular preacher and pastor of the "drive-in church" in Pasadena, Florida; published many books of sermons; strong in imagination and illustration; applied biblical truth to human needs, but was somewhat weak on doctrinal content

Hamilton, Patrick (1503-1528). Scottish preacher; influenced by Tyndale's New Testament and Martin Luther's friendship; had to flee Scotland; returned to preach Reformation doctrine and later martyred

Hare, Julius (1795-1855). British Anglican; archdeacon of Lewes; very liberal; an able preacher

Harlow, William (1500-1575). Scottish Presbyterian; leader in Scotland when John Knox was in exile; not a great preacher, but a beloved leader

Harms, Claus (1778-1855). German Lutheran revivalist; "a born preacher"; pietistic; known as a devoted pastor

Harms, Ludwig (Louis) (1809-1866). German Lutheran pastor and founder of a missionary training school

Harris, Howell (1714-1773). Welsh Calvinistic Methodist; lay preacher who was an associate of George Whitefield; "a man of extraordinary gifts"; more than 20,000 people attended his funeral

Henderson, Alexander (c. 1583-1646). Scottish Presbyterian; one of the leading Covenanters; drafted "The Solemn League and Covenant"; second only to John Knox and Andrew Melville in preaching and leadership in the Scottish Reformation

Henry, Matthew (1662-1714). English Nonconformist; ordained Presbyterian; served twenty-five years as a pastor in Chester; preached expository sermons; his church services often lasted all day; known for his *Expositions of Holy Scripture*

Henry of Lausanne (c. 1085-1145). Italian itinerant preacher who majored on repentance in his messages

Henson, Herbert Hensley (1863-1947). Bishop of Durham; influential preacher with strong ecumenical leanings; did not hesitate to preach in Nonconformist churches; involved himself in politics and social questions; gave the Yale Lectures (1909), *The Liberty of Prophesying*

Hill, Rowland (1744-1833). Nonconformist English preacher; "full of fire in the pulpit"; built the Surrey Chapel in London in 1783

Hillis, Newell Dwight (1858-1929). American Presbyterian; succeeded Henry Ward Beecher at Plymouth Congregational Church in Brooklyn; pulpit orator; emphasized the richness and fullness of the Christian life

Hinton, John H. (1791-1873). English Baptist; known for missionary and antislavery sermons

Hippolytus (c. 170-236). Ante-Nicene Father (Western group); prolific writer

Hodge, Charles (1797-1878). American Presbyterian; taught systematic theology at Princeton; Benjamin Warfield succeeded him

Houghton, William Henry (1887-1947). American Baptist; president of Moody Bible Institute (1934-46); evangelist and radio preacher

Hofacker, Ludwig (1798-1828). Popular German Lutheran preacher

Hog, Thomas (1628-1692). Scottish evangelical preacher; imprisoned for his faith; buried at the door of his church at Kiltearn with a stone bearing an inscription warning the church against ever calling an ungodly pastor

Hook, Walter F. (1798-1875). Dean of Chichester; very popular preacher who built large congregations in Coventry and Leeds

Hooker, Richard (1553-1600). Church of England scholar known for his *Laws of Ecclesiastical Polity*

Hooker, Thomas (1586-1647). Left the State church to become Congregationalist; founded the colony of Hartford, Connecticut; preached using illustrations and popular style; known for his graphic denunciation of sin

Hooper, John (c. 1495-1555). Bishop of Gloucester; popular preacher with Reformed views; martyred

Hopkins, Samuel (1721-1803). American Congregationalist; moderate Calvinist; served for thirty-three years as pastor of First Congregational Church in Newport, Rhode Island; generally conceded to be a dull preacher with poor delivery

Horne, Charles Sylvester (1865-1914). English Congregationalist; popular preacher with social and political emphases; known for a "beautiful voice"; gave the Yale Lectures (1914), *The Romance of Preaching*

Horton, Robert Forman (1855-1934). English Congregationalist; pastored in London for fifty years; gave the Yale Lectures (1893), *Verbum Dei*

Howe, John (1630-1706). English Nonconformist; "The Platonic Puritan"; philosophical preacher with doctrinal emphasis; tried, but failed, to unite British Presbyterians and Independents

Hübmaier, Balthasar (c. 1480-1528). German Anabaptist leader; known for his sermonic style and delivery; burned at the stake

Hugo of St. Victor (1097-1141). French Roman Catholic mystic; ministered in Paris

Hus, John (c. 1373-1415). Bohemian reformer before the Reformation; evangelical; used allegory; burned at the stake

Hutton, John A. (1868-1947). British Congregationalist; Bible preacher and influential editor; delivered many sermons on Bible characters

Hyde, William DeWitt (1858-1917). American Congregationalist; educator and author; gave the Yale Lectures (1916), *The Gospel of Good Will*

I

Ignatius (of Antioch) (d. 117). Bishop of Antioch; apostolic Father; known for his strong love for Christ; martyred

Inge, William Ralph (1860-1954). Dean of St. Paul's in London; "the gloomy dean"; intellectual preacher; gave the Yale Lectures (1925), series not published

Innocent III (1161-1216). Pope from 1198-1216; brought the papacy to its greatest power

Irenaeus (c. 130-202). Bishop of Lyons; apologist

Ironside, Henry Allan (1876-1951). American Brethren; Known as "Harry" or simply "H.A.I."; Bible teacher and prolific author; pastored Moody Memorial Church (1930-48); sermons were verse-by-verse expositions of a Bible book; used many personal illustrations and much poetry; his sermons followed the explain, illustrate, and apply pattern

Irving, Edward (1792-1834). Scottish Presbyterian; assistant to Thomas Chalmers; popular eloquent preacher; deposed from the presbytery because of his views on apostolic gifts; his followers founded the Catholic Apostolic church

Ivo (of Chartres) (1040-1116). Bishop of Chartres; expert in theology and canon law

J

Jacks, Laurence Pearsall (1860-1955). British Unitarian; believed, however, in the resurrection of Jesus Christ; founder and editor of *The Hibbert Journal*; principal of Manchester College, and then Oxford; gave the Yale Lectures (1933), *Elemental Religion*

James, John Angell (1785-1859). British Congregationalist; pastored Carr's Lane Church in Birmingham for more than fifty years; succeeded by R. W. Dale

Jasper, John (1812-1901). American; Baptist; eloquent Black preacher; born into slavery; his closing prayer at a fellow slave's funeral was so moving that he was also asked to preach; "the most original, dramatic and effective orator" of all the Black preachers; had a creative use of imagination

Jay, William (1769-1853). British Congregationalist; "boy preacher" who attracted large crowds; known for good textual analysis and practical application

Jefferson, Charles Edward (1860-1937). American Congregationalist; pastored Broadway Tabernacle in New York; known for his doctrinal preaching; concerned the social issues of the day; gave the Yale Lectures (1910), *The Building of the Church*

Jerome (of Prague) (1379-1416). Bohemian reformer and friend of John Hus; a layman and popular orator; martyred

Jewel, John (1522-1571). Bishop of Salisbury; popular preacher of Reformation doctrine

Joachim of Fiore (c. 1135-1202). Italian Roman Catholic mystic

John of Capistrano (1386-1456). Franciscan leader

John of Damascus (c. 675-749). Greek theologian and allegorical preacher

Johnson, Gustaf Frederick (1873-1959). American Free church (Scandanavian) and Covenant church; "one of the truly outstanding preachers of his generation"; had magnetic ability in the pulpit

Jonas, Justus (1493-1555). German Reformation scholar and associate of Martin Luther; hymnwriter

Jones, Edgar DeWitt (1876-1956). American; Disciples of Christ; for many years pastor of Central Woodward Christian Church in Detroit; wrote many of books on preachers and preaching; especially noted for *The Royalty of The Pulpit* (1951), a study of the men who gave the Yale Lectures

Jones, Eli Stanley (1884-1973). American Methodist missionary to India; devotional writer and conference speaker

Jones, Griffith (1683-1761). Welsh Episcopal preacher; established many charity schools

Jones, John Daniel (1865-1942). British Congregationalist; pastored many years at Bournemouth; had a quiet pulpit delivery

Jones, David (1796-1841). Welsh missionary to Madagascar

Jones, Rufus (1863-1948). American Quaker educator, writer, and preacher

Jones, Samuel Porter (1847-1906). American Methodist evangelist and orator

Jones, Robert ("Bob") Reynolds, Sr. (1883-1968). American; Methodist evangelist and educator; founder of Bob Jones University; called "the greatest evangelist of all time" by Billy Sunday; known for his biblical preaching with emphasis on decision

Jowett, John Henry (1864-1923). British Congregationalist; followed G. Campbell Morgan at Westminster Chapel in London; emphasized the doctrine of grace; had a quiet delivery; a master of words; gave the Yale Lectures (1912), *The Preacher: His Life and Work*

Justin Martyr (c. 100-165). Apologist and teacher; opened the first Christian school in Rome; trained in rhetoric and philosophy; martyred in Rome

K

Kagawa, Toyohiko (1888-1960). Japanese evangelist and social worker who sought to apply the gospel to the needy people in the cities

Keach, Benjamin (1640-1704). British Baptist; preacher and prolific writer; introduced congregational singing into his services; in London, pastored the church that Charles Haddon Spurgeon later pastored

Keble, John (1792-1866). British Anglican; hymnwriter; friend of John Henry Newman; author of *The Christian Year*

Kelman, John (1864-1929). British Presbyterian; assistant to Alexander Whyte; pastored Fifth Avenue Church in New York; closed his ministry at St. Andrew's Presbyterian Church, Hampstead, London; Yale Lectures (1919), *The War and Preaching*

Ketcham, Robert (1889-1978). American; Baptist; founder of the General Association of Regular Baptist Churches that withdrew from the Northern (now American) Baptist Convention; gifted preacher who was a self-taught man

King, Martin Luther, Jr. (1929-1968). American; Baptist preacher and civil rights leader; pastored churches in Montgomery, Alabama and Atlanta, Georgia; sought to apply Christian principles to social problems; applied Gandhi's "civil disobedience" philosophy to the race problems; assassinated

Kingsley, Charles (1819-1875). British Anglican; preacher, novelist, and Christian socialist leader

Kirk, Edward N. (1802-1874). American Presbyterian; pastored in Albany, New York; in 1844 founded Mount Vernon Church in Boston; was D. L. Moody's pastor when Moody joined the church; pastored in Boston for thirty years

Kirkland, John T. (1770-1840). American Congregationalist; moral and ethical preacher who promoted liberal doctrines; served as pastor of New South Church in Boston (1793-1810); had Unitarian leanings; president of Harvard University (1810-1828)

Kirwen, Walter Blake (1754-1805). Church of Ireland; pulpit orator; famous for "charity sermons" to raise funds; not too strong in evangelical emphasis

Knox, John (c. 1514-1572). Scottish Reformer; responsible for the triumph of Calvinism in Scotland; strong doctrinally, and had evangelistic emphasis

Knox, Ronald A. (1888-1957). British Roman Catholic preacher who began as an evangelical Anglican; quiet biblical preacher; scholarly

Krummacher, Friedrich (1796-1868). German Reformed leader and powerful preacher; devotional author

Kuyper, Abraham (1837-1920). Dutch Reformed theologian and preacher who broke with the liberal school; emphasized topical rather than expository preaching; taught preaching and theology; became Dutch prime minister (1901-1905)

L

Lacordaire, Jean-Baptiste Henri (1802-1861). French Roman Catholic orator

Lactantius, Lucius (c. 240-320). Italian rhetorician and apologist; "the Christian Cicero"

Landels, William (1823-1899). Scottish Baptist; served twenty-eight years as pastor of the Baptist church in Regent's Park in London; opposed Charles Spurgeon on the "Down Grade Controversy"

Latimer, Hugh (c. 1485-1555). English Reformer and martyr; "father of the English pulpit"; vivid and forceful preacher

Lawson, James (1538-1584). Successor to John Knox at St. Giles' in Edinburgh, Scotland; his evangelical zeal sometimes made him intolerant; forced to flee Scotland

Lee, Robert Greene (1886-1978). American Southern Baptist; an eloquent preacher; pastored Bellevue Baptist Church in Memphis, Tennessee for thirty-five years; famous sermon "Pay Day Someday"

Leighton, Robert (1611-1684). Archbishop of Glasgow; expounded Scripture; wrote a detailed commentary on 1 Peter

Leland, John (1691-1766). Born in England and reared in Dublin, Ireland; served as a pastor in Dublin; great foe of the Deists; wrote many books; known for his courageous preaching

Leo I (the Great) (c. 400-461). "Founder of the papacy"; dedicated to preaching

Lever, Thomas (1521-1577). British Anglican whose doctrinal convictions forced him to flee from England to Geneva, Switzerland, where he came under John Calvin's influence; returned to England, served in Coventry and Durham; deprived of his offices because of Nonconformist views; very outspoken in his preaching

Lewis, Clive Staples (C. S.) (1898-1963). British Anglican; layman; professor at Oxford and Cambridge; classical scholar; greatest modern apologist for Christianity

Lewis, Howell Elvet (1860-1953). Welsh Congregationalist; eloquent as preacher, poet, and hymnwriter

Liddon, Henry Parry (1829-1890). British Anglican; canon of St. Paul's in London (1870-90); high-church doctrine; preached theological sermons

Livingstone, John (1603-1672). Scottish preacher and Hebrew scholar; when twenty-seven years old, he preached a sermon that converted 500 people in one meeting; people thronged to hear him

Lloyd-Jones, David Martyn (1895-1981). Welsh Presbyterian; associate of and successor to G. Campbell Morgan at Westminster Chapel in London; expositor of the Puritan school; Calvinistic; wrote *Preachers and Preaching*

Lorimer, George C. (1838-1904). American; Baptist; twice pastor of Tremont Temple in Boston; also pastored First Baptist and Immanuel Baptist in Chicago, and Madison Avenue Baptist in New York; a former actor, he had a remarkable memory and a dramatic style

Lucar, Cyril (1572-1638). Patriarch of Constantinople; Calvinistic in theology; murdered by Muslims

Luccock, Halford E. (1885-1961). American Methodist; taught homiletics at Yale Divinity School; gave the Yale Lectures (1954), *Communicating the Gospel*; mastery of words and style; life-centered preaching; excellent illustrations

Luther, Martin (1483-1546). One of the greatest preachers of all time; his sermons were biblical, doctrinal, and practical; leader of the Reformation; expounded the Scriptures so that the common people could understand

M

MacAlpine, John (1505-1577). Scottish Dominican; influenced by Martin Luther; eloquent preacher; became a Danish Lutheran pastor in Copenhagen, Denmark

MacArthur, Robert S. (1841-1923). Canadian Baptist; pastor of Calvary Baptist Church in New York for forty-one years

Macartney, Clarence E. (1879-1957). American Presbyterian; preached strong biblical sermons without notes; excelled in biographical preaching; made good use of historical illustrations; one of the conservative leaders in the fundamentalist-modernist controversy of the 1930s; published many books of sermons

MacBean, Angus (1656-1688). Scottish pastor at Inverness; imprisoned for his opposition to the state church; a fearless preacher with extraordinary power

Machen, J. Gresham (1881-1937). American Presbyterian; scholar, author, and preacher; founder of Westminster Theological Seminary in Philadelphia; professor of New Testament at Princeton Seminary; one of the leaders in the fundamentalist-modernist controversy of the 1930s

McCheyne, Robert Murray (1813-1843). Scottish Presbyterian; known for his holy life; pastored St. Peter's at Dundee, Scotland, where he is buried

McConnell, Francis John (1871-1953). American Methodist leader; gave the Yale Lectures (1930), *The Prophetic Ministry*

McCracken, Robert James (1904-1973). Scottish-born preacher who ministered and taught in Canada, then succeeded Harry Emerson Fosdick at Riverside Church in New York; Baptist; professor of theology and philosophy of religion at McMaster University in Hamilton, Ontario

McDowell, Benjamin (1739-1824). Irish Presbyterian; ministered in Dublin, Ireland; a great defender of the faith

McDowell, William Fraser (1858-1937). American Methodist; gave the Yale Lectures (1917), *Good Ministers of Jesus Christ*; possessed unusual gifts of imagination and illustration

McNeill, John (1854-1933). Scottish Presbyterian; powerful preacher and evangelist known around the world; unusual wit; was able to make Bible history and characters come alive through imaginative preaching; called "the Scottish Spurgeon"

Mackenzie, Lachlan (1754-1819). Scottish Presbyterian preacher known for his courageous preaching against sin

Maclaren, Alexander (1826-1910). British Baptist; known for his expository messages; "the prince of expository preachers"; pastored Union Chapel in Manchester (1858-1903); a man with a scholar's mind and a pastor's heart; first president of the Baptist World Alliance

MacLaren, Ian (1850-1907). Pen name of John Watson (q.v.)

MacLaurin, John (1693-1754). Scottish preacher who was a friend of Jonathan Edwards; one of the first to use the modern approach to sermon structure; doctrinal preacher

Macleod, Norman (1812-1872). Church of Scotland preacher; pastored Barony Church in Glasgow, Scotland from 1851 to his death

Magee, William C. (1821-1891). Irish Protestant; one of the three greatest orators of the nineteenth century; emphasized the arrangement of the sermon for greatest effect

Maier, Walter A. (1893-1950). American Lutheran (Missouri Synod); professor of Hebrew and Old Testament at Concordia Seminary in St. Louis; radio preacher (1930-50) on "The Lutheran Hour" with an audience of 20 million listeners; invested one hour of preparatory study for each minute that he preached on the radio

Manning, Henry Edward (1808-1892). British Roman Catholic; archbishop of Westminster; became cardinal in 1875

Marshall, Peter (1902-1949). Scottish Presbyterian; known for his ministry at New York Avenue Church in Washington, D.C., and as chaplain of the United States Senate; also widely recognized for his superior diction and ability to communicate truth imaginatively

Marshall, Stephen (c. 1594-1655). English Presbyterian; Puritan leader; a powerful preacher who was not afraid to deal with political matters

Martin of Tours (c. 335-400). Founder of the Gallican church and defender of the Nicene Creed

Martin, Samuel (1817-1878). English Congregationalist; built Westminster Chapel in London, and filled its large sanctuary week after week; pastored Westminster from 1841 to his death

Martineau, James (1805-1900). English Unitarian; preacher and writer; known for his philosophical sermons

Mason, John Mitchell (1770-1829). American Presbyterian and Reformed; great pulpit orator with a rich voice and an effective delivery

Massillon, Jean Baptiste (1663-1742). French Roman Catholic; known for beauty of sermonic style; preached before Louis XIV, and famous for his funeral sermon for that monarch

Mather, Cotton (1663-1728). American Congregationalist; Puritan leader; produced more than 400 publications during his lifetime; doctrinal preacher, but also preached on political and social issues of his day

Mather, Increase (1639-1723). American Congregationalist; youngest son of Richard Mather; pastor of North Church in Boston from 1664 to his death; president of Harvard College; strong evangelistic preacher

Mather, Richard (1596-1669). Congregationalist; father of Increase, grandfather of Cotton Mather

Matheson, George (1842-1906). Church of Scotland; blind preacher, devotional writer, and hymnwriter of "O Love That Wilt Not Let Me Go"

Matthew, Theobald (1790-1856). Irish Roman Catholic preacher who toured the land preaching against sin (especially drunkenness), and sought to help the poor; known for the moving pathos of his preaching

Matthew, Edward (1813-1892). Welsh Calvinistic Methodist; known for his dramatic style

Matthews, Mark A. (1867-1940). American Presbyterian; popular Bible preacher and fundamentalist leader; trained as a lawyer; crusader for moral issues; strong evangelistic emphasis

Maurice, John Frederick Denison (1805-1872). English Anglican preacher; one of the leaders of the Christian Socialist movement

Maximus of Turin (380-465). Bishop of Turin; greatly influenced by the preaching of Ambrose; left 116 sermons and 118 homilies

Meade, William (1789-1862). American Episcopal; founded the Virginia Theological Seminary in Alexandria, Virginia

Melito (d. 190). Bishop of Sardis

Melville, Henry (1798-1871). English evangelical Anglican; wrote out his sermons several times before preaching them; Charles Spurgeon called him "The Demosthenes of London"

Melville, Andrew (1545-1622). Successor to John Knox; "Father of the Scottish Presbyterian church"

Menno Simons (c. 1496-1561). Anabaptist leader and founder of the Mennonites

Methodius (815-885). With the help of his brother, Cyril, an "apostle to the southern Slavs"

Meyer, Frederick B. (1847-1929). British Baptist; devotional and biographical preacher; greatly influenced by D. L. Moody; his preaching emphasized the deeper life

Milic, John (Jan of Kromeriz) (d. 1374). Moravian reformer whose bold preaching led to his arrest; believed also in a ministry to the needy

Monod, Adolphe Theodore (1802-1886). French evangelical leader and one of the founders of the Reformed church in France; gave deeply spiritual messages

Moody, Dwight Lyman (1837-1899). American lay-evangelist used greatly in campaigns in the United States and Great Britain; founder of Moody Bible Institute and Northfield schools; served as a YMCA worker

Moorehead, William Gallogly (1836-1914). American Presbyterian; professor and president of Xenia Seminary in Xenia, Ohio; contributing editor to the *Scofield Reference Bible*

Morgan, George Campbell (1863-1945). British Congregationalist; "the prince of Bible expositors"; associated with D. L. Moody during the Northfield Bible Conference lectures; twice pastored Westminster Chapel in London; author of many Bible study books

Morgan, William (c. 1541-1604). Welsh bishop and Bible translator

Morris, David (1744-1791). Welsh Methodist preacher who drew hugh crowds

Morris, Ebenezer (1769-1825). Calvinistic Welsh Methodist; son of David Morris

Morrison, Charles Clayton (1874-1966). American Disciples of Christ; founded *Christian Century* magazine; gave the Yale Lectures (1939), *What is Christianity?*

Morrison, Henry Clay (1857-1942). American Methodist; emphasized sanctification; followed Wesley in attacking social evils; strong promoter of missions

Morrison, George Herbert (1866-1928). Scottish Presbyterian; assisted Alexander Whyte in Edinburgh; pastored Wellington Church in Glasgow, Scotland, where he drew large crowds; published many volumes of sermons

Moule, Handley Carr Glynn (1841-1920). British Anglican; bishop of Durham; scholar and preacher; author of several devotional commentaries based on the Greek text

Mozley, James Bowling (1813-1878). British Anglican active in the Oxford Movement

Mühlenberg, Henry Melchior (1711-1787). American Lutheran; came from Germany; had a pietistic emphasis

Muller, Julius (1801-1878). German theologian; opposed the rationalistic tendencies of his day

Murray, Andrew (1828-1917). Scottish; became Dutch Reformed minister in South Africa; author of many devotional books on prayer and revival

Myconius, Oswald (1488-1552). Swiss Reformer; friend of Erasmus; was never ordained

Mylne, Walter (1476-1558). Scottish Roman Catholic who embraced Reformed doctrine; was burned at the stake

N

Nee, Watchman (1903-1972). Chinese Christian preacher and writer whose "Little Flock" movement reached many; prolific writer, best known for *The Normal Christian Life*

Nestorius (d. 451). Patriarch of Constantinople; a popular preacher who confronted the heretics; died in exile

Newman, John Henry (1801-1890). Originally Anglican evangelical; founder of the Oxford Movement; joined the Roman Catholic church and eventually became a cardinal; wrote the hymn "Lead, Kindly Light"; preached to large and appreciative audiences at St. Mary's Church in Oxford

Newton, John (1725-1807). British evangelical Anglican; former slave trader; wrote "Amazing Grace"; ministered at Olney where he enjoyed the friendship of the hymnwriter William Cowper

Newton, Joseph Fort (1880-1950). American; changed from Southern Baptist to Congregationalist, and finally to Episcopalian; pastored City Temple in London for a brief time; fervent, realistic preaching; closed his ministry in Philadelphia; author of many books of sermons and essays

Nicholas (of Cusa) (c. 1401-1464). German Roman Catholic mystic and philosopher

Nicoll, William Robertson (1851-1923). Scottish Presbyterian; forced to leave pastoral ministry because of ill health; became England's leading editor; edited *Expositor's Bible, The Expositor's Greek New Testament,* and many more scholarly works

Niebuhr, Karl Paul Reinhold (1893-1971). American United Church of Christ; neo-orthodox; emphasized social needs and problems; gave the Yale Lectures (1945), *Faith and History*

Niebuhr, Helmut Richard (1894-1962). American; neo-orthodox; professor of Christian ethics at Yale; younger brother of Reinhold

Niemoller, Martin (1892-1967). German Protestant leader who opposed Hitler, and was imprisoned at Dachau; served as leader of Evangelical church after the war; officer in World Council of Churches

Niles, Daniel T. (1907-1970). Methodist; ecumenical leader from Ceylon; Methodist; worked in YMCA; gave the Yale Lectures (1958), *The Preacher's Task and the Stone of Stumbling*; emphasized the resurrection of Christ; preached with great vitality

Nitzsch, Karl (1787-1868). German Lutheran theologian

Norbert (1080-1134). German Roman Catholic preacher and founder of a monastic order; canonized in 1582

Nott, Eliphalet (1773-1866). American Presbyterian; president of Union College for sixty-two years

O

Ochino, Bernardino (1487-1564). Popular Italian Roman Catholic preacher

Oecolampadius (1482-1531). German Reformer; gifted linguist and popular preacher

Oman, John Wood (1860-1939). British Presbyterian; principal of Westminster College in Cambridge; wrote on theology, philosophy, and the ministry (*Concerning the Ministry,* 1937)

Orchard, William Edwin (1877-1955). British preacher who began as an Anglican, became a Presbyterian, and then pastored the King's Weigh House in London, a Congregational church made famous by Thomas Binney; he then joined the Roman Catholic church

Origen (c. 185-254). Alexandrian theologian and preacher; "the father of expository preaching"

Owen, John (1616-1683). British Congregationalist preacher and Puritan leader; theologian; known for his detailed exposition of texts

Oxnam, Garfield Bromley (1891-1963). American Methodist bishop; pastored in Baltimore, Evanston (Illinois), and New York City; liberal in his theology, he tried to apply biblical truths to "a revolutionary age"; emphasized the social gospel; gave the Yale Lectures (1944), *Preaching in a Revolutionary Age*

P

Palamus, Gregory (1296-1359). Greek mystical preacher and writer; archbishop of Thessalonica

Paley, William (1743-1805). Anglican scholar and apologist; his *Natural Theology* and *Evidences of Christianity* were standard texts

Palmer, Benjamin Morgan (1818-1902). American Presbyterian; pastored First Presbyterian Church in New Orleans (1856-1902)

Parker, Joseph (1830-1902). British Congregationalist; pastored City Temple in London; preached through the Bible in seven years; conducted large Thursday noon services for people in the city; known for his imagination and daring; autobiography, *A Preacher's Life* (1899)

Parker, Matthew (1504-1575). Became Archbishop of Canterbury in 1559; popular pulpiteer, but weak doctrinally

Parker, Theodore (1810-1860). American Congregationalist who became Unitarian; emphasized social reform

Parkhurst, Charles Henry (1842-1933). American Presbyterian; preached the sermon that led to the investigation of New York City politics and the fall of Tammany Hall; gave the Yale Lectures (1913), *The Pulpit and The Pew*

Parsons, James (1799-1877). British Congregationalist; "the barrister of the pulpit"; trained for law, he preached for a verdict; pastored Lendal Chapel (1822-1839), and Salem Chapel (1839-1870), both in York; "Parsons of York" was known throughout England

Patrick (Patricius) (c. 389-461). "Apostle of the Irish"; founder of the Celtic church; missionary preacher

Patton, Francis Landey (1843-1932). American Presbyterian; president of Princeton University and Seminary; staunch champion of orthodoxy

Peabody, Francis Greenwood (1847-1936). American Unitarian; gave the Yale

Lectures (1905), *Jesus Christ and the Christian Character*; Scottish field preacher ejected from his church because he would not submit to the bishop; drew large crowds

Penry, John (1559-1593). Welsh Puritan; itinerant preacher; martyred

Perkins, William (1558-1602). English Puritan leader; wrote the first work on homiletics in the English language

Peter of Blois (c. 1130-1204). French theologian; Archbishop of Canterbury; sermons were allegorical and mystical

Peter of Bruys (d. 1140). French Roman Catholic reformer; martyred

Peter of Damian (1007-1072). Italian Roman Catholic reformer

Peter the Hermit (c. 1050-1115). Preacher of the First Crusade; able to arouse people but not direct them; effective open-air preacher with powerful delivery

Peter of Lombard (c. 1095-1159). Bishop of Paris; "Father of Roman Catholic systematic theology"; his famous *Four Books of Sentences* was the basic textbook in schools in the Middle Ages

Peter of Ravenna (1205-1252). "Peter the Martyr"; Roman Catholic Dominican who won many to Catholicism; assassinated by his enemies

Photius (of Constantinople) (c. 820-891). Patriarch of Constantinople

Pidgeon, George Campbell (1872-1971). United Church of Canada; first moderator; for thirty-three years pastor of Bloor Street United Church in Toronto; used expository preaching; his motto: "find the central thought of the text . . . enforce it"

Pierson, Arthur Tappan (1837-1911). American Presbyterian; Bible expositor associated with C. I. Scofield; missions leader; interim pastor of Spurgeon's Metropolitan Tabernacle in London; author of many books of Bible studies and sermons

Pike, James Albert (1913-1969). American Episcopalian; trained as lawyer; bishop of California; emphasized the intellectual and social; became involved in spiritualism in 1960s

Pink, Arthur W. (1886-1952). British independent itinerant Bible teacher and writer; pastored churches in California, Kentucky, South Carolina, and Colorado; retired to the Isle of Lewis, Scotland in 1934, and devoted himself to writing; published the periodical *Studies in the Scriptures* for many years; began as an ardent dispensationalist, but gradually moved to the Puritan position

Polycarp (c. 70-160). Bishop of Smyrna; knew the apostle John; had a pietistic emphasis; died at the stake

Poteat, Edwin McNiel (1892-1955). American; Baptist; missionary to China (1917-1926); professor and president of Colgate Rochester Divinity School

Powell, Vavasor (1617-1670). "The George Whitefield of Wales"; Welsh Puritan leader with tireless evangelistic zeal

Produls (Proclus) (c. 410-485). Patriarch of Constantinople; renowned preacher whose sermons precipitated the Nestorian controversy

Punshon, William Morley (1824-1881). Eloquent British Methodist preacher; pastored churches in London, Bristol, and in Canada; 1875 General Secretary of the Wesleyan Missionary Society; old-fashioned homiletical style with innumerable divisions; just before he died he said, "Christ is to me a bright reality!"

Pusey, Edward Bouverie (1800-1882). Anglican theologian and professor active in the Oxford Movement; the term "Puseyite" used to identify followers of the high church movement

Q

Quadratus (Second century). Bishop of Athens; known for his defense of the faith

Quayle, William (1860-1925). American Methodist; preacher, writer, educator (at one time the youngest college president in the world); bishop; known for evangelistic zeal and emphasis on pastoral work; wrote *The Pastor-Preacher*

R

Rabanus, Maurus (c. 776-856). Archbishop of Mainz; member of the Benedictine order

Rainy, Robert (1826-1906). Church of Scotland; preacher and educator; professor of church history and later principal of New College in Edinburgh; friend of Alexander Whyte

Rauschenbusch, Walter (1861-1918). American Baptist; pastor and seminary professor; emphasized the social gospel

Rees, Henry (1798-1869). Calvinistic Methodist; born in Wales; for thirty-three years superintendent of Calvinistic Methodist work in Liverpool; known for his searching communion addresses

Rees, Morgan (1760-1804). Welsh preacher and educator; encouraged the founding of Sunday schools and night schools; promoter of religious liberty; emigrated to America and established a Welsh church in Pennsylvania

Rees, William (Rhys) (1802-1883). Welsh Congregational; powerful preacher and theologian; editor

Reinhard, Franz Volkmar (1752-1812). One of the ablest German Lutheran preachers of his time; court preacher at Dresden for twenty years; produced thirty-nine volumes of sermons

Renwick, James (1662-1688). Last of the Scottish Covenanter martyrs; protested the crowning of James II

Rice, Merton Stacher (1872-1943). American Methodist; "Poet of the Pulpit"; vivid use of illustrations; used "folksy" preaching that encouraged the hearer

Ridley, Nicholas (c. 1500-1555). English Reformer; able theologian and preacher; bishop of London; burned at the stake with Hugh Latimer at Oxford

Roberts, Evan (1875-1951). Welsh Calvinistic Methodist; revivalist; prayed eleven years for revival that came in 1904 and led to the salvation of an estimated 100,000 people

Roberts, Robert (1762-1802). Welsh Calvinistic Methodist; had only fifteen years of ministry; brought new life to Welsh congregations

Roberts, William (1809-1853). Welsh Calvinistic Methodist; preached in Wales and the United States where he founded churches; preached carefully prepared messages from the original languages; known for simplicity and power

Robertson, Frederick William (1816-1853). British Anglican; known for his two-point sermons; memorized most of the New Testament in both Greek and English; ministered only six years at Brighton, and died thinking himself a failure; his published sermons were distributed widely and have been influential

Robinson, James Herman (1907-1972). American Presbyterian; first Black minister to give the Yale Lectures (1955), *Adventurous Preaching*; ministry was centered in one church in New York City

Robinson, John (c. 1575-1625). English Separatist; pastor of the Pilgrim Fathers in Holland; known for his statement, "The Lord has more truth yet to break forth out of His Holy Word"

Robinson, Ezekiel Gilman (1815-1894). American; Baptist; liberal in his theology; president of Brown University; gave the Yale Lectures (1882), *Lectures on Preaching*

Rogers, John (c. 1500-1555). English Reformer; worked on Old Testament with William Tyndale; published *Matthew's Bible* in 1537; burned at the stake by Queen Mary

Rollock, Robert (1555-1598). First principal and professor of theology at Edinburgh University; his expositions drew people to church at 7 A.M.; wrote several commentaries

Romaine, William (1714-1795). Evangelical Anglican; friend of George Whitefield; noted Hebrew scholar; his preaching attracted large crowds

Rough, John (1510-1557). Scottish Reformer who helped "discover" John Knox; burned at the stake in England

Rowland, Daniel (c. 1713-1790). Cofounder of the Welsh Calvinistic Methodist church; magnetic preacher whose lengthy sermons held the attention of large congregations

Ruchrath, John (or Rucherat) (c. 1400-1481). German Roman Catholic reformer; cathedral preacher at Worms; arrested and deposed for his views; died in an Augustinian cloister

Rutherford, Samuel (c. 1600-1661). Scottish Presbyterian; exiled from his church at Anwoth; his *Letters* written at that time are a devotional classic; a delegate to the Westminster Assembly

Ryle, John Charles (1816-1900). Evangelical Anglican; bishop of Liverpool; prolific writer, best known for his *Expository Thoughts on the Gospels*

S

Sandys, Edwin (c. 1516-1588). Archbishop of York; helped to translate the *Bishop's Bible*

Sangster, William Edwyn (1900-1960). British Methodist; pastored Westminster Central Hall during World War II and turned it into a bomb shelter in which he ministered to needy people; popular preacher and evangelist; author of many books on preaching and Christian living

Saurin, Jacques (1677-1730). "Greatest 17th Century French Protestant preacher"; his sermons were not logical in their arrangement; addressed the emotions; a powerful orator

Savonarola, Girolamo (1452-1498). Italian Roman Catholic; one of the greatest preachers of all time; courageous civic reformer; used allegory; appealed to the emotions; drew large congregations in Florence; excommunicated for denouncing the pope and preaching reform; tried for heresy and burned at the stake

Scarborough, Lee Rutland (1870-1945). American Southern Baptist: president of Southwestern Baptist Seminary at Fort Worth, Texas; had a passion for the lost and used strong evangelistic preaching

Scherer, Paul Ehrman (1892-1969) American Lutheran; pastor of Holy Trinity Lutheran Church in New York City (1920-1945); gave the Yale Lectures (1943), *For We Have This Treasure*; professor of homiletics at Union Seminary in New York (1945-61) and at Princeton Seminary (1961); a gifted preacher and teacher of preachers

Sclater, John Robert Paterson (1876-1949). Preached in the Scottish tradition; served Old St. Andrew's United Church in Toronto, Canada for many years; emphasized worship; gave the Yale Lectures (1927), *The Public Worship of God*

Schleiermacher, Friedrich (1768-1834). German theologian who revolted against traditional orthodox theology and German pietism; emphasized religious experience; published ten volumes of sermons

Scholarius, George (c. 1400-1468). Patriarch of Constantinople; teacher of philosophy; resigned to live in a monastery; author of more than one hundred books

Scholasticus, Honorius (c. 1090-1156). "Honorius of Autun"; Christian Platonist and writer

Scofield, Cyrus Ingersoll (1843-1921). American Congregationalist; trained as a lawyer; worked with D. L. Moody; leader in the Bible conference ministry and the dispensational school of interpretation; editor of the famous *Scofield Reference Bible*

Scott, Thomas (1747-1821). Anglican; converted from Unitarianism to evangelical position; his commentary on the Bible was very popular

Scroggie, William Graham (1877-1959). British Baptist; pastored Charlotte Chapel in Edinburgh, Scotland, and Spurgeon's Metropolitan Tabernacle; tireless Bible student who wrote many valuable books; was active in the Keswick movement

Seabury, Samuel (1729-1796). American Episcopalian; first bishop in America; emphasized preaching as a part of church worship

Selwyn, George (1809-1878). Anglican; first bishop of New Zealand

Seiss, Joseph Augustus (1823-1904). American Lutheran; preacher and writer; his commentary on Revelation is still popular

Semler, Johann Salomo (1725-1791). German Lutheran; scholar and textual critic; father of higher criticism

Semple, Gabriel (1632-1706). Scottish field preacher; declared a traitor and jailed for three months; had the ability to preach familiar truths with new power and meaning

Sharp, James (1613-1679). Church of Scotland archbishop of St. Andrew's; betrayed the Covenanters

Sheen, Fulton John (1895-1979). American Roman Catholic; popular radio and TV speaker; taught philosophy; converted several famous people to Catholicism; author of many books

Sheppard, Hugh Richard (1880-1937). Known as "Dick" Sheppard; colorful Anglican preacher; pastored St. Martin's-in-the-Field in London; popular radio speaker; had a pacifistic emphasis

Shields, Thomas Todhunter (1873-1955). Canadian Baptist; pastored Jarvis Street Baptist Church in Toronto for over forty years; "the Spurgeon of Canada"; a controversial preacher who attacked Romanism and liberalism

Shoemaker, Samuel Moor (1893-1963). American Episcopalian; popular preacher and lecturer; famous for his mid-week services; one of the founders of Alcoholics Anonymous

Simeon, Charles (1759-1836). Evangelical Anglican; pastored Holy Trinity Church in Cambridge for fifty years; sent out Henry Martyn; published twenty-one volumes of sermon outlines covering the entire Bible; greatly influenced Cambridge students

Simpson, Matthew (1811-1884). American Methodist; famous orator; strong opponent of slavery; served as bishop; friend of Abraham Lincoln; patterned his preaching after Wesley; gave the Yale Lectures (1879), *Lectures on Preaching*

Simpson, Albert Benjamin (1843-1919). American Presbyterian; founder of The Christian and Missionary Alliance; author of many books on the Spirit-filled life, healing, and missions

Singh, Sadhu Sundar (1889-1929). Indian Christian leader known as "the Sadhu"; associated with the Anglican church; traveled widely in his ministry; emphasized the love of God; had a somewhat mystical approach

Sizoo, Joseph Richard (1885-1966). American Reformed Church; pastored the St. Nicholas Collegiate Reformed Church in New York and New York Avenue Presbyterian Church in Washington, D.C.; president of New Brunswick Seminary in New Jersey; applied reformed theology to current issues

Smellie, Alexander (1857-1923). Scottish Free Church; pastored a small congregation, yet his books influenced the church at large; a quiet, conversational, although powerful preacher

Smith, George Adam (1856-1942). English Old Testament scholar and writer; leaned toward the liberal school of theology; gave the Yale Lectures (1899), *Modern Criticism and the Preaching of the Old Testament*

Smith, Henry (1550-1591). English Puritan preacher known as "the silver-tongued"; preached to great crowds

Smith, Rodney ("Gipsy") (1860-1947). English Wesleyan evangelist and singer; emphasized God's love; won many to Christ

Sockman, Ralph Washington (1889-1970). American Methodist; popular preacher on "National Radio Pulpit"; known for his use of illustrations; gave the Yale Lectures (1941), *The Highway of God*

South, Robert (1634-1716). Anglican; known for clarity, simplicity, and fervor; made doctrine interesting

Spellman, Francis Joseph (1889-1967). American; Roman Catholic cardinal in New York City

Spener, Philipp (1635-1705). German Lutheran; "father of pietism"; expounded entire books of the Bible and emphasized biblical preaching

Spurgeon, Charles Haddon (1834-1892). British Baptist; self-taught; evangelistic; had strong Calvinistic emphasis; perhaps the greatest preacher of modern times; built the Metropolitan Tabernacle in London; his sermons were published weekly, even after his death; founded Pastors' College

Stalker, James (1848-1927). Scottish United Free church; professor; friend of D. L. Moody; interest in social concerns, but evangelistic; wrote popular books on the life of Christ and Paul; gave the Yale Lectures (1891), *The Preacher and His Models*

Stanley, Arthur P. (1815-1881). Anglican dean of Westminster Abbey; belonged to the "Broad Church" school; scholarly; sympathetic with German liberalism

Stidger, William Leroy (1885-1949). American Methodist; gifted poet, writer, and speaker; ministered in Boston; emphasized hope, optimism, confidence, and good will; wrote *Preaching Out of the Overflow* (1929)

Stier, Rudolf Ewald (1800-1862). German Lutheran preacher and commentator; ministry was doctrinal, but also mystical

Stillingfleet, Edward (1635-1699). Anglican bishop of Worcester; dean of St. Paul's; beloved pastor; expert on religious controversies; chaplain to the king

Stoddard, Solomon (1643-1729). American Congregationalist; grandfather of Jonathan Edwards; effective preacher and revivalist

Stone, John Timothy (1868-1954). American Presbyterian; pastor of Fourth Presbyterian Church in Chicago (1909-1930); president of McCormick Seminary in Chicago

Storrs, Richard (1821-1900). American Congregationalist; pastored the Church of the Pilgrims in Brooklyn, New York for fifty-four years

Straton, John Roach (1875-1929). American; Baptist; pastor of Calvary Baptist in New York City; fundamentalist leader

Sunday, William Ashley ("Billy") (1862-1935). American Presbyterian; famous evangelist heard by more than 100 million people; saw over one million "hit the sawdust trail"; assisted by Homer Rodeheaver, soloist and song leader; retired to Winona Lake, Indiana, where a large tabernacle is named in his memory

Swing, David (1830-1894). American Presbyterian; pastored Fourth Presbyterian Church in Chicago; left the denomination to start the Central Church in Chicago; his sermons were published in local newspapers for years; tried for heresy, but acquitted

T

Talmage, Thomas DeWitt (1832-1902). American Presbyterian; pastored Brooklyn Tabernacle; his sermons were syndicated in newspapers; a master in the use of rhetoric and illustration

Tauler, Johann (c. 1300-1361). German Dominican; mystic; used allegory; had evangelistic emphasis

Tausen, Hans (1494-1561). Danish bishop; Reformer; popular preacher

Taylor, Jeremy (1613-1667). British Anglican; "the Poet of the Pulpit"; "the Shakespeare of divines"; eloquent, with grandiose style; used many illustrations

Taylor, William Mackergo (1829-1895). Scottish Congregationalist; pastored Broadway Tabernacle in New York City (1872-92); a traditional expositor in the Scottish style; gave the Yale Lectures twice, *The Ministry of the Word* (1875-76), and *The Scottish Pulpit* (1886)

Temple, Frederick (1821-1902). Anglican; Archbishop of Canterbury (1896-1902); emphasized social action

Temple, William (1881-1944). Anglican; Archbishop of Canterbury (1942-44); philosopher and theologian; emphasized church union and social action

Tennent, Gilbert (1703-1764). American Presbyterian; preached a sermon that led to a division in the Presbyterian movement; famous sermon "The Danger of an Unconverted Ministry"; son of William Tennent

Tennent, William (1673-1746). American Presbyterian; founder of the "log college," later to become Princeton College; worked with George Whitefield; helped to train many ministers

Tertullian (c. 160-220). Latin church Father in North Africa; apologist; dramatic delivery; trained as a lawyer; a born orator

Theodore of Mopsuestia (c. 350-428). Antiochene; exegete and theologian; opposed an allegorical approach to the Bible

Theodoret of Cyrrhus (c. 390-458). Bishop of Cyrrhus; diligent pastor; wrote brief commentaries

Theophilus of Antioch (Late second century). Bishop and apologist

Tholuck, Friedrich August (1799-1877). Evangelical German Lutheran; exegete and theologian; had a doctrinal emphasis

Thomas, William Henry Griffith (1861-1924). British Anglican; evangelical; principal of Wycliffe Hall in Oxford; professor of Wycliffe College in Toronto, Canada; conference speaker and author of many Bible study books and commentaries; associated with R. A. Torrey and James M. Gray in various ministries; one of the founders of Dallas Theological Seminary

Tillich, Paul (1886-1965). German existential theologian and professor; published a systematic theology and several books of sermons

Tillotson, John (1630-1694). Anglican; Archbishop of Canterbury (1691-94); most influential homiletician in English church; emphasized arrangement, simplicity, and a good homiletical pattern; not strongly evangelistic; had an ethical emphasis

Tittle, Ernest Fremont (1885-1949). American; served for thirty-one years at First Methodist Church in Evanston, Illinois; his sermons interpreted world events in the light of Scripture; took vocal exercises all his life; considered preaching an act of worship; gave the Yale Lectures (1932), *Jesus After Nineteen Centuries*

Torrey, Reuben Archer (1856-1928). American Congregationalist; discovered by D. L. Moody and became superintendent of Moody's school in Chicago; toured the world with soloist Charles Alexander in great evangelistic meetings; helped to found the Bible Institute of Los Angeles (Biola) and the Church of the Open Door in Los Angeles; author of many Bible study books

Truett, George Washington (1867-1944). American Southern Baptist; pastored First Baptist Church in Dallas, Texas for forty-seven years; eloquent Bible preacher with the heart of an evangelist; preached to cowboys each year; a great leader in his denomination and for the Baptist World Alliance

Trumbull, Henry Clay (1830-1903). American Congregationalist; founder of *The Sunday School Times*

Tucker, William Jewett (1839-1926). American Congregationalist; followed Bushnell at North Church in Hartford, Connecticut; gave the Yale Lectures (1898), *The Making and the Unmaking of the Preacher*

U

Ulfilias (c. 311-381). Apostle to the Goths; translated Scripture into their language

Urban II (c. 1042-1099). French Roman Catholic; pope from 1088-99; preached the First Crusade

Ussher, James (1851-1933). Irish Anglican; archbishop of Armagh; had strong

Calvinistic leanings; scholar known for his biblical chronology that dates the creation 4004 B.C.

V

Van Dyke, Henry (1852-1933). American Presbyterian; pastor of the Brick Church in New York City (1883-99); author and hymnwriter; professor at Princeton University; used poetical preaching with very little doctrine; appointed ambassador to the Netherlands by President Woodrow Wilson; his sermons were known for their literary polish; participated Yale Lectures (1896), *The Gospel for an Age of Doubt*

Van Ruysbroeck, Jan (1293-1381). Flemish mystic and spiritual counselor; author of *The Spiritual Espousals*

Varley, Henry (1835-1912). Nondenominational British preacher and evangelist; was never ordained; greatly used in Britain, United States, and Canada; influenced D. L. Moody with the statement, "The world has yet to see what God can do with, and for, and through, and in a man who is fully and wholly consecrated to Him."

Van Dusen, Henry P. (1897-1975). American Presbyterian; president of Union Seminary, New York City; an ecumenical leader

Vaughan, Bernard J. (1847-1922). English Roman Catholic; as popular in his day as Charles Spurgeon and Joseph Parker; served eighteen years at Holy Name Church in Manchester; his sermons drew large crowds that included Protestants and nonbelievers; boldly attacked the sins of society; did open-air preaching in the slum areas; known for his humor

Vaughan, Charles John (1816-1897). Welsh Anglican of the Broad Church school; highly esteemed for his preaching; expounded the Bible and published commentaries and books of sermons

Venn, Sir Henry (1725-1797). For twelve years pastor of the Anglican Church in Huddersford, Yorkshire, where his ministry stirred the city; recognized as an excellent preacher; George Whitefield held him in high esteem and called him "a son of thunder"

Vinet, Alexander (1797-1847). Swiss Reformed; theologian and preacher; appealed to the conscience; displayed good use of illustrations

Viret, Pierre (1511-1571). Swiss Reformed; recognized as an effective preacher

von Frank, Franz Hermann Reinhold (1827-1894). German Lutheran; apologist and theologian

von Staupitz, Johann (1469-1524). German Augustinian who influenced Martin Luther

W

Waldo, Peter (d. c. 1217). French founder of "the poor men of Lyons," an itinerant preaching order

Walther, Carl F. W. (1811-1887). American Lutheran; organized the Evangelical Lutheran Synod of Missouri; president of Concordia Theological Seminary; emphasized the teaching ministry of the pulpit and the priesthood of believers

Watson, John (1850-1907). Scottish Presbyterian; pastored churches in Scotland; for twenty-five years pastor of the wealthy Sefton Park Church in Liverpool; very popular as preacher, lecturer, and writer; used the pen name Ian Maclaren; gave the Yale Lectures (1897), *The Cure of Souls*

Wayland, Francis (1796-1865). American; Baptist; president of Brown University for twenty-five years; preached famous sermon: "The Moral Dignity of the Missionary Enterprise"; a great missionary leader

Weatherhead, Leslie Dixon (1893-1976). English Methodist; famous for the use of psychology in pastoral work and preaching; pastor of City Temple in London (1936-60); gave the Yale Lectures (1949), *The Minister's Relation to the Community*

Welsh, John ("of Ayr") (1570-1622). Son-in-law of John Knox; a courageous preacher who defied King James and was exiled and persecuted; preached daily in Ayr to a crowded church; the ban against his preaching lifted when he was on his deathbed, so he arose, went to the church and preached, returned home, and died two hours later

Welsh, John ("of Irongray") (1624-1681). Grandson of Welsh of Ayr; charged with treason, he became an itinerant preacher who often preached to huge crowds in the open air; died while visiting in London; his funeral was the greatest London had seen in many years

Wesley, John (1703-1791). English Anglican; with George Whitefield, founded what became the Methodist church; evangelistic; had amazing power to control large crowds; adopted Whitefield's open-air preaching ministry; his sermons were based on the Bible; an excellent scholar and prolific author, he preached more than 40,000 sermons

Whately, Richard (1786-1863). Anglican; archbishop of Dublin; although a very poor preacher, he left sixty volumes of sermons and essays; author of a well-known work on rhetoric

White, John (1570-1615). English Puritan; chaplain to King James I; lively and popular style; strongly Calvinistic and monarchial; an outspoken enemy of Catholicism

Whitefield, George (1714-1770). Founder of the Calvinistic Methodist church; ordained in the Church of England, but worked with other evangelical groups; "the greatest preacher England ever produced"; a pioneer open-air preacher, he could be heard clearly by 30,000 people; preached over 18,000 sermons during his ministry; made seven evangelistic visits to America and shared in the Great Awakening; founder of the University of Pennsylvania; buried at the First Presbyterian Church at Newburyport, Massachusetts

Whyte, Alexander (1837-1921). Free Church of Scotland; "The last of the Puritans"; minister of Free St. George's Church in Edinburgh for thirty-nine years; known for his "surgical sermons" on sin; excellent biographical preacher; emphasized study and hard work in the ministry

Wilberforce, Samuel (1805-1873). Anglican; "high church" bishop

Williams, Peter (1722-1796). Welsh Calvinistic Methodist; published a Welsh family Bible, commentary, and concordance, that was found in almost every home; went on many preaching tours; expelled from his denomination for heresy, but the charges were probably exaggerated

Williams, Roger (c. 1603-1683). Anglican, but became a Separatist and Baptist; champion of religious liberty; founded Rhode Island

Williams, William (1717-1791). Welsh Methodist preacher, author of ninety books; hymnwriter ("Guide Me, O Thou Great Jehovah")

Williams, William ("of Werm") (1788-1840). Welsh Congregationalist; known for his quiet and persuasive preaching style

Willock, John (1512-1585). Assistant to John Knox; pastored in London, but had to flee to the Continent; in 1559 became pastor of St. Giles Church in Edinburgh; in 1562 left to pastor a church in England

Wishart, George (c. 1513-1546). Scottish Reformer; his preaching influenced John Knox, who served as his bodyguard for a time; burned at the stake

Wiseman, Nicholas Patrick Stephen (1802-1865). Leading English Roman Catholic prelate; first archbishop of the Westminster Cathedral in London; helped to reestablish the Roman Catholic church in Britain; an eloquent preacher with Irish humor

Witherspoon, John (1723-1794). Born in England, ministered in the Presbyterian church in the United States; the only cleric to sign the Declaration of Independence; president of the College of New Jersey (now Princeton University) for twenty-five years

Woolman, John (1720-1772). Quaker preacher and itinerant minister whose *Journal* is a spiritual classic; supported himself as a tailor; opposed slavery; had a mystical approach to Scripture

Wroth, William (1576-1642). "Apostle to South Wales"; "Father of Welsh nonconformity"; served his congregation at Llanfaches for forty years

Wulfstan (c. 1012-1095). Bishop of Worcester; known for humility and Christian grace; opposed the slave trade in Britain

Wycliffe, John (c. 1329-1384). "Morning star of the Reformation"; translated the Latin Vulgate into English; a gifted lecturer and preacher with a doctrinal emphasis

X

Xavier, Francis (1506-1552). Spanish Jesuit missionary who baptized thousands of converts

Y

Yorke, Peter C. (1864-1925). Roman Catholic prelate; born in Ireland, but ministered in the United States; effective in his use of humor; involved in social problems and labor disputes; strong appeal to the laboring men

Young, Dinsdale Thomas (1861-1938). English Methodist; pastored Westminster Central Hall in London, and drew great crowds; aimed to reach the popular mind and emphasized simplicity in preaching

Youngdahl, Reuben Kenneth (1911-1968). American Lutheran; served for thirty-one years the pastor of Mount Olivet Church in Minneapolis—the largest Lutheran church in the world at that time; known for his pastoral preaching with heart and conviction

Z

Zinzendorf, Nickolaus Ludwig (1700-1760). Founder of the Moravian church; a mystical Pietist

Zwemer, Samuel M. (1867-1952). American; Presbyterian and Reformed church; gave his life as a missionary to the Moslem world; a forceful preacher and an effective missionary statesman

Zwingli, Ulrich (1484-1531). Swiss Reformer; widely read in the classics; a gifted preacher who expounded books of the Bible; known for his delivery, arrangement, style, and use of illustrations

Part 4
AN ILLUSTRATIONAL PERSPECTIVE

16

How to Use Biographical Illustrations Effectively

We use illustrations in sermons to achieve several goals. We may want to *enlighten the mind* and make the material we are presenting easier to understand. A story is a good way to bring abstract truth down to concrete experience. Or we may want to *stir the emotions* and help our listeners *feel* the truth as well as understand it. If we bypass the emotions in our preaching, we may end up delivering a lecture instead of proclaiming God's message. Illustrations also help us to *capture attention*. They add variety and balance to a sermon and help to relieve the tension that can come from listening to a sustained line of reasoning or argument. An interesting story is a good bridge between major divisions in a sermon, enabling the listener to relax for a moment and prepare for the next encounter of truth.

Illustrations from biography are especially good because they grow out of the experiences of life. However, this kind of material has its own built-in hazards. For example, persons who are well-known to the studious preacher may be complete strangers to a congregation. Just as there arose a generation that knew not Joseph, so there arises a generation that never heard of Balthasar Hübmaier or W. Graham Scroggie. For that reason, the preacher should follow these simple suggestions.

BE SURE THE STORY IS RELEVANT TO THE MESSAGE

This rule applies to *all* illustrations, of course, but it is especially true for biographical illustrations. A "good story" is not always a good illustration. It may be interesting, amusing, even illuminating, but unless it relates to the matter at hand, it will become a detour instead of a highway.

BE SURE THAT THE SUBJECT OF THE STORY IS INTRODUCED TO THE LISTENERS

Never build an illustration around a stranger. Do not even assume that your congregation knows such famous preachers as G. Campbell Morgan, Charles Spurgeon, or even John Wesley. Those may be similar names to most Christians, but perhaps not to the new believer or unsaved friend in the congregation. Why take a chance on excommunicating them from the flow of the sermon? It is important that we introduce those great preachers and tell why it is important to know them.

Of course, our approach is not to be encyclopedic; for example, "John Wesley was born in 1703 and died in 1791," and so on. we can identify a preacher of the past and make him more interesting and important to our listeners by following these guidelines:

Relate the person to someone or something already known. That is, use the old principle of starting from the familiar and moving to the unfamiliar. Mentioning the familiar hooks the listener and arouses his interest. For example: "This morning we sang 'Love Divine, All Loves Excelling,' a hymn written by Charles Wesley. As you know, Charles had a famous brother named John. About the time of the Revolutionary War, John and Charles were ministering in Great Britain and founded what we know as the Methodist church. One day John sprained his ankle . . . ," and that leads into your story.

Try to avoid phrases such as "I'm sure you do not know" or "You probably have not heard of." If the listener does know about the person mentioned, you have insulted the listener's intelligence. If he does not know, you are putting yourself above him and perhaps alienating him. It is better to use *positive* and *inclusive* statements such as: "Most of us remember from our American history class . . . " or "You will probably recall that during the blackout in New York City a few years ago . . . "

Tie your illustration to a basic human need or experience. Arouse interest and then give information. "Did you ever sprain your ankle and end up getting married? John Wesley did, and it may well have been the worst series of events in his life!" Love and hate, failure and success, hope and despair, faith and unbelief are all seen in the lives of the great preachers; and it should not be too difficult to relate those experiences to the people to whom we minister the Word of God.

Admit that the person is unfamiliar and build on that fact. For example, "Quite frankly, I had never heard of Dan Crawford. He was very famous in his day, which was about the turn of the century. You see, Dan Crawford was a missionary to Africa . . . ," and then go into the illustration. If you identify with the members of the congregation in such a "learning experience," they will stay with you and get the point.

The important thing is that you relate the person in the story to the people in the congregation. If you do not, there will be little impact from the illustration; after all, who will respond enthusiastically to an anonymous individual?

BE SURE YOU HAVE THE FACTS AND STATE THEM ACCURATELY

Stories have a way of moving from illustration book to illustration book and undergoing elaborate changes. An experience that happened to Charles Spurgeon is soon told about Joseph Parker. That is why it is best to get your illustrations from the official biographies of the preachers and not from compilations. The material in this book has been carefully checked with the best biographical sources available.

Also, be sure you can correctly pronounce the name of the person who is central to the illustration. *Webster's Biographical Dictionary* is your best help here, and it will also give you the important historical data about the person's life and work. To supplement Webster, use *The New International Dictionary of the Christian Church* edited by J. D. Douglas. It does not give pronunciation, but it does contain an amazing amount of factual information. The *Eerdmans' Handbook to the History of Christianity* is helpful to those who are a bit foggy on church history. You should also refer to the biographical section of this book.

Be sure you do not confuse your leading man or woman with another person of the same name. A preacher (who should have known better) once confused the Swiss Reformer Johann Heinrich Bullinger with the Anglican minister and author Ethelbert Bullinger. The fact that those two men lived three centuries apart did not seem to bother him!

DO NOT BE LONG AND TEDIOUS

If you have to make a short story long, drop it from the sermon. Too many details will only confuse the congregation. An effective illustration is an arrow to the heart, not a time-release capsule. Read the story several times and think it through. Aim for conciseness and you will do more good.

So much for rules. Now let's take a story and show what can be done with it.

> John Henry Jowett was born in Great Britain in 1864. He was converted as a youth and joined the church. He was fascinated by politics and politicians, and often traveled to hear great political speakers. He decided he wanted to become a lawyer and eventually enter politics. His father had made all the arrangements for his training. The day before the papers were to be signed, Jowett met his Sunday school teacher J. W. Dewhirst on the street. Jowett eagerly told Dewhirst of his career decision, and the man replied, "I had always hoped that you would go into the ministry." Jowett was profoundly struck by that statement and thought seriously about it all the way home. He came to the conclusion that he was drawn to the ministry. He became one of England's most famous preachers and was known as "the greatest preacher in the English-speaking world."

As that story stands, it is not in shape for public presentation. But we cannot "put it into shape" until we know what we are going to do with it. What truth do we want to illustrate? Consider the possibilities; the power of the words (James 3); the influence of friendship; the influence of a Sunday school teacher; the providence of God; the call to the ministry; and the importance of decision. One of the obvious lessons of the story is the importance of using our "casual contacts" for the Lord. Dewhirst did not have an appointment with Jowett; they met "by accident" on the street. Our Lord always used His casual contacts to help people, and so should we.

Let's assume that we are preparing a message for a Sunday school worker's conference, and that we want to emphasize the importance of doing all to the glory of God.

A Sunday school worker is never "off duty." We are on the job "in season and out of season." Never underestimate opportunities, even in the casual contacts of life. For all you may know, you may have a great preacher or missionary in your class. Did you ever hear of J. W. Dewhirst? He's a man we need to meet! He was a Sunday school teacher in a church in England. He had in his class a boy named John Henry Jowett. One day Dewhirst met John Henry Jowett on the street—not an accidental meeting, a providential meeting.

And then lead into your story.

Or suppose we are preaching from James 3 on the power of the tongue.

The tongue is like a bit and a rudder—it has the power to direct. The bit leads the horse; the rudder guides the ship. The words that we can speak can lead people in the right direction or get them off on a detour out of God's will. Even causal conversation can be used of God to direct someone's life.

Now you can move on into the story.

Because each story has several possible applications, we have not classified these two accounts into the usual categories. As you read them, you may want to pigeonhole them, but do not let your categories become too rigid. Each new reading may suggest new applications to life.

One final word of caution: *Do not use stories about the same person week after week.* For several months I read books about Dwight L. Moody and often quoted him or told stories about him. The congregation wondered if he had become one of my assistants! For that matter, biographical illustrations ought to be balanced with other material as we prepare messages week after week. Sameness leads to tameness.

17

Anecdotes from the Lives of Great Preachers

These anecdotes are included so that you may get better acquainted with some of the great preachers of the past. They may be read for entertainment, for historical interest, or for use as illustrations in sermons.

It is unfortunate that some of the great preachers did not live what we would call "eventful lives." For that reason, one of your favorite preachers may be missing from this section. On the other hand, some men—such as Charles Spurgeon and Dwight L. Moody—provide a vast storehouse of material for the student of preaching.

AMBROSE

Ambrose (A.D. 340-397) was trained as a lawyer and was given an excellent position as a Roman civil governor in Milan. When he left to take his new office, he jokingly said, "I will fulfill it like a bishop!"

Some time later, the bishop of Milan died. Because he was not true to the faith (he was an Arian), the people asked for an orthodox bishop. A riot began to brew in the town, so Ambrose went down to quiet the people. When he got to the church where the people had gathered, he did his utmost to get them under control. Then the voice of a child was heard: "Ambrose for bishop! Ambrose for bishop!" The people took up the cry, and within eight days, Ambrose was baptized and consecrated as bishop of Milan.

It was through the preaching of Ambrose that Augustine was converted.

"Out of the mouths of babes and sucklings" God sometimes directs the affairs of men and nations!

ANTHUSA

One of the godly mothers found in church history is Anthusa, the mother of John of

Damascus (better known as John Chrysostom). When John was young, his father died, leaving only his mother to raise him. She was offered many opportunities for marriage but turned them all down. She lived for her son and his faith, and would not wed an unbeliever. One of her disappointed suitors said, "Behold, what women these Christians have!"

AUGUSTINE

The conversion of Augustine is another evidence of the power of the Word of God and prayer. His mother, Monica, prayed fervently for her son, and Ambrose preached the Word to him in Milan. One day, while struggling with his sins and the claims of the gospel, Augustine heard a child's voice say, "Take—read! Take—read!" Augustine opened his New Testament, and it fell to Romans 13:14 ("But put on the Lord Jesus Christ, and make no provision for the flesh in regard to its lusts" [NASB].) The light dawned in his heart, he trusted Christ, and was born again. He became one of the greatest leaders of the church, both as a theologian and a preacher.

ANDREW BONAR

Queen Victoria visited Edinburgh, and Andrew Bonar took his two youngest daughters to see her. They met a friend, Mr. Walker from Perth, and Bonar said to him: "You see, I've brought my children in to see the queen. We saw her, but we were not changed; but 'when we see Him, we shall be like Him.'"[1]

Late one night, Andrew Bonar was going home from a meeting and lost his way. As he wandered about, he asked, "Can I give thanks for this?" After a short time, he came to a house and was about to knock on the door and ask for directions, when a girl came out and exclaimed, "Mr. Bonar! You're the very person I want to see!" She had been under great conviction of soul, and Bonar was able to lead her into peace through faith in Christ. He had lost his way but found a soul![2]

WILLIAM BOOTH

William Booth, founder of the Salvation Army, was brushing his manelike white hair when his son Bramwell stepped into the room.

"Bramwell!" he cried. "Did you know that men sleep out all night on the bridges?"

"Well, yes," the son replied. "A lot of poor fellows I suppose do that."

"Then you ought to be ashamed of yourself to have known it and to have done nothing for them!" his father retorted. And when the son began to talk about the Poor Law program, General Booth waved a hand and said, "Go and do something! We *must* do something!"

"What can we do?"

"Get them a shelter!"

1. Marjory Bonar, *Andrew Bonar—A Diary and Life* (London: Banner of Truth, 1960), 478.
2. Ibid., 411.

"That will cost money," replied Bramwell.

"Well, that is your affair. Something must be done. Get hold of a warehouse and warm it, and find something to cover them. But mind, Bramwell, no coddling!"

That was the beginning of the Salvation Army shelters. It all started when General Booth came home very late one night and witnessed the plight of the men sleeping on the bridges in London.[3]

* * *

During the early days of the Salvation Army, William Booth and his associates were bitterly attacked in the press by religious leaders and government leaders alike. Whenever his son, Bramwell, showed Booth a newspaper attack, the General would reply, "Bramwell, fifty years hence it will matter very little indeed how these people treated us; it will matter a great deal how we dealt with the work of God."[4]

* * *

The Salvation Army was accustomed to opposition, but the most ridiculous attack came from the great Earl of Shaftesbury, one of the leaders of the evangelical wing of the Church of England and a great politician. He announced that, after much study, he was convinced the Salvation Army was clearly antichrist! Then, some admirer of the Earl announced that in his own studies, he learned that the "number" of William Booth's name added up to 666![5]

* * *

One Sunday evening, William Booth was walking in London with his son, Bramwell, who was then twelve or thirteen years old. The father surprised the son by taking him into a saloon! The place was crowded with men and women, many of them bearing on their faces the marks of vice and crime; some were drunk. The fumes of alcohol and tobacco were poisonous.

"Willie," Booth said to his son, "these are our people; these are the people I want you to live for and bring to Christ."

Years later, Bramwell Booth wrote, "The impression never left me."[6]

* * *

One day Bramwell Booth asked one of the officers, "How did you come into the Army?"

The story of his conversion was remarkable. The man was in a miserable state and one evening was wandering aimlessly across Hyde Park in London when he saw a crowd gather around a speaker. It was a Salvation Army open-air meeting. The man stood at the edge of the crowd a few minutes and then started to go away; and at that

3. Bramwell Booth, *Echoes and Memories* (New York: George H. Doran, 1925), 1-2.
4. Ibid., 8.
5. Ibid., 27.
6. Ibid., 41.

moment, the speaker shouted: "Now, remember what I said," and he quoted a Bible verse adding in a loud voice, "JOHN THREE AND SIXTEEN."

The words "John three and sixteen" electrified the man. He went home and was not able to sleep. Finally, in desperation he turned to Christ and was saved.

"What was there about the words 'John three and sixteen' that convicted you?" Booth asked.

"Well, you see, Chief," the man replied, "my name is John, I have been married *three* times, and I have *sixteen* children!" God still works in mysterious ways.[7]

* * *

A man wandered into a Salvation Army all-night prayer meeting in Stratford, England, listened for a time to the sermon, and then fell asleep. Suddenly he was aroused from his sleep by a very loud snore! The man woke up startled and, not knowing where he was, stumbled out of his seat and into the aisle.

"Here's another soul for Jesus!" shouted an officer.

Before he could protest, the man was led to the sinner's bench where he found himself on his knees. As he reflected on his life, and the part of the sermon he had listened to earlier in the meeting, the man came under conviction of sin. Ultimately, he gave his heart to Christ and joined the Army.

He liked to tell people that he was saved by a snore![8]

* * *

One day a man walked into the London Salvation Army office and told the officer in charge that he wanted to give a check for a thousand pounds to the work of the Army.

The officer thanked him and asked him what prompted him to make such a generous donation.

"I was walking down Aldersgate Street," the man said, "and I saw a laborer loading sacks of scrap iron. One of the sacks was too heavy for him and he didn't know what to do. Just then, a tall man wearing a silk hat stepped up and loaded the sack for the weary old man. I was so struck by the deed that I asked a policeman who the tall man was. 'Oh, don't you know?' the policeman replied. 'That's General Booth!'"

"If that is the spirit of the Salvation Army," the man said, "then I shall help it as I have opportunity."[9]

* * *

Cecil Rhodes helped to carve out the politics and business of South Africa. He was wealthy, famous, and powerful. One evening, he happened to be in the company of Bramwell Booth, son of the founder of the Salvation Army. General Booth was in the next compartment of the train, and the son and Rhodes were together.

Booth leaned over to Rhodes and asked, "Mr. Rhodes, are you a happy man?" The man seemed to be surrounded by depression and gloom.

7. Ibid., 97.
8. Ibid., 98.
9. Ibid., 103.

Rhodes gripped the arms of the seat and said, "Happy? I, happy? No!"

Booth then told the powerful world figure that there was only one place to find real happiness. "That is down at the feet of the crucified Savior, because it is only there we can be freed from our sins."

"Yes," Rhodes said quietly, and then he added: "I would give all I possess to believe what that old man in the next carriage believes!"[10]

* * *

The coronation of Edward VII of Great Britain was postponed because the monarch had to undergo emergency surgery. Of course, all the important people of government, church, and society were expected to be present in Westminster Abbey wearing court dress.

Bramwell Booth, general of the Salvation Army, was invited, but he felt it was not right for him to wear court dress. The Army was recognized by its distinctive uniform and he did not want to change. On August 5, Booth wrote to the king and explained his plight. He wanted to be present to help honor the King, but he did not want to abandon his witness as a Salvation Army officer.

The next day, he received a telegram from the king stating that Booth could attend in uniform! He did not need to lay aside the uniform that honored the King of kings.[11]

PHILLIPS BROOKS

A young man in Boston lived in a boarding house with his wife and small child, and occasionally attended Trinity Church, where Phillips Brooks preached. The child died suddenly, and the shock deranged the young mother to the extent that she refused to give up the little dead body of her child. She held it and rocked the baby as though it were still alive.

The landlady encouraged the distraught father to visit Phillips Brooks. When he did, he discovered that the great preacher welcomed him warmly, listened to his story, and said, "I will go with you."

At the boarding house, Brooks looked at the child and said, "What a beautiful child! Would you let me rock him for a little while?"

The mother relinquished the baby and Brooks sat in the chair and rocked the child. At a signal from Brooks, the husband gently led his wife out of the room where she was properly cared for. Brooks not only attended the funeral but also sent flowers to the service.[12]

OSWALD CHAMBERS

Oswald Chambers and a friend, Arthur Green, were walking down a street in Cincinnati, Ohio, when Green shouted, "I hate the devil!" Chambers replied at the top

10. Ibid., 151-52.
11. Ibid., 215-16.
12. Lyman Abbott, *Silhouettes My Contemporaries* (New York: Doubleday, 1922), 252-53.

of his voice, "So do I!" Suddenly a man rushed up to them and asked them the way of salvation, and they pointed him to Christ.[13]

*   *   *

When a teenager, Oswald Chambers went with his father to hear Charles Spurgeon preach. As they were walking home in London, Chambers told his father that he would have given himself to Christ had Mr. Spurgeon given him the opportunity. "You can do it now, my boy," said the father, and there in the street, Chambers trusted Christ and was born again.[14]

DAN CRAWFORD

Dan Crawford (1870-1926) spent most of his adult life serving as a missionary in Africa. When it was time to return home to Britain, Crawford described to an old Bantu the kind of world he was about to return to. He told him about ships that ran under the water, on the water, and even those that flew above the water. He described English houses with all of their conveniences, such as running water and electric lights. Then Crawford waited for the old African to register his amazement.

"Is that all, Mr. Crawford?" the aged man asked.

"Yes, I think it is," Crawford replied.

Very slowly and very gravely, the old Bantu said: "Well, Mr. Crawford, you know, that to be better off is not to be better."[15]

R. W. DALE

R. W. Dale, in his day Britain's leading Congregationalist minister, did not believe in eternal punishment. Yet, before he died, Dale sighed and said, "No one fears God nowadays."[16]

HENRY DRUMMOND

Henry Drummond taught natural science at Edinburgh University and was recognized far and wide as a great spiritual counselor. One mother, deeply concerned about her son, who was a student at the University, begged Drummond to talk to him. Drummond was not too happy about such forced interviews, but finally gave in. The lad came in, and the look on his face gave proof that he was disgusted and resentful. But Drummond totally disarmed the boy, and finally won him when he smiled and said, "I suppose you know that this is all a put-up job?" That broke the ice, and before long the boy was assisting Drummond in his ministry to the students.[17]

---

13. Gertrude Chambers, ed., *Oswald Chambers* (London: Simkin Marshall, Ltd., 1933), 97.
14. Ibid., 19.
15. Arthur Porritt, *The Best I Remember* (London: Cassell and Co., Ltd., 1922), 83.
16. Ibid., 3.
17. Ibid., 101.

WILFRED GRENFELL

Wilfred Grenfell served as a missionary doctor in Labrador for many years, and achieved great distinction. He wrote to a friend:

> Mrs. Grenfell and I have been persuaded to take a Sabbatical year. My directors almost compelled me to, and I think of going around the world with her. We want change of scene and thought, and yet personally I hate the idea of losing a day on mere sight-seeing when life is so brief.

Paul probably had the same idea when he was left in Athens and decided to witness![18]

JOHN HUSS

In 1414 Sigismund, the emperor of Bohemia, called a council at Constance and ordered the "heretic" John Huss to be there. Sigismund gave Huss a letter of protection, but failed to honor it. In the council, Huss showed the letter and called on the emperor to acknowledge his signature and seal. "Sigismund turned pale and then blushed with shame," but he refused to protect Huss. His argument was that it was not necessary for an emperor to keep faith with a heretic. Huss was imprisoned and later led to the burning stake.[19]

ARCHBISHOP LEIGHTON

People criticized Archbishop Leighton because he "did not preach to the times." His reply was: "While so many are preaching to the times, may not one poor brother preach for eternity?"[20]

JOHN HENRY JOWETT

When John Henry Jowett was pastor at Newcastle-on-Tyne, England, he began a series of children's meetings. At the very first meeting, four boys with penny whistles upset the meeting by playing tunes while Jowett was speaking. An usher rounded up the boys and took them to the vestry where they faced Jowett.

"Can't you fellows play tin whistles any better than that?" Jowett asked. "If you can't, I shall have to get Mrs. Jowett to give you some lessons."

A few weeks later, the four boys gave a concert with Mrs. Jowett accompanying them on the piano.[21]

---

18. Porritt, *More and More of Memories* (London: George Allen & Unwin, Ltd., 1947), 140.
19. Edwin C. Dargan, *A History of Preaching* (Grand Rapids: Baker, 1974), 1:347-48.
20. J. D. Jones, *Three Score Years and Ten* (London: Hodder and Stoughton, 1940), 289.
21. Porritt, *The Best I Remember,* 101.

JUSTIN MARTYR

As a youth Justin Martyr (c. A.D. 100-165) tried every philosophical system but found no peace. One day he wandered down by the sea to think and he met a kind, old man who spoke to him. The man was a Christian and shared his faith with Justin. Justin was converted and became a great defender of the faith. God uses "anonymous servants" to accomplish great things.

JOHN KELMAN

When John Kelman was assistant to Alexander Whyte at Free Street George's Church, Edinburgh, he wondered whether his pulpit ministry was what it ought to be. His own approach to preaching was quite different from that of Whyte. One Sunday, Kelman preached a sermon patterned after Whyte's style. In the vestry after the service, Whyte walked up and down the room, then turned to Kelman, put a hand on his shoulder, and said, "John, preach your own message."[22]

MARTIN LUTHER

On a hot day in July 1505, Martin Luther, then a young university student, was walking near the village of Sotternheim when a summer storm suddenly blew up. A bolt of lightning struck near him and knocked him to the ground. Filled with terror, Luther cried, "St. Anne, help me! I will become a monk!" That was his "call" to Christian service.[23]

*   *   *

"I was a good monk," wrote Martin Luther, "and I kept the rule of my order so strictly that I may say that if ever a monk got to heaven by his monkery it was I. All my brothers in the monastery who knew me will bear me out. If I had kept on any longer, I should have killed myself with vigils, prayers, reading, and other work."

And yet, after all the works he had no peace of heart or assurance of salvation.[24]

*   *   *

In 1510, Martin Luther visited Rome and anticipated receiving great spiritual help, but he was disappointed. He climbed Pilate's Staircase on his hands and knees, kissing each step and repeating the "Our Father" for each step. At the top of the staircase, he said, "Who knows whether it is so?" He came seeking certainties, but returned home only with doubts.[25]

*   *   *

22. W. Y. Fullerton, *F. B. Meyer: A Biography* (London: Marshall, Morgan & Scott, n.d.), 32.
23. Roland H. Bainton, *Here I Stand* (Nashville: Abingdon, 1950), 15.
24. Ibid., 34.
25. Ibid., 38.

"If it had not been for Dr. Staupitz," said Martin Luther, "I should have sunk in hell."

It was Staupitz who pointed the terrified Luther to the merits of Jesus Christ. Sometimes Luther spent six hours in the confessional, examining his heart and naming his sins. "Man, God is not angry with you!" the weary confessor exclaimed. "You are angry with God."

Dr. Staupitz assigned Luther to earn his doctor's degree so that he might teach Bible at the university. Luther gave fifteen reasons he could not undertake the assignment, the main one being that it would kill him. "Quite all right," Staupitz replied. "God has plenty of work for clever men to do in heaven."

Because of those studies in the Bible, Luther discovered justification by faith and spearheaded the Reformation.[26]

* * *

Martin Luther believed in the preaching of the Word of God. While in Wittenberg he preached three services each Sunday (services at five and nine in the morning, and a service in the afternoon). He preached in the church each day of the week, climaxing with a Saturday evening service. He always balanced his messages, using the gospels, Paul's epistles, the catechism, and the Old Testament. In 1528 Luther preached 195 sermons over the course of 145 days. There are about 2300 of Luther's sermons in his complete works.[27]

* * *

For family devotions, Martin Luther once read the account of Abraham offering Isaac on the altar in Genesis 22. His wife, Katie, said, "I do not believe it. *God* would not have treated his son like that!"

"But, Katie," Luther replied, *"He did."*[28]

GEORGE MATHESON

We have heard of George Matheson, the blind minister and hymnwriter, composer of "O Love that Wilt Not Let Me Go" and "Make Me a Captive, Lord." But how many of us know William Pulsford, minister of Trinity Church, Glasgow? It was Pulsford who was used of God to awaken spiritual life in Matheson.

"The man of all others that shaped my personality was Pulsford," Matheson said. "I met him only once, but I never heard a man who so inspired me; he set me on fire, and, under God, he was my spiritual creator."[29]

* * *

During the second year of his ministry, George Matheson went through a period of doubt and skepticism. "I found myself an absolute atheist," he said. He offered his

26. Ibid., 40, 45.
27. Ibid., 272-73.
28. Ibid., 290.
29. D. Macmillan, *The Life of George Matheson* (London: Hodder and Stoughton, 1907), 75.

resignation to the board of his church, but they refused to accept it. They told him that many young ministers went through such experiences and that he would come out of it and would change. Their prediction came true. Matheson came through the storm and his faith never faltered again.[30]

* * *

The beloved hymn "O Love That Wilt Not Let Me Go" was written on the evening of June 6, 1882, by the blind minister, George Matheson. It was the day of his sister's marriage and his family was in Glasgow, so he was alone in his manse. He wrote the hymn in perhaps five minutes. The inspiration for the hymn came from a personal experience that gave Matheson "the most severe mental suffering." He never told anybody what it was, but it was certainly *not* because his fiancé had broken their engagement because he was going blind! Matheson had suffered from poor eyesight since he was eighteen months old, and he himself affirmed that he had never been in love, and certainly he had never been engaged.[31]

* * *

One winter's evening George Matheson went to his church at Innellan to preach and found a very small congregation. He was a bit disappointed because he had worked especially hard on the sermon. He did his best and left the results with the Lord. In that congregation was a visitor, Dr. Currie, who was deeply moved by the message. A few years later when St. Bernard's Church, Edinburgh, was seeking a pastor, Dr. Currie remembered Matheson and suggested his name. As a result, he was called to the church and had a wonderful ministry there.

"Make every occasion a great occasion, for you can never tell when somebody may be taking your measure for a larger place."[32]

F. B. MEYER

The famous evangelist J. Wilbur Chapman was greatly influenced by F. B. Meyer's life and ministry. Chapman and Meyer were guests at D. L. Moody's home, and Chapman asked Meyer if he could explain why his (Chapman's) spiritual experience seemed so intermittent. Sometimes he felt power in his ministry, and at other times he was weak.

Meyer asked Chapman, "Have you ever tried to breathe out three times without breathing in once?"

Chapman tried the experiment and failed.

"Don't you know you must always breathe in before you breathe out, and the one must be in proportion to the other?"[33]

* * *

30. Ibid., 120-24.
31. Ibid., 181, 310-11.
32. Ibid., 224-26.
33. Fullerton, F. B. Meyer, 190.

A girl working in a bookbinding establishment became interested in one of F. B. Meyer's books as she folded the pages. She hid some of the pages in her clothing, took them home, read them that night, and returned them the next day. She read enough to see her need to trust Jesus Christ! When she had saved enough money, she bought a copy of the book. Later, she openly confessed Christ and became a member of a local church.[34]

* * *

F. B. Meyer was scheduled to preach at Chiswick Baptist Chapel, but when he arrived, he discovered the church door shut and locked. Somebody had made a mistake and announced the meeting for the following Thursday, and the pastor's letter to Meyer had arrived too late to prevent Meyer from coming.

In reply to the pastor's letter of apology, Meyer wrote: "Do not trouble, nothing happens by chance, and the rather long walk, in the calm autumn air, did me good."[35]

* * *

F. B. Meyer once confided to his friend F. A. Robinson of Toronto, "I do hope my Father will let the river of my life go flowing fully until the finish. I don't want it to end in a swamp."[36]

When F. B. Meyer was pastoring Christ Church in London, Charles Spurgeon was preaching at Metropolitan Tabernacle, and G. Campbell Morgan was at Westminster Chapel. Meyer said, "I find in my own ministry that supposing I pray for my own little flock, 'God bless me, God fill my pews, God send me a revival,' I miss the blessing; but as I pray for my big brother, Mr. Spurgeon, on the right-hand side of my church, 'God bless him'; or my other big brother, Campbell Morgan, on the other side of my church, 'God bless him'; I am sure to get a blessing without praying for it, for the overflow of their cups fills my little bucket."[37]

* * *

F. B. Meyer was a constant traveler who read the train schedules carefully and sought to make the best use of his time. Taking the train to Hitchin one day, he waited until the last minute to board, and then discovered that the train did not stop at Hitchin! Immediately, he went to his knees in the compartment and committed the matter to the Lord. As the train approached Hitchin, it slowed down and stopped long enough for him to jump off![38]

* * *

Pastor F. A. Robinson of Toronto was to meet Meyer at the Bonaventure station in Montreal, but on his way to the station he decided to go to the Windsor Station instead

34. Ibid., 185.
35. Ibid., 184.
36. Ibid., 168.
37. Ibid., 132.
38. Ibid., 102.

and meet the train on the Canadian Pacific line. He sent a friend to the other station. When Robinson arrived at the Windsor station, he saw Meyer in the crowd! "I knew there had been a bungle and that I had been put into the wrong train," said Meyer, "so I told God about it, and said, 'Please, Father, let Mr. Robinson meet me in Montreal,' and I knew it would be all right. Oh, God is so good, so good, my friend!"[39]

* * *

During one of F. B. Meyer's American tours of ministry, his message so impressed one man that the man followed Meyer to the next city and took a room at the same hotel. He had his meals at the next table and, as it were, "shadowed" Meyer for days. Finally, the man went to Pastor Curtis Lee Laws and reported that F. B. Meyer lived what he preached.[40]

* * *

A miserable-looking woman recognized F. B. Meyer on the train and ventured to share her burden with him. For years she had cared for a crippled daughter who brought great joy to her life. She made tea for her each morning, then left for work, knowing that in the evening the daughter would be there when she arrived home.

But the daughter had died, and the grieving mother was alone and miserable. Home was not "home" anymore.

Meyer gave her wise counsel.

"When you get home and put the key in the door," he said, "say aloud, 'Jesus, I know You are here!' and be ready to greet Him directly when you open the door. And as you light the fire, tell Him what has happened during the day; if anybody has been kind, tell Him; if anybody has been unkind, tell Him, just as you would have told your daughter. At night, stretch out your hand in the darkness and say, 'Jesus, I know You are here!'"

Some months later, Meyer was back in that neighborhood and met the woman again, but he did not recognize her. Her face radiated joy instead of announcing misery. "I did as you told me," she said, "and it has made all the difference in my life, and now I feel I know Him."[41]

* * *

Stanley Smith and C. T. Studd, two of the "Cambridge Seven" who had volunteered to serve in China, ministered at Melbourne Hall at the request of F. B. Meyer, the pastor. Little did the men realize that their message of surrender and spiritual power was exactly what Meyer himself needed. Their message of victory was not new to Meyer, but somehow it had come across with new force.

One night, Meyer wrestled with God about things in his life that needed to be settled. He was unwilling to give them up. "It was a long struggle," he said. "At last, I said

39. Ibid., 170.
40. Ibid., 76.
41. Ibid., 182-83.

feebly, 'Lord, I am willing to be made willing.'" He was able to yield himself completely to the Lord, and that was a turning point in his life and ministry.

He used to illustrate that decision by referring to the "keys of his life." He had given the Lord the bunch of keys, but had kept just one for himself. As the Lord turned to leave, Meyer realized what a mistake he was making; so he gave that last key to Christ, and peace and victory followed.[42]

* * *

As pastor of the Victoria Road Church, Leicester, F. B. Meyer was not at all happy. The church resisted his efforts to win lost souls. They wanted him to maintain a respectable church and not stir things up. Finally he resigned. A number of churches wrote to him to secure his services, and he decided to accept the call from a church in Sheffield. He wrote the letter of acceptance, but it was never mailed.

As he walked to the post office he had no idea that he would meet Arthur Rust, a devoted Christian layman, just outside the office. He showed Rust the letter, and Rust told the pastor that a group of believers had already met and decided to begin a new work in Leicester! They wanted Meyer to be their pastor. The result was the erection of Melbourne Hall and the beginning of an amazing ministry that led to the salvation of many souls.[43]

* * *

F. B. Meyer often ministered at Moody's Northfield Bible Conference, and he always drew great crowds. When G. Campbell Morgan began to preach at Northfield, his stirring Bible studies attracted larger audiences. Meyer confessed to some of his close friends that he was tempted to be envious of Morgan. "The only way I can conquer my feelings," Meyer said, "is to pray for him daily, which I do."[44]

* * *

F. B. Meyer was the first minister to welcome D. L. Moody to England. Moody and Sankey had come to England in 1873 at the invitation of W. Pennefather and Cuthbert Bainbridge, only to discover that both men had died! Moody recalled the name of a Mr. Bennet in York, so he contacted Bennet who, in turn, contacted Meyer, who was then pastoring the Baptist Chapel on Priory Street. Bennet and Meyer sent Moody the message: "Come on!"

Meyer felt drawn to Moody and learned much from him. Moody taught Meyer to be himself, to seek to win men and women to Christ, and to love all of God's people.[45]

* * *

F. B. Meyer preached his first sermon at Tunbridge Wells, when he was visiting an

---

42. Ibid., 57-58.
43. Ibid., 46-49.
44. Ibid., 37.
45. Ibid., 31-32.

uncle. He was only sixteen at the time and his text was Psalm 84:11: "The Lord will give grace and glory."[46]

* * *

When he was sixteen, F. B. Meyer told his mother of his desire to enter the ministry. She reminded him that his decision would involve sacrifice, and she suggested that if it did not work out, he could always make a change.

"Never!" the son replied, looking straight into her face. "That would be putting my hand to the plow and looking back!" [cf. Luke 9:62].[47]

* * *

At sixteen years of age, F. B. Meyer was convinced that God had called him to the ministry. However, he was uncertain about his gifts; he especially doubted his ability to speak. He prayed for God's guidance and opened his Bible. It opened to the first chapter of Jeremiah.

"I saw the seventh verse," he said, "which I had never seen before. With indescribable feelings I read it again and again, and even now never come on it without a thrill of emotion. It was the answer to all my perplexing questionings."

The verse reads: "But the Lord said unto me, Say not, I am a child: for thou shalt go to all that I shall send thee, and whatsoever I command thee thou shalt speak" [KJV].[48]

* * *

Never underestimate the ministry of a child. One Sunday evening young F. B. Meyer was "playing church" in the dining room and something he said in his "sermon" reached the heart of one of the housemaids who turned to Christ.[49]

* * *

Throughout his life, F. B. Meyer maintained a humility that honored Christ. "I am only an ordinary man," he would say. "I have no special gifts. I am no orator, no scholar, no profound thinker. If I have done anything for Christ and my generation, it is because I have given myself entirely to Christ Jesus, and then tried to do whatever He wanted me to do."

He suggested two texts that described his life: the man that "had received two talents came" (Matt. 25:22), and "John did no miracle: but all things that John spake of this man were true" (John 10:41).[50]

* * *

One evening when F. B. Meyer was only five years old, he added this request to his

46. Ibid., 15.
47. Ibid., 14.
48. Ibid., 13.
49. Ibid., 11.
50. Ibid., 10.

regular prayers: "Put Thy Holy Spirit in me to make my heart good, like Jesus Christ was."

The day before he died Meyer was asked by a friend if he had experienced any new vision of the Savior. "No," the saintly man replied, "just the constant interchange between Him and me."[51]

* * *

Near the close of his ministry F. B. Meyer said, "My outlook for the next world is summed up in the words, 'His servants shall serve Him.' If I had a hundred lives, they should be at Christ's disposal. In His service is perfect freedom, and I am satisfied that, for me, the best avenue of service was the ministry of His holy Gospel."[52]

* * *

Charles Spurgeon said of F. B. Meyer, "Meyer preaches as a man who has seen God face to face."[53]

* * *

F. B. Meyer had a special burden for the workingman and a gift for reaching him with the gospel. A bus driver saw Meyer preaching in an open-air meeting and said, "I ain't religious and I can't stomach parsons. But him, well, he's different. There's something human about him. And let me tell you, when you've been listening to him for a bit, a kind of clean feeling takes ahold on you—same as if it were your day off and you'd had a hot bath and got your Sunday clothes on. Take it from me, that bloke's one in a million!"[54] [The original is in Cockney. We have taken the liberty of translating it into English.]

* * *

When F. B. Meyer was pastor of the Victoria Road Baptist Church, Leicester, he discovered that the church was rich, respectable, and spiritually dead. Undaunted, Meyer preached the gospel with fervency and sought to win lost souls. One evening, Meyer was conducting an after-service for inquirers, and a deacon burst into the meeting protesting, "We cannot have this sort of thing here! This is not a Gospel shop!"[55]

* * *

An American preacher described F. B. Meyer as he ministered at Northfield, Massachusetts:

51. Ibid., 9.
52. A. Chester Mann, *F. B. Meyer: Preacher, Teacher, Man of God* (London: George Allen & Unwin, 1929), 165.
53. Ibid., 75.
54. Ibid., 56.
55. Ibid., 42.

The best thing about him is that you almost instantly forget him. His soul singles you out and speaks to your soul. He speaks with marvellous deliberation, but you never think of him being slow. He does not dazzle you with a long array of Scripture passages, but the few he uses are unfolded to you in a new light of the throne. . . . He makes a man know himself as never before. He speaks more like what I suppose our Lord would than any man I have ever heard.[56]

* * *

The next time you hear the word *hooligan,* think of F. B. Meyer. When he was pastoring Christ Church in London he started a special evangelistic effort among the boys in the district. One family, whose name was Hooligan, was known for its supply of children, who seemed to do nothing but cause trouble. When some of the church workers found that their coats had been stolen Meyer said, "We have evidently got ahold of the right sort at last!" But as a result of the church's ministry, many needy boys found Christ.[57]

* * *

Early in his ministry, F. B. Meyer had been a topical preacher. One day Mr. Birrell of Liverpool said to him: "Meyer, that was quite a good sermon you preached, but it was on a topic. There will come a time when you will have spoken on all the topics and the newspapers will have excelled you. Where will you be then? You had better learn to expound the Word of God."[58]

Dwight L. Moody

D. L. Moody called it the biggest blunder of his life.

It happened on October 8, 1871, during a preaching series in Farwell Hall, Chicago. His text was "What then shall I do with Jesus which is called Christ" (Matt. 27:22). At the conclusion of the sermon Moody said he would give the people one week to make up their minds about Jesus. He then turned to Ira Sankey for a solo, and Sankey sang "Today the Saviour Calls."

But by the third verse Sankey's voice was drowned out by the noise outside the hall. The great Chicago fire had begun, and the flames were even then sweeping toward the Hall. The clanging of the fire bells and the noise of the engines made it impossible to continue the meeting.

In the years that followed, Moody wished that he had called for an immediate decision for Christ.[59]

* * *

56. M. Jennie Street, *F. B. Meyer: His Life and Work* (Philadelphia: American Baptist Publication Society, 1902), 151.
57. Ibid., 98.
58. Fullerton, *F. B. Meyer*, 201.
59. Richard K. Curtis, *They Called Him Mister Moody* (New York: Doubleday, 1962), 150.

When the Chicago fire crossed the river, D. L. Moody and his wife knew they would have to flee. They bundled up their two children and tried to salvage whatever valuables they could. Mrs. Moody took her husband's portrait from the parlor wall and gave it to him to carry. He refused.

"Take my own picture!" he argued. "Well, that would be amusing! Suppose I am met on the street by friends . . . and they say, 'Hello, Moody, glad you have escaped. What's that you have saved and cling to so affectionately?' Wouldn't it sound well to reply, 'Oh, I've got my own portrait.'"

His wife ripped it out of the frame, rolled it up, and carried it herself while her husband pushed the baby carriage.[60]

* * *

After the great Chicago Fire, a friend approached D. L. Moody and said, "I hear you lost everything."

"Well, you understand it wrong," the evangelist replied.

"How much have you left?"

"I can't tell you; I have a good deal more left than I lost," said Moody.

"You can't tell how much you have?" the man asked.

"No."

"I didn't know you were ever that rich."

"I suppose you didn't!"

"What do you mean?" the perplexed friend inquired.

Moody opened his Bible to Revelation 21:7: "He that overcometh shall inherit all things; and I will be his God."[61]

* * *

After the Chicago fire, D. L. Moody went to the East Coast to rest and reflect. He felt a sterility in his ministry and needed a new touch from God. While he was conducting Bible readings in Brooklyn, an event took place that led to one of the great spiritual experiences in Moody's life.

Douglas Russell, a British evangelist friend, visited the meetings and gave a study on Galatians 4. He pointed out that whereas all Christians were born of the Spirit, not all Christians were filled with the Spirit. The thought struck Moody, who said, "I never saw that before! Been troubled about that for years."

The next day, Moody was walking down Wall Street, meditating on this truth, when God met him in a special way. Moody said:

"Oh, what a day! I cannot describe it; I seldom refer to it; it is almost too sacred an experience to name. . . . I can only say that God revealed Himself to me, and I had such an experience of His love that I had to ask Him to stay His hand."

The new power that came to the evangelist lit a flame in the meetings, and more than one hundred sinners found Christ.[62]

60. Ibid., 152-53.
61. Ibid., 198.
62. Ibid., 155-56.

* * *

It was in 1873, in Dublin, that D. L. Moody heard British evangelist Henry Varley utter those life-changing words: "The world has yet to see what God can do with and for and through and in a man who is fully and wholly consecrated to Him."

It was after an all-night prayer meeting in Dublin, at the home of Henry Bewley. Varley did not even remember making the statement when Moody reminded him of it a year later.

"As I crossed the wide Atlantic," Moody said, "the boards of the deck . . . were engraved with them, and when I reached Chicago, the very paving stones seemed marked with them." The result: Moody decided he was involved in too many ministries to be effective and therefore began to concentrate on evangelism.[63]

* * *

After the 1873 Glasgow campaign, D. L. Moody and Ira Sankey took the train to Edinburgh for a three-day meeting. Sankey was reading the paper, looking for some news from America; but all he found that interested him was a religious poem in the corner of a page of advertising. He read it to Moody who, absorbed in a letter from home, heard nothing.

At the noon meeting a day or two later Moody spoke on the "The Good Shepherd," and then asked Sankey to close with an appropriate song. All the singer could think of was the poem on the parable of the lost sheep, so he put the newspaper clipping on the organ, lifted a silent prayer, struck an *A*-flat, and began to sing.

"Note by note the tune was given," Sankey wrote in later years. "As the singing ceased a great sigh seemed to go up from the meeting, and I knew that the song had reached the hearts of my Scotch audience."

Moody was greatly stirred by the song and asked Sankey where he had found it. "I never heard the like of it in my life!" he said. Sankey explained that it was the poem he had read to Moody from the newspaper during their train ride.[64]

* * *

D. L. Moody was never ordained. He was a layman who was wholly yielded to Christ, and preaching and winning souls was "important business" to him. Those who have analyzed his preaching tell us that his sermons averaged about half-an-hour in length. He used short sentences, averaging about seventeen words, and short words, 80 percent of them monosyllables. He used few adjectives and adverbs, but majored on verbs with a lot of action. He used the language of the marketplace and sought to reach the common man.

"We have too many orators," he said. "I am tired and sick of your 'silver-tongued orators.' I used to mourn because I couldn't be an orator. I thought, *Oh, if I could only have the gift of speech like some men.*"[65]

63. Ibid., 159-61.
64. Ibid., 184-85.
65. Ibid., 192.

* * *

It was in 1875, during Moody's great British campaign, that former Prime Minister William Gladstone took Matthew Arnold, the famous writer and critic, to hear D. L. Moody preach. After the meeting, Gladstone said: "I thank God that I have lived to see the day when He should bless His church on earth by the gift of a man able to preach the Gospel of Christ as we have heard it preached this afternoon!"

The intellectual Arnold replied, "Mr. Gladstone, I would give all I possess if I could only believe it!"[66]

* * *

In 1884 D. L. Moody returned to Britain, and one day was involved with the famous cricketer C. T. Studd in a meeting at a theater. A young London intern was attracted to the meeting, but when he walked in he found that a man was leading in prayer and apparently never going to finish it. But as the young doctor arose to leave, he heard an American voice say, "Let us sing a hymn while one brother finishes his prayer!" It was Moody. The doctor was so impressed that he stayed for the rest of the service and then returned for another meeting. As a result, the doctor, Wilfred Grenfell, gave his heart and life to Christ, and his missionary work in Labrador earned him knighthood from King George V.[67]

* * *

One of the special features of the 1893 Columbian Exposition in Chicago was the Parliament of Religions. D. L. Moody decided that he would use the world's fair and the parliament as an opportunity to proclaim Christ. His more conservative friends criticized him for "joining" with other religions, especially those that denied Christ; but Moody was persistent.

"I am not going to attack it," Moody explained. "I am going to make Jesus Christ so attractive . . . that men will turn to Him."

His one concern was to reach the lost, and he would not allow man-made barriers to hinder him. He said: "I'll preach Christ crucified anywhere I can find lost men, on the street, in the open air, in tents or in saloons, in beer gardens or in missions, in theaters or halls, in churches or in the Parliament of Religions."[68]

* * *

At Northfield, Massachusetts, D. L. Moody founded several schools for the training of underprivileged children. Whenever students arrived at the train station, if Moody was in town, he would take his buggy and meet them. One rainy day a man and two women arrived at the station and looked around for someone to take them to the hotel. Seeing a man in a buggy, the visitor insisted that he drive them to the hotel. "I'm waiting for some seminary girls," Moody explained.

66. Ibid., 211.
67. Ibid., 220-21.
68. Ibid., 275.

The visitor was offended. "These girls are not the only people to be served!" he said. "Now, you just take us right up to the hotel!"

Meekly the driver obeyed, left them at the hotel, and drove off before he could be paid.

"Who was that driver?" the visitor asked the bellboy.

"Mr. D. L. Moody," the boy replied.

The visitor was shocked, because he was at Northfield to ask Moody to take his daughter into the school. The next day the man apologized, and Moody had a great deal of fun over it.[69]

*   *   *

A man once testified in one of D. L. Moody's meetings that he had lived "on the Mount of Transfiguration" for five years.

"How many souls did you lead to Christ last year?" Moody bluntly asked him.

"Well," the man hesitated, "I don't know."

"Have you saved any?" Moody persisted.

"I don't know that I have," the man admitted.

"Well," said Moody, "we don't want that kind of mountaintop experience. When a man gets up so high that he cannot reach down and save poor sinners, there is something wrong."[70]

*   *   *

The children that D. L. Moody recruited for his Chicago Sunday school were among some of the worst characters in the city, boys with nicknames like "Red Eye," "Madden the Butcher," "Rag Breeches Cadet," and the ringleader of the gang, "Butcher" Kilroy. Moody never condescended to them, always treated them with firmness and love, and sought to win them to Christ. When "Butcher" Kilroy first attended the school, he was dressed like a beggar: a man's old overcoat around his body, papers around his legs, and a big pair of shoes on his feet. Moody treated him as though he were the best-dressed child in the school. The gang of rough boys was known as "Moody's Bodyguard." He promised them each a new suit if they faithfully attended Sunday school, and twelve of the fourteen boys earned their suits.

Moody had a photographer take "before and after" shots, which were labeled: "Will it pay?" and "It does pay!"[71]

*   *   *

D. L. Moody had a keen memory for names and faces. If one of his children was missing from Sunday school, he knew it, and he would do everything possible to find out why. One day he saw an absentee coming down the street, so the took off after her. She ran down the sidewalk, across the street, and through an alley into a saloon, up the stairs to a back apartment, into the bedroom, and then dived under the bed. Moody went

69. Ibid., 294.
70. Ibid., 316.
71. Ibid., 67-68.

after her, and just as he was claiming his prize, the mother showed up.

Panting from the exertion, Moody simply explained, "I'm Moody." He said that he had missed the girl and would be happy if all the family could come to the services. Within a few weeks he had every child in the family in his school.[72]

* * *

A man named Stillson was one of D. L. Moody's assistants in his mission Sunday school ministry in Chicago. Stillson noted that Moody was not really preparing his Sunday school addresses. He would have prayer with the leaders, choose a Bible verse "to depart from," and tell stories from his previous week's experiences in witnessing and visiting.

"Moody," Stillson told him one day, "if you want to draw wine out of a cask . . . put some in. You are all the time talking, and you ought to begin to study."

Stillson lined up some books for Moody to read, but when Stillson left Chicago and returned to his Rochester, New York home, the training process ceased. Moody was a great learner, but he learned more from life than from books.[73]

* * *

While making a visit in a home, D. L. Moody persuaded the wife to get rid of her husband's whiskey. In fact, Moody emptied the jug in the street! When he returned the next afternoon to take the children to North Market Mission Hall, he found himself confronting several irate men who threatened to beat him.

"See here now, my men," said Moody, "if you are going to whip me for spilling the whiskey, you might at least give me time to say my prayers." The men thought that his praying would just add more fun to the event, so Moody knelt down to pray. He prayed as they had never heard a man pray before, and the longer he prayed, the more their hearts softened. When he arose from his knees, he found the men giving him their hands and saying that he was not such a bad fellow after all! Safely delivered, Moody was soon marching the children to the mission![74]

* * *

The Roman Catholic children were breaking the windows in D. L. Moody's Mission Hall, so Moody decided to pay a visit to the bishop of Chicago, James Duggan. After hearing Moody's appeal, the bishop promised to do what he could to restrain the children. Then Moody introduced a new subject: his own ministry to the Roman Catholics.

"I often come across sick people who are Roman Catholics. I should be glad to pray with them and relieve them, but they are so suspicious of me that they will not allow me to come near them. Now, Bishop, won't you give me a good word to those people; it will help amazingly in my work."

The bishop replied that Moody, of course, would have to join the Roman Catholic

72. Ibid., 68-69.
73. Ibid., 70.
74. Ibid., 74-75.

church to get any kind of recommendation. But Moody argued that such a move would then hinder his work among the Protestants, but the bishop said it would not.

"What?" said Moody. "Do you mean that I could go to the noon prayer meetings, and pray with all kinds of Christian people . . . just as I do now?"

The bishop said that he could. At that point Moody asked the bishop to pray for him, and then Moody prayed for the bishop! One writer claimed that in another ten minutes, Moody would have had the bishop teaching in his Sunday school! In fact, the North Side Roman Catholics called him "Father Moody."[75]

* * *

One of D. L. Moody's Sunday school teachers was absent one Sunday, and Moody visited him to discover the problem. The man explained that his doctor had told him he had but a short time to live because he was bleeding in his lungs, and the man was planning to go home to his widowed mother to die. However, his great concern was not himself, but rather the spiritual condition of the children in his class.

Moody offered to go with the man to visit each child. In spite of his physical weakness, the teacher would call on each pupil and then with tears implore him to come to Christ. At the close of ten days of visiting, Moody and the teacher saw the last child yield to Christ. The entire class, now born again, met at the railroad station to see the dying teacher off the next day.

Moody called the experience "the most memorable I have ever known," because it increased his personal concern for lost souls.[76]

* * *

While greeting people as they left the evening service at North Market Hall, Moody was approached by a man who deliberately insulted him. Moody pushed the man away only to send him tumbling down the stairs to the lower vestibule.

When Moody went to the platform to start the second service, he said: "Friends, before beginning tonight, I want to confess that I yielded just now to my temper, out in the hall, and I have done wrong. . . . If that man is present here, . . . I want to ask his forgiveness, and God's. Let us pray."[77]

* * *

D. L. Moody's businesslike, New England honesty showed up in strange ways.

A man who was a constant troublemaker in Moody's Chicago ministry approached the evangelist to shake his hand. Moody hesitated, and then shook the man's hand, saying to him, "I suppose if Jesus Christ could eat the Last Supper with Judas Iscariot, I ought to shake hands with you."[78]

* * *

75. Ibid., 76-77.
76. Ibid., 79-80.
77. Ibid., 81.
78. Ibid.

D. L. Moody was never afraid to do something new or to risk ridicule from people, even other Christians.

"There's a class," he said, "very much afraid of being called 'peculiar.' They hesitate to work for Christ because they will be considered peculiar. You will notice that when God has some work to do, He generally calls peculiar people to do it."

In Chicago, Moody was called "Crazy Moody." Even the newspapers printed stories and jokes about him.[79]

* * *

D. L. Moody made an covenant with God that he would witness for Christ to at least one person each day. One night, about ten o'clock, he realized that he had not yet witnessed; so he went out in to the street and spoke to a man standing by a lamppost, asking him, "Are you a Christian?"

The man flew into a violent rage and threatened to knock Moody into the gutter. Later, that same man went to an elder in the church and complained that Moody was "doing more harm in Chicago than ten men were doing good." The elder begged Moody to temper his zeal with knowledge.

Three months later, Moody was awakened at the YMCA by a man knocking at the door. It was the man he had witnessed to. "I want to talk to you about my soul," he said to Moody. He apologized for the way he had treated Moody and said that he had had no peace ever since that night on Lake Street when Moody witnessed to him. Moody led the man to Christ and he became a zealous worker in the Sunday school.[80]

* * *

On April 25, 1855, Edward Kimball led young Dwight L. Moody to faith in Christ in the back of Samuel Holton's shoe store in Boston where Moody was employed. (Holton was Moody's uncle.)

Kimball was Moody's Sunday school teacher at the Mount Vernon Church and he said, "I have seen few persons whose minds were spiritually darker than was his when he came into my . . . class."

Kimball admitted that he himself was hesitant about approaching young Moody concerning his soul. He walked past the store, stopped, and then "determined to make a dash for it and have it over at once." The Spirit was working, Moody was ready and he trusted Christ.

"I was in a new world," Moody said in later years when he told the story of his conversion. "The next morning the sun shone brighter and the birds sang sweeter, . . . the old elms waved their branches for joy, and all Nature was at peace. . . . It was the most delicious joy that I'd ever known."[81]

* * *

Young D. L. Moody did not have an easy time becoming a member of the Mount

79. Ibid., 82.
80. Ibid., 90-91.
81. Ibid., 51-53.

Vernon Church in Boston. He knew he was converted, but he was unable to express his thoughts the way the seasoned saints expected. So zealous was he in the witnessing of his faith that one of the deacons took him aside and said, "Young man, you can serve the Lord better by keeping still."

Edward Kimball, who had led Moody to Christ, said that the membership committee had seldom met an applicant for membership who was more unlikely to be a good member and a useful worker than D. L. Moody. How wrong they were! After a year of special preparation, Moody was finally admitted into the membership of the church. [82]

* * *

D. L. Moody was quite frank with people when they spoke publicly and were out of line. After a prayer meeting, Moody said to a man, "You ought not to have said what you did tonight, and besides, your record is all bad, and you ought not to take part at all."

"Sir, you hurt my feelings," the man replied.

"Well," Moody returned, "you hurt mine. I have feelings as well as you, and you hurt the feelings of five hundred other people besides." [83]

* * *

As a young Christian in Chicago, Moody wanted to serve God. He rented five pews at the Plymouth Congregational Church and filled them with young men each Sunday, but he wanted to do more. He happened to stop in a little mission on North Wells Street where he asked the superintendent if he could teach a Sunday school class. The man admitted that he already had more teachers than scholars (there were only sixteen students in the entire school). But if Moody rounded up his own class, he would be allowed to teach it. The next Sunday, Moody showed up with eighteen ragged and dirty boys, and more than doubled the Sunday school! "That was the happiest day I have ever known," said Moody. "I had found out what my mission was." [84]

* * *

Mr. and Mrs. Moody often had guests in their Chicago home. One evening, after a very demanding day, Moody asked a visiting Christian to lead in family devotions. The man waxed eloquent as he expounded the symbolism in a difficult chapter of the Bible. Then he prayed at great length. When the worship was over, Mrs. Moody and the guest got up from their knees, but Moody remained bowed in prayer. The guest thought that he was praying, but Mrs. Moody soon detected that her husband was—asleep. [85]

* * *

One New Year's day, Moody took the deacons of his Illinois Street Independent

82. Ibid., 55-57.
83. Ibid., 56.
84. Ibid., 66.
85. Ibid., 112-13.

Church on a marathon visitation ministry. They made 200 calls in one day! The problem was that the deacons could not keep up with Moody; and many of them "fell aside" as the day progressed.

Moody would rush up the stairs to an apartment and introduce himself and the deacons with him. Then he would quickly inquire of the family's spiritual state and whatever material needs they had. He would then pray for the family and be off to the next house. The entire visit would consume less than two minutes.

Moody believed in keeping in contact with his people. One day, he made five visits and reported, "In every home I found a broken heart."[86]

* * *

D. L. Moody received an invitation to attend the grand opening of a "magnificent pool hall" on the west side of Chicago. Before the opening, Moody called on the owners to see if he could bring a friend with him. Skeptical of Moody, the partners wanted to know who his "friend" was, but he refused to name him. "Well, I'll ask him to forgive you."

"We don't want any praying!" the men replied.

"You've given me an invitation, and I am coming," said Moody.

The men tried to argue with Moody, but he would not give in. Finally, he suggested that perhaps he should pray right then and there. Anxious to get rid of their problem, the partners agreed. Moody went to his knees and asked God to "bless their souls and . . . break their business to pieces."

Within a few months, their business was on the rocks.[87]

* * *

At a meeting of the London (England) Sunday School Union, the vice-chairman introduced D. L. Moody as "their American cousin, the Rev. Mr. Moody of Chicago."

Moody responded by saying: "The vice-chairman has made two mistakes. To begin with, I'm not 'the Reverend' Mr. Moody at all. I'm plain Dwight L. Moody, a Sabbath school worker. And then I'm not your 'American cousin.' By the grace of God I'm your brother who is interested with you in our Father's work for His children."[88]

* * *

D. L. Moody not only won sinners to Christ, but he won Christians for service. He was traveling through rural Indiana with another Christian layman, and they passed a schoolhouse. "Do they ever hold religious meetings in that schoolhouse?" he asked a woman whose house was next door. She said that there had been no meetings there.

"Well, tell all your neighbors there will be prayer meetings in that schoolhouse every night next week!" Moody said.

Then Moody contacted the teacher of the school and asked that the announcement be sent home with all of the students. Moody's friend knew that Moody was booked up for

86. Ibid., 118-19.
87. Ibid., 119-20.
88. Ibid., 131.

that entire week, so he casually asked, "Who is going to conduct these meetings?"

"You are!" Moody replied.

"I?" the man responded, aghast. "I never did such a thing in my life!"

"It's time you had, then," said the evangelist. "I have made the appointment, and you will have to keep it."

The man did, and the result was another moving of God that brought souls to Christ.[89]

*   *   *

D. L. Moody first met Ira Sankey at a YMCA convention in Indianapolis in June 1870. It was at a prayer meeting in a Baptist church at six in the morning. Sankey had arrived late and discovered a man was leading in an interminable prayer. A friend whispered to Sankey, "The singing here has been abominable. I wish you would start up something when that man stops praying—if he ever does."

The man finally stopped and immediately Sankey started singing "There Is A Fountain Filled with Blood." The rest of the crowd, relieved at a new voice and a change of pace, enthusiastically joined in. Afterward, the friend introduced Sankey to Moody who immediately asked him a number of personal questions about himself, his job, his family, and his work.

Moody then announced that Sankey would have to give up his job to come to Chicago and help him in his ministry!

Sankey argued. After all, he had a job, a wife and two small children, and was working for the government. He could not come.

"You must," Moody replied. "I have been looking for you for the last eight years."

The next day, Sankey got word that Moody wanted to meet him at a certain street corner at six that evening. When Sankey arrived, Moody put him on a soap box and told him to sing. The song gathered a large crowd of working men and gave Moody a congregation for the preaching of the gospel.[90]

*   *   *

It was the converted English ex-prizefighter, Harry Moorehouse, who taught Moody to preach *from* the Bible, not *about* the Bible, and to emphasize the love of God to sinners. Moody had met Moorehouse in Dublin and casually invited him to preach at his church, should he ever be in Chicago. One day, Moody received word that Moorehouse was on his way! He arranged for him to preach (Moody was to be out of the city anyway), and when Moody returned, he discovered that the young evangelist was making a great impact on the people. He had used the same text (John 3:16) for every sermon!

Rather skeptical, Moody went to the meetings and saw that the church was packed and the people were carrying Bibles. Moorehouse told them to bring their Bibles so they could check up on the preacher! He announced John 3:16 as his text, and then led the people through the Bible, from Genesis to Revelation, and showed them the love of God for sinners.

89. Ibid., 146-47.
90. Ibid., 142-45.

Moody called this experience his "second conversion." Up to then, he had preached God's hatred for sinners and His terrible wrath; but now he saw that his message was "God is love." "This heart of mine began to thaw out," he said. "I could not hold back the tears." Using his concordance, he studied *love* in the Bible. (Moorehouse also taught him topical Bible study and introduced him to *Cruden's Concordance*.) "I got full of it. It ran out my fingers," Moody said. He decided to stop trying to frighten men into the kingdom of God, but instead to woo them with God's love.[91]

* * *

"Some day," D.L. Moody used to say, "you will read in the papers that D. L. Moody of East Northfield is dead. Don't believe a word of it! At that moment I shall be more alive than I am now!"

He preached his last sermon in Kansas City on November 23, 1899, from the text Luke 14:18: "And they all with one consent began to make excuse."

When he gave the invitation, fifty stood to their feet and went across the street into the inquiry room.

He was too ill to continue the Kansas City campaign, so he took the train back to Northfield. On Friday, December 22, he went "home."

Five years before his homegoing Moody had said, "If it can be said, faithfully said, over my grave, 'Moody has done what he could,' that will be the most glorious epitaph." Instead, 1 John 2:17 was chosen: "He that doeth the will of God abideth forever."[92]

G. CAMPBELL MORGAN

During World War I, when Dr. G. Campbell Morgan was pastor of Westminster Chapel in London, he often met with important government people who wanted spiritual counsel and encouragement. Sometimes he attended "official meetings" for key pastors and government leaders. In June 1914 Morgan first met Winston Churchill.

"You should try flying, Dr. Morgan," said Churchill at the dinner table. "Have you ever been up?"

"No," replied Morgan, "and I never expect to until I go up for the last time."

Churchill was ready with his reply. "But I shall have the advantage over you," he said, "for I shall have had more practice!"[93]

* * *

While he always kept abreast of the activities of the church, Campbell Morgan detested committee work. He told a friend, "I would prefer to preach three sermons a day rather than spend half an hour at a deacon's meeting discussing who ought to keep the keys to the door."[94]

91. Ibid., 132-35.
92. Ibid., 332-34.
93. Jill Morgan, *A Man of the Word* (Grand Rapids: Baker, 1972), 205.
94. Ibid., 198.

* * *

People often asked Campbell Morgan for the "secret" of his effective Bible-teaching ministry, and his answer was always, "Work—hard work, and again, work!" He was up early in the morning studying God's Word, even when he was involved in a difficult itinerant ministry. He rose early and retired late. He did not permit minor demands to keep him from the study. He devoted his mornings to the study of the Word and permitted no one to interrupt him until lunchtime. While not every pastor or missionary can afford the luxury of such a schedule, it is a worthwhile goal to strive for![95]

* * *

While ministering at Northfield, Morgan was riding in D. L. Moody's buggy with the evangelist holding the reins. Suddenly Moody said, "What is character anyhow?"

Morgan knew that Moody had a thought he wanted to share so he said, "Well, what is it?"

Moody replied, "Character is what a man is in the dark."[96]

* * *

During the early years of his pastoral ministry Campbell Morgan was uneasy about his own lack of academic training. A self-taught student of the Bible, Morgan attended neither college nor seminary.

When he became pastor of Westminster Road Congregational Church in Birmingham, England, Morgan visited the leading pastor of that city, R. W. Dale of Carr's Lane Church. He told Dale that he felt his (Morgan's) qualifications were inadequate for the ministry, and Dale reassured him by saying: "Never say that you are untrained. God has many ways of training men. I pray that you may have much joy in His service."[97]

* * *

So popular and effective was Campbell Morgan's ministry that he was given all kinds of offers from many different places and people. John Wanamaker, the great merchant of Philadelphia, offered to build Morgan a million dollar church if he would become its pastor. Morgan turned him down, something the wealthy Wanamaker was not accustomed to in his dealings with people. "I am God's man," said Morgan. "If I did that I would become John Wanamaker's man."[98]

* * *

On May 2, 1888, young Campbell Morgan showed up at the Lichfield Road Church, Birmingham, England, where he was to preach a trial sermon in preparation for entering the Methodist ministry. There were but a few people in the large auditorium and the atmosphere was certainly not conducive to the preaching of a stirring message.

95. Ibid., 105, 325.
96. Ibid., 93.
97. Ibid., 77-78.
98. Ibid., 71.

As a consequence, Morgan preached poorly and was rejected.

He sent a one-word wire to his father, who was also a minister: "Rejected!" He wrote in his diary, "Very dark everything seems. Still, He knoweth best." Morgan's father wired back: "Rejected on earth. Accepted in heaven."

In later years, Morgan said: "God said to me, in the weeks of loneliness and darkness that followed, 'I want you to cease making plans for yourself, and let Me plan your life.'"

Morgan surrendered to God's leading and finally entered the Congregationalist ministry. He became one of the greatest preachers of his day, and his books still teach the Word to God's people.[99]

* * *

Before entering the ministry, Morgan taught at a private school that prepared Jewish boys for their Barmitzvah. He always had a special love for the Jewish people. Years later, when Morgan lived in Athens, Georgia, he had many friends among the orthodox Jews of the city. Sometimes they came to hear him preach. One Jewish visitor said to one of Morgan's sons, "If I believed what you believe, I would not rest till I had told everyone about it!"[100]

* * *

G. Campbell Morgan had already enjoyed some success as a preacher by the time he was nineteen years old. But then he was attacked by doubts about the Bible. The writings of various scientists and agnostics disturbed him (e.g., Charles Darwin, John Tyndall, Thomas Huxley, and Herbert Spencer). As he read their books and listened to debates, Morgan became more and more perplexed.

What did he do? He cancelled all preaching engagements, put all the books in a cupboard and locked the door, and went to the bookstore and bought a new Bible. He said to himself, "I am no longer sure that this is what my father claims it to be—the Word of God. But of this I *am* sure. If it *be* the Word of God, and if I come to it with an unprejudiced and open mind, it will bring assurance to my soul of itself."

The result? "That Bible *found* me!" said Morgan.

That new assurance in 1883 gave him the motivation for his preaching and teaching ministry. He devoted himself to the study and preaching of God's Word.[101]

* * *

G. Campbell Morgan was known as "the prince of expositors." Even as a teenager, he knew he had a gift for preaching and could exert a strong influence over his listeners. He might have been lost to the cause of Christ were it not for a friend, David Smith, with whom Morgan often ministered in cottage meetings.

Morgan spoke at a meeting in Birdlip, using Isaiah 51:6 as his text. During the six-

99. Ibid., 57-60; John Harries, *G. Campbell Morgan: The Man and His Ministry* (New York: Revell, 1930), 35-36.
100. Morgan, *Man of the Word,* 43.
101. Ibid., 39-40.

mile walk home, Smith gently spoke to Morgan about his pride in using preaching opportunities as occasions to display his abilities. At first Morgan resented the loving criticism, but then he gave in.

Later, Morgan and Smith returned to the same cottage for a meeting, and Morgan spoke on Matthew 11:28-30. He was so overwhelmed that he broke down and could not finish the sermon; but as a result of his ministry there, two or three persons present trusted Christ.[102]

*   *   *

G. Campbell Morgan was conducting an evangelistic mission in one of the Midlands towns of England, and a ragpicker came into the inquiry room, a man [Morgan said] who had "grown hoary in the service of sin and Satan." Morgan knelt by him and showed him the Savior in the Word.

Then, someone touched Morgan's shoulder and asked if he would speak with another man who had come into the place of prayer. It turned out it was the mayor of the town! The mayor just a few weeks before had sentenced the ragpicker to a month of hard labor. Morgan led the mayor to faith in Christ, and when the man finished praying, he arose and went over to the ragpicker.

"Well, the last time we met, it was not *here*," the mayor said.

When the ragpicker discovered it was the mayor, he said, "No, and we never *shall* meet where we met last time, thank God!"

Morgan said that the same gospel message was sufficient for both men.[103]

*   *   *

Early in his ministry, when he was pastor of the Congregational Church at Rugeley, Campbell Morgan studied hard and preached often. He was discovering and developing the gift of Bible exposition that later made him the prince of expositors. His preaching made him popular.

One evening, as he sat in his study, he felt God saying to him, "What are you going to be, a preacher or My messenger?" As Morgan pondered the question, he realized that his desire to become "a great preacher" was hindering his work. For several hours, Morgan sat there struggling with God's call and human ambition. Finally he said, "Thy messenger, my Master—Thine!"

He took the precious outlines of his sermons, messages that he was proud of, and laid them in the fireplace where they burned to ashes. That was when the victory was won. As the outlines were burning, Morgan prayed: "If Thou wilt give me Thy words to speak, I will utter them from this day forward, adding nothing to them, taking naught away. Thine whole counsel I will declare, so help me God!"[104]

*   *   *

A Presbyterian deacon once asked one of Campbell Morgan's grandsons if he

102. Ibid., 37-38.
103. Harries, *G. Campbell Morgan*, 107.
104. Ibid., 45-46.

intended to become a preacher like his grandfather, his father, and his uncles. (All of Morgan's four sons went into the ministry.)

"No, sir!" said the lad. "I'm going to work!"[105]

* * *

A group of speakers was gathered around Will Moody's table at Northfield, all of them participants in the Northfield summer conference founded by D. L. Moody. Will Moody passed a daily devotional book around the table and suggested that each one look up his birth date and read the text assigned. F. B. Meyer read his, J. Stuart Holden read his, but Campbell Morgan merely opened to the page, closed the book, and passed it on.

At this point, it must be explained that Morgan was a tall, thin man at that time, very angular in appearance.

Will Moody was interested to know why Morgan had refused to read the verse, so he looked up "December 9" and read the text: "Can these dry bones live?" (Ezek. 37:3).[106]

ORIGEN

Origen (A.D. 185-154) was born into a godly home, and his father was martyred when Origen was about seventeen. The lad wanted to be martyred as well, and his mother hid his clothes so he would not foolishly tempt the enemy. He grew up to become one of the greatest of the Greek Fathers in the church and a theologian of great repute.

JOSEPH PARKER

The story has been told about several famous preachers, but it actually happened to Joseph Parker, minister of the City Temple in London.

An old lady waited on Parker in his vestry after a service to thank him for the help she received from his sermons.

"You do throw such wonderful light on the Bible, doctor," she said. "Do you know that until this morning, I had always thought that Sodom and Gomorrah were man and wife?"[107]

* * *

When the Woolrich Tabernacle in England was to be dedicated, the officers invited three "distinguished and famous ministers" to speak on three successive Wednesday evenings.

Joseph Parker was the first. After the service, the church treasurer asked Parker what his fee was. The genial preacher said, "Oh, just give me enough to pay my expenses!"

---

105. Morgan, 390.
106. Ibid., 258.
107. Porritt, *The Best I Remember*, 68.

The treasurer asked if a guinea would suffice (worth about $3.00 in American currency) and Parker said, "Amply, amply."

When the treasurer asked each of the next two speakers the same question, each one replied, "Well, you had Joseph Parker here, so just give me whatever amount you gave him." They were expecting, of course, to receive a large honorarium, but received instead only a guinea![108]

* * *

Joseph Parker stepped into the pulpit of the City Temple in London for his Thursday sermon and announced that he was under some trepidation that day because of a letter he had received. It seemed that a gentleman wrote to tell Parker that he would be in the congregation that day for the express purpose of making a philosophical analysis of the sermon.

After a long pause, Parker said, "I may add that my trepidation is somewhat mitigated by the fact that the gentleman spells philosophical with an *f*."[109]

POLYCARP

Polycarp (A.D. c. 70-155) was bishop of Smyrna and a godly man. He had known the apostle John personally. When he was urged by the Roman proconsul to renounce Christ, Polycarp said: "Eighty and six years have I served Him, and He never did me any injury. How then can I blaspheme my King and my Savior?"

"I have respect for your age," said the official. "Simply say, 'Away with the atheists!' and be set free." The aged Polycarp pointed to the pagan crowd and said, "Away with the atheists!"

He was burned at the stake and gave joyful testimony of his faith in Jesus Christ.

WILLIAM SANGSTER

When William Sangster began to preach in his student days, he had somewhat of a London "cockney" accent, which he worked hard to overcome. He often practiced in his room at college, repeating phrases over and over: "Is it raining? Noooo—is it raining? Noooo!"

One day he repeated "Who shall deliver me from the body of this death?" so often that the student in the adjoining room came to the door and asked, "Will *I* do?"[110]

* * *

William Sangster visited a young girl in the hospital who was going blind. "God is going to take my sight away," she told the pastor.

After a long pause, Sangster said, "Don't let Him, Jessie. Give it to Him. Try to pray

108. Jones, *Three Score Years and Ten*, 65-66.
109. Porritt, *The Best I Remember*, 70.
110. Paul Sangster, *Dr. Sangster* (London: Epworth, 1962), 54.

this prayer: 'Father, if for any reason I must lose my sight, help me to give it to you.'"

When Jessie returned to church she had a guidedog with her. The dog used to sleep during the first twenty minutes of the sermon and then wake up and howl. When it saw that its howling did not silence the preacher, it went back to sleep![111]

* * *

Early in his ministry William Sangster experienced a spiritual crisis and severe depression. He carefully examined his own heart and life, listing his failures and noting what he must do to obtain victory.

"Pray. Pray. Pray. The secret is in prayer," he wrote. "Strive after holiness like an athlete prepares for a race. The secret is in prayer."[112]

* * *

When he pastored the Methodist church in Scarborough, William Sangster had an eccentric member who tried to be a zealous Christian. Unfortunately, the man was mentally deficient and usually did the wrong thing.

While working as a barber the man lathered up a customer for a shave, came at him with the poised razor, and asked, "Are you prepared to meet your God?" The frightened man fled with the lather on his face![113]

* * *

During the years of World War II William Sangster pastored Westminster Central Hall in London, which seated more than 3,000 people. It was regularly nearly full and on special days was filled to capacity.

One Easter day a rather "self-important" lady arrived at Central Hall about five minutes before the service was to begin. She asked for a seat at the end of a row (so she could depart quickly!) and was told that there were no such seats available!

"If that's the way you treat visitors," she said in an indignant voice, "no wonder the churches are empty!"[114]

* * *

William Sangster preached and practiced the philosophy "remember to forget." He was often criticized, but he tried to "remember to forget" and go right on with his work.

His wife saw him completing the addressing of his Christmas cards and was astonished at one of the addresses. "Surely you are not sending a greeting to *him*!" his wife remarked, and then she started to remind Sangster of what the man had done to him eighteen months before.

Sangster recalled what the man had done, but he also recalled that at that time, he had

111. Ibid., 88.
112. Ibid., 91.
113. Ibid., 107.
114. Ibid., 140.

resolved to "remember to forget." And he actually had forgotten!

"I posted the card," said Sangster.[115]

* * *

During World War II the attendant at St. James's Park in London dutifully asked the public to leave each evening and then, just as dutifully, locked the gates. But there was no fence around the park! All the metal had been conscripted for the war effort. However, the man did his job faithfully and let nothing stop him![116]

* * *

During World War II William Sangster ministered in air raid shelters as did many other London ministers. One evening during a heavy raid a man came into the shelter, and seeing Sangster's clerical garb, bitterly began to attack life and faith. He said that the war had made him an atheist.

Sangster asked him, "If you are an atheist, you won't read the Bible, will you?" The man said that he would not. Sangster then asked him about prayer, attending church, and partaking in the Holy Communion; the man affirmed that he would have nothing to do with any of those practices.

"Tell me now," said Sangster, "have you been doing any of those things up till now?" The man admitted that he had not.

"Well, don't worry overmuch, old fellow," said Sangster. "Being an atheist won't make much difference to you."[117]

* * *

During a concert at Westminster Central Hall, London, a comedian tried to entertain the crowd by telling a number of obscene stories. When the man finished, William Sangster, pastor at the Hall, marched to the front and began to tell some stories of his own. Before long the people were laughing uproariously. Sangster then silenced them and said, "You see? You can be funny *and clean.*"[118]

* * *

When William Sangster's son Paul was lying in a darkened hospital ward, Sangster stood at the end of the bed and whispered: "I can't help you. Why can't I help you? Son, I'd go to hell for you if it would help!"[119]

* * *

William Sangster thought primarily of helping others. One of his friends said, "Whenever he (Sangster) met a person, his attitude seemed to be, "How can I help

115. Ibid., 169.
116. Ibid., 196-97.
117. Ibid., 216.
118. Ibid., 326.
119. Ibid., 335.

him?'" When Sangster died, his widow received nearly 1,400 letters from people who cared, and more than 1,000 letters mentioned some specific help Dr. Sangster had given.[120]

* * *

When William Sangster was told he was dying of progressive muscular atrophy, he made four resolutions and faithfully kept them: (1) I will never complain; (2) I will keep the home bright; (3) I will count my blessings; (4) I will try to turn it to gain.[121]

SAVONAROLA

Savonarola (1452-1498) started out to be a doctor, but then joined the Dominicans and became a preacher. He began his ministry in his hometown of Ferrara, but there he had little success. In 1481 he was sent to Florence to minister at the famous old church of San Lorenzo, but he failed miserably as a preacher. His sermons simply did not reach the people and the congregation dwindled to twenty-five weary listeners. It is difficult to believe that such a powerful preacher started out as a failure in the pulpit. In later years great crowds came to hear him, and he has gone down in church history as one of the great preachers and reformers of his era.[122]

CHARLES SIMEON

While waiting in a cemetery to conduct a funeral service Charles Simeon walked among the graves, looking at the epitaphs. He found one that arrested him.

> When from the dust of death I rise,
> To claim my mansion in the skies,
> E'en then shall this be all my plea—
> "Jesus hath lived and died for me."

He was so impressed with that gospel message that he looked for someone in the cemetery with whom he might share it. He saw a young woman, obviously distressed, and called her over to read the epitaph. He took her address and visited her the next day. The home was a scene of poverty and squalor. The woman's old mother was dying of asthma, and two little children, very dirty, were trying to warm themselves by a small fire. Simeon prayed with the family, visited them again, and found assistance for them. Later, the young woman told Simeon that she had been in the cemetery five hours and was contemplating suicide when he called her to read the epitaph. Because of his concern she trusted Christ and the family situation was changed.[123]

* * *

120. Ibid., 338.
121. Ibid., 351.
122. Dargan, *A History of Preaching,* 1:350-58.
123. Hugh Evan Hopkins, *Charles Simeon of Cambridge* (Grand Rapids: Eerdmans, 1977), 54.

In his early years of ministry in Cambridge, Charles Simeon was the object of much ridicule and persecution. One day, hoping to get some relief, he went for a walk and prayed that God would give him some comfort from the Word. He opened the New Testament to the first text that caught his eye. It was Matthew 27:32: "And as they came out, they found a man of Cyrene, Simon by name: him they compelled to bear his cross."

Simeon said, "You know Simon is the same as Simeon. What a word of instruction was here—what a blessed hint for my encouragement! To have the Cross laid upon me, that I might bear it after Jesus—what a privilege! It was enough. Now I could leap and sing for joy as one whom Jesus was honoring with a participation in his sufferings. . . . I henceforth bound persecution as a wreath of glory around my brow."[124]

CHARLES H. SPURGEON

On October 7, 1857, Charles Spurgeon preached at the Crystal Palace to a congregation of 23,654 persons, perhaps the largest congregation ever addressed by a gospel preacher in London up to that time. But a few days before, Spurgeon had gone to the Crystal Palace to test out the acoustics. He stood on the platform and said, "Behold the lamb of God, which taketh away the sin of the world" (John 1:29). A workman, painting in one of the upper galleries, heard those words and came under deep conviction. Later, he found salvation in Christ. The same Word that speaks to the multitudes also speaks to the individual sinner.[125]

* * *

Once when Charles Spurgeon was weary in body and depressed in spirit, he took a holiday in the country and on the Lord's Day worshiped at a Methodist chapel. The minister's message deeply affected Spurgeon and he felt a new surge of spiritual power. He went to the minister and thanked him for the sermon. When the minister asked him who he was and heard it was the great Charles Spurgeon, he turned red and stammered, "Why, it was one of your sermons that I preached this morning!"

"Yes," said Spurgeon, "I know it was, but that was the very message that I wanted to hear, because I then saw that I did enjoy the very Word I myself preached."[126]

* * *

People in Charles Spurgeon's day often asked, "When Mr. Spurgeon dies, who will take his place?" To that the great preacher replied: "As if God could not raise up servants when He would, or as if we ought to neglect our present duty, because of something which may happen in fifty years' time!"

He added: "At any rate, when I am proposing to commence a plan, I never think about whether I should live to see it finished, for I am certain that, if it is God's plan, He

---

124. Ibid., 81.
125. Ernest W. Bacon, *Spurgeon: Heir of the Puritans* (Grand Rapids: Eerdmans, 1968), 59-60.
126. Charles Ray, *A Marvellous Ministry* (London: Passmore and Alabaster, 1905), 45-46.

will surely finish it, even if I should have to leave the work undone."[127]

* * *

A man who had been converted through Charles Spurgeon's ministry had a wife who was religious but lost. She continued to attend her church and refused to go hear Spurgeon.

One Sunday evening the woman decided to attend Metropolitan Tabernacle, but she did not want to be recognized. She put on a heavy veil and shawl and made her way into the upper gallery. Just as she entered the gallery, Spurgeon read his text and pointed right at her: "Come in, thou wife of Jeroboam; why feignest thou thyself to be another? for I am sent to thee with heavy tidings" (1 Kings 14:6).

The words arrested her and the sermon that followed convicted her. When she arrived home, she blamed her husband for telling the minister about her! He assured her that he himself did not even know she was in the building. We are not told whether she trusted the Lord.[128]

* * *

At a Monday evening prayer meeting, Charles Spurgeon suddenly interrupted his sermon, pointed in a certain direction, and said, "Young man, those gloves you are wearing have not been paid for; you have stolen them from your employer!"

After the meeting a young man came to the vestry and begged to see Spurgeon. Pale and trembling, the young man confessed that he had stolen the gloves he was wearing! He promised never to steal again and begged Spurgeon not to expose him to his employer.[129]

* * *

One Sunday morning President and Mrs. James A. Garfield worshiped in London at the Metropolitan Tabernacle. Charles Spurgeon's text that morning was Job 14:14. Garfield was greatly impressed with the huge congregation and with the powerful sermon. He wrote in his journal: "God bless Mr. Spurgeon! He is helping to work out the problem of religious and civil freedom for England, in a way that he knows not of."[130]

* * *

A British high churchman attended a service at Spurgeon's Tabernacle and wrote an interesting article explaining the reasons for Spurgeon's success. They are worth noting.

1. "He has taken the measure of his congregation's taste and capacity, and adapts himself to it."

2. He is "mighty in the Scriptures. This is his deep well, and he is not sparing of its resources."

127. Charles Haddon Spurgeon, *The Full Harvest,* 1861-1892 (London: Banner of Truth, 1962), 40.
128. Ibid., 59-60.
129. Ibid., 60.
130. Ibid., 60-61.

3. "He is evidently a man of prayer."

4. "He is gifted in body and voice and knows how to use his gifts. He holds himself entirely under control."

5. "Careful study and long cultivation."

6. "His energy is prodigious, and his earnestness bears all the appearance of sincerity and truth."[131]

*   *   *

One day Charles Spurgeon rebuked one of his deacons rather sharply.

"Well, that may be so," the man replied, "but I tell you what, sir, *I would die for you any day*."

"Bless your heart," Spurgeon said, "I am sorry I was so sharp, but, still, you did deserve it, did you not?"

The man smiled and admitted that he had deserved the rebuke, "and there the matter ended," said Spurgeon.[132]

*   *   *

During a serious illness, Charles Spurgeon's spirits fell and he began to worry about his financial situation. There was really no cause for anxiety, but the combination of intense pain and weakness made him a good target for the Enemy.

One of Spurgeon's deacons visited him and tried to encourage him not to be anxious. Finally, the deacon went home and returned with a packet of stocks, bonds, and other financial holdings. He put them on the bed and said to his pastor: "There, my dear pastor, I owe everything I have in the world to you, and you are quite welcome to all I possess. Take whatever you need and do not have another moment's anxiety."

Of course, Spurgeon did not use the assets; but the unselfish expression of the man's love and devotion to his pastor was medicine to his soul.[133]

*   *   *

The officers of a small country church wrote to Charles Spurgeon requesting that he suggest a minister for their empty pulpit. When Spurgeon learned of the meager salary they paid their pastor, he wrote: "The only individual I know, who could exist on such a stipend, is the angel Gabriel. He would need neither cash nor clothes; and he could come down from heaven every Sunday morning, and go back at night, so I advise you to invite him."[134]

*   *   *

When Charles Spurgeon sent his ministerial students out to pastor churches, he gave this charge: "Cling tightly with both your hands; when they fail, catch hold with your

131. Ibid., 68-69.
132. Ibid., 70.
133. Ibid., 72.
134. Ibid., 108.

teeth; and if they give way, hang on by your eyelashes!"[135]

* * *

Few men endured the abuse and criticism that Charles Spurgeon endured during his early years in London. Yet, he was able to thank God for it as he prayed and told God he would be willing to yield even his reputation for the cause of Christ. He admitted that it was difficult to bear up under almost constant slanders, but that one good thing can come of it: you can discover your weak points!

One day a man met Spurgeon on the street, took off his hat and bowed, and said, "The Rev. Mr. Spurgeon—a great humbug!" Spurgeon took of his hat and replied, "Thank you for the compliment. I am glad to hear that I am a great anything!"[136]

* * *

Faithfulness in seemingly small ministries is preparation for ministry in large places (Matt. 25:21).

Charles Spurgeon preached to thousands in London each Lord's Day, yet he started his ministry by passing out tracts and teaching a Sunday school class as a teenager. When he began to give short addresses to the Sunday school, God blessed his ministry of the Word. He was invited to preach in obscure places in the countryside, and he used every opportunity to honor the Lord. He was faithful in the small things, and God trusted him with the greater things.

"I am perfectly sure," he said, "that, if I had not been willing to preach to those small gatherings of people in obscure country places, I should never have had the privilege of preaching to thousands of men and women in large buildings all over the land. Remember our Lord's rule, "Whosoever exalteth himself shall be abased; and he that humbleth himself shall be exalted.'"[137]

* * *

Charles Spurgeon often suffered intense pain because of gout. After one of his periods of illness he went out for a short drive, still wearing bandages on his hand and foot, and met one of his neighbors. The man pointed to the bandages and scornfully said, "Whom the Lord loveth, he chasteneth. I would not have such a God as that!"

Spurgeon felt himself boiling with indignation and replied: "I rejoice that I have such a God as that; and if He were to chasten me a thousand times worse than this, I would still love Him; yea, though He slay me, yet will I trust Him."[138]

* * *

Although he looked robust, Charles Spurgeon was not a healthy man. From the age of 35 he was laid low with one kind of illness or another almost every year until his death at age 57. Because of illness approximately one-third of the time, Spurgeon was

135. Ibid., 114.
136. Ibid., 129-30.
137. Ibid., 130.
138. Ibid., 186.

out of his pulpit often during his last 22 years of ministry.

Often Spurgeon wrestled with the Lord in prayer, asking for deliverance from pain. "I talked to the Lord as Luther would have done," he said, "and pleaded His Fatherhood in real earnest."

His constant experience with pain and with God's grace made him sympathetic with those who suffered, and his tender heart is seen often in his sermons.[139]

* * *

Charles Spurgeon suffered many painful afflictions during the latter years of his life; including gout, rheumatism lumbago, and sciatica. From his own experience of pain, he wrote:

> In the matter of faith-healing, health is set before us as if it were the great thing to be desired above all other things. Is it so? I venture to say that the greatest earthly blessing that God can give to any of us, is health, *with the exception of sickness.* Sickness has frequently been of more use to the saints of God than health has. . . . Trials drive us to the realities of religion.[140]

* * *

While preaching in the Metropolitan Tabernacle one Sunday evening, Charles Spurgeon said, "Dear mother, if you have never talked with your daughter about her soul, do it this very night. 'But,' you reply, 'when I get home, she will be in bed.' If so, then wake her up, but do talk and pray with her tonight; and then let her fall asleep again."

One woman present took the admonition to heart, went home, awakened her daughter, and talked to her about the Savior. The girl said, "Oh, Mother! I am glad you have spoken to me about Jesus; for months I have been wishing you would do so." In a short time the mother brought the daughter to Spurgeon to inquire about uniting with the church.[141]

* * *

Although Charles Spurgeon did not give a public altar call at the close of his sermons, he always urged people to trust Jesus Christ and not delay. One time, he requested that his listeners spend a quiet time at home thinking about their spiritual condition. If they were not saved, they should take a piece of paper and write CONDEMNED on it. If they were saved, they should write FORGIVEN.

A number of people came to Christ as the result of that unusual suggestion. One young man wrote CONDEMNED and then began to weep. He threw the paper in the fire, trusted Jesus Christ, took another piece of paper and wrote FORGIVEN. He came and told Spurgeon the news and asked to be received into the church.

Another man went home and told his wife what Spurgeon had said. He took a piece of paper and said he was going to write CONDEMNED, but his wife pleaded with him

139. Ibid., 194, 197.
140. Ibid., 385, 414.
141. Ibid., 240-41.

to trust Christ. Just as he was about to write the letter *C,* his little daughter caught hold of his hand and said, "No, Father, you shall not write it." The man was brought to the Savior, and he and his family became faithful members at the Tabernacle.[142]

* * *

Charles Spurgeon had some definite views on leadership.

> Wherever anything is to be done, either in the Church or in the world, you may depend upon it, it is done by one man. The whole history of the Church, from the earliest ages, teaches the same lesson. A Moses, a Gideon, an Isaiah, and a Paul are from time to time raised up to do an appointed work; and when they pass away, their work appears to cease. Nor is it given to everyone, as it was to Moses, to see the Joshua who is destined to carry on his work to completion. God can raise up a successor to each man, but the man himself is not to worry about that matter, or he may do harm.
>
> One great object of every religious teacher should be to prevent the creation of external appliances to make his teaching appear to live when it is dead.[143]

* * *

On a wall in his bedroom Charles Spurgeon had a plaque with Isaiah 48:10 on it: "I have chosen thee in the furnace of affliction."

"It is no mean thing to be chosen of God," he wrote. "God's choice makes chosen men choice men. . . . We are chosen, not in the palace, but in the furnace. In the furnace, beauty is marred, fashion is destroyed, strength is melted, glory is consumed; yet here eternal love reveals its secrets, and declares its choice."[144]

* * *

Charles Spurgeon never permitted his heavenly citizenship to make him lax in civic responsibilities. He arrived at a preaching appointment a bit late and explained that he had been delayed because he took time to vote.

"To vote!" exclaimed the pastor. "But my dear brother, I thought you were a citizen of the New Jerusalem!"

"So I am," Spurgeon replied, "but my 'old man' is a citizen of this world."

"Ah, but you should mortify your old man," the pastor argued.

"That is exactly what I did," said Spurgeon; "for my old man is a Tory, and I made him vote for the Liberals!"[145]

* * *

Although he took care not to cheapen his message, Charles Spurgeon often used humor in his preaching, and with good effect. One listener objected to something humorous Spurgeon had said, and Spurgeon replied: "If you had known how many

142. Ibid.
143. Ibid., 392.
144. Ibid., 402.
145. Ibid., 437.

others I kept back, you would not have found fault with that one, but you would have commended me for the restraint I had exercised."

He never planned to make humorous remarks; they came to him unbidden. But he learned that many who were attracted by some bit of humor often heard the message and were converted. He compared his humor to the bait that conceals the hook that catches the fish.[146]

* * *

Charles Spurgeon was not timid when it came to proclaiming his faith or attacking what he thought was false doctrine. He preached a particularly strong sermon against baptismal regeneration and aroused the furor of many ministers.

"I hear that you are in hot water," a friend said to Spurgeon.

"Oh, dear, no!" he replied. "It is the other fellows who are in the hot water; I am the stoker, the man who makes the water boil!"[147]

* * *

A mother took her little boy to hear Charles Spurgeon preach. After listening for a quarter of an hour, the lad said to his mother, "Mother, is Mr. Spurgeon speaking to *me*?" No matter how large the congregation might be, Spurgeon preached as though he were speaking to one person.[148]

* * *

At the close of one of the Tabernacle services, a poor woman accompanied by two neighbors, visited Charles Spurgeon in his vestry. The woman's husband had deserted her and fled the country. Spurgeon suggested that they immediately kneel down and pray for the man's conversion, which they did.

Some months later, the woman reappeared at the vestry, and this time her husband was with her—and he was a converted man! On the very day that Spurgeon had prayed for him the man was aboard ship, far out to sea. But he had found one of Spurgeon's printed sermons, read it, and trusted Jesus Christ! Both the man and his wife united with the church and served God faithfully.[149]

* * *

While Charles Spurgeon was preaching at the Surrey Music Hall he received an anonymous communication each week through the mail that listed all his mistakes made on Sunday. The writer listed mispronunciations, grammatical errors, and various other errors. If Spurgeon repeated himself the writer told him about it. Spurgeon was prone to quote often the line "Nothing in my hand I bring," and his anonymous critic wrote, "We are sufficiently informed of the vacuity of your hand."

146. Ibid., 440.
147. Ibid.
148. Booth, *Echoes and Memories*, 34.
149. Ray, *A Marvellous Ministry*, 58-60.

Instead of resenting that weekly criticism, Spurgeon said he welcomed it and profited from it. His only regret was that his correspondent was anonymous, because he wanted to thank the critic for his help![150]

* * *

October 19, 1856, was a crisis night for Charles Spurgeon. He was scheduled to preach at the Surrey Music Hall for several months while the New Park Street Chapel facilities were undergoing remodeling and expansion. Some ten to twelve thousand people crowded into London's chief place of amusement to hear Spurgeon preach. Several groups of troublemakers came for the purpose of opposing the gospel. Some of them cried "Fire!" and the great crowd turned into a confused mob. "The galleries are giving way!" some shouted. "The place is falling!" Seven people were trampled to death and many others injured.

The young preacher was crushed with despair and spent several days in dark solitude. He and his wife retreated to the home of one of the deacons and sought to find God's peace. As they were walking in the garden Spurgeon suddenly turned and said: "Dearest, how foolish I have been! Why, what does it matter what becomes of me, if the Lord shall be but glorified! If Christ be exalted, let Him do as He pleases with me; my one prayer shall be, that I may die to self, and live wholly for Him and for His honor. Oh, wifey, I see it all now! Praise the Lord with me!" The burden had been lifted.

The Lord used the devices of the enemy to magnify Spurgeon's name throughout London; and this one He used to greatly expand Spurgeon's ministry.[151]

* * *

Charles Spurgeon usually prepared his Sunday morning sermon on Saturday evening. One Saturday, he was working hard on a sermon on Psalm 110:3, but the message just would not come. He sat up late, but no light came. His wife suggested that he go to bed and get his much needed rest, promising to awaken him early so he could make a fresh beginning.

During the early morning hours, she heard him talking in his sleep! He was actually expounding the text! His wife listened attentively and prayed that God would help her recall the points. Then she fell asleep and failed to give him the promised early call.

When Spurgeon awakened he was distressed that he had overslept, but then his wife told him what had happened and gave him the message she had heard him preach. "Why, that's just what I wanted!" he said and went to his study to finalize the message. He preached it that morning.[152]

* * *

Charles Spurgeon often preached thirteen or fourteen times a week, and as a result, had to do much traveling. One morning as he was preparing to leave on a long journey, he saw his wife weeping and looking very discouraged.

150. Charles Spurgeon, *The Early Years, 1834-1860* (Carlisle, Pa.: Banner of Truth, 1976), 533.
151. Ibid., 423-51, *passim.*
152. Ibid., 419-20.

·"Wifey," he said to her, "do you think that, when any of the children of Israel brought a lamb to the Lord's altar as an offering to Him, they stood and wept over it when they had seen it laid there?"

"Why, no!" she replied. "Certainly not! The Lord would not have been pleased with an offering reluctantly given."

"Well," he said, "don't you see, you are giving me to God in letting me go to preach the gospel to poor sinners, and do you think He likes to see you cry over your sacrifice?"

In later years, whenever she looked sad as he was leaving for ministry elsewhere, Spurgeon would say, "What! Crying over your lamb, wifey?"[153]

*   *   *

Every minister has problems with interruptions. Charles Spurgeon was working on Saturday afternoon on his Sunday morning message when a man arrived who wanted to see him. "Tell Mr. Spurgeon that a servant of the Lord wishes to see him," he said, but he would not give his name.

Spurgeon sent back the message: "Tell the gentleman that I am so busy with his Master, that I cannot attend to the servant."

Then the visitor gave his name; he was the author of *Glimpses of Jesus*, a book that had especially helped Spurgeon. Spurgeon rushed out and greeted the man with, "Come in, thou blessed of the Lord!"

We never know when we are entertaining angels unawares![154]

*   *   *

Listen to Charles Spurgeon on the subject of preaching.

> The quarry of Holy Scripture is inexhaustible, I seem hardly to have begun to labor in it, but the selection of the next block, and the consideration as to how to work it into form are matters not so easy as some think. Those who count preaching and its needful preparations to be slight matters, have never occupied a pulpit continuously month after month, or they would know better.
>
> Let those preach lightly who dare do so; to me, it is "burden of the Lord"—joyfully carried as grace is given; but still, a burden which at times crushes my whole manhood into the dust of humiliation, and occasionally, when ill-health unites with the mental strain, into depression and anguish of heart.
>
> Preaching Jesus Christ is sweet work, joyful work, Heavenly work. . . . Scarcely is it possible for a man, this side the grave, to be nearer heaven than is a preacher when his Master's presence bears him right away from every care and thought, save the one business in hand, and that the greatest that ever occupied a creature's mind and heart.[155]

*   *   *

On August 20, 1854, Charles Spurgeon preached from the text 1 Samuel 12:17, and the sermon was printed in the *Penny Pulpit* series. In 1855 he began to publish and

153. Ibid., 418.
154. Ibid., 414-15.
155. Ibid., 403.

distribute his own sermon series with a sermon on Malachi 3:6. When Spurgeon died in 1892, thirty-seven annual volumes of sermons had been published, with fifty-two sermons in each one! And there was sufficient material available to continue publishing one sermon a week until May 10, 1917! The final sermon was numbered 3,563![156]

* * *

Not all of the students at Spurgeon's Pastors' College turned out to be successful preachers. One student prayed at the Monday evening prayer meeting: "O Thou that art encinctured with an auriferous zodiac!" Spurgeon immediately became concerned about the man, and his fears proved to be well-grounded. The man changed denominations, then became a playwright and an actor. He abandoned his wife, and Spurgeon helped to support her for several years.[157]

* * *

T. W. Medhurst was converted early in 1854 after hearing Charles Spurgeon preach. Almost immediately, Medhurst began to seek to win the lost and started preaching in the streets. Some of the members of New Park Street Chapel complained to Spurgeon that Medhurst was untrained, somewhat rustic, and perhaps would turn people against the gospel. When Spurgeon spoke to the young man, he said, "I must preach, sir! And I shall preach unless you cut off my head!" It was then that Spurgeon decided to educate Medhurst, and this was the start of the famous Pastors' College.

Three months later Medhurst complained to Spurgeon that he had been preaching for three months and had seen no one saved.

"Do you expect the Lord to save souls every time you open your mouth?" Spurgeon asked.

"Oh, no, sir!" said Medhurst.

"Then that is just the reason why you have not had conversions: 'According to your faith be it unto you.'"

One day Spurgeon himself preached at the open-air meeting usually conducted by Medhurst. "How did you like Mr. Spurgeon?" one listener asked another. "Oh, very well, but I should have enjoyed the service more if he hadn't imitated our dear Mr. Medhurst so much."[158]

* * *

Charles Spurgeon was returning to London on the train after ministering in the country and discovered that he had lost his ticket. The only other person in the compartment, a distinguished-looking man, noticed that Spurgeon was fumbling about in his pockets, and he asked what was wrong. The preacher explained that he had lost his ticket and that he had neither watch nor money on his person.

"But I am not at all troubled," Spurgeon said, "for I have been on my Master's business, and I am quite sure all will be well."

The gentleman seemed interested and they conversed quite profitably during the trip.

156. Ibid., 393-94.
157. Ibid., 390.
158. Ibid., 388-89.

When the agent came to get the tickets, the gentleman said, "All right, William!" and out he went. When Spurgeon asked why the agent had not asked for his ticket, the man explained, "I am the General Manager of this line, and it was no doubt Divinely arranged that I should happen to be your companion just when I could be of service to you."[159]

*   *   *

Charles Spurgeon was scheduled to preach at Haverhill in Suffolk, but a railway delay made him late. As he approached the meeting, Spurgeon heard another man preaching, and discovered it was his grandfather! As Charles entered the church, his grandfather said, "Here comes my grandson. He may preach the gospel better than I can, but he cannot preach a better gospel, can you, Charles?"

The younger preacher urged his grandfather to continue the message, but the elder Spurgeon insisted that Charles take over. The text was Ephesians 2:8, so Charles Spurgeon picked up the thread of the sermon and went on. When Charles came to the part about the sinfulness of human nature, his grandfather interrupted.

"I know much about that, dear friends," he said and then spoke for about five minutes on human depravity.

Then Charles took up the text again and finished the sermon.

In a sense, all gospel preachers are preaching the same message and ought to be preaching together and not competing with each other.[160]

*   *   *

A group of hyper-Calvinist critics descended on Charles Spurgeon after he had preached, and they found fault with his theology.

"How can a dead sinner cry out to God?" they asked. "The Bible declares that the prayer of a sinner is abomination unto the Lord."

Spurgeon replied that, as an unconverted boy, he had often cried out to God; and certainly God answered, for he was saved. And as for the "quotation" about the prayer of the unconverted, Spurgeon said he could not find it anywhere in his Bible, nor could anybody else.

At that point an old woman pushed into the circle and told the critics to keep still. "The psalmist did say, 'He giveth to the beast his food, and to the young ravens which cry' (see Ps. 147:9). Is there any grace in *them*? If God hears the cry of the ravens, don't you think He will hear the prayers of those who are made in His own image? You don't know anything at all about the matter, so leave the young man alone, and let him go on with his Master's work."

The critics quickly departed.[161]

*   *   *

We influence each other. Charles Spurgeon gladly confessed that his ideal and model

159. Ibid., 369-70.
160. Ibid., 363-64.
161. Ibid., 362.

for preaching was George Whitefield. "Often as I have read his life," Spurgeon wrote, "I am conscious of distinct quickening whenever I turn to it. He *lived*. Other men seem to be only half-alive, but Whitefield was all life, fire, wing, force. My own model, if I may have such a thing in due subordination to my Lord, is George Whitefield, but with unequal footsteps must I follow in his glorious track."[162]

* * *

The attacks against Charles Spurgeon only served to keep him in submission before the Lord. He wrote to a friend:

> Now, my Master is the only one who can humble me. My pride is so infernal that there is not a man on earth who can hold it in, and all their silly attempts are futile: but then my Master can do it, and He will. Sometimes I get such a view of my own insignificance that I call myself all the folly in the world for even letting pride pass my door without frowning at him.[163]

* * *

During one particularly trying time in his ministry, Charles Spurgeon wrote to a friend: "Friends firm. Enemies alarmed. Devil angry. Sinners saved. Christ exalted. Self not well."[164]

* * *

Any ministry that is blessed of God is bound to be attacked, and Charles Spurgeon's ministry was no exception. Articles and booklets were printed about him, debating whether or not he was really born again, or whether his ministry was honoring to God. He was called an actor, a comet that would appear and be gone. His preaching was called vulgar and profane. One critic said, "He has gone up like a rocket, and ere long will come down like a stick."

Mrs. Spurgeon saw how those unjust attacks affected her husband, so she had Matthew 5:11-12 printed and framed, and put it up where he would see it first thing each morning. The promise did its work, and Spurgeon was able to sail through the storms successfully.[165]

* * *

As Charles Spurgeon's ministry grew, he became the target of many slanderous attacks. His enemies criticized his preaching, his pulpit manner, and even his character. One day a particularly slanderous attack came to his ears, and it crushed him with despair. To think that he was faithfully preaching the gospel and serving Christ, and yet people were maligning his character!

He fell to his knees in prayer. "Master, I will not keep back even my character for

162. Ibid., 348.
163. Ibid., 342.
164. Ibid., 341.
165. Ibid., 303-27, *passim*.

Thee. If I must lose that, too, then let it go; it is the dearest thing I have, but it shall go, if, like my Master, they shall say I have a devil, or am mad, or, like Him, I am a drunken man and a wine-bibber."

Jesus was made of no reputation for us. Shall we hold back our reputation for Him?[166]

* * *

In 1854 the neighborhood around the New Park Street Chapel, where Charles Spurgeon preached, was visited by Asiatic cholera. The young pastor had been there only a year, yet he found himself visiting many people who were seriously ill, and he buried many dead. It was a difficult and demanding time, and the pastor became discouraged.

He was returning home from a funeral when he noticed a paper fixed to the window of a shoemaker's shop in Great Dover Road. Spurgeon was curious and went over to read it. It said:

> Because thou hast made the Lord, which is my
> refuge, even the Most High, thy habitation; there
> shall no evil befall thee, neither shall any
> plague come nigh thy dwelling.

That quotation from Psalm 91:9-10 struck Spurgeon with new power. "Faith appropriated the passage as her own," he wrote. "I felt secure, refreshed, girt with immortality."

The shoemaker was Mr. W. Ford. Little did Mr. Ford realize how God would use that simple ministry.[167]

* * *

When Charles Spurgeon began his ministry at New Park Street Chapel, London, the congregation was small; but before long, the building was crowded. In the evenings, when the gas jets were lit, the atmosphere became stifling. Spurgeon compared it to "the Black Hole of Calcutta," and he suggested to the deacons that the upper panes in the windows be removed to give added oxygen. Nothing was done about the matter. Then one Monday the deacons discovered all the panes gone! Spurgeon suggested they offer a reward for the culprit who had smashed the windows, but the reward was never claimed.

It was Spurgeon himself who did the deed! "I have walked with the stick which let the oxygen into that stifling structure," he wrote.

On another occasion, while preaching, Spurgeon shouted: "By faith, the walls of Jericho fell down, and by faith, this wall at the back shall come down too!" One of the old deacons told him never to say that again, but Spurgeon persisted. Eventually the church voted to remodel and expand the building.[168]

* * *

166. Ibid., 303-4.
167. Ibid., 272-73.
168. Ibid., 270-71.

One Sunday evening when Charles Spurgeon was preaching at New Park Street Chapel in London, he announced the hymn before the sermon and opened the Bible to the prepared text. When he did, a text on the opposite page jumped out at him "like a lion from a thicket" with compelling power.

As the people sang, Spurgeon debated; should he preach the message he prepared or should he launch out by faith on the new text? He decided on the latter course and went along with blessing—and then the lights went out!

He told the people to sit quietly, because the gas would be relit in a short time. Because he was preaching without any notes or prepared manuscript, the darkness was no threat to him. While the lights were out and the people listened attentively, he preached about the child of light walking in the darkness.

The results? A few church meetings later, two persons presented themselves as new believers. One had been saved as a result of the first message, and the second from the message Spurgeon preached in the dark![169]

* * *

When Charles Spurgeon was pastor at New Park Street in London, God used his words to bring about amazing changes in the lives of people.

A man who was on his way to get some gin saw the crowd at the church door and pushed his way in to see what was going on. At that moment, Spurgeon turned and faced the man and said that there was a man in the gallery who had a gin bottle in his pocket and had come with no good motive. The startled man listened to the rest of the message and was converted.

One evening a prostitute, on her way to Blackfriars Bridge to commit suicide, stopped at the church, hoping to hear some word that would prepare her to meet her maker. Spurgeon was preaching from Luke 7:36-50, the story of the prostitute who wiped Jesus feet with her tears. His text was verse 44: "Seest thou this woman?" As Spurgeon preached, the woman saw herself but also saw the grace of God and trusted Christ.[170]

* * *

Sheridan Knowles was a famous actor and playwright in Charles Spurgeon's day. He had been converted and had become instructor in speech at the Baptist College, Stepney. He said to his students one day:

> Go, and hear him at once if you want to know how to preach. His name is Charles Spurgeon. He is only a boy, but he is the most wonderful preacher in the world. He is absolutely perfect in his oratory; and, beside that, a master in the art of acting. He has nothing to learn from me, or anyone else. He is simply perfect. He knows everything. He can do anything.
>
> Now, mark my word, boys, that young man will live to be the greatest preacher of this or any other age. He will bring more souls to Christ than any man who ever proclaimed the gospel, not excepting the apostle Paul. His name will be known everywhere, and his sermons will be translated into many of the languages of the world.[171]

169. Ibid., 268.
170. Ibid., 266-67.
171. Ibid., 260-61.

*   *   *

As a young and zealous preacher, Charles Spurgeon sometimes was too bold in his preaching, and some people were offended. A Mr. King, an officer of the Baptist Chapel in Waterbeach, thought the young preacher needed some counsel, so he put a pin in Spurgeon's Bible at Titus 2:8: "Sound speech, that cannot be condemned; that he that is of the contrary part may be ashamed, having no evil thing to say of you."

"Nothing could have been in better taste," Spurgeon said. "The wise rebuke was well deserved and lovingly taken."[172]

*   *   *

Not everyone in the Baptist Chapel at Waterbeach approved of young Charles Spurgeon's pointed sermons. Spurgeon was having Sunday dinner with one of the old men of the church who reproved him for preaching *invitation sermons*. But as Spurgeon pressed the man to tell him what kind of sermons ought to be preached, the old fellow admitted that his daughter and his son-in-law had been converted because of Spurgeon's gospel appeals!

"Don't you take any notice of an old man like me," the man said. "As long as God blesses you, you go on in your own way."[173]

*   *   *

After Charles Spurgeon had preached as pastor of the Baptist Chapel in Waterbeach for some months, it was suggested that he might want to enroll in the Baptist College at Stepney. It was arranged that he meet Dr. Angus, the tutor of the college, at the home of a Mr. Macmillan in Cambridge.

At the appointed time, Spurgeon went to the house and was shown to a room where he waited for Dr. Angus to appear. After a couple of hours he became a bit impatient and asked why the interview was delayed. Spurgeon had to leave to take care of his school responsibilities (he was still an assistant teacher), and only then discovered that Dr. Angus had been taken to another room in the house. Since he had to catch a train, Dr. Angus had departed when Spurgeon did not appear for the interview.

It was not God's will that Spurgeon get his training in the usual fashion. That afternoon he considered writing the school and applying, but as he walked to a preaching engagement he heard the words from Jeremiah 45:5 ringing in his soul: "And seekest thou great things for thyself? seek them not." Spurgeon decided not to enter college. He was a great believer in ministerial training and in his later years started a college for pastors; but Spurgeon himself was trained of God in a different way.[174]

*   *   *

Charles Spurgeon was invited to preach at a Baptist chapel in Waterbeach,

172. Ibid., 223.
173. Ibid., 222.
174. Ibid., 207-12.

Cambridge, and the text of his sermon was Matthew 1:21. One of the deacons later said, "He looked so white, and I thought to myself, *he'll* never be able to preach—what a boy he is." But when Spurgeon began to read and expound the Scriptures, the deacon changed his mind. The forty members of the little church called him to be their pastor, and soon the work was growing and souls were coming to Christ.

Spurgeon's first convert at the church was a laborer's wife. When he heard about it, he asked one of the deacons to drive him to her house where he encouraged her in the Lord. "I prize each one whom God has given me," Spurgeon wrote, "but I prize that woman most. . . . She was the first seal to my ministry, and a very precious one. . . . I would rather be the means of saving a soul from death than be the greatest orator on earth. . . . To win a soul from going down into the pit, is a more glorious achievement than to be crowned in the arena of theological controversy."[175]

* * *

Not every preacher would dare to prepare his messages the way Spurgeon did, but we must remember that he was saturated with the Bible and theology. He was an avid reader, and he was greatly gifted by God. We can learn some valuable principles from his description of how he prepared.

> When I have had to preach two or three sermons in a day, I have asked Him for the morning subject, and preached from it; and I have asked Him for the afternoon's topic or the evening's portion, and preached from it, after meditating on it for my own soul's comfort—not in the professional style of a regular sermon-maker, but feasting upon it for myself. Such simple food has done the people far more good than if I had been a week in manufacturing a sermon, for it has come warm from the heart just after it has been received in my own soul; and therefore it has been well spoken, because well known, well tasted, and well felt.[176]

* * *

James Vinter was a deacon at the St. Andrew's Street Chapel in Cambridge where Charles Spurgeon served in the Sunday school. He was a godly man who had a gift for discovering and developing young men for Christian service, and he had his eye on young Spurgeon. He asked Spurgeon to accompany an older man to a cottage meeting on a Sunday evening in Teversham, and Spurgeon agreed.

As Spurgeon and the man walked over to the meeting, Spurgeon expressed the hope that his friend would know the power of God as he preached. It was then that Spurgeon discovered that *he* was the preacher of the evening! Spurgeon had given several Sunday school addresses, but he had never preached a sermon before. As he walked along, he prayed for God's help and selected as his text 1 Peter 2:7: "Unto you therefore which believe he is precious."

God did assist the young preacher and he gave a message that touched the hearts of the rural folks in the meeting. No sooner did the meeting end when some of the folks asked, "How old are you?"

175. Ibid., 196-98.
176. Ibid., 189.

"I am under sixty," the lad replied.

"Yes, and under sixteen!" someone said.

"Never mind my age," said Spurgeon. "Think of the Lord Jesus and His preciousness."[177]

* * *

A strong Calvinist, Charles Spurgeon rejoiced in the doctrine of election and preached it with power. An Arminian brother once told Spurgeon that he had read through the Bible more than a score of times and could never find the doctrine of election. In fact, he had even read the Word on his knees!

Spurgeon told him, "I think you read the Bible in a very uncomfortable posture, and if you had read it in your easy chair, you would have been more likely to understand."[178]

* * *

As a new believer, Charles Spurgeon's first ministry was putting gospel tracts in envelopes and distributing them to various districts in the city. He also began to teach a Sunday school class. It was from those small beginnings that God developed "the prince of preachers." Because Spurgeon was faithful in a few small things, God entrusted him with greater things (Matt. 25:21).

He wrote:

> It may be that, in the young dawn of my Christian life, I did imprudent things in order to serve the cause of Christ, but I still say, give me back that time again, with all its impudence and with all its hastiness, if I may but have the same love to my Master, the same overwhelming influence in my spirit, making me obey my Lord's commands because it was a pleasure to me to do anything to serve my God.

He also wrote:

> Many of our young folks want to commence their service for Christ by doing great things, and therefore do nothing at all. . . . He who is willing to teach infants, or to give away tracts, and so to begin at the beginning, is far more likely to be useful than the youth who is full of affectations, and sleeps in a white necktie, who is aspiring to the ministry, and is touching up certain superior manuscripts which he hopes are long to read from the pastor's pulpit.[179]

* * *

Charles Spurgeon once tried to help a man who had been a Christian forty years but had never been baptized. The man kept quoting Isaiah 28:16: "He that believeth shall not make haste." Spurgeon countered with Psalm 119:60: "I made haste, and delayed not to keep thy commandments."[180]

* * *

177. Ibid., 182-84.
178. Ibid., 166.
179. Ibid., 156, 184.
180. Ibid., 146.

Charles Spurgeon was saved on January 6, 1850, and on February 1 he wrote the following prayer of consecration:

> O great and unsearchable God, who knowest my heart, and triest all my ways; with a humble dependence upon the support of Thy Holy Spirit, I yield up myself to Thee; as Thy own reasonable sacrifice, I return to Thee Thine own. I would be for ever, unreservedly, perpetually Thine; whilst I am on earth, I would serve Thee; and may I enjoy Thee and praise Thee for ever! Amen.

He signed his name to that prayer of consecration and by God's grace fulfilled it throughout a fruitful life and ministry.[181]

* * *

Charles Spurgeon once said:

> I have found, in my own spiritual life, that the more rules I lay down for myself, the more sins I commit. The habit of regular morning and evening prayer is one which is indispensable to a believer's life, but the prescribing of the length of prayer, and the constrained remembrance of so many persons and subjects, may gender unto bondage, and strangle prayer rather than assist it.[182]

* * *

When he was a young believer Charles Spurgeon often had evil thoughts that tortured him. He spoke to his grandfather about them and confessed that perhaps he was not even a child of God because he was having such evil thoughts.

"Nonsense, Charles," the man explained, "it is just because you are a Christian that you are thus tempted. These blasphemies are no children of yours; they are the devil's brats, which he delights to lay at the door of a Christian. Don't you own them as yours, give them neither house-room nor heart-room."[183]

* * *

An outbreak of fever at the school where Charles Spurgeon was teaching made it necessary to close the school early for the winter holidays. A terrible storm prevented him from going to church with his father, so he attended a primitive Methodist chapel on Artillery Street near their home on Hythe Hill, Colchester. Perhaps twelve or fifteen people attended that winter morning. The preacher did not show up, so a layman gave the sermon.

"He was obliged to stick to his text, for the simple reason that he had little else to say," Spurgeon commented. The text was Isaiah 45:22: "Look unto me, and be ye saved, all the ends of the earth." After about ten minutes of "rambling around the text," the substitute preacher looked straight at Spurgeon and said, "Young man, you look very miserable, and you always will be miserable—miserable in life, and miserable in

181. Ibid., 125.
182. Ibid., 103.
183. Ibid., 102.

death—if you don't obey my text; but if you obey now, this moment, you will be saved. Young man, look to Jesus Christ! Look! Look! Look! You have nothin' to do but to look and live."

Charles Spurgeon did look to Christ by faith, and at that very moment he was born again. Nobody knows the name of that rustic preacher, but God used him to win a choice trophy of grace for Christ. In later years three men claimed to have been the preacher, but Spurgeon could not recognize any of them.

That evening, Spurgeon attended the Baptist church and heard a sermon on the text "accepted in the beloved" (Eph. 1:6). He said that in that text he found peace and pardon after finding salvation that morning.[184]

* * *

"Let none despise the strivings of the Spirit in the hearts of the young," wrote Charles Spurgeon. "Let not boyish anxieties and juvenile repentance be lightly regarded. He incurs a fearful amount of guilt who in the least promotes the aim of the evil one by trampling upon a tender conscience in a child. No one can guess at what age children become capable of conversion. I, at least, can bear my personal testimony to the fact that grace operates on some minds at a period almost too early for recollection. When but young in years, I felt with much sorrow the evil of sin. . . . Our Heavenly Father does not usually cause us to seek the Saviour till He has whipped us clean out of all our confidence; He cannot make us in earnest after Heaven till He has made us feel something of the intolerable tortures of an aching conscience, which is a foretaste of hell."[185]

* * *

When Spurgeon was a teenager, he served as an assistant teacher in a school in Newmarket, Cambridgeshire, kept by John Swindell. The cook in the house was Mary King, a devout Christian with strong Calvinist beliefs. When Spurgeon was experiencing deep conviction he talked with her, and she explained what she knew of the Word. Spurgeon wrote, "From her I got all the theology I ever needed." Mary King is one of the forgotten heroes of church history who influenced such a mighty man of God.[186]

* * *

In 1844 the missionary Richard Knill was doing deputation work for the London Missionary Society, and he stayed at the parsonage in Stambourne where Charles Spurgeon lived as a child. Knill took an interest in the boy and even awakened him at six o'clock one morning to talk to him about Jesus and to pray with him.

All the family was gathered at morning prayer one day, when Knill took Charles on his knee and said: "This child will one day preach the gospel, and he will preach it to great multitudes. I am persuaded that he will preach in the chapel of Rowland Hill" [a famous London church]. The missionary then promised to give Charles sixpence if he

184. Ibid., 78-88, 110.
185. Ibid., 58.
186. Ibid., 39-40.

would learn the hymn "God Moves in a Mysterious Way," and if he would promise to have that hymn sung when he preached at Hill's chapel.

The prediction was fulfilled. Years later, when he was a famous London preacher, Spurgeon was called on at the last minute to substitute at the Chapel of Rowland Hill because the visiting preacher had become ill. He agreed, provided the children would sing "God Moves in a Mysterious Way."[187]

* * *

Charles Spurgeon's brother had weak ankles and frequently his father was quite unhappy with him. Finally, his father warned him that he would be whipped if he came home showing signs of falling down.

Years later, Spurgeon reminded his father of that warning. "Yes, it was so," said his father, "and he was completely cured from that time."

Spurgeon replied, "Ah, so you thought, yet it was not so, for he had many a tumble afterwards, but I always managed to wash his knees, and to brush his clothes, so as to remove all traces of his falls."

What a picture of the truth of Galatians 6:1![188]

* * *

When Charles Spurgeon was fourteen he attended a Church of England school where several clergymen regularly interrogated the students. One conversation with Spurgeon went like this:

"What is your name?"

"Spurgeon, sir."

"No, no. What is your name?"

"Charles Spurgeon, sir."

"No, you should not behave so, for you know I only want your Christian name."

"If you please, sir, I am afraid I haven't got one."

"Why, how is that?"

"Because I do not think I am a Christian."

"What, are you, then—a heathen?"

"No, sir, but we may not be heathens, and yet be without the grace of God, and so not be truly Christians."[189]

* * *

There is no getting around the influence of a godly family. "The faith I hold bears upon it marks of the blood of my ancestors," said Charles Spurgeon.

In later years, when asked the reason for the position God had given him, Spurgeon would reply: "My mother, and the truth of my message."[190]

* * *

187. Ibid., 27-28.
188. Ibid., 24.
189. Ibid., 34.
190. Ibid., 22.

When you read Spurgeon's sermons you are impressed with the way he presents his material, with each point clearly stated and developed. It is easy to follow his train of thought. An experience in his childhood helps to explain this neatness and orderliness in his sermon preparation and delivery.

His mother sent him off to the store to purchase a pound of tea, a quarterpound of mustard, and three pounds of rice. He put those items into his basket and started home; but on the way, he saw a pack of hounds after a fox. He "felt it necessary to follow them over hedge and ditch," and had a grand time in the chase. But when he arrived home he discovered that "all the goods were amalgamated—tea, mustard, and rice—into one awful mess."

He said that he learned the necessity of packing up his subjects "in good stout parcels." "People will not drink mustardy tea, nor will they enjoy muddled-up sermons."[191]

* * *

Charles Spurgeon believed in the gospel and in the power of preaching. He wrote:

> I do not look for any other means of converting men beyond the simple preaching of the gospel and the opening of men's ears to hear it. The moment the Church of God shall despise the pulpit, God will despise her. It has been through the ministry that the Lord has always been pleased to revive and bless His Churches.[192]

* * *

When Charles Spurgeon was a boy he lived with his grandfather, who pastored in Stambourne. One of the members of the church was a man named Roads who had the habit of visiting the local pub. Charles noticed that the man's conduct was a great burden to his grandfather, and the lad took it to heart.

"I'll kill old Roads, that I will!" Charles said to his grandfather one day.

His grandfather tried to calm him down and warned him that he must not do anything wrong.

"I shall not do anything bad, but I'll kill him though, that I will," the boy replied.

A few days later, he announced that he had "killed Roads" and that the man would never grieve his grandfather again. Sure, enough, Roads showed up at the pastor's house, very repentant, to ask forgiveness for his conduct. Then he told what had happened. He had been sitting in the pub when young Charles came in, pointed at him with his finger, and asked. "What doest thou here, Elijah? Sitting with the ungodly; and you a member of a church, and breaking your pastor's heart. I'm ashamed of you. I wouldn't break my pastor's heart, I'm sure."

The words pierced the man's heart, he left his pipe and beer, went off to a private place, and settled the matter with the Lord. In the years that followed, Roads proved to be a faithful Christian and church member.[193]

* * *

191. Ibid., 19-20.
192. Ibid., v.
193. Ibid., 11-12.

On Sunday morning, June 7, 1897, Charles Spurgeon stood for the last time on the platform at the Metropolitan Tabernacle, and delivered his last sermon from that pulpit. His text was 1 Samuel 30:21-25 and was published in the *Metropolitan Tabernacle Pulpit* series as number 2,208.[194]

* * *

Charles Haddon Spurgeon died at five minutes past eleven on Sunday evening, January 31, 1892. He was at Mentone, in southern France.

More than 100,000 persons attended the various memorial services that were held at the Metropolitan Tabernacle from Sunday, February 7, to Thursday, February 11, when the interment took place. His pulpit Bible was open on the casket to Isaiah 45:22, the text God used to bring him to Christ.

During his ministry in London, he had preached to at least twenty million people. He had received 14,691 persons into the fellowship of the church. The membership of the church at his death was 5,311.

On the day of the funeral as Spurgeon was laid to rest the congregation sang:

> Dear dying Lamb, Thy precious blood,
> Shall never lose its power,
> Till all the ransomed Church of God
> Be saved to sin no more.[195]

C. T. STUDD

C. T. Studd, the wealthy cricketer, gave everything up to serve Jesus Christ on the mission field. He told Arthur Porritt one day, "I have had one long honeymoon with Christ in the mission field."[196]

J. HUDSON TAYLOR

Even before his birth, James Hudson Taylor had been the object of his mother's prayers. In June 1849, when Taylor had just turned seventeen, those prayers were answered.

His mother was away from home, visiting friends, and she felt a strong compulsion to pray for her son. At that hour Taylor was in his father's library, looking for a book to read. He picked up a gospel tract, thinking there would at least be an interesting story at the beginning; but the more he read, the more interested he became.

He came to the phrase "the finished work of Christ" and it arrested him. "Why does the author use this expression?" he asked himself; and then the words "It is finished" leaped into his mind. He realized that the work of salvation had been completed by Christ on the cross.

"If the whole work was finished and the whole debt paid," he told himself, "then

194. Spurgeon, *The Full Harvest*, 499.
195. Ibid., 504-8.
196. Porritt, *More and More of Memories*, 71.

what is there left for me to do?" He realized that all he could do was receive God's gift and thank Him for it! He fell to his knees in grateful praise. When his mother returned from her visit, she greeted him with the news that she already knew he had been saved. Taylor also discovered that his sister had made a covenant to pray for him until he trusted Christ.[197]

* * *

As a young man preparing to go to China, Hudson Taylor determined to learn to live by faith alone while he was still in England. His resolve was "to learn before leaving England to move man through God by prayer alone."

He worked for a doctor and was paid quarterly. When the time drew near to receive his salary, Taylor was disturbed that his employer said nothing about it. Taylor had only one half-crown piece, but he determined not to break his resolution and ask for his salary. While visiting a needy home on the Lord's Day, Taylor felt led of God to give his last coin to the needy family. The next day he received an anonymous gift through the mail, four times what he had given to the poor!

The following Saturday, the doctor finished up his work and said, "Taylor, is not your salary due again?" Taylor told him that it was and became disappointed when he learned that the doctor had forgotten about the salary due and sent all his funds to the bank! He prayed about the matter (for he had bills of his own to pay) and left it with the Lord. That evening, the doctor visited him and said that one of his richest patients had come over *after hours* to pay his bill! He gave the money to Taylor, who rejoiced. He had learned he could trust God and therefore go to China as a missionary.[198]

* * *

In 1853, when young Hudson Taylor was making his first voyage to China, his vessel was delayed near New Guinea because the winds had stopped. A rapid current was carrying the ship toward some reefs and the situation was becoming dangerous. Even the sailors using a longboat could not row the vessel out of the current.

"We have done everything that can be done," said the captain to Taylor. But Taylor replied, "No, there is one thing we have not done yet." There were three other believers on the ship, and Taylor suggested that each retire to his own cabin and pray for a breeze. They did, and while he was at prayer, Taylor received confidence from God that the desperately needed wind would be sent.

He went up on deck and suggested to the first officer, an unbeliever, that he let down the mainsail because a breeze was on its way. The man refused, but then they saw the corner of the sail begin to stir. The breeze had come! They let down the sail and in a short time were on their way![199]

* * *

197. Dr. & Mrs. Howard Taylor, *Biography of James Hudson Taylor* (London: China Inland Mission, 1965), 6-7.
198. Ibid., 29-34.
199. Ibid., 56-57.

At a "Jesus Hall" in Shanghai, Hudson Taylor preached a gospel message on John 3:14-17. The Holy Spirit spoke to a Mr. Nyi, a businessman who had come into the meeting. Mr. Nyi stood and gave witness of his faith in Christ. "In Confucianism, Buddhism, Taoism, I have found no rest," he said, "but I do find rest in what we have heard tonight. Henceforward I am a believer in Jesus."

Shortly after his conversion, Mr. Nyi introduced Hudson Taylor to the members of a society to which he belonged, and at the same time the new believer gave a clear testimony of his faith in Christ. As a result, one of Nyi's friends trusted Christ.

One day, Mr. Nyi asked Taylor, "How long have you had the glad tiding in England?"

Taylor evasively told him that England had known the gospel for several hundreds of years.

"What!" exclaimed Nyi. "Several hundreds of years! It is possible that you have known about Jesus so long and only now have come to tell us? My father sought the truth for more than twenty years and died without finding it. *Oh, why did you not come sooner?*" [200]

* * *

Hudson Taylor had gone with friends to Brighton, England, to get some rest at the seaside. Burdened by the sight of so many careless Christians in the church service, he wandered out by the shore to watch the waves and to pray. God spoke to him about the founding of a mission to work in inland China. It was a challenge to his faith, but he had learned that whenever God leads He always provides. Taylor wrote on a flyleaf of his pocket Bible, "Prayed for twenty-four willing skillful laborers at Brighton, June 25, 1865." Two days later he opened an account at the London & County Bank in the name of The China Inland Mission. His first deposit was only ten pounds, but God multiplied it greatly in the years that followed. [201]

* * *

Hudson Taylor was traveling by Chinese junk from Shanghai to Ningpo and met a Chinese gentleman named Peter, who seemed interested in the gospel. As the boat neared the city of Sungkiang, Peter fell overboard! The men on the ship refused to do anything to help save the man.

Taylor saw some fishermen nearby and begged them to drag the water to find the drowning man. "It is not convenient," they replied. Taylor begged them, but they only said, "We are busy fishing." Finally, he offered to pay them, but they only delayed more by haggling over the price. They wanted thirty dollars! All Taylor had was fourteen dollars, but he offered to give it all to them if only they would help save his friend.

The men agreed and brought up the man's body on their first attempt. Taylor did all he could to try to restore respiration, but it was too late. The man was dead and perhaps

200. Ibid., 138-40.
201. Ibid., 162-63.

lost forever, only because of the careless indifference of those who could have rescued him.[202]

* * *

It was a stormy night in Birmingham, England, and Hudson Taylor was to speak at a meeting at the Severn Street schoolroom. His hostess assured him that nobody would attend on such a stormy night, but Taylor insisted on going. "I must go, even if there is no one but the doorkeeper."

Less than a dozen people showed up, but the meeting was marked with unusual spiritual power. Half of those present either became missionaries or gave their children as missionaries; and the rest were faithful supporters of the China Inland Mission for years to come.[203]

* * *

Hudson Taylor had definite convictions against strong promotion for financial support. His policy was to share the burden of missions with the people and let God tell them what to give and when to give.

At a meeting in Herfordshire, the chairman announced that there would be opportunity for giving, but Taylor interrupted and quietly told the group that money was not the greatest need. The greatest need was for workers. Instead of sending a contribution to some missionary society, perhaps they ought to pray about giving themselves as God's willing servants, Taylor said.

His host gently reprimanded him that evening for not allowing an offering. "We might have had a good collection," the man said, seemingly deaf to Taylor's explanation of the mission's financial policy.

But the next morning at breakfast the man had a different attitude. God had dealt with him all that night, and he had spent much time in prayer. Finally, he had asked the Lord, "What wilt thou have me to do?" The answer was a check for five hundred pounds given to the mission.

"If there had been a collection," he said honestly, "I would have given a five-pound note!"[204]

* * *

During one especially trying time in the work of the China Inland Mission, Hudson Taylor wrote to his wife, "We have twenty-five cents—and all the promises of God!"[205]

* * *

What kind of candidates did Hudson Taylor want for the China Inland Mission? Taylor wrote:

202. Ibid., 165.
203. Ibid., 178.
204. Ibid., 180.
205. Ibid., 237.

While thankful for any educational advantages that candidates may have enjoyed, we attach far greater importance to spiritual qualifications. We desire men who believe in eternity and live for it. . . . If you want hard work and little appreciation; if you value God's approval rather than fear man's disapprobation; if you are prepared to take joyfully the spoiling of your goods, and seal your testimony, if need be, with your blood; if you can pity and love the Chinese, you may count on a harvest of souls now and a crowd of glory hereafter "that fadeth not away," and on the Master's "Well done."[206]

* * *

Hudson Taylor and George Nicoll, one of the China Inland Mission workers, were in the Chinkiang office of the mission when a packet of letters arrived that told of serious trouble in the various mission stations. Because of rioting, their fellow workers were in serious danger.

As Nicoll began to leave the room, he heard Hudson Taylor whistling! It was Taylor's favorite hymn, "Jesus, I am resting, resting, in the joy of what Thou art. . . . "

"How *can* you whistle when our friends are in such danger?" Nicoll asked Taylor.

"Would you have me anxious and troubled?" Taylor replied. "That would not help them, and would certainly incapacitate me for my work. I have just to roll the burden on the Lord."

The opposition actually was used of God to bring about greater outreach for the mission.[207]

* * *

Hudson Taylor had definite convictions about how God's work should be done. We can make our best plans and try to carry them out in our own strength. Or, we can make careful plans and ask God to bless them. "Yet another way of working is to begin with God; to ask His plans, and to offer ourselves to Him to carry out His purposes."[208]

* * *

Hudson Taylor was scheduled to speak at a large Presbyterian church in Melbourne, Australia. The moderator of the service introduced the missionary in eloquent and glowing terms. He told the large congregation all that Taylor had accomplished in China, and then presented him as "our illustrious guest."

Taylor stood quietly for a moment, and then opened his message by saying, "Dear friends, I am the little servant of an illustrious Master."[209]

SAMUEL TIPPLE

Samuel A. Tipple was a somewhat eccentric British Baptist preacher. In fact, it was his heretical preaching that aroused Charles Spurgeon and precipitated the "Down-

206. Ibid., 242.
207. Ibid., 247.
208. Ibid., 271.
209. Ibid., 316.

grade Controversy," which finally led to Spurgeon's leaving the Baptist Union.

Tipple used to keep a list posted on the bulletin board in the church vestibule of books he wanted in his library. Donors could purchase the books, give them to him, and then cross the titles off the list![210]

HENRY VAN DYKE

Henry van Dyke was pastor of the Brick Presbyterian Church in New York City. We know him primarily as the author of *The Story of the Other Wise Man*. Rather aristocratic, van Dyke enjoyed attention. One journalist said that van Dyke was the only man he knew who could strut sitting down.

Two ladies arrived late at the Brick Church and were ushered to the pulpit stairs because no other seats were available. "But won't we be conspicuous?" they asked. The usher replied, "When Dr. van Dyke preaches, no one is conspicuous."[211]

* * *

Dr. van Dyke owned a fishing chalet in the New England mountains, not far from a popular resort hotel. One summer, a lady gave birth to a baby in the hotel and wanted to have it weighed. No scale was available, but someone remembered that van Dyke owned a fishing scale. A man went down to the chalet and secured the scales. The baby weighed twenty-eight pounds![212]

LESLIE WEATHERHEAD

When Leslie Weatherhead became pastor of the Methodist church in Manchester he found the congregation small and struggling. An aged member of the church told him, "In my father's day, young man, the church was full, and the street was lined with carriages!"

In a short time the church was full again and the street was lined with automobiles.

"This must remind you of your father's day," Weatherhead said to the old fellow.

"Young man, don't be carried away by numbers!" the aged saint replied. "They are no sign of success!"[213]

JOHN WESLEY

John Wesley preached his last sermon on February 17, 1791, in Lambeth on the text "Seek ye the Lord while He may be found, call ye upon Him while He is near" (Isa. 55:6).

The following day, a very sick man, he was put to bed in his home on City Road.

210. Porritt, *More and More of Memories*, 186-88.
211. Ibid., 228.
212. Ibid.
213. A. Kingsley Weatherhead, *Leslie Weatherhead: A Personal Portrait* (Nashville: Abingdon, 1975), 64.

During the days of his illness, he often repeated the words from one of his brother's hymns:

> I the chief of sinners am,
> But Jesus died for me!

His last words were: "The best of all is, God is with us!" He died March 2, 1791.[214]

* * *

People greeted Wesley respectfully in his latter years. He usually answered by quoting his favorite text, "Little children . . . love one another" (John 13:33-34). When he visited an assembly of believers, he often said: "Love the brotherhood. Fear God. Honour the King" (1 Pet. 2:17).[215]

* * *

John Wesley practiced Galatians 6:1: "Brethren, if a man be overtaken in a fault, ye which are spiritual, restore such an one in the spirit of meekness."

William Shent was a barber who had been converted and had become a Methodist preacher. But he fell into sin, and the society in Keighley had to deal with him.

Hearing that the society had been unusually hard on Shent, Wesley wrote the members a letter.

> I have a few questions which I desire may be proposed to the Society at Keighley.
>
> Who was the occasion of the Methodist preachers first setting foot in Leeds? William Shent. Who received John Nelson into his house at his first coming hither? William Shent. Who was it that invited me and received me when I came? William Shent. Who was it that stood by me while I preached in the street with stones flying on every side? William Shent.
>
> Who was it that bore the storm of persecution for the whole town and stemmed it at the peril of his life? William Shent. Whose word did God bless for many years in an eminent manner? William Shent. By whom were many children now in paradise begotten in the Lord and many now alive? William Shent.
>
> Who is he that is ready now to be broken up and turned into the street? William Shent.
>
> And does nobody care for this? William Shent fell into sin and was publicly expelled [from] the Society; but must he be also starved? Must he with his grey hairs and all his children be without a place to lay his head? Can you suffer this? O tell it not in Gath! Where is gratitude? Where is compassion? Where is Christianity? Where is humanity? Where is concern for the cause of God? Who is a wise man among you? Who is concerned for the gospel? Who has put on bowels of mercy? Let him arise and exert himself in this matter. You here all arise as one man and roll away the reproach. Let us set him on his feet once more. It may save both him and his family. But what we do, let it be done quickly.[216]

* * *

214. Ingvar Haddal, *John Wesley* (Epworth, 1961), 168-69.
215. Ibid., 168.
216. Ibid., 151-52.

A nomad at heart, John Wesley did not believe a preacher should remain too long in the same place of ministry. "I have too great an interest in my preachers' bodies and souls to allow them to confine their labors to one place," he said. He feared that the people might get lulled into apathy if they heard the same minister all the time.

It was reported to him that one of the societies had decreased in membership from 160 to 50 in one year. "Such is the fruit of a single preacher's staying a whole year in one place!" was his comment.[217]

* * *

John Wesley had a balanced view of preaching. He told the preachers they should invite, convince, offer Christ, and build up the saints. Every sermon should have each of those elements "in some measure."[218]

* * *

While crossing a bridge in London, John Wesley stumbled and sprained his ankle. Some friends carried him to the house of Mrs. Mary Vazeille on Threadneedle Street. She was a widow with several children. She cared for Wesley and his response to her concern was to ask her to marry him.

If we were writing fiction we might say that the sprained ankle was God's providential way to bring those people together. But the marriage was a disaster, and Mary finally left John. Had Wesley consulted with his brother Charles, and asked for the prayers of the brethren, he might have avoided that unfortunate situation. Mary was accustomed to her quiet home, and it was difficult for her to travel with her husband and stay in uncomfortable inns.

It is unfortunate that Mary was not content just to ignore John's ministry; she actually opposed it. She gave certain personal letters to his enemies and even made additions to them that made them worse! Once she even pulled her husband around on the floor by his hair! "I felt as though I could have knocked the soul out of her!" one of Wesley's friends said.

Wesley concluded that his unhappy marriage encouraged him to work harder and not complain about missing the comforts of a home. Certainly it encouraged him to be away from home more![219]

* * *

Often Wesley had to put up with interruptions and distractions while he was preaching. Sometimes they would ring the church bells and try to drown him out. His enemies even hired people to sing in the street, play the drum, or blow trumpets! In London, one man tried to drive his herd of cows right through the listening crowd! "The brutes were wiser than their masters," Wesley wrote, "they went another way!" (See Isa. 1:3.)

One particular day, a number of the troublemakers in London attended a meeting at

217. Ibid., 151.
218. Ibid., 149.
219. Ibid., 143-74.

the Foundry Chapel, and several trusted Christ. "I wonder the devil has not wisdom enough to discern that he is destroying his own kingdom," said Wesley.[220]

* * *

The preacher needs discernment in his choice of texts. Sometimes Wesley embarrassed people by the texts he chose, but God always vindicated him.

Once, he addressed a group of wealthy people from the text, "O generation of vipers, who hath warned you to flee from the wrath to come?" (Matt. 3:7).

"You should use that text in the slums," said his listeners.

"Oh, no," Wesley replied, "there I shall preach on: "Behold, what manner of love the Father hath bestowed upon us, that we should be called the sons of God" (1 John 3:1).[221]

* * *

Wesley was not an advocate of sensationalism in preaching. But on one occasion, he interrupted his own sermon and shouted, "Lord, is Saul also among the prophets? Is James Watson here? If he be, show Thy power!" And James Watson dropped to the floor and began to cry loudly for God's mercy![222]

* * *

Wesley's simple style of preaching was not natural to him. He had to develop it by hard work. When he first began to preach, his vocabulary was so academic and difficult that the simple listeners sat with their mouths open, wondering what he was talking about. Finally, Wesley read his sermons privately to an intelligent maidservant and told her to stop him whenever he uttered something she could not understand. She cried "Stop, sir!" so often that Wesley became irritated. But it helped him learn to phrase his thoughts in ways that would interest and teach the simple people who came to hear him preach.

He considered the first epistle of John to be "the deepest part of Holy Scripture," and he modeled his own style after that epistle. "Here are sublimity and simplicity together," he said, "the strongest sense and the plainest language!"[223]

* * *

It has been estimated that John Wesley traveled 250,000 miles in his ministry, which averages to about eighteen miles a day. Keep in mind that he traveled by horse or by a carriage.

He wrote 231 books and preached about 40,000 sermons!

A book alone could be written about Wesley's travels. He often had problems with incompetent blacksmiths who made his horse lame, and once he even had his horse lie down and die!

220. Ibid., 124.
221. Ibid., 121.
222. Ibid., 119.
223. Ibid., 118-19.

He rarely allowed the weather to stop him. One day he was told that it was impossible to ride because of the snowstorm. "At least we can walk twenty miles a day," Wesley replied, and off he went, leading his horse.

When he was 83 years old, he had the same courage and determination. He was to preach at St. Ives and encouraged his coachman to cross a stretch of sand that had been covered by the tide. A fisherman begged them not to attempt the crossing, but Wesley would not miss his appointment. Before long, the horses were swimming! Wesley leaned out the window and shouted, "What is your name, driver?" "Peter," the man answered. "Peter, fear not; thou shalt not sink!"

They made it safely across and Wesley preached at St. Ives.[224]

* * *

In 1742 Wesley began to discover that, like it or not, he was a controversial figure. Of course, many of the people who condemned him had never met him or heard him preach. It was just a popular thing to criticize the Methodist leader.

While riding one day, Wesley overtook another traveler and they began to converse on various topics. Before long, the stranger let Wesley know where he stood on matters of religious faith. As they rode along, the man became more and more vehement, and finally said that his companion (whom he did not know was Wesley) must be a follower of John Wesley who was "rotten at heart."

"No, I am not his follower," said John. "I *am* John Wesley."

At that, the stranger attempted to get away; but Wesley had the better horse and kept close to him, sharing the truth of the Word.[225]

* * *

Among the forgotten men of church history are Thomas Maxfield and John Cennick. They were laymen Wesley appointed to help supervise the Methodist societies—Maxfield in London and Cennick in Kingswood. He gave them permission to expound the Word, but they were not allowed to preach in the formal sense. Wesley was still strongly influenced by his Anglican respect for church order.

While away on a trip Wesley heard that Maxfield was *preaching* the Word, that great crowds were coming to hear, and that many were being saved. John rushed home to investigate and met his mother in his rooms. "Thomas Maxfield has turned preacher, I find!" John told her, and she could see his agitation.

"John, you know what my sentiments have been," she said. "You cannot suspect me of favoring readily any thing of this kind. But take care what you do with respect to that young man, for he is as surely called of God to preach as you are. Examine what have been the fruits of his preaching, and hear him also yourself."

When Wesley listened to Maxfield preach, he was so excited he joyfully said, "It is the Lord; let Him do what seemeth Him good!" That was the beginning of lay ministry in the Methodist societies, a ministry greatly blessed of God.[226]

224. Ibid., 112-14.
225. Ibid., 105-6.
226. Ibid., 104-5.

* * *

Early in his ministry, Wesley had fellowship with and often preached at a German United Brethren meeting in Fetter Lane. He was most distressed at the spirit of disunity among the people, and often had to act as mediator in their disputes. While Wesley was out of the city on a trip, a French "prophetess" took over the meetings; when John returned, he had her dismissed. He had investigated her life and discovered she was living in sin.

Then there appeared in the group some false teaching concerning the work of the Holy Spirit. On June 22, 1740, Wesley preached a sermon on Jeremiah 6:16: "Stand ye in the ways, and see, and ask for the old paths." The group soon decided that Wesley could not preach to them again! About a month later Wesley warned them again of their dangerous doctrines and asked all who were warned to obey the truth to follow him. About eighteen people left the meeting with Wesley and that was the nucleus for the first Methodist society. They met in an abandoned cannon foundry that still stands on City Road in London and is known today as "The Foundry Chapel."

Three years later there were nearly 2,000 members in Wesley's group, whereas the United Brethren had 72![227]

* * *

For many years Samuel Wesley, John's father, labored on a commentary on the book of Job, working on it up to the day of his death. If any member of the family criticized the book or questioned his labors, that child was immediately in disfavor! The book was almost considered to be another member of the family. The family discussed it at meals and hoped the father would complete it soon.

After Samuel's death the book was published and John Wesley went to London to present a copy to Queen Caroline. She received it somewhat carelessly, examined it superficially, and put it on a shelf, remarking, "It is very prettily bound."

It is unlikely that many people read the book, but it did accomplish one great thing: it brought John Wesley to London. On that visit he met James Oglethorpe, governor of the colony of Georgia. Wesley's voyage to North America and the subsequent events are written in modern church history; and that all turned on the tiny hinge of a man's forgotten book![228]

* . * *

Samuel Wesley died on April 25, 1735, and his son John was at his side to pray for him. Samuel said to his daughter Emeila, "Do not be concerned at my death. God will then begin to manifest Himself to my family." Then to John he said: "Be steady. The Christian faith will surely revive in the kingdom. You shall see it though I shall not." Both of his predictions came true.[229]

* * *

227. Ibid., 94-95.
228. Ibid., 46.
229. Ibid.

Bishop Joseph Butler was a learned man, but he had no sympathy with John Wesley's message or ministry. In 1739, when Wesley showed up in his territory, the Bishop opposed him. "Sir, you have no business here," he said. "You are not commissioned to preach in this diocese. Therefore, I advise you to go hence."

Wesley replied: "My lord, my business on earth is to do what good I can. Wherever, therefore, I think I can do most good, there must I stay, so long as I think so. At present I think I can do most good here; therefore, here I stay. As to my preaching here, a dispensation of the gospel is committed to me, and woe is me if I preach not the gospel wherever I am in the habitable world!"[230]

* * *

In 1749 Wesley was preaching at Bolton, and a mob attacked the house where he was staying. Two of his associates managed to quiet the crowd, and then Wesley himself walked right into the crowd unafraid. He recorded in his journal: "I called for a chair. The winds were hushed, and all was calm and still. My heart was filled with love, my eyes with tears, and my mouth with arguments. They were amazed, they were ashamed, they were melted down, they devoured every word. What a turn was this!"

Wesley often had to preach while standing on a chair so that he might better be seen, for he was a very short man.[231]

* * *

John Wesley's father, Samuel, was a dedicated pastor, but there were those in his parish who did not like him. On February 9, 1709, a fire broke out in the rectory at Epworth, possibly set by one of the rector's enemies. Young John, not yet six years old, was stranded on an upper floor of the building. Two neighbors rescued the lad just seconds before the roof crashed in. One neighbor stood on the other's shoulders and pulled young John through the window.

Samuel Wesley said, "Come, neighbors, let us kneel down. Let us give thanks to God. He has given me all my eight children. Let the house go. I am rich enough."

John Wesley often referred to himself as "a brand plucked out of the fire" (Zech. 3:2; Amos 4:11). In later years he often noted February 9 in his journal and gave thanks to God for His mercy.

Samuel Wesley labored for forty years at Epworth and saw very little fruit; but consider what his family accomplished![232]

* * *

John Wesley once told his friend Adam Clarke, "If I were to write my own life, I should begin it before I was born."[233]

* * *

230. Skevington Wood, *The Burning Heart* (Grand Rapids: Eerdmans, 1967), 106-7.
231. John Wesley, *Journal*, (October 18, 1749).
232. Wood, *The Burning Heart*, 29.
233. Ibid., 19.

Wesley reports his mother's death as follows:

> About three in the afternoon, I went to my mother, and found her change was near. . . . Her look was calm and serene, and her eyes fixed upward, while we commended her soul to God. From three to four, the silver cord was loosing, and the wheel breaking at the cistern [Ecclesiastes 12:6]; and then, without any struggle, or sigh, or groan, the soul was set at liberty. We stood round the bed and fulfilled her last request, uttered a little before she lost her speech: "Children, as soon as I am released, sing a psalm of praise to God."[234]

[For an accurate report of Susanna Wesley's "Rules for Raising her Family," see the *Journals* for Sunday, August 1, 1742.]

* * *

After a service at All-Saints Church in Bristol, Wesley started riding to Kingswood, but his horse fell; and when he tried to raise him, the horse again fell, this time on Wesley. Several women came out of a neighboring house to assist him, and they took him into the house. In the house were three persons whom he knew, people who had professed faith in Christ but were now in a backslidden condition. Wesley ministered to them, they all repented, and Wesley reported "not one of them has looked back since."[235]

* * *

Wesley and Whitefield had their theological differences, and the enemy tried to magnify them and create division in the various Methodist societies. One Sunday Wesley came to the Foundry Chapel in London to preach and discovered that someone, without permission, had printed one of Whitefield's letters to Wesley and was having them distributed at the door of the chapel!

Wesley secured a copy and explained the matter to the congregation. Then he said, "I will do just what I believe Mr. Whitefield would do were he here himself." And he tore the letter to pieces. Everybody in the congregation followed his example, and within two minutes not a copy was to be found.[236]

[For a copy of the letter itself, see page 97 of *John Wesley*, by Ingvar Raddal (Abingdon).]

* * *

While riding to Oxford, John Wesley was overtaken by a young gentleman who asked him if he had seen Whitefield's *Journals*. Wesley said that he had.

"And what do you think of them?" the gentleman asked, adding critically that they were full of hypocrisy and enthusiasm.

"Why do you think so?" Wesley inquired.

"Why," said the young man, "he talks so much about joy and stuff, and inward

234. Wesley, *Journal*, (August 23, 1742).
235. Ibid., (October 25, 1741).
236. Ibid., (February 1, 1741).

feelings. As I hope to be saved, I cannot tell what to make of it."

Wesley took the opportunity to explain the gospel to him and then warned him that he beware of criticizing something about which he personally knew nothing.[237]

* * *

Susanna Wesley is another of God's great women, and an example for Christian mothers everywhere. Her son John told how she found assurance of salvation.

> I talked largely with my mother, who told me, that, till a short time since, she had scarce heard such a thing mentioned, as having forgiveness of sins now, or God's Spirit bearing witness with our spirit: much less did she imagine that this was the common privilege of all true believers.

It occurred at a communion service when the cup was handed to her, and the pastor (her son, Hall) said, "The blood of our Lord Jesus Christ, which is given for thee," that she found assurance. The words struck her heart and (she said) "I knew God for Christ's sake had forgiven *me* all *my* sins."[238]

* * *

Weary in body, John Wesley went to Wapping to speak to a religious gathering. He had intended to speak on Romans 3:19 but seemed unable to give the message. While the congregation was singing, Wesley was praying for wisdom from God to know what to say. A statement from Hebrews went through his mind, but he could not pin it down. He opened his Bible to Hebrews 10:19 and began to preach about entering "into the holiest" and taking advantage of the "new and living way."

God began to work. People began to call on the Lord for salvation. Twenty-six people promised to call on Wesley the next day, but only eighteen came. Wesley examined each of their experiences carefully and concluded that many of them had truly been saved.[239]

* * *

John Wesley's favorite subject was, "Christ Jesus, who of God is made unto us wisdom, and righteousness, and sanctification, and redemption" (1 Cor. 1:30).

He wrote: "I went with Mr. Whitefield to Blackheath, there were, I believe, twelve or fourteen thousand people. He a little surprised me, by desiring me to preach in his stead; which I did (though nature recoiled) on my favorite subject."

He added an interesting observation: "I was greatly moved with compassion for the rich that were there, to whom I made a particular application. Some of them seemed to attend [pay attention], while others drove away their coaches from so uncouth a preacher."[240]

* * *

237. Ibid., (November 12, 1739).
238. Ibid., (September 3, 1739).
239. Ibid., (June 15, 1739).
240. Ibid., (June 14, 1739).

All of his life, John Wesley had believed that the preaching of the Word had to be done in a consecrated building. When his friend George Whitefield began to preach in the open fields, Wesley at first was critical. Wesley met Whitefield in Bristol and recorded this in his journal: "I could scarce reconcile myself at first to this strange way of preaching in the fields . . . having been all my life (till very lately) so tenacious of every point relating to decency and order, that I should have thought the saving of souls almost a sin, if it had not been done in a church."

Two days later Wesley did his first outdoor preaching and recorded the event in his journal: "At four in the afternoon, I submitted to be more vile, and proclaimed in the highways the glad tidings of salvation, speaking from a little eminence in a ground adjoining to the city, to about three thousand people." His text was Luke 4:18-19.[241]

* * *

While visiting at Hernhuth, Germany, John Wesley witnessed the burial of a child and was deeply moved. As the procession moved from the chapel to the cemetery, the people sang a hymn. The child's body was committed to the earth as the father stood watching.

"How do you find yourself?" Wesley asked the man.

"Praised be the Lord, never better!" the man replied. "He has taken the soul of my child to himself. . . . And I know that when it is raised again, both he and I shall be ever with the Lord."[242]

* * *

One morning John Wesley awoke at five o'clock and opened his Greek New Testament to 2 Peter 1:4 and translated: "There are given unto us exceeding great and precious promises, even that ye should be partakers of the divine nature."

As he left the room to go about his work he opened the New Testament again, this time to Mark 12:34, and again translated: "Thou art not far from the kingdom of God."

Later that day, he attended a service at St. Paul's Cathedral, and the choir sang the anthem based on Psalm 130:1: "Out of the Deep Have I Called unto Thee, O Lord."

That evening he went "very unwillingly" to a meeting in Aldersgate Street where someone was reading aloud the preface to Martin Luther's *Commentary on Romans*.

Wesley wrote in his journal:

> About a quarter before nine, while he was describing the change which God works in the heart through faith in Christ, I felt my heart strangely warmed. I felt I did trust in Christ, Christ alone for salvation: And an assurance was given me, that he had taken away my sins, even *mine,* and saved *me* from the law of sin and death.[243]

* * *

John Wesley visited his brother Charles in Oxford, and there met Peter Bohler, a German Christian whose ministry convinced Wesley of his lack of faith.

241. Ibid., (March 31 and April 2, 1739).
242. Ibid., (August 8, 1738).
243. Ibid., (May 24, 1738).

"How can you preach to others, who have not faith yourself?" he said to himself. He asked Bohler what he should do, and the man replied: "Preach faith *till* you have it; and then, *because* you have it, you will preach faith."

Wesley began to preach "this new doctrine," and offered salvation to a condemned prisoner named Clifford, even though for years Wesley had opposed "death-bed repentance."[244]

* * *

As he was returning to England after his missionary service in America, John Wesley wrote in his journal:

> I went to America to convert the Indians; but O! who shall convert me? who, what is he that will deliver me from this evil heart of unbelief? I have a fair summer religion. I can talk well; nay, and believe myself, while no danger is near: But let death look me in the face, and my spirit is troubled. Nor can I say, "To die is gain."[245]

* * *

While ministering as a missionary in Georgia, John Wesley wrote a will for a man who was very ill. Wesley asked the man what he thought of paradise. "To be sure, it is a fine place," the dying man said. "But I don't mind that; I don't care what place I am in. Let God put me where He will, or do with me what He will, so I may but set forth His honor and glory."

Wesley declared this to be a perfect example of "disinterested love."[246]

* * *

In 1736 John Wesley arrived in America and settled in Savannah, Georgia. The day after he arrived he was introduced to one of the German Moravian pastors who questioned Wesley about his personal faith.

"Have you the witness within yourself?" he asked the Anglican missionary. "Does the Spirit of God bear witness with your spirit that you are a child of God?"

Wesley was surprised, and did not know how to answer.

"Do you know Jesus Christ?" the Moravian asked.

"I know He is the Savior of the world," Wesley replied after a pause.

"True," the pastor said, "but do you know He has saved you?"

Wesley answered, "I hope He has died to save me."

"Do you know yourself?" the German persisted.

"I do," Wesley replied, but he added in his journal, "I fear they were vain words."[247]

* * *

As John Wesley was sailing to America, his ship went through terrifying storms. One of the storms broke and was more violent than the others. Every ten minutes there was

244. Ibid. (March 4-6, 1738).
245. Ibid. (January 24, 1738).
246. Ibid. (June 1, 1736).
247. Ibid. (February 7, 1736).

such a shock in the stern of the ship that the passengers wondered if it would remain together. A young child was brought to Wesley to be received into the church.

He wrote in His journal: "It put me in mind of Jeremiah's buying the field, when the Chaldeans were on the point of destroying Jerusalem, and seemed a pledge of the mercy God designed to show us."

A group of German Moravians was on board, and Wesley was impressed with their peace in the midst of the storm. While the Germans were holding a service, a huge wave swept over the deck and split the main sail in pieces. The English passengers began to scream, but "the Germans calmly sang on." Wesley asked one of the Moravians later whether or not he had been afraid during the storm, and the man replied, "I thank God, no."

"But were not your women and children afraid?" asked Wesley.

"No; our women and children are not afraid to die," the Moravian replied.

God used that witness to awaken Wesley to his own spiritual needs.[248]

GEORGE WHITEFIELD

There was a drinking club that had as its waiter a boy who had a gift of mimicking people. One day the members asked the boy to mimic George Whitefield, but the boy refused. Being pressed by the men, the boy finally stood up and, impersonating Whitefield, said: "I speak the truth in Christ; I lie not; except you repent you will all be damned!"

That short sermon broke up the club, which never met again.[249]

* * *

A man in Boston went to hear George Whitefield preach only for the purpose of hearing something he could make fun of at the tavern. But the crowd was so densely packed that the man could not move; so he had to remain during the entire sermon. Later, under conviction, he talked to Whitefield personally and was led to faith in Christ.[250]

* * *

Although George Whitefield disagreed with John Wesley on some theological matters, he was careful not to create problems in public that could be used to hinder the preaching of the gospel. When someone asked Whitefield if he thought he would see Wesley in heaven, Whitefield replied: "I fear not, for he will be so near the eternal throne and we at such a distance, we shall hardly get sight of him."[251]

* * *

When George Whitefield arrived as a student in Oxford, he heard about the Wesley

248. Ibid. (January 25, 1736).
249. Arnold A. Dallimore, *George Whitefield*, 2 vols. (London: Banner of Truth, 1970), 1:500-501.
250. Ibid., 2:196.
251. Ibid., 2:353.

brothers and their "religious society," and he wanted to meet them and become a part of their work, but the opportunity did not present itself.

One day Whitefield heard about a woman in one of the poorhouses who had tried to commit suicide by cutting her throat. Whitefield sent a message to Charles Wesley and suggested that perhaps someone would want to minister to the woman, and in that way the friendship began. The poor woman had tried to destroy herself, yet God overruled and used the event to build His church. [252]

ALEXANDER WHYTE

When Alexander Whyte was a boy working on the farm, he caught his right arm in a threshing machine. Everyone thought at first that he would have to have the limb amputated, but a neighbor named Margaret cautioned them to wait.

The next day the pain was so severe that Whyte's mother called in the neighbor, who said, "I like the pain, Janet; I like the pain." It was proof that the arm was healing, and heal it did.

Whyte often used this story to illustrate that the pain of conviction for sin is a good sign and can lead to spiritual recovery. [253]

* * *

Although a Puritan in the area of theology, Alexander Whyte was more broadminded when it came to appreciating the preaching of those with whom he disagreed. In particular, he appreciated the sermons of Cardinal Newman. Whyte gave a volume of Newman's sermons to a young friend and wrote on the flyleaf, "The finest of the wheat." Apparently one of Whyte's more critical elders saw the inscription one day and so he wrote under it, "The worst of the chaff!" [254]

* * *

Alexander Whyte heard of a young minister whose little son had just died, so he wrote him a letter, recalling the death of his own little boy twenty years before.

> Dear friend—
> I have been thinking of you all morning and of the funeral day of our little George. I stepped in before the undertaker's man, and could scarcely let him screw down the little coffin lid. By these things men live and ministers preach. I go out far from home alone this afternoon. You may be sure I will not forget you. Tenderest sympathy for your dear wife.
>   Alexander Whyte [255]

* * *

In 1908, Rev. E. Jenkins, a Methodist pastor, wrote to Alexander Whyte that he was

252. Haddal, *John Wesley*, 44-45.
253. G. F. Barbour, *Life of Alexander Whyte* (London: Hodder and Stoughton, 1923), 19-20.
254. Ibid., 173.
255. Ibid., 269.

discouraged in the ministry and thinking of resigning.

Whyte wrote back: "Never think of giving up preaching! The angels around the throne envy your great work."[256]

* * *

When baptizing the child of one of his ministerial colleagues at Free St. George's, Edinburgh, Alexander Whyte remarked, "He'll teach you more, sir, than any of your college professors did!"[257]

* * *

Dr. John Duncan was the revered Hebrew professor at New College in Edinburgh when Alexander Whyte was a student there. The scholar was known familiarly as "Rabbi" Duncan, and he was a man with a keen mind and a warm heart.

One Sunday Duncan was assisting in the Lord's Supper and noted a woman near the front of the church weeping and refusing to take the cup from the elder. The great scholar left his place at the table, took the cup from the elder, and gave it to the woman, saying, "Take it, woman—it's for sinners!"[258]

* * *

After preaching an especially powerful New Year's sermon, Alexander Whyte was visited in the vestry by one of his fine members. The man thanked his pastor for the sermon. "It went to my heart as if you had come straight from the Audience-chamber."

"And perhaps I did," was Whyte's solemn reply.[259]

* * *

BIBLIOGRAPHY

Abbott, Lyman. *Silhouettes of My Contemporaries*. New York: Doubleday, 1922.

Bacon, Ernest W. *Spurgeon: Heir of the Puritans*. Grand Rapids: Eerdmans, 1968.

Bainton, Roland H. *Here I Stand: A Life of Martin Luther*. Nashville: Abingdon, 1950.

Barbour, G. F. *The Life of Alexander Whyte*. London: Hodder and Stoughton, 1923.

Bonar, Marjory, ed. *Andrew A Bonar: Diary and Life*. London: Banner of Truth, 1960.

Booth, Bramwell. *Echoes and Memories*. New York: George H. Doran, 1925.

Chambers, Gertrude, ed. *Oswald Chambers: His Life and Work*. London: Simkin Marshall, Ltd., 1933.

Curtis, Richard K. *They Called Him Mister Moody*. New York: Doubleday, 1962; paperback edition, Grand Rapids: Eerdmans, 1967.

Dallimore, Arnold A. *George Whitefield*, 2 vols. London: Banner of Truth, 1970.

Dargan, Edwin C. *A History of Preaching*, 2 vols. Grand Rapids: Baker, 1974.

Fullerton, W. Y. *F. B. Meyer: A Biography*. London: Marshall, Morgan & Scott, nd.

Haddal, Ingvar. *John Wesley*. London: Epworth, 1961.

Harries, John. *G. Campbell Morgan: The Man and His Ministry* New York: Revell, 1930.

Hopkins, Hugh Evan. *Charles Simeon of Cambridge*. Grand Rapids: Eerdmans, 1977.

Jones, J. D. *Three Score Years and Ten*. London: Hodder and Stoughton, 1940.

256. Ibid., 307-8.
257. Ibid., 311.
258. Ibid., 310.
259. Ibid., 317.

Macmillan, D. *The Life of George Matheson*. London: Hodder and Stoughton, 1907.

Mann, A. Chester *F. B. Meyer: Preacher, Teacher, Man of God* London: George Allen & Unwin, Ltd., 1929.

Morgan, Jill. *A Man of the Word*. Grand Rapids: Baker, 1972.

Murray, Iain H. *The Forgotten Spurgeon*. London: Banner of Truth, 1966.

Porritt, Arthur *The Best I Remember*. London: Cassell and Co., Ltd., 1922.

——————————. *More and More of Memories*. London: George Allen & Unwin, Ltd., 1947.

Ray, Charles. *A Marvellous Ministry: The Story of C. H. Spurgeon's Sermons, 1855-1905*. London: Passmore and Alabaster, 1905.

Sangster, Paul. *Dr. Sangster*. London: Epworth, 1962.

Spurgeon, Charles Haddon. *The Early Years*. London: Banner of Truth, 1962.

——————————. *The Full Harvest*. London: Banner of Truth, 1973.

Street, M. Jennie. *F. B. Meyer, His Life and Work*. Philadelphia: American Baptist Publication Society, 1902.

Taylor, Dr. & Mrs. Howard *Biography of James Hudson Taylor*. London: China Inland Mission, 1965.

Turnbull, Ralph G. *History of Preaching*, vol. 3. Grand Rapids: Baker, 1974.

Weatherhead, A. Kingsley *Leslie Weatherhead: A Personal Portrait*. Nashville: Abingdon, 1975.

Wesley, John. *The Works of John Wesley*. Grand Rapids: Zondervan, n.d.

Wood, Skevington. *John Wesley—The Burning Heart*. Grand Rapids: Eerdmans, 1967.

Bibliographies

GREAT PREACHERS: THEIR METHODS AND MESSAGE

Ashley, John M. *Augustine the Preacher*. London: J. T. Hayes, 1877.
——————. *Origen the Preacher*. London: J. T. Hayes, 1878.
Baring-Gould, Sabine. *Post-Medieval Preachers*. London: Rivington's, 1865.
Baxter, B. B. *The Heart of the Yale Lectures*. New York: Macmillan, 1947.
Blackwood, Andrew W. *The Protestant Pulpit*. New York: Abingdon-Cokesbury, 1957.
Blaikie, W. G. *The Preachers of Scotland from the 6th to the 19th Century*. Edinburgh: T. & T. Clarke, 1888.
Blench, J. W. *Preaching in England*. New York: Barnes and Noble, 1964.
Bond, Albert C. *The Master Preacher: A Study of the Homiletics of Jesus*. New York: American Tract Society, 1910.
Brastow, Lewis O. *The Modern Pulpit*. New York: MacMillan, 1906.
——————. *Representative Modern Preachers*. New York: Macmillan, 1904.
Brilioth, Yngve. *A Brief History of Preaching*. Philadelphia: Fortress, 1965.
Broadus, John A. *Lectures on the History of Preaching*. New York: Sheldon, 1876.
Crocker, Lionell. *Henry Ward Beecher's Art of Preaching*. Chicago: U. of Chicago, 1934.
Crowe, Charles M. *Great Southern Preaching*. New York: Macmillan, 1926.
Currier, Albert. *Nine Great Preachers*. Boston: Pilgrim, 1912.
Dargan, Edward Charles. *The Art of Preaching in the Light of Its History*. New York: George H. Doran, 1922.
——————. *A History of Preaching*. Grand Rapids: Baker, 1954.
Dodd, C. H. *The Apostolic Preaching and Its Development*. London: Hodder and Stoughton, 1936.
Duffield, Guy. *Pentecostal Preaching*. New York: Vantage, 1957.
Fish, H. C. *History and Repository of Pulpit Eloquence*. New York: M. W. Dodd, 1856.

Gammie, Alexander. *Preachers I Have Heard*. London: Pickering and Inglis, 1945.

Garvie, Alfred E. *The Christian Preacher*. New York: Scribner's, 1921.

—————————. *The Preachers of the Church*. London: J. Clarke & Co., 1926.

Higgins, Paul. *Preachers of Power*. New York: Vantage, 1950.

Horn, Howard. *Princes of the Christian Pulpit*. Nashville: Cokesbury, 1927.

Horne, Charles. *The Romance of Preaching*. New York: Revell, 1914.

Hoyt, Arthur S. *The Pulpit and American Life*. New York: Macmillan, 1921.

Humpstone, John. *Man and Message*. Philadelphia: Judson, 1927.

James, Fleming. *The Message and the Messengers*. New York: Thomas Whittaker, 1897.

Jeffs, Ernest H. *Princes of the Modern Pulpit*. Nashville: Cokesbury, 1931.

Jones, Edgar DeWitt. *American Preachers of Today*. Indianapolis: Bobbs-Merrill, 1933.

—————————. *Royalty of the Pulpit*. New York: Harper and Brothers, 1951.

Kerr, Hugh T. *Preaching in the Early Church*. New York: Revell, 1942.

Kerr, John. *Lectures on the History of Preaching*. London: Hodder & Stoughton, 1888.

Kleiser, Grenville. *Christ the Master Speaker*. New York: Funk & Wagnalls, 1920.

—————————. *The World's Greatest Sermons*. 10 vols. New York: Funk & Wagnalls, 1908.

Kulandran, Sabapathy. *Message and Silence of the American Pulpit*. Boston: Pilgrim, 1949.

Macartney, C. E. *Great Sermons of the World*. Grand Rapids: Baker, 1958.

—————————. *Six Kings of the American Pulpit*. Philadelphia: Westminster, 1945.

—————————. *Sons of Thunder*. New York: Revell, 1929.

McGraw, James. *Great Evangelical Preachers of Yesterday*. New York: Abingdon, 1961.

Mitchell, William F. *English Pulpit Oratory*. New York: Macmillan, 1932.

Neale, John M. *Medieval Preachers and Medieval Preaching*. London: J. & C. Mozley, 1856.

Nicoll, W. Robertson. *Princes of the Church*. London: Hodder & Stoughton, 1921.

Owst, Gerald. *Preaching in Medieval England*. Cambridge: University Press, 1926.

—————————. *Preaching in a Revolutionary Age*. New York: Abingdon, 1944.

Pattison, T. Harwood. *The History of Christian Preaching*. Philadelphia: American Baptist Publication Society, 1912.

Petry, C. Ray. *No Uncertain Sound*. Philadelphia: Westminster, 1948.

Pierson, Arthur T. *Pulpit Power and Eloquence*. Cleveland: F. M. Barton, 1901.

Richardson, Alan. *English Preachers and Preaching*. New York: Macmillan, 1928.

Rosser, John. *Paul the Preacher*. New York: American Tract Society, 1916.

Ryle, J. C. *The Christian Leaders of the Last Century*. London: Nelson and Sons, 1960.

Shepherd, William. *Great Preachers as Seen by a Journalist*. New York: Revell, 1924.

Simons, Laird. *Half Hours with the Great Preachers*. Philadelphia: Porter and Coates, 1871.

Smyth, Charles. *The History of Preaching*. London: Society for the Promulgation of Christian Knowledge, 1940.

Sprague, W. B. *Annals of the American Pulpit*. 9 vols. New York: Carter, 1858-1861.

Sumner, John B. *Apostolic Preaching*. New York: Protestant Episcopal, 1830.

Taylor, William M. *The Scottish Pulpit from the Reformation to the Present Day*. New York: Harper, 1867.

Thompson, Ernest T. *Changing Emphasis in American Preaching*. Philadelphia: Westminster, 1943.

Turnbull, Ralph G. *Jonathan Edwards the Preacher*. Grand Rapids: Baker, 1958.

Turnbull, Robert. *The Pulpit Orators of France and Switzerland*. New York: R. E. Carter, 1848.

Wagner, Don. *The Expository Methods of Campbell Morgan*. Westwood, N.J.: Revell, 1957.

Waterbury, J. B. *Sketches of Eloquent Preachers*. New York: American Tract Society, 1864.

Webber, F. R. *A History of Preaching*. 3 vols. Milwaukee: Northwestern, 1957.

Wilkinson, William. *Modern Masters of Pulpit Discourse*. New York: Funk & Wagnalls, 1905.

Zawart, Anscan. *History of Franciscan Preaching*. New York: J. F. Wagner, 1928.

ANTHOLOGIES OF PREACHING

Abernathy, William, et al. *What We Preach*. Philadelphia: Judson, 1929.

————————. *American Pulpit Series*. New York: Abingdon, 1945.

————————. *The Anglican Pulpit of Today*. London: Hodder & Stoughton, 1886.

Atkins, Gaius. *Master Sermons of the 19th Century*. Chicago: Willett Clark and Co., 1940.

Baxter, B. B. *Preachers of Today*. Nashville: Christian, 1952.

Belcher, Joseph. *The Baptist Pulpit of the United States*. New York: Edward Fletcher, 1850.

Brastow, Lewis. *Representative Modern Preachers*. New York: Macmillan, 1904.

Brawley, E. M. *Negro Baptist Pulpit*. Philadelphia: American Baptist, 1890.

Butler, Paul. *Best Sermons*. New York: Harper, 1947-1950.

Clark, Davis. *The Methodist Episcopal Pulpit*. New York: Lane & Scott, 1848.

————————. *Classic Preachers of the English Church*. New York: Dutton, 1877.

Crows, Charles M. *Great Southern Preaching*. New York: Macmillan, 1926.

Engstrom, T. *Great Sermons by Great American Preachers*. Grand Rapids: Zondervan, 1953.

————————. *Great Sermons from Master Preachers*. Grand Rapids: Zondervan, 1951.

Fish, H. C. *Pulpit Eloquence: History and Repository of Pulpit Eloquence*. New York: M. W. Dodd, 1855.

————————. *Pulpit Eloquence of 19th Century*. New York: Dodd, Mead, 1871.

Frost, S. E. *The World's Great Sermons*. Garden City, N.Y.: Halcyon, 1943.

Gifford, Frank. *The Anglican Pulpit Today*. New York: Morahouse Gorhan, 1953.

Humbert, Jessel. *Great Sermons by Great Preachers*. Philadelphia: John Winston, 1927.

Kleiser, Glenville. *The World's Great Sermons*. 10 Vols. New York: Funk & Wagnalls, 1908.

Macartney, Clarence. *Great Sermons of the World*. Grand Rapids: Baker, 1958.

Marchant, James. *If I Had Only One Sermon to Preach*. New York: Harpers, 1928.

McKeehan, Hobart. *Anglo-American Preaching*. New York: Harper and Brothers, 1928.

_____. *Great Modern Sermons*. New York: Revell, 1923.

Moore, W. T. *Living Pulpit of the Christian Church*. St. Louis: Christian, 1867.

Morrison, Charles. C. *The American Pulpit*. New York: Macmillan, 1925.

Newton, Joseph F. *Preaching in New York*. New York: George H. Doran, 1924.

_____. *Some Living Masters of the Pulpit*. New York: George H. Doran, 1923.

Poling, Dan. *Treasury of Great Sermons*. New York: Greenbury, 1944.

Scott, Robert and Stiles, William. *Modern Sermons by World Scholars*, New York: Funk & Wagnalls, 1909.

_____. *Sermons of Power*. Nashville: Cokesbury, 1930.

Simpson, Hubert. *Twenty Sermons by Famous Preachers*. New York: Doran, 1924.

Smythson, William T. *The Methodist Pulpit South*. Washington: W. T. S., 1859.

Stamm, Frederick. *The Reformed Church Pulpit*. New York: Macmillan, 1928.

Stiles, Robert, & Stiles, William. *Modern Sermons by World Scholars*. New York: Funk & Wagnalls, 1909.

Suddards, W. *The British Pulpit*. Philadelphia: Gregar & Elliot, 1836.

Wallis, Charles. *Notable Sermons from Protestant Pulpits*. New York: Abingdon, 1958.

Young, William H. *Great Canadian Preaching*. New York: George H. Doran, 1929.

ANCIENT ORATORS AND THEORIES OF SPEECH

BACKGROUND (GREECE)

Gomperz, Theodor. *Greek Thinkers*, authorized ed., London: Murray, 1901-12.

Grote, George. *History of Greece,* 10 vols. London: J. Murray, 1888.

Zimmern, Alfred. *The Greek Commonwealth*. 5th ed. rev. Oxford: Clarendon, 1931. (Part II, Politics).

BEGINNINGS OF RHETORIC

Baldwin, C. A. *Ancient Rhetoric and Poetic*. New York: Macmillan, 1924, 2-7.

Croiset, Alfred. *History of Greek Literature*. Translated by George Hethelbower. New York: Macmillan, 1904.

Platz, Mabel. *History of Public Speaking*. New York: Noble & Noble, 1935.

Roberts, W. Rhys. *Greek Rhetoric and Literary Criticism*. New York: Longmans, 1928.

Sandy, J. E. *Cicero's Orator*. Cambridge: University Press, 1885.

Wilkins, Augustus S. *Cicero's De Oratore*. Oxford: Clarendon, 1895, 26-56.

PLATO

Cooper, Lane. *Plato: Phaedrus, Ion, Gorgias, Symposium, Republic and Laws*. London: Oxford U., 1938.

Hunt, E. L. "Plato and Aristotle on Rhetoric and Rhetoricians," in *Studies in Rhetoric and Public Speaking in Honor of J. A. Winans*. New York: Century, 1925, 3-60.

ARISTOTLE

Cooper, Lane. *The Rhetoric of Aristotle*. New York: D. Appleton, 1932.
————————. *The Poetics of Aristotle, Its Meaning and Influence*. Boston: Marshall Jones, 1923.
Cope, E. M. *An Introduction to Aristotle's Rhetoric*. London: Macmillan, 1861.

THE ATTIC ORATORS

Dobson, J. F. *Greek Orators*. New York: E. P. Dutton, 1919.
Jebb, Richard C. *The Attic Orators*. London: Macmillan, 1893.

WORKS ON STYLE

Roberts, W. Rhys, ed. *Dionysius of Halicarnassus: The Three Literary Letters*. London: Cambridge U., 1901.

RHETORICAL BACKGROUND MATERIAL

Baldwin, Charles S. *Ancient Rhetoric and Poetic*. New York: Macmillan, 1924.
Hardwicks, Henry. *History of Oratory and Orators*. New York: G. P. Putnam's Sons, 1896.
Platz, Mable. *The History of Public Speaking*. New York: Noble and Noble, 1935.
Wilkins, Augustus S. *Ciceronis de Oratore*. Oxford: Clarendon, 1890-1893.
Thonssen, Lester. *Selected Readings in Rhetoric and Public Speaking*. New York: H. W. Wilson, 1942.

HISTORICAL BACKGROUND

Gibbon, Edward. *The Decline and Fall of the Roman Empire*. New York: Bigelow, Brown and Co., 1923.
Plutarch. *Lives*. Translated John Dryden. New York: Bigelow, Brown, 1917.

RHETORICAL WORKS

Butler, H. E., tran. *The Institutio Oratoria of Quintilian*. London: William Heinemann; New York: G. P. Putnam's Sons, 1921-1922.
Cicero.
Cicero's rhetorical works are available in various translations. The following are his major rhetorical works.
De Inventione. An early work dealing primarily with invention and secondarily with arrangement. Obviously designed as a rhetorical handbook.
Oratorical Partitions. Cicero's advice to his son. Dealt primarily with arrangement.

The Orator. Work of political expediency. Written to seek favor with Cato. It emphasized style and delivery.

Topics. A repetition from memory of Aristotle's *Topics*. Dealt primarily with argument on legal cases.

De Optimo Genera. On the best style of orators. Prepared as a preface to an edition of the Crown Debate.

De Oratore. A complete theory of rhetoric written from the standpoint of the accomplished orator discussing the secret of his art. Emphasized adequate understanding of subject matter.

Wilkins, Augustus S., ed. *Ad Herennium*. In M. Tulli, *Ciceronis de Oratore*, Oxford: Clarendon, 1890-1893.   .

SPEECHES

Bryan, W. J. *The World's Famous Orations*. New York: Funk and Wagnalls, 1906.

Lee, Guy Carleton. "History of Oratory." In his *Principles of Public Speaking*. New York: G. P. Putnam's Sons, 1899.

Morris, Charles. *The World's Great Orators and Their Orations*. Philadelphia: J. C. Winston, 1902.

Platz, Mabel. *Anthology of Public Speeches*. New York: H. W. Wilson, 1940.

MEDIEVAL, RENAISSANCE, AND EARLY BRITISH AND AMERICAN RHETORIC

The authors and their books in this section are listed in chronological order.

REVIEW OF THE FIRST CENTURY A.D.

Seneca (56 B.C.-A.D. 39). *Controversiae and Suasoriae*.
Quintilian (c. A.D. 35-100). *Institutio Oratoria*.
Tacitus (c. 55-120). *Dialogue on Oratory*.

THE SECOND SOPHISTIC (100-649) (DECLAMATIO)

Philostratus (c. 238). *Lives of the Sophists*.
Lucian (c. 125-?). *Professor of Public Speaking*.
Hermogenes (c. 170). *Elementary Exercises*; *De Rhetorica*.
Ausonius (c. 310-393). *Declamatio*.
Victor, Julius (c. 350). *Art of Rhetoric*.
Augustine (354-430). *De Doctrina Christiana*.
Fortunatianus (4th century). *Art of Rhetoric*.
Capella (c. 425). *Marriage of Philology and Mercury*.
Sidonius (c. 475). *Letters and Poems*.
Boethius (475-525). *Topics*; *De Divisione*; *Categorical and Hypothetical Syllogisms*. Translation of Aristotle's *Organon*.
Cassiodorus (485-575). *Institutiones*.
Isidore of Seville (560-636). *Etymologiarum*.

THE CAROLINGIAN (CHARLEMAGNE) PERIOD (650-999) (GRAMMAR)

Alcuin (735-804). *Disputatio de Rhetorica and de Virtutibus* (*Dialogue of Alcuin and Charlemagne*). Translated by Wilbur S. Howell.

Marus, Rabanus (776-856): *De Clericorum Institutione*.

Labeo, Notker (c. 940-1022). *De Arte Rhetorica*. Based on the work of Otto A. L. Dieter.

THE SCHOLASTIC PERIOD (1000-1399) (DIALECTIC)

St. Victor, Hugh of (1096-1141). *Lore of Teaching*.

Salisbury, John of (1120-1180). *Metalogicus* (Dictamen).

Lille, Alain de (1128-1202). *Anticlaudianus*.

Beauvais, Vincent of (1210-1264). *Peculum Doctrinale*.

Latini, Brunetto (1220-c. 1294). *Tresor*.

THE RENAISSANCE PERIOD (1400-1649)

Fifteenth Century

Trapezuntius. *The Art of Rhetoric*.

Agricola. *De Inventione Dialectica*.

Fifteenth and Sixteenth Centuries

Erasmus. *De Rhetorica*.

Sixteenth Century

Cox. *The Crafte of Rhetoryke*. The first rhetoric in English. Melanchthon was the principal source used by Cox.

Melanchthon. *Elements of Rhetoric*.

Rainolde. *A Book Called the Foundation of Rhetoric*.

Ramus. *Dialecticae Partitiones*.

Talaeus or Talon. *Institutiones Dialecticae* and *Institutiones Oratoriae*.

Sherry. *Treatise of Schemems and Tropes*.

Wilson, Thomas. *Arte of Rhetorique*. Edited by G. H. Mair.

Sixteenth and Seventeenth Centuries

Ascham. *The Schoolmaster*.

Bacon, Francis. *The Advancement of Learning,* and *Novum Organum*.

Butler. *Rameae Rhetoricae Libri Duo* (revised), and *Oratoriae Libri Duo*.

Hoskins. *Directions for Speech and Style*.

Peacham. *The Garden of Eloquence*.

Fraunce. *Lawier's Logic* and *Arcadian Rhetoric*.

Seventeenth Century

Barton. John. *The Art of Rhetorick Concisely Handled* (1634). "Rhetorick is the skill of using daintie words, and comely deliverie, whereby to work upon men's affections. It hath two parts, adornation and action."

Farnaby, Thomas. *Index Rhetoricus et Oratoribus*. Most widely used rhetoric textbook in England during the seventeenth century. A highly compact, convenient, and inclusive treatment. Most significant English work from Wilson's *Arte of Rhetorique* to 18th century.

Vicars. *Manuductio ad Artem Rhetoricam* (1619). Small handbook of rhetoric (128 pages) in the form of questions and answers for students at Oxford. His treatment and emphasis accord with classical practice.

THE LATER ENGLISH PERIOD (1650-1849)

Eighteenth Century

Burgh, James. *Art of Speaking* (1761). This was the first speech work published in America (1775). It included an essay on elocution and much material for practice. A good portion of the material on action is quoted directly from Thomas Sheridan.

Campbell, George. *Philosophy of Rhetoric*.

_____. *Lectures on Pulpit Eloquence* (n.d.).

Lawson, John. *Lectures Concerning Oratory* (1752). Evidently based on Aristotle and Cicero.

Priestley, Joseph. *Lectures on Rhetoric and Belles Lettres* (1783), 4th ed., London, 1790.

Sheridan, Thomas. *Lectures on Eloquence* (1759). Lectures delivered at Oxford, Cambridge, London.

Steele, Joshua. *Prosodia Rationalis* (1775). Mechanistic. It attempted to set the speech of the orator as rigid. The work was concerned solely with reading.

Walker, John. *Elements of Elocution* (1781). The mechanical school received its most detailed and influential treatment up to this time. Most of the discussion of gesture was concerned with what not to do.

_____. *Hints for Improvement in the Art of Reading* (1783).

_____. *Rhetorical Grammar* (1785). Walker believed this was his greatest work. It emphasized delivery.

_____. *Melody of Speaking Delineated*, or *Elocution Taught Like Music* (1787).

_____. *The Academic Speaker* (1801).

_____. *The Teacher's Assistant* (1787).

Ward, John. *System of Oratory* (1759).

Eighteenth and Nineteenth Centuries

Austin, Gilbert. *Chironomia* (1806).

Luxton. *Elements of Rhetoric* (1811).

Rippingham, John. *Art of Extempore Speaking* (1813). Supplemented the elocutionary training then prevalent.

Nineteenth Century

Whately, Richard (19th century): *Elements of Logic* (1859).

_____. *Elements of Rhetoric* (1881). An analysis of the laws of moral evidence and of persuasion.

RHETORICAL THEORY IN AMERICA (1636-1850)

Eighteenth Century

Witherspoon, John. *Lectures on Moral Philosophy and Eloquence.* This was the first American rhetoric. It was largely influenced by the classical writers.

Eighteenth and Nineteenth Centuries

Adams, John. *Lectures on Rhetoric and Oratory.*

Nineteenth Century

Channing. *Lectures on Rhetoric and Oratory.*

Day, Henry. *Elements of the Art of Rhetoric.*

————————. *Art of Discourse.*

Goodrich, Chauncey A. *Lectures on Rhetoric and Public Speaking.*

Hope, M. B. *The Princeton Textbook in Rhetoric* (1859). He was professor of rhetoric at Princeton. It was written to replace Whately at Princeton. Hope believed Whately was weak on the subject of belle lettres and also weak on the discussion of the validity of arguments. Rhetoric is the art of enabling men to produce at will conviction and persuasion.

Newman. *A Practical System of Rhetoric.*

Litch. *A Concise Treatise on Rhetoric.* A rhetoric published early in the nineteenth century in America. It provided anything new and dealt only with style.

Porter. *Lectures on Eloquence and Style.*

Shedd, William G. T. Translation of Theremin's *Eloquence a Virtue.*

Additional Readings in Rhetoric

The Art of Speaking. Read in America as early as 1755. This is one of the earliest works in English to present a complete treatment of all aspects of delivery and to be assigned as a school text. Author not known.

Bain, Alexander. *The Senses and the Intellect.* London: Longman, Green, Longman, Roberts, and Green, 1864 (640 pages). Of particular interest is the section "Illustrative Comparisons and Literary Art."

Bayly, Anselm. *The Alliance of Music, Poetry, and Oratory.* London: J. Stockdale, 1789 (384 pages). Under the heading of poetry is considered the alliance and nature of the epic and dramatic poem, as it exists in the Iliad, Aeneid, and Paradise Lost.

Beeson, C. H. *A Primer of Medieval Latin.* Chicago: Scott & Foresman, 1926.

Blount, Thomas. *Academy of Eloquence.* London: T. Johnson, 1670 (232 pages). Blount believed thought was largely dependent on a smooth-flowing style. "Quaint and fluent stile" attained by fifty-three figures and tropes, forty-three commonplaces, and numerous *formulae minores.* He concluded with directions for letterwriting.

Bouhours, Dominique. *The Arts of Logick and Rhetoric*. Bouhours was more of a critic than a rhetorician.

Brehaut, Ernest. *An Encyclopedist of the Dark Ages: Isidore of Seville*. New York: Columbia U., 1912 (274 pages).

Bulwer, John. *Chirologia*. London: T. Harper, 1644. 2 vols. According to Bulwer: "The natural language of the hand. Composed of the speaking motions, and discoursing gestures thereof. Whereunto is added Chironomia: or the art of manual rhetoricke. Consisting of the natural expressions, digested by art in the hand, as the chiefest instrument of eloquence, by historical manifesto's, exemplified out of the authentic registers of common life, and civil conversation. With types, or chyrograms: a long-wish'd for illustration of this argument." *Chironomia* explained fifty "canons" of the hand and thirty "canons" of the fingers.

Campbell, George. *Philosophy of Rhetoric*. New York: Harper and Brothers, 1851 (435 pages).

Clark, Donald L. *Rhetoric and Poetry in the Renaissance*. New York: Columbia U., 1922 (166 pages). Traced the influence of classical rhetoric on the criticisms of poetry published in England between 1553 and 1641. It treated the influence of rhetoric on the general theory of poetry within the period and its influence on the Renaissance formulation of the purpose of poetry.

Cockin, William. *The Art of Delivering Written Language*. London: H. Hughes for J. Dodsley, 1775 (152 pages). This contribution developed mainly a body of elocutionary principles. Delivery was the principal topic of concern.

Colson, F. H. *Institutio Oratoria of Quintilian (Book I)*, 1917. Proceedings of Classical Association (British), 14:149-73. Some considerations on the influence of rhetoric on history.

Cooper, Lane. *Phaedrus, Ion, Gorgias, and Symposium*. London: Oxford U., 1938 (436 pages). Translation with introduction and notes.

Crane, William G. *Wit and Rhetoric in the Renaissance*. New York: Columbia U., 1937 (285 pages). This study was confined to indicating the relation of wit to rhetoric and to presenting the more important rhetorical practices of the Renaissance.

Crawford, John. *Rhetoric of George Campbell*. Commentary on Campbell's *Philosophy of Rhetoric*.

Crocker, Lionel F. *Argumentation and Debate*. Substituted analogy for reasoning as evidence. Omitted sign completely.

Demetrius. *Rhetores Selecti*. Selection of excerpts from rhetorical writings.

De Quincey, Thomas. *Rhetoric*. London: Henry Frowde, 1909 (pp. 37-89). A review suggested by Whately's *Elements of Rhetoric*. Contains in part De Quincey's ideas on rhetoric and public speaking. Also found in Masson's edition of the *Collected Writings of Thomas De Quincey* (London, 1897).

Edward, William A. *The Suasoriae of Seneca, The Elder*. London: Cambridge U., 1928 (160 pages). Introductory essay, text, translation, and explanatory notes.

Enfield, William. *The Speaker*. 1774. "To follow nature is certainly the fundamental law of oratorys." It has an essay on elocution and then much practice material. Communications is stressed.

Fenelon. *Dialogues on Eloquence*. Boston: Farrand, Mallory and Co., 1810 (174 pages). Translated by William Stevenson. A translation of this work is found in *The Preacher and Pastor* by Edward Park (New York: M. D. Dodd, 1849) (468 pages).

Fisher, George. *The American Instructor*. "Rhetoric is the art of speaking in the most elegant and persuasive manners." This work used elocution in the sense of delivery.

Genung, John F. *The Practical Elements of Rhetoric*. Boston and New York: Ginn, 1886 (488 pages). A comprehensive treatment of the parts of rhetoric, with numerous examples and exercise material. Contains a section on argumentation.

Gibbons, Thomas. *Rhetoric*. London: J. and W. Oliver, for J. Buckland and J. Payne, 1767 (478 pages). A view of the principal tropes and figures in their origin and powers, with a variety of rules to escape errors and blemishes and attain property and elegance in composition.

Gregory, George. *Letters On Literature, Taste, and Composition*. Philadelphia: Bradford and Inskeep, 1809 (363 pages). Addressed to his son. Letters xvi-xix contain general observations on oratory, and the parts of an oration. Letter xx discusses generally the narrator's art and the importance of narrative in writing and speaking.

Hermogenes. *Elementary Exercises De Rhetorica*. c. 170.

Herries, John. *The Elements of Speech*. London: E. and C. Dilly, 1773 (259 pages). Correction manual and drill book.

Hobbes, Thomas. *Whole Art of Rhetorick*. 1637. 2d ed. Oxford: D. A. Talboys, 1833 (273 pages). An analysis of rhetoric. Analytical questions on rhetoric, with a brief and idiomatic translation of Aristotle's *Rhetoric*. Hobbes added a section called "The

Art of Rhetorick," in which, inconsistently enough, he defined rhetoric as the art of speaking "finely." It consisted of two parts: garnishing of the speech (elocution), and garnishing of the manner of utterance (pronunciation).

Home, Henry (of Kames). *The Elements of Criticism.* Edited by James R. Boyd. New York and Chicago: A. S. Barnes, 1855 (486 pages). A work originally published in 1751. Dealt with the fundamental principles of the fine arts and set up a standard of good taste. Valuable as a study of style. The work as a whole presents a critical analysis of "the faculty of perception, and the result of its exercise upon the tastes and emotions." Boyd's notes and analyses are helpful.

Hoole. *New Discovery of the Old Art of Teaching School.* 1660.

Howell, Wilbur S. *Fenelon's Dialogues on Eloquence.*
_____. *The Rhetoric of Alcuin and Charlemagne.*

Hudson, Hoyt H. *Directions For Speech and Style by John Hoskins.* Princeton, N.J.: Princeton U., 1935 (122 pages).

Jamieson, Alexander. *Grammar of Rhetorical and Polite Literature.* New Haven: A. H. Maltby, 1818 (306 pages). Dealt with the comprehension of the principles of language and style and the elements of taste and criticism with rules for the study of composition and eloquence. Illustrated by appropriate examples, selected chiefly from the British classics. It was elementary and devoted almost exclusively to style.

Johnson, Samuel. *The Art of Speaking.* 1755. Later works were also accepted in America as readily as in England.

Mason, John. *Essay on Elocution.* 1748. Mason derived his material largely from Quintilian and was of the "Natural School." "Follow nature and avoid affectation." Mason was copied by many others both in America and England.

Matthews, Lyman. *Memoir of the Life and Character of Ebenezer Porter.* Philadelphia: Perkins and Marvin, 1837 (396 pages).

Mill, John Stuart. *A System of Logic, Ratiocinative and Inductive.* New York: Harper, 1859.

O'Connor, John B. *Isidore of Seville.* New York: Encyclopedia Press, 1913.

Pemble, William. *Enciridion Oratorium.* 1633. This little book (78 pages) treated invention and disposition and recognized traditional aims, kinds, divisions, but was not certain of memory. Treatment was preponderantly logica, schematic, and overanalyzed. Resembled work by Leonard Cox.

Tacitus, *Dialogue on Public Address*. Translated by William Peterson. London: Heinemann and New York: G. P. Putnam's Sons, 1920.

Rahskoph, Horace G. *John Quincy Adams*. Edited by Albert Craig Baird. Iowa City, Iowa: U. of Iowa, September 1936. Dealt with the theory and practice of public speaking.

Rand, E. K. *Founders of the Middle Ages*. Cambridge, Mass.: Harvard U., 1928.

Rice, John. *An Introduction To the Art of Reading with Energy and Propriety*. London: J. and R. Tonson, 1765 (322 pages).

Sandys, John E. *Ciceronis Ad M. Brutum*. London: Cambridge U., 1885 (257 pages). Analytical notes on Cicero's works on rhetoric; summary of Cicero's *The Orator*; and a short treatment of the history of rhetoric.

Schmidt, Robert M. *Hugh Blair*. New York: Kings Crown, 1948.

Scott, William. *Lessons in Elocution*. Edinburgh: C. Elliot, 1789 (398 pages). A selection of pieces in prose and verse for the improvement of young people in reading and speaking and for the perusal of persons of taste.

Smith, John. *Mysterie of Rhetorique Unveiled*. London: R. Clavel, 1688 (244 pages). More than 130 of the tropes and figures are severally derived from the Greek into English, together with lively definitions, and a variety of Latin, English, and spiritual examples pertinent to each of them.

Spedding, James, ed. *Popular Edition*. Boston; Houghton, Mifflin & Co., 1860.

Spencer, Herbert. *The Philosophy of Style*. New York: John B. Alden, 1888 (40 pages).

Spredding, Ellis, and Spredding, Heath. *The Words of Francis Bacon*. 1857-1859. They are translated (where necessary) and more readily available in *Popular Edition*. Edited by James Spedding. Boston: Houghton, Mifflin, c. 1860.

Taylor, Henry O. *The Medieval Mind*. New York: Macmillan, 1925.

Thompson, James W. *The Middle Ages—300-1500*. New York: Knopf, 1931.

Thonssen and Baird. *Speech Criticism*. New York: Ronald Press, 1948. Contains 150 pages on the history of rhetoric.

Turnbull, Robert. *Pulpit Orators of France and Switzerland*. New York: Robert Carter, 1848.

Victor, Julius. *Art of Rhetoric*.

Wright, A.; and Sinclair, T. A. *A History of Later Latin Literature from the Middle of the Fourth to the End of the Seventeenth Century*. London: Routledge, 1931.

DISSERTATIONS

Lang, Robert A. *The Development of Rhetorical Theory in French College, 1550-1709*. Ph.D. diss., Northwestern University, 1950.

Ostler, Margaret. *The Rhetoric of Gaius Julius Victor*. Master's thesis, Northwestern University, 1938.

Sandford, William P. *English Theories of Public Address 1530-1828*. H. L. Hedrick, Columbus, 1938.

Vandraegen, Daniel. *Report on "The Natural School of Oral Reading In England, 1748-1828."* Ph.D. diss., Northwestern University, 1949.

Wallace, Karl R. *Bacon On Communication and Rhetoric*. Ithaca, N.Y: Cornell U., 1933. Bacon's theory of public address.

MISCELLANEOUS

Clark, Donald L. "Progymnasmata in the Grammar Schools (16th & 17th Century)." Appears in *Speech Monographs* 19, no.4 (November 1952): 259-63.

Nadeau, Ray. "The Progymnasmata of Apthonius." *Speech Monographs* 19, no. 4 (November 1952): 264-85.

Paul, Wilson. "John Witherspoon." *Speech Monographs* 16 (September 1949).

Sears, Floyd S. *St. Isidore and Medieval Science*. Rice Institute Pamphlet, vol. 23 (April 1936) 2: 75-105.

Wallace, Karl R. "Bacon's Conception of Rhetoric." *Speech Monographs* 3 (1936): 21-48. Deals with the Patristic period

Appendix 1

This section deals with American homiletics educators and supplies information concerning authors and teachers: their outstanding literary contribution; denomination; and seminary or institution affiliation.

Alexander, James Waddell (1804-1859); Presbyterian
Born: Gordonsville, Virginia
Princeton Theological Seminary
Thoughts on Preaching Being Contributions to Homiletics. New York: Charles Scribner, 1861 (514 pages).

Atkins, Gaius Glenn (1868-1956); Congregationalist
Born: Mount Carmel, Indiana
Auburn (New York) Theological Seminary; professor of homiletics
Preaching and the Mind of Today. New York: Round Table, 1934 (227 pages).

Baughman, Harry Fridley (1892-   ); United Presbyterian
Born: Everett, Pennsylvania
Lutheran Theological Seminary; professor of the art of preaching
Preaching from the Propers. Philadelphia: Muhlenberg, 1949 (120 pages).

Baxter, Batsell Barrett (1916-   ); Church of Christ
Born: Cordell, Oklahoma
David Lipscomb College; professor of speech and homiletics
Speaking for the Master. New York: Macmillan, 1954 (134 pages).

Blackwood, Andrew Watterson (1882-1968); United Presbyterian
Born: Clay Center, Kansas

Princeton Theological Seminary and Temple University
The Preparation of Sermons. New York and Nashville: Abingdon-Cokesbury, 1948
(272 pages).

Booth, Henry M. (1843-1899); Presbyterian
Born: New York, New York
Auburn (New York) Theological Seminary; professor of practical theology
The Man and His Message. Addresses delivered at Auburn Seminary. New York:
Revell, 1899 (163 pages).

Bowie, Walter Russell (1882-1968); Episcopalian
Born: Virginia
Protestant Episcopal Seminary and Union Theological Seminary (New York)
Preaching. Nashville: Abingdon, 1954 (224 pages).

Brastow, Lewis Orsmond (1834-1912); Congregationalist
Born: Brewer, Maine
Yale Divinity School
The Work of the Preacher: A Study of Homiletic Principles and Methods. Boston and
New York: Pilgrim, 1914 (434 pages).

Breed, David Riddle (1848-1931); Presbyterian
Born: Pittsburgh, Pennsylvania
Western Theological Seminary (Pittsburgh)
Preparing to Preach. New York: George H. Doran, 1911 (455 pages).

Broadus, John Albert (1827-1895); Baptist
Born: Culpeper County, Virginia
Southern Baptist Theological Seminary
A Treatise on the Preparation and Delivery of Sermons. New York: A. C. Armstrong
and Son, 1889 (514 pages).

Brown, Charles Reynolds (1862-1950); Congregationalist
Born: Bethany, West Virginia
Yale Divinity School; professor of homiletics
The Art of Preaching. New York: Macmillan, 1922 (250 pages).

Burrell, David James (1844-1926)
Born: Pennsylvania
Princeton Theological Seminary; professor of homiletics
The Sermon: Its Construction and Delivery. New York: Revell, 1913 (329 pages).

Caldwell, Frank Hill (1902-   ); Presbyterian
Born: Corinth, Mississippi
Louisville Presbyterian Seminary
Preaching Angles. Nashville: Abingdon, 1954 (126 pages).

Coffin, Henry Sloan (1877-1954); Presbyterian
Born: New York City, New York
Union Theological Seminary (New York)
Communion Through Preaching: The Monstrance of the Gospel. New York: Scribner's, 1953 (124 pages).

Dabney, Robert Lewis (1820-1898); Presbyterian
Born: Louisa County, Virginia
Union Theological Seminary (Virginia)
Sacred Rhetoric: Lectures on Preaching. New York: Anson D. F. Randolph and Co., 1870 (361 pages).

Davis, Ozora Stearns (1866-1949); Congregationalist
Born: Wheelock, Vermont
University of Chicago Theological Seminary
Principles of Preaching. Chicago: U. of Chicago, 1924 (270 pages).

English, John Mahan (1845-1927); Baptist
Born: Tarrytown, Pennsylvania
Andover Newton Theological Seminary (Masssachusetts); professor of homiletics
For Pulpit and Platform. New York: Macmillan, 1919 (143 pages).

Ferris, Theodore Parker (1908-1972); Episcopalian
Born: Port Chester, New York
Episcopal Theological School (Massachusetts)
Go Tell the People. New York: Scribner's, 1951 (116 pages).

Fisk, Franklin Woodbury (1820-1901); Congregationalist
Born: Hopkinton, Vermont
University of Chicago Theological Seminary; professor of sacred rhetoric
A Manual of Preaching. New York: A. C. Armstrong and Son, 1895 (337 pages).

Fritz, John Henry Charles (1874-1953); Lutheran
Born: Ohio
Concordia Seminary; Institute in Homiletics
Essentials of Preaching. St. Louis: Concordia, 1948 (73 pages).

Fry, Jacob (1834-1920); Lutheran
Born: Trappe, Pennsylvania
Evangelical Lutheran Theological Seminary
Elementary Homiletics. Reading, Penn.: Henry H. Bieber, 1893 (57 pages).

Gardner, Charles Spurgeon (1859-   ); Baptist
Born: Gibson County, Tennessee
Southern Baptist Theological Seminary
Psychology and Preaching. New York: Macmillan, 1918 (389 pages).

Garrison, Webb Black (1919-   ); Methodist
Born: Covington, California
Vanderbilt University and Emory University
The Preacher and His Audience. Westwood, N.J.: Revell, 1954 (285 pages).

Gibson, George Miles (1896-1932); Presbyterian
Born: Missouri
McCormick Theological Seminary; professor of homiletics
Planned Preaching. Philadelphia: Westminster, 1954 (140 pages).

Graves, Henry C. (1830-1917); Baptist
Born: Deerfield, Massachusetts
Gordon Bible and Missionary Training School (Boston)
Lectures on Homiletics. Philadelphia: American Baptist Publication Society, 1906 (156
    pages).

Hall, Charles Cuthbert (1852-1908); Presbyterian
Born: New York City, New York
Union Seminary (New York); professor of practical theology
Qualifications for Ministerial Power. Hartford, Conn.: Hartford Seminary, 1895 (241
    pages).

Hoppin, James Mason (1820-1906); Congregationalist
Born: Providence, Rhode Island
Yale Divinity School; professor of homiletics and pastoral charge
The Office and Work of the Christian Ministry. New York: Sheldon and Co., 1869 (620
    pages).

Hoyt, Arthur Stephen (1851-1924); Presbyterian
Born: Meridian, New York
Auburn (New York) Theological Seminary
The Work of Preaching. New York: Macmillan, 1905 (335 pages).

Hutchins, William James (1871-1958); Presbyterian
Born: Brooklyn, New York
Oberlin Graduate School of Theology; professor of homiletics
The Preacher's Ideals and Inspirations. New York: Revell, 1917 (187 pages).

Jefferson, Charles Edward (1860-1937); Congregationalist
Born: Cambridge, Ohio
Union Theological Seminary (New York)
Quiet Hints to Growing Preachers in My Study. New York: Thomas Y. Crowell, 1901
    (214 pages).

Johnson, Herrick (1832-1913); Presbyterian
Born: Kaughnewaga, New York

McCormick Theological Seminary (Chicago) and Auburn (New York) Theological
   Seminary; professor of homiletics, sacred rhetoric, and pastoral theology
The Ideal Ministry. New York: Revell, 1908 (500 pages).

Jones, Bob, Jr. (1911-   )
Born: Montgomery, Alabama
Bob Jones University
How to Improve Your Preaching. New York: Revell, 1945 (126 pages).

Jordan, Gerald Ray (1896-1964); Methodist
Born: Kingston, North Carolina
Emory University (Georgia)
You Can Preach. Westwood, N.J.: Revell, 1951 (256 pages).

Kennedy, Gerald Hamilton (1907-1980); Methodist
Born: Benzonia, Michigan
Pacific School of Religion; professor of homiletics
His Word Through Preaching. New York: Harper and Brothers, 1947 (234 pages).

Kern, John Adam (1846-1926); Methodist
Born: Frederick County, Virginia
Vanderbilt University
The Ministry to the Congregation. New York: Jennings and Graham, 1897 (551 pages).

Kidder, Daniel Parrish (1815-1891); Methodist
Born: New York City, New York
Garrett Biblical Institute and Drew Theological Seminary; professor of practical
   theology
A Treatise on Homiletics. New York: Carlton and Porter, 1864 (504 pages).

Kirkpatrick, Robert White (1908-   ); Presbyterian
Born: Austin, Texas
Union Seminary (Virginia)
Creative Delivery of Sermons. New York: Macmillan, 1947 (235 pages).

Littorin, Frank T. (1900-   ); Baptist
Born: Chicago, Illinois
Gordon Divinity School (Massachusetts)
How to Preach the Word with Variety. Grand Rapids: Baker, 1953 (157 pages).

Luccock, Halford Edward (1885-1961); Methodist
Born: Pittsburgh, Pennsylvania
Yale Divinity School
In the Minister's Workshop. Nashville: Abingdon-Cokesbury, 1944 (254 pages).

MacLennan, David Alexander (1903-   ); United Presbyterian
Born: Boston, Massachusetts
Yale Divinity School; professor of preaching and pastoral care
Preacher's Primer. New York: Oxford, 1950 (113 pages).

Montgomery, Richmond Ames (1870-1950); Presbyterian
Born: Hindrick County, Indiana
Presbyterian Theological Seminary
Preparing Preachers to Preach. Grand Rapids: Zondervan, 1939 (249 pages).

Moore, William Thomas (1832-1926)
Born: Kentucky
College of the Bible (Lexington, Ky.); professor of sacred rhetoric
Preacher Problems. New York: Revell, 1907 (387 pages).

Noyes, Morgan Phelps (1891-1972); Presbyterian
Born: Warner, Pennsylvania
Union Theological Seminary (New York); associate professor of practical theology
Preaching the Word of God. New York: Scribner's, 1943 (219 pages).

Oxnam, Garfield Bromley (1891-1963); Methodist
Born: California
University of Southern California and Boston University School of Theology;
    professor of practical theology
Preaching in a Revolutionary Age. New York: Abingdon-Cokesbury, 1944.

Patton, Carl S. (1866-1939); Congregationalist
Born: Greenville, Michigan
Pacific School of Religion
The Preparation and Delivery of Sermons. New York: Willett, Clark and Co., 1938 (191
    pages).

Pease, Theodore Claudius (1853-1920); Congregationalist
Born: New York City, New York
Andover Newton Theological Seminary; professor of sacred rhetoric
The Christian Ministry. Boston: Houghton, Mifflin, 1894 (140 pages).

Phelps, Arthur Stevens (1863-1948); Baptist
Born: New Haven, Connecticut
Berkeley Baptist Divinity School; professor of public speaking
Speaking in Public. New York: Richard R. Smith, 1930 (232 pages).

Phelps, Austin (1820-1890); Congregationalist
Born: West Brookfield, Massachusetts

Andover Newton Theological Seminary; professor of sacred rhetoric
The Theory and Practice of Preaching. New York: Scribner's, 1894 (610 pages).

Pittenger, William (1840-1894); Methodist
Born: Jefferson County, Ohio
National School of Elocution (Philadelphia)
Oratory: Sacred and Secular. New York: Samuel R. Wells, 1868 (220 pages).

Pond, W. Enoch (1791-1882); Congregationalist
Born: Wrentham, Massachusetts
Bangor (Maine) Theological Seminary
The Young Pastor's Guide. Bangor, Maine: E. F. Duren, 1844 (377 pages).

Porter, Ebenezer (1772-1834); Congregationalist
Born: Cornwall, Connecticut
Andover Newton Theological Seminary (Massachusetts)
Lectures on Homiletics and Preaching on Public Prayer. Andover and New York:
   Flagg, Gould and Newman, 1834 (428 pages).

Ray, Jefferson Davis (1860-1951); Baptist
Born: Victoria, Texas
Southwestern Baptist Seminary
Expository Preaching. Grand Rapids: Zondervan, 1940 (123 pages).

Riley, William Bell (1861-1947)
Born: Green County, Indiana
Northwestern schools (Minneapolis)—Bible Training School, Evangelical Seminary,
   and College of Liberal Arts Baptist
The Preacher and His Preaching. Wheaton, Ill.: Sword of the Lord, 1948 (146 pages).

Ripley, Henry Jones (1798-1875); Congregationalist
Born: Boston, Massachusetts
Andover Newton Theological Seminary (Massachusetts)
Sacred Rhetoric. Boston: Gould, Kendall, and Lincoln, 1849 (259 pages).

Robbins, Howard Chandler (1876-1952); Episcopalian
Born: Philadelphia, Pennsylvania
General Theological Seminary
Preaching the Gospel. New York: Harper and Brothers, 1939 (151 pages).

Schenck, Ferdinand Schureman (1845-1925); Reformed
Born: New York City, New York
Princeton Theological Seminary and New Brunswick Theological Seminary; professor
   of practical theology
Modern Practical Theology. New York: Funk & Wagnalls, 1903 (311 pages).

Scherer, Paul Ehrman (1892-1969); Lutheran
Born: Mt. Holly Springs, Pennsylvania
Union Theological Seminary (New York) and Mount Airy Lutheran Seminary;
    professor of homiletics
For We Have This Treasure. New York: Harper and Brothers, 1944 (212 pages).

Shedd, William Greenough Thayer (1820-1894); Presbyterian
Born: Acton, Massachusetts
Union Theological Seminary (New York) and Andover Theological Seminary;
    professor of sacred rhetoric and pastoral theology
Homiletics and Pastoral Theology. New York: Scribner's, 1867 (429 pages).

Skinner, Thomas Harvey (1791-1871); Presbyterian
Born: Harvey's Neck, North Carolina
Andover Newton Theological Seminary (Massachusetts)
Aids to Revealing and Hearing. New York: J. S. Taylor, 1839 (305 pages).

Sperry, Willard Learoyd (1882-1954); Congregationalist
Born: Peabody, Massachusetts
Harvard Divinity School and Andover Newton Theological Seminary (Massachusetts)
We Prophesy in Part. New York: Harper and Brothers, 1938 (201 pages).

Stidger, William LeRoy (1886-1949); Methodist
Born: Moundsville, West Virginia
Boston University School of Theology
Preaching Out of the Overflow. Nashville: Cokesbury, 1929 (238 pages).

Tilroe, William Edwin (1861-1940); Methodist
Born: Michigan
Maclay School of Bolig and University of Southern California; professor of practical
    theology
Sent Forth. New York: Abingdon, 1923 (255 pages).

Townsend, Luther Tracey (1838-1922); Methodist
Born: Orono, Maine
Boston University School of Theology
Pulpit Rhetoric. New York: Chautauqua, and Boston: Franklin, 1882 (86 pages).

Tucker, William Jewett (1839-1926); Congregationalist
Born: Griswold, Connecticut
Andover Newton Theological Seminary (Massachusetts)
The Making and the Unmaking of the Preacher. Boston and New York: Houghton
    Mifflin, 1898 (224 pages).

Vance, James Isaac (1862-1939); Presbyterian
Born: Tennessee
Vanderbilt University; professor of homiletics
Being a Preacher. New York: Revell, 1923 (171 pages).

Weatherspoon, Jesse Burton (1886-1964); Baptist
Born: Durham, North Carolina
Southern Baptist Seminary
Sent Forth to Preach. New York: Harper and Brothers, 1954 (182 pages).

Whitesell, Faris Daniel (1895-   ); Baptist
Born: Indiana
Northern Baptist Seminary
The Art of Biblical Preaching. Grand Rapids: Zondervan, 1950 (160 pages).

Appendix 2

AMERICAN HOMILETICS TEXTBOOKS WRITTEN BY AMERICAN HOMILETICS
TEACHERS BETWEEN 1834 AND 1954

This section treats American homiletics texts published between 1834 and 1954 inclusively. The books are presented in chronological order of publication to show the growth and development of the study and teaching of homiletics in America.

This material is taken from Perry, Lloyd M., "Trends and Emphases in the Philosophy, Materials, and Methodology of American Protestant Homiletical Education as Established by a Study of Selected Trade and Textbooks Published Between 1834 and 1954." Ph.D. diss., Northwestern University, 1961, which is available in its entirety on microfilm from University Microfilms International, 300 North Zeeb Road, Ann Arbor, Michigan 48106.

AMERICAN HOMILETICS TEXTBOOKS 1834-1954

1. Porter, Ebenezer. *Lectures on Homiletics and Preaching and on Public Prayer*. Andover and New York: Flagg, Gould, and Newman, 1834 (428 pages).
2. Skinner, Thomas Harvey. *Aids to Revealing and Hearing*. New York: J. S. Taylor, 1839 (305 pages).
3. Pond, W. Enoch. *The Young Minister's Guide*. Bangor, Maine: E. F. Duren, 1844 (377 pages).
4. Ripley, Henry Jones. *Sacred Rhetoric*. Boston, Mass.: Gould, Kendall, and Lincoln, 1849 (259 pages).
5. Alexander, James Waddell. *Thoughts on Preaching*. New York: Charles Scribner, 1861 (514 pages).
6. Widder, Daniel Parrish. *A Treatise on Homiletics*. New York: Carlton and Porter, 1864 (504 pages).
7. Shedd, William Greenough Thayer. *Homiletics and Pastoral Theology*. New York: Scribner's, 1867 (429 pages).

8. Pittenger, William. *Oratory, Sacred and Secular*. New York: R. Wells, 1868 (220 pages).

9. Hoppin, James Mason. *The Office and Work of the Christian Ministry*. New York: Sheldon and Co., 1869 (620 pages).

10. Dabney, Robert Lewis. *Sacred Rhetoric: Lectures on Preaching*. New York: Amson D. F. Randolph and Co., 1870 (361 pages).

11. Anderson, Galusha. *Notes on Homiletics*. Boston: Rockwell & Churchill Printers, 1872 (69 pages).

12. Townsend, Luther Tracy. *Pulpit Rhetoric*. New York: Chautauqua Press and Boston: Franklin Press, 1882 (86 pages).

13. Broadus, John Albert. *A Treatise on the Preparation and Delivery of Sermons*. New York: A. C. Armstrong and Son, 1889 (514 pages).

14. Fry, Jacob. *Elementary Homiletics*. Reading. Pa.: Henry H. Bieber, 1893 (57 pages).

15. Pease, Theodore Claudius. *The Christian Ministry*. Boston: Houghton, Mifflin, 1894 (140 pages).

16. Phelps, Austin. *The Theory of Preaching*. New York: Scribner's, 1930 (232 pages).

17. Fisk, Franklin Woodbury. *A Manual of Preaching*. New York: A. C. Armstrong and Son, 1895 (337 pages).

18. Hall, Charles Cuthbert. *Qualifications for Ministerial Power*. Hartford, Conn.: Hartford Seminary Press, 1895 (241 pages).

19. Kern, John Adam. *The Ministry to the Congregation*. New York: Jennings and Graham, 1897 (551 pages).

20. Tucker, William Jewett. *The Making and the Unmaking of the Preacher*. Boston and New York: Houghton, Mifflin, 1898 (224 pages).

21. Booth, Henry M. *The Man and His Message*. (Addresses delivered before the students and alumni of the Auburn (New York) Theological Seminary. New York: Revell, 1899 (163 pages).

22. Jefferson, Charles Edward. *Quiet Hints to Growing Preachers in My Study*. New York: Thomas Y. Crowell & Co., 1901 (214 pages).

23. Schenck, Ferdinand Schureman. *Modern Practical Theology*. New York: Funk & Wagnalls, 1903 (311 pages).

24. Hoyt, Arthur Stephen. *The Work of Preaching*. New York: Macmillan, 1905 (355 pages).

25. Graves, Henry C. *Lectures on Homiletics*. Philadelphia: American Baptist Publications Society, 1906 (156 pages).

26. Moore, William Thomas. *Preacher Problems*. New York: Revell, 1907 (387 pages).

27. Johnson, Herrick. *The Ideal Ministry*. New York: Revell, 1908 (500 pages).

28. Breed, David Riddle. *Preparing to Preach*. New York: George H. Doran, 1911 (455 pages).

29. *Burrell, David James. The Sermon: Its Construction and Delivery*. New York: Revell, 1913 (329 pages).

30. Brastow, Lewis Orsmond. *The Work of the Preacher: A Study of Homiletic Principles and Methods*. Boston and New York: Pilgrim, 1914 (434 pages).

31. Hutchins, William James. *The Preacher's Ideals and Inspirations*. New York: Revell, 1917 (187 pages).

32. Gardner, Charles Spurgeon. *Psychology and Preaching*. New York: Macmillan, 1918 (389 pages).

33. English John Mahan. *For Pulpit and Platform*. New York: Macmillan, 1919 (143 pages).

34. Brown, Charles Reynolds. *The Art of Preaching*. New York: Macmillan, 1922 (250 pages).

35. Tilroe, William Edwin. *Set Forth*. New York: Chautauqua, and Boston: Franklin Press, 1882 (86 pages).

36. Vance, James Isaac. *Being a Preacher*. New York: Revell, 1923 (171 pages).

37. Davis, Ozora Stearns. *Principles of Preaching*. Chicago: U. of Chicago, 1924 (270 pages).

38. Stidger, William LeRoy. *Preaching Out of the Overflow*. Nashville: Cokesbury, 1929 (238 pages).

39. Phelps, Arthur Stevens. *Speaking in Public*. New York: Richard R. Smith, 1930 (232 pages).

40. Atkins, Gaius Glenn. *Preaching and the Mind of Today*. New York: Round Table, 1934 (227 pages).

41. Patton, Carl S. *The Preparation and Delivery of Sermons*. New York: Willett, Clark, and Co., 1938 (191 pages).

42. Sperry Willard L. *We Prophesy in Part: A Re-examination of the Liberty of Prophesying*. New York: Harper and Brothers, 1938 (201 pages).

43. Montgomery, Richmond Ames. *Preparing Preachers to Preach*. Grand Rapids: Zondervan, 1939 (249 pages).

44. Robbins, Howard Chandler. *Preaching the Gospel*. New York: Harper and Brothers, 1939 (151 pages).

45. Ray, Jefferson Davis. *Expository Preaching*. Grand Rapids: Zondervan, 1940 (123 pages).

46. Noyes, Morgan Phelps. *Preaching the Word of God*. New York: Scribner's, 1943 (219 pages).

47. Kirkpatrick, Robert White. *Creative Delivery of Sermons*. New York: Macmillan, 1947 (235 pages).

48. Luccock, Halford Edward. *In the Minister's Workshop*. Nashville: Abingdon-Cokesbury, 1944 (254 pages).

49. Oxnam, Garfield Bromley. *Preaching in a Revolutionary Age*. New York: Abingdon-Cokesbury, 1944.

50. Scherer, Paul Ehrman. *For We Have This Treasure*. New York: Harper and Brothers, 1944 (212 pages).

51. Jones, Bob, Jr. *How to Improve Your Preaching*. New York: Revell, 1945 (126 pages).

52. Kennedy, Gerald Hamilton. *His Word Through Preaching*. New York: Harper and Brothers, 1947 (234 pages).

53. Blackwood, Andrew Watterson. *The Preparation of Sermons*. New York and Nashville: Abingdon-Cokesbury, 1948 (272 pages).

54. Fritz, John H. C. *Essentials of Preaching*. St. Louis: Concordia, 1948 (73 pages).

55. Riley, William Bell. *The Preacher and His Preaching*. Wheaton, Ill.: Sword of the Lord, 1948 (146 pages).

56. Baughman, Harry Fridley. *Preaching from the Propers*. Philadelphia: Muhlenberg, 1949 (120 pages).

57. MacLennan, David Alexander. *Preacher's Primer*. New York: Oxford, 1950 (113 pages).

58. Whitesell, Faris Daniel. *The Art of Biblical Preaching*. Grand Rapids: Zondervan, 1950 (160 pages).

59. Ferris, Theodore Parker. *Go Tell the People*. New York: Scribner's, 1951 (116 pages).

60. Jordan, Gerald Ray. *You Can Preach*. Westwood, N.J.: Revell, 1951 (256 pages).

61. Coffin, Henry Sloane. *Communion Through Preaching*. New York: Scribner's, 1953 (124 pages).

62. Littorin, Frank T. *How to Preach the Word with Variety*. Grand Rapids: Baker, 1953 (157 pages).

63. Baxter, Batsell Barrett. *Speaking for the Master*. New York: Macmillan, 1954 (134 pages).

64. Bowie, Walter Russell. *Preaching*. Nashville: Abingdon, 1954 (224 pages).

65. Caldwell Frank Hill. *Preaching Angles*. Nashville: Abingdon, 1954 (126 pages).

66. Garrison, Webb Black. *The Preacher and His Audience*. Westwood, N.J.: Revell, 1954 (285 pages).

67. Gibson, George M. *Planned Preaching*. Philadelphia: Westminster, 1954 (140 pages).

68. Weatherspoon, Jesse Burton. *Sent Forth to Preach*. New York: Harper and Brothers, 1954 (182 pages).

Appendix 3

This section treats homiletics textbooks published in and after 1954. The thirty-seven most-used texts are presented and evaluated on the basis of their frequency of use. Frequency was determined by a survey in which questionnaires were sent to 137 members of the American Association of Theological Seminaries.* This survey is not necessarily an evaluation of the best homiletics texts, but is primarily an indication of the most-used homiletics texts by those members of the AATS.

Number of Responses   Author and Title

76	Davis, Henry Grady. *Design for Preaching*. Philadelphia: Muhlenberg, 1958.
38	Broadus, John A. *A Treatise on the Preparation and Delivery of Sermons*. 4th ed. Edited by Vernon Stanfield. San Francisco: Harper & Row, 1979.
37	Blackwood, Andrew W. *The Preparation of Sermons*. New York: Abingdon, 1948.
35	Jones, Illion T. *Principles and Practices of Preaching*. Nashville: Abingdon, 1956.
31	Miller, Donald G. *The Way to Biblical Preaching*. New York: Abingdon, 1957.
30	Abbey. Merrill R. *Preaching to the Contemporary Mind*. New York: Abingdon, 1963.
27	Robinson, Haddon W. *Biblical Preaching*. Grand Rapids: Baker, 1980.
26	Sangster, William E. *The Approach to Preaching*. Philadelphia: Westminster, 1952.

*Survey taken from R. Kent Hughes, "A Quantitative Analysis of Selected General Homiletical Trade and Textbooks" (Ph.D. diss., Trinity Evangelical Divinity School, 1983), 10-11.

25	Stott, John R. W. *Between Two Worlds*. Grand Rapids: Eerdmans, 1982.
21	Baumann, J. Daniel, *An Introduction to Contemporary Preaching*, Baker, 1972.
19	Killinger, John. *The Centrality of Preaching in the Total Task of the Ministry*. Waco, Tex.: Word, 1969.
18	Haselden, Kyle. *The Urgency of Preaching*. New York: Harper & Row, 1963.
15	Bartlett, Gene E. *The Audacity of Preaching*. New York: Harper & Row, 1962.
	Koller. Charles W. *Expository Preaching Without Notes*. Grand Rapids: Baker, 1962.
	Lenski, R. C. H. *The Sermon, Its Homiletical Construction*. Grand Rapids: Baker, 1968.
14	McCracken, Robert J. *The Making of the Sermon*. New York: Harper, 1956.
	Perry, Lloyd M. *Biblical Preaching for Today's World*. Chicago: Moody, 1973.
	Stevenson, Dwight E. *In the Biblical Preacher's Workshop*. Nashville: Abingdon, 1967.
13	Lloyd-Jones, D. Martyn. *Preaching and Preachers*. Grand Rapids: Zondervan, 1971.
	Kennedy, Gerald H. *God's Good News*. New York: Harper and Brothers, 1955.
12	Malcomson, William R. *The Preaching Event*. Philadelphia: Westminster, 1968.
11	Hall, Thor. *The Future Shape of Preaching*. Philadelphia: Fortress, 1971.
	Reid, Clyde. *The Empty Pulpit: A Study in Preaching and Communication*. New York: Harper & Row, 1967.
10	Brown, Henry Clifton, Jr. *The Quest for Reformation in Preaching*. Waco, Tex.: Word, 1968.
	Brown, Henry Clifton, Jr.; Clinard, H. Gordon, and Jesse J. *Steps to the Sermon*. Nashville: Broadman, 1963.
6	Evans, William. *How to Prepare Sermons*. New York: Sheed & Ward, 1963.
4	Unger, Merrill F. *Principles of Expository Preaching*. Grand Rapids: Zondervan, 1955.
3	Skinner, Craig. *The Teaching Ministry of the Pulpit*. Grand Rapids: Baker, 1973.
2	Gibbs, Alfred P. *The Preacher and His Preaching*. Topeka, Kan.: Walterick, 1958.
	Mark, Harry Clayton. *Patterns for Preaching: The Art of Sermon Making*. Grand Rapids: Zondervan, 1959.
	O'Neal, Glenn. *Make the Bible Live*. Winona Lake, Ind.: BMH Books, 1972.

1   Caldwell, Frank H. *Preaching Angles*. New York: Abingdon, 1954.

Drury, Ronan. *Preaching*. New York: Sheed and Ward, 1963.

Hogue, Wilson T. *A Handbook of Homiletics and Pastoral Theology*. Winona Lake, Ind.: Free Methodist, 1954.

Appendix 4

HOMILETICAL CONCEPTS IN THE HISTORY OF PREACHING

1. Allegory
2. Argumentative
3. Application
4. Arrangement
5. Author
6. Bible content
7. Biographical
8. Delivery
9. Doctrinal
10. Eloquence
11. Evangelistic
12. Expository
13. Extemporaneous
14. Humor
15. Illustrations
16. Imagination
17. Law training
18. Life-situation preaching
19. Logic
20. Long pastorate
21. Manuscript preaching
22. Martyrs
23. Memorized sermons
24. Missionaries
25. Mystics
26. Open-air preachers
27. Pastor
28. Persuasion of audience
29. Prayer
30. Professors
31. Radio and TV preachers
32. Speech training or teacher
33. Style and originality
34. Textual
35. Topical
36. Unique features

1. Allegory

Lancelot Andrews (1565-1624). Allegorical interpretation.
Anthony of Padua (1195-1231).
Thomas Aquinas (1227-1274).
Bede the Venerable (672-735).

Bonaventura (John Fidanza) (1221-1274).
Columba (521-597).
Cyprian (200-255).
Gregory of Nyssa (329-394).
Gregory the Great (540-604).
John Huss (1373-1415). Excellent allegories.
John of Damascus (700-745).
Origen (182-251). Used allegory extensively.
Savonarola (1452-1498).
John Tauler (1300-1361). Fanciful allegory.

2. Argumentative

Robert S. Candlish (1806-1873). Master of argumentative preaching.
John Chrysostom (347-407). A lawyer; used argument.
Jean Claude (1619-1687). Departed from textual of his day to a more topical arrangement.
Balthasar Hubmaier (1480-1528). Excellent in argumentation.
Justin Martyr (100-165). Noted for arguing in favor of Christ.
Jacques Saurin (1677-1730). Argumentative in the body of the message.
Jeremy Taylor (1613-1667). Used clear arguments.

3. Application

Lyman Beecher (1775-1863). Doctrinal but practical.
Phillip Brooks (1835-1893). Put theology into life.
Charles Gore (1853-1932). Stressed the obligations of Christianity.
William Jay (1769-1853). Combined doctrinal, experimental, and practical applications.
Robert Murray McCheyne (1813-1843). Matchless applications.
Karl Nitzsch (1787-1868). Combined doctrine and duty.
Stephen Olford (1918-   ). Excellent applications.

4. Arrangement

James Alexander (1804-1859). Main points simple and clear.
Anthony of Padua (1195-1231). Analytical method.
Thomas Aquinas (1227-1274). Three major divisions.
Richard Baxter (1615-1691). Had minute sermon divisions.
Berthold of Regensberg (1220-1272). Outline clear and well arranged.
Bonaventura (John Fidanza) (1221-1274). Skilled in analyzing his subject; outlines were simple and bare.
Thomas Boston (1677-1732). Good order and arrangement.
John Bradford (1510-1555). Sermon outlines consisted of three questions.
Phillips Brooks (1835-1893). Clear construction.

John Calvin (1509-1564).

J. Wilbur Chapman (1859-1918). Strong sermon outline (evangelistic).

John Chrysostom (347-407). Drawn out description, introduction, exposition, and application.

Theodore Cuyler (1822-1909).

Dominic (1170-1221). Began with a story and then wove a sermon into the story.

DuBosc (1623-1692). Unique conclusions

Francis Fenelon (1651-1715). Used a carefully prepared plan.

Thomas Guthrie (1803-1873). Sermons carefully prepared.

Robert Hall (1764-1831).

Hippolytus (170-236). Eloquent and suggestive.

Balthasar Hübmaier (1488-1528). Good sermon arrangement.

Harry A. Ironside (1876-1951). Explain; illustrate; apply.

William Jay (1769-1853). Practical textual analysis.

Charles Koller (1896-   ). Propositional preaching.

H. P. Liddon (1829-1890). Master of sermon construction.

George C. Lorimer (1838-1904). Clear divisions.

Halford Luccock (1885-1961). Logical structure.

Martin Luther (1483-1546). Stressed the body of the sermon, not the introduction or conclusion.

Robert Murray McCheyne 1813-1843). Good divisions and subdivisions.

Harold John Ockenga (1905-   ). Outlines are clear and concise.

Stephen Olford (1918-   ). Well organized; alliteration.

Harold Cooke Phillips (1892-1966). Emphasized sermon preparation.

A. T. Pierson (1837-1911). Strong on sermon divisions.

Frederick W. Robertson (1816-1853). Two-point sermons.

Robert South (1634-1716). Noted for good sermon arrangement but not for spirituality.

John Tillotson (1630-1694). Good homiletical pattern.

John Wesley (1703-1791). A great arranger of thought.

5. Authors

Albert the Great (1193-1280). Most voluminous author of thirteenth century.

Ambrose (340-397). Homilies; hymns; letters; funeral orations; Ambrosian chant and ritual.

Lancelot Andrews (1565-1624). Devotional literature.

Thomas Aquinas (1227-1274). Wrote *Summa Theologiae*.

Athanasius (293-373). Wrote against Arianism.

Augustine of Hippo (354-430). *De Doctrina Christiana*.

Donald G. Barnhouse (1895-1962). Founded *Eternity* magazine.

Richard Baxter (1615-1691). Wrote *Saints' Everlasting Rest* (1650); *The Reformed Pastor*; *Call to the Unconverted*.

The Venerable Bede (672-735). Wrote several commentaries.

Bernard of Clairvaux (1090-1153). Hymnwriter.

Oscar F. Blackwelder (1878-   ). Galatians Commentary; Interpreter's Bible.

Andrew Blackwood (1882-1968). Wrote twenty books in practical theology.

John S. Bonnell (1893-   ). Wrote *What Are You Living For?*

Frank W. Boreham (1871-1959). Wrote more than fifty books.

John Albert Broadus (1827-1895). Wrote a famous textbook on the history of preaching.

Charles R. Brown (1862-1950). Author of a textbook.

John Bunyan (1628-1688). Wrote *Pilgrim's Progress* and *Grace Abounding*.

George A. Buttrick (1892-1980).

John Calvin (1509-1564). Wrote *The Institutes of the Christian Religion*.

B. H. Carroll (1843-1914). Wrote *Interpretation of the English Bible* (6 vols.).

John Chrysostom (347-407). Wrote the first treatise on homiletics—*On the Priesthood*.

Jean Claude (1619-1687). Wrote an essay on the composition of a sermon.

Clement of Rome (30-100). Wrote *Epistle to the Corinthians* and *Epistle of Clement*.

Harry Sloane Coffin (1887-1954). Wrote twelve books.

James Denney (1856-1917). Wrote studies in theology.

Henry Drummond (1857-1897). Famous sermon on 1 Corinthians 13 delivered in 1887.

Andrew Fairbairn (1838-1912). Published a number of theological works.

Herbert Henry Farmer (1714-1787). Wrote doctrinal books.

Theodore Ferris (1909-1968). Wrote nine books of which *Go Tell the People* was most popular.

P. T. Forsyth (1848-1921). Wrote many books including *Positive Preaching and the Modern Mind*.

Thomas Fuller (1608-1661). A better writer than preacher.

A. J. Gordon (1836-1895). Author of *When I Came to Church* and *The Ministry of the Spirit*.

Gregory of Nazianzus (329-390). Wrote five great theological discourses.

Gregory the Great (540-604). Wrote *Rules for Pastors*.

Thomas Richard Hooker (1553-1600). Wrote *Laws of Ecclesiastical Polity*; influenced the development of English prose.

Lynn Harold Hough (1877-1971). Wrote at least thirty-seven books.

John Howe (1630-1705). Wrote many doctrinal treatises.

Harry A. Ironside (1876-1951).

Rufus Jones (1863-1948). Wrote a book a year.

D. Martyn Lloyd-Jones (1895-1981). Wrote *Preaching and Preachers*.

Halford Luccock (1885-1961).

Clarence Macartney (1879-1957). Books of sermons.

David A. MacLennan (1903-   ). Wrote several homiletical works.

Cotton Mather (1663-1728). Published 382 works.

F. B. Meyer (1847-1929). Wrote 70 books with 5 million copies printed.

G. Campbell Morgan (1863-1945). Wrote ninety books.

W. Robertson Nicoll (1851-1923). Author of *Expositor's Bible*; read an average of two books a day.

Joseph Parker (1830-1902). Author of *People's Bible*.

William Perkins (1558-1602). Wrote first work on homiletics in the English language— *The Art of Prophesying*.

Peter of Lombard (1105-1164). Wrote one of the first theological textbooks—*Four Books of Sentences* (A.D. 1152).

William Alfred Quayle (1860-1925). Wrote twenty books.

Paul Rees (1900-   ).

William Edwin Sangster (1900-1960). Wrote fifteen books.

Fulton J. Sheen (1895-1979). Wrote a column that appeared in sixty newspapers.

Samuel Shoemaker III (1893-1963). Wrote thirty books.

Richard Storrs (1821-1900). Wrote *Preaching without Notes*.

Tertullian (170-240). Wrote on moral and theological subjects.

Thomas a Kempis (1380-1471). Wrote *Imitation of Christ*.

George W. Truett (1867-1944). Wrote many books.

John Wesley (1703-1791). Wrote 273 books and 23 hymnbooks.

John Wycliffe (1324-1384). Wrote many books.

6. Bible Content

Lancelot Andrews (1565-1624). Bible translator of KJV.

Francis Asbury (1745-1816).

Donald G. Barnhouse (1895-1962).

The Venerable Bede (672-735).

John S. Bonnell (1893-   ).

Frank W. Boreham (1871-1959). Bible content but not an expositor.

Bossuet (1627-1704). Many Bible quotations.

George A. Buttrick (1892-1980).

Clovis Chappell (1882-1972). But not an expositor.

John Chrysostom (347-407). Good Bible student; not knowledgeable in Hebrew, therefore, defective in his Old Testament interpretation.

Clement of Rome (30-100). Used Scriptures extensively in his sermons.

James Denney (1856-1917). Bible preacher.

David Dickson (1583-1663). Sermons based on three or four verses.

Phillip Doddridge (1702-1751). A Bible preacher.

John Donne (1573-1631).

August Herman Franke (1663-1727). Used both Old and New Testaments.

A. J. Gordon (1836-1895). Good spiritual insight.

William (Billy) Graham (1918-   ).

Gregory of Nazianzus (329-390). Good knowledge of the Bible.

Joseph Hall (1574-1656). Forced biblical interpretations; combined philosophical thought and biblical truth.

Matthew Henry (1662-1714). A notable pulpit Bible expositor.

Oswald Hoffman (1913-   ).

John Howe (1630-1705). Good Bible student.

John A. Hutton (1868-1947).

Harry A. Ironside (1876-1951). A verse by verse expositor.

William Jay (1769-1853).

John Knox (1505-1572).

Hugh Latimer (1485-1555).

R. Leighton (1611-1684). Stayed with one passage for a sermon.

Martin Luther (1483-1546). Strong use of the Bible.

Clarence Macartney (1879-1957).

Walter A. Maier (1893-1950). Averaged using a Bible verse a minute.

Justin Martyr (100-165). Stressed Bible reading in the church.

Andrew Melville (1545-1622). Followed the text closely.

D. L. Moody (1837-1899).

John Newton (1725-1807). Bible preacher.

Harold John Ockenga (1905-   ). Emphasis on doctrinal themes.

Origen (182-251). Memorized Bible content at mother's knee; preached mostly from Old Testament; pioneered in textual study.

John Owen (1616-1683). Anchored to the Scriptures.

Harold Cooke Phillips (1892-1966). Stressed the need for preaching the Bible.

A. T. Pierson (1837-1911). Wrote on Bible study.

Frederick W. Robertson (1816-1853). Sermons were biblical and practical.

Edwin Sandys (1516-1588). Bible translator and noted preacher.

Charles Simeon (1759-1836). Sought the plain meaning of Scripture.

Henry Smith (1550-1591). Great emphasis on Old Testament.

Philip Spener (1635-1705). Emphasized the use of the Bible and was the father of Pietism.

Charles H. Spurgeon (1834-1892). Messages saturated with Scripture.

Tertullian (170-240). Devoted to Scripture.

George W. Truett (1867-1944). Exalted and defended the Bible.

John Wesley (1703-1791). His sermons were filled with Scriptures.

John Wycliffe (1324-1384). Bible translator and emphasized the importance of Scripture; felt preachers must know their Bibles.

Ulrich Zwingli (1484-1531). Preached serially on the books of the Bible.

7. Biographical

Clovis G. Chappell (1882-1972). Old Testament biography.

Joseph Hall (1574-1656). Strong use of biographical material.

John A. Hutton (1868-1947). Preached many sermons on Bible characters.

Clarence Macartney (1879-1957).

F. B. Meyer (1847-1929).

George Matheson (1842-1906).

Alexander Whyte (1836-1921). Bible character messages.

8. Delivery

Ambrose (340-397). Outstanding orator.

Anthony of Padua (1195-1231). Once preached to 30,000 men.

Thomas Aquinas (1227-1274). Preached without a manuscript.

Augustine of Hippo (354-430). Preached to laborers at noon.

Richard Baxter (1615-1691). Spoke directly to the people.

The Venerable Bede (672-735). Extemporaneous.

Henry Ward Beecher (1813-1887). Fearless; dramatic.

Lyman Beecher (1775-1863). Magnetic; emotional; tempestuous.

Bernard of Clairvaux (1090-1153).

John S. Bonnell (1893-   ). Used dramatic dialogue.

Bossuet (1627-1704).

Phillips Brooks (1835-1893). Read his sermons well; had a very rapid delivery.

George A. Buttrick (1892-1980). Dramatic and fascinating.

John Calvin (1509-1564). Very little humor or human touch; used no notes.

Thomas Chalmers (1780-1847). Preaching saturated with personality.

John Chrysostom (347-407). "The golden mouthed."

Cyprian (200-258). Very eloquent.

Robert W. Dale (1829-1895). Shifted from extemporaneous to manuscript.

Pierre Didon (1840-1900). Impassioned eloquence.

Dominic (1170-1221).

John Donne (1573-1631). Wept while preaching; noted for good eye contact.

DuBosc (1623-1692). Had a pleasant voice.

Jonathan Edwards (1703-1758). Had an unattractive voice; argumentative; used few gestures; read, holding arms up in front of his face.

Francis Fenelon (1651-1715). Preached without notes.

Charles G. Finney (1792-1875). Dignified.

Harry Emerson Fosdick (1878-1969). Excellent eye contact; conversational style; preached from a manuscript.

Bernard Gilpin (1517-1583). A bold preacher.

Washington Gladden (1836-1918). Flowery introductions.

Thomas Goodwin (1600-1680). No wit or affectation.

Frank W. Gunsaulus (1856-1921). Used the technique of role playing in his preaching.

Thomas Guthrie (1803-1873). Great platform speaker.

Joseph Hall (1574-1656). Great pulpit orator.

Robert Hall (1764-1831). Spoke from an outline; produced transcribed sermon by dictation.

Lynn Harold Hough (1877-1971). An explosive delivery.

R. Leighton (1611-1684). Extemporaneous delivery.

H. P. Liddon (1829-1890). Good sermon delivery.

Halford Luccock (1885-1961). Preached from an outline.

Clarence Macartney (1879-1957). Preached without notes.

John Mitchell Mason (1770-1829). Extemporaneous; conversational tone.

Mark A. Matthews (1867-1940). Preached extemporaneous, 45-minute sermons

D. L. Moody (1837-1899). Spoke 200 words a minute.

G. Campbell Morgan (1863-1945). Excellent voice; good diction; dramatic.

Harold John Ockenga (1905-   ). Modest, not overly dynamic

Garfield B. Oxnam (1891-1963). Friendly but business-like manner; dynamic.

Joseph Parker (1830-1902). Oratorical; theatrical.

Peter the Hermit (1050-1115). Remembered for his gestures; drew pictures with his hands; magnetism in his eyes.

Polycarp (68-160). Warm earnestness.

Bishop William Quayle (1860-1925). An orator.

Jacques Saurin (1677-1730). An orator.

Charles Simeon (1759-1836). Lively and earnest; his mannerisms and gestures were often awkward.

Henry Smith (1550-1591). Great orator.

Ralph Sockman (1889-1970). Deep melodious voice.

Charles H. Spurgeon (1834-1892). Clear and powerful voice.

T. Dewitt Talmage (1832-1901). Poor use of gestures.

Leslie D. Weatherhead (1893-1976). Conversational delivery.

George Whitefield (1714-1770). His voice could be heard unamplified by 30,000 people.

Alexander Whyte (1836-1921). Dramatic delivery.

9. Doctrinal

Peter Abelard (1079-1142).

Lancelot Andrews (1565-1624).

Anselm of Canterbury (1033-1109).

Thomas Aquinas (1227-1274).

Athanasius (293-373). Championed the Nicene Creed; expounded the Trinity.

Augustine of Hippo (354-430).

D. M. Baille (1887-1954).

Karl Barth (1886-1968). Preached the theology of crisis.

Basil the Great (330-397). Had ability to define doctrine but practical.

Richard Baxter (1615-1691). Studied theology.

Henry Ward Beecher (1813-1887).

Lyman Beecher (1775-1863). Doctrinal but practical.

Bernard of Clairvaux (1090-1153). Theologian; preached the cross.

Thomas Binney (1798-1874). At home with theological questions.

Bonaventura (1221-1274). Theologian to the Franciscans.

Yngve Brilioth (1891-1964).

Phillips Brooks (1835-1893). Put theology into life.

Charles R. Brown (1862-1950). Biblical theologian.

Emil Brunner (1889-1966). Biblical doctrine of Genesis and natural revelation.

Rudolph Bultmann (1884-1976). Doctrinal preaching but not evangelical.

John Bunyan (1628-1688).

Horace Bushnell (1802-1876). Trinity (mediating in theology).

John Calvin (1509-1564). Sound doctrine.

Thomas Chalmers (1780-1847). Sermons on Romans.

William E. Channing (1780-1842). Liberal.

Clement of Alexandria (350-222). An outstanding theologian.

Oscar Cullman (1902-   ). Exegetical theologian influenced by form criticism.

Robert W. Dale (1829-1895). The great doctrinal preacher of 19th century.

Martin Dibelius (1883-1947). Radical form criticism.

Frederick Dillistone (1903-   ).

James Denney (1856-1917). Theologian of the cross.

John Donne (1573-1631). Became a Protestant by studying doctrine; strong on doctrine of redemption.

Timothy Dwight (1752-1817). A firm evangelical; published good models of doctrinal discourses.

Jonathan Edwards (1703-1758).

Andrew M. Fairbairn (1838-1912). Doctrine of God.

Herbert Henry Farmer (1892-1981). Lecturer on doctrine.

Nels Ferre (1908-1971). Theologian and philosopher; preached radical theology.

Charles G. Finney (1792-1875). Stressed the deity of Christ.

E. Flechier (1632-1710).

Peter Taylor Forsyth (1848-1921). Preached theology; cross and love of God; emphasized grace.

Francis of Assisi (1182-1226). Preached and wrote about the doctrine of Christ.

August Herman Franke (1663-1727). Preached on all the doctrines of the Bible.

Andrew Fuller (1754-1815). Formulated Calvinism in strong, simple language.

Thomas Goodwin (1600-1680). Emphasized Christ; a Calvinist.

A. J. Gordon (1836-1895). Doctrine of the Holy Spirit.

George A. Gordon (1853-1929). Earnest Trinitarian, but inclined toward liberalism.

Charles Gore (1853-1932). Had power in presenting the doctrine and obligations of Christianity.

Arthur J. Gossip (1873-1954). Cross was centered in his sermons.

William (Billy) Graham (1918-   ). Emphasized redemption but not noted for doctrinal preaching.

I. M. Haldeman (1845-1933). The "second coming" preacher.

Joseph Hall (1574-1656). Emphasized the cross of Christ.

Robert Hall (1764-1831). Popular, pleasing presentation of doctrine.

Robert Horton (1885-1934). Denied the infallibility of Scripture.

John Howe (1630-1705). A philosophical theologian.

Charles Edward Jefferson (1860-1937). Preached doctrine but avoided doctrinal terms.

John D. Jones (1797-1840). Holiness of God, redemption, forgiveness and immortality.

Charles Hodge (1797-1878).

H. P. Liddon (1829-1890). Preached sacramental doctrine.

Martin Luther (1483-1546). Emphasized duty founded on doctrine; emphasis on repentance and faith.

J. Gresham Machen (1887-1937). Preached doctrine simply.

Alexander MacLaren (1826-1910). Preached Christ.

Cotton Mather (1663-1728). Sermons based on doctrine; stressed Christ as mediator.

Robert Murray McCheyne (1813-1843).

John H. Newman (1801-1890). Doctrinal sermons but not technical.

Karl Nitzsch (1787-1868). Combined doctrine and duty in his preaching.

Harold John Ockenga (1905-   ). Emphasized the Holy Spirit and salvation.

Stephen Olford (1918-   ). Stressed person and work of Christ.

Origen (182-251). Greatest contribution through the logos doctrine; outstanding theologian.

John Owen (1616-1683). Many doctrinal writings.

Joseph Parker (1830-1902). Redemption was the center of his preaching.

Nicholas Ridley (1500-1555). Good theologian and preacher.

Jacques Saurin (1677-1730). Mostly doctrinal and ethical.

William G. T. Shedd (1820-1894). Calvinistic doctrine.

Paul Scherer (1892-1969). Doctrinal preacher; could phrase doctrine in fresh language.

Charles H. Spurgeon (1834-1892). Calvinist; preaching was doctrinal.

John Tauler (1300-1361). Preached Christ and against sin.

Jeremy Taylor (1613-1667). Good theologian.

Tertullian (170-240). First Christian theologian to write in Latin; not systematic.

I. R. Watson (1781-1833). Formulated Methodist theology.

Benjamin B. Warfield (1851-1921).

John Wesley (1703-1791). Arminian theology; expounded doctrine because of its practical value to listeners.

George Whitefield (1714-1770). Calvinistic doctrine.

10. Eloquence

Thomas Adams (1580-1653).

Cyprian (200-258).

Pierre Didon (1840-1900). Impassioned eloquence.

Frank W. Gunsaulus (1856-1921). Noted for charming rhetoric.

Leo the Great (390-461).

John McNeill (1854-1933).

Cotton Mather (1663-1728).

Joseph Parker (1830-1902). Natural eloquence without education.

Jeremy Taylor (1613-1667).

Francis Wayland (1796-1865).

11. Evangelistic

Augustine of Hippo (354-430).

Richard Baxter (1615-1691).

William Biederwolf (1867-1939).

Bernard of Clairvaux (1090-1153). Emphasized repentance; led thousands to Christ.

Berthold of Regensberg (1220-1272). Franciscan evangelist.

Jacques Bridaine (1701-1767). Sermons only in French.

John Bunyan (1628-1688).

John Calvin (1509-1564).

Thomas Chalmers (1780-1847). Greatest nineteenth century soulwinner.

J. Wilbur Chapman (1859-1918).

Christmas Evans (1766-1838).

Charles G. Finney (1792-1875). Invited sinners to come to the "anxious bench."

Arthur John Gossip (1873-1954). Called for pastoral evangelism.

William (Billy) Graham (1918-   ).

Gregory of Nyssa (329-394). Strong desire to win souls.

Hugh Latimer (1485-1555).

John Livingstone (1603-1672). Won 500 to Christ in one sermon.

Walter A. Maier (1893-1950).

Increase Mather (1639-1723). Lamented the age of decreasing conversions.

Dwight L. Moody (1837-1899).

Stephen Olford (1918-   ). Man of great compassion.

A. T. Pierson (1837-1911). Won thousands to Christ.

Alan Redpath (1907-   ). Evangelist in England with a youth group.

William Edwin Sangster (1900-1960).

Lee R. Scarborough (1870-1945). Never lost his passion for souls; professor of evangelism.

Samuel Shoemaker III (1893-1963). Known also to be evangelistic.

Rodney (Gypsy) Smith (1860-1947).

Charles H. Spurgeon (1834-1892). Had a consistent audience of 5,400 at Metropolitan Tabernacle in London.

William A. (Billy) Sunday (1863-1945).

Reuben A. Torrey (1856-1928).

George W. Turnett (1867-1944).

George Whitefield (1714-1770).

12. Expository

Thomas Adams (1580-1653).

Athanasius (293-373). Followed Origen's idea of expository preaching.

Augustine of Hippo (354-430).

Donald G. Barnhouse (1895-1962).

The Venerable Bede (672-735). Bible translator.

James M. Boice (1938-   ).

Charles R. Brown (1862-1950).

John Calvin (1509-1564). Verse by verse.

Thomas Chalmers (1780-1847). Special emphasis on Romans.

Clement of Alexandria (150-222). Strong exegete of Scripture.

John Colet (1466-1519). Devoted to the the Word of God; expository in a day of allegorical preaching.

Robert W. Dale (1829-1895). Sermons were expository and doctrinal.

Andrew Fuller (1754-1815).

Thomas Goodwin (1600-1680). Excellent exegetical preacher.

Harry A. Ironside (1876-1951). Verse by verse.

D. Martyn Lloyd-Jones (1895-1981).

R. Leighton (1611-1684). Preached on one passage.

Alexander MacLaren (1826-1910).

John M. Mason (1770-1829). Verse by verse.

F. B. Meyer (1847-1929).

G. Campbell Morgan (1863-1945). Analysis, synthesis, and application.

Stephen Olford (1918-   ). Well organized.

Origen (182-251). Stressed exposition.
W. Graham Scroggie (1877-1959).
Ulrich Zwingli (1484-1531). Great expositor.

13. Extemporaneous (without notes)

The Venerable Bede (672-735). Extemporaneous.
John Calvin (1509-1564). Used no notes.
Robert W. Dale (1829-1895). Shifted from extemporaneous to manuscript.
Francis Fenelon (1651-1715). Preached without notes.
Hugh Latimer (1485-1555). Preached without notes.
R. Leighton (1611-1684). Extemporaneous delivery.
Halford Luccock (1885-1961). Preached from an outline.
Clarence Macartney (1879-1957).
John Mitchell Mason (1770-1829). Conversational tone; without notes.
Mark A. Matthews (1867-1940). Preached 45-minute messages.
Joseph Parker (1830-1902).

14. Humor

Lancelot Andrews (1565-1624). Used puns.
John Bunyan (1628-1688). Homely humor.
James Cleland (1903-1978). Kindly sense of humor.
Thomas Fuller (1608-1661). Known for his wit.
Joseph Hall (1574-1656). Noted for his great wit.
C. Oscar Johnson (1886-1965). Remembered for his sense of humor.
Hugh Latimer (1485-1555). Had a lively wit.
H. P. Liddon (1829-1890). Rich humor and strong sarcasm.
Martin Luther (1483-1546). Great sense of humor.
John McNeill (1854-1933).
Dwight Lyman Moody (1837-1899).
Joseph Parker (1830-1902).

15. Illustrations

Lancelot Andrewes (1565-1624). Noted for his puns.
Anthony of Padua (1195-1231).
Augustine of Hippo (354-430).
Isaac Barrows (1630-1677). Student of the classics.
Basil the Great (330-397). Used many illustrations.
Henry Ward Beecher (1813-1887).
William Biederwolf (1867-1939). Illustrations from art, history, and science (7 vols.).
John S. Bonnell (1893-   ). Good illustrations; many quotes.
Phillips Brooks (1835-1893).
J. Wilbur Chapman (1859-1918). Bible and experience illustrations.

Clovis G. Chappell (1882-1972). Used many illustrations.

John Chrysostom (347-407). Long descriptions; drew illustrations from everything.

Russell Conwell (1843-1925). Wrote *Acres of Diamonds*; sermons were 95 percent illustrations.

Dominic (1170-1221). Good use of illustrations and fables.

Washington Gladden (1836-1918). Used Scriptural illustrations.

Arthur John Gossip (1873-1954). Good use of illustrations.

Gregory of Nazianzus (329-390). Poet.

Harry A. Ironside (1876-1951). Used a lot of poetry in sermons.

John Henry Jowett (1864-1923). Noted for unusual illustrations.

George C. Lorimer (1838-1904). Incorporated poetry and literature in sermons; had been an actor.

Clarence Macartney (1879-1957). Illustrations from Bible, life, and history.

Alexander Maclaren (1826-1910). Freshness in his illustrations.

F. B. Meyer (1847-1929). Graphic illustrations.

D. L. Moody (1837-1899).

Harold John Ockenga (1905-   ). Many historical references; places and people.

Stephen Olford (1918-   ). Personal and biblical illustrations.

Ralph Sockman (1889-1970). Excellent illustrations.

Charles H. Spurgeon (1834-1892). Rich illustrations.

T. Dewitt Talmage (1832-1901). Great storyteller; confused illustration with argument.

John Tauler (1300-1361). Used many illustrations.

Jeremy Taylor (1613-1667). Good variety and many illustrations; used many quotations from the classics.

Alexander Vinet (1797-1847). Illustrations were apt and forceful.

Leslie D. Weatherhead (1893-1976). Personal experiences.

Alexander Whyte (1836-1921).

Ulrich Zwingli (1484-1531). Classical illustrations.

16. Imagination

Henry Ward Beecher (1813-1887).

John S. Bonnell (1893-   ). Used dramatic dialogue.

Frank W. Boreham (1871-1959).

Phillip Brooks (1835-1893). More imaginative than profound.

John Bunyan (1628-1688). Good imagination.

George A. Buttrick (1892-1980).

Christmas Evans (1766-1838).

Washington Gladden (1836-1918).

Arthur Gossip (1873-1954).

George C. Lorimer (1838-1904).

Martin Luther (1483-1546). Good imagination.

Gregory of Nazianzus (329-390). Eloquence and imagination in preaching.

Newell Dwight Hillis (1858-1929). Vivid imagination.

Clarence Macartney (1879-1957). Great powers of description.

Jacques Saurin (1677-1730). Powerful imagination.

Girolamo Savonarola (1452-1498). Used good imagination.

T. Dewitt Talmage (1832-1901). A florid and ill-balanced imagination.

Tertullian (170-240).

Leslie D. Weatherhead (1893-1976). Strong use of visual imagination.

Alexander Whyte (1836-1921). Vivid imagination.

17. Law Training

John Chrysostom (347-407).

Charles G. Finney (1792-1875).

Richard Fuller (1804-1876).

Mark A. Matthews (1867-1940).

James Albert Pike (1907-1969).

Richard Storrs (1821-1900).

Tertullian (170-240).

18. Life-situation Preaching

Basil the Great (330-397). Preached on temperance.

Albert W. Beaven (1882-1943). Preventive preaching.

Henry Ward Beecher (1813-1887). Leader in anti-slavery.

Adolphus J. F. Behrends (1839-1900).

Thomas Binney (1798-1874). Started the trend toward life-situation preaching.

Hugh Black (1868-1953).

John S. Bonnell (1893-   ). Leader in pastoral psychology movement.

Walter Russell Bowie (1882-1968). Tried to know his people personally.

Horace Bushnell (1802-1876). Wanted to know people personally.

George A. Buttrick (1892-1980). Visited all once a year.

William E. Channing (1780-1842). Doctrinal preaching applied to life situations; strong on ethics.

Clement of Rome (30-100). Known for his ethical sermons.

Henry Sloane Coffin (1887-1954). Applied Christian ethics to social problems.

Theodore Ferris (1908-1972). Preached to needs of the people.

Jack Finegan (1908-   ). Preached to student needs; had private interviews with them.

Harry Emerson Fosdick (1878-1969). Combined counseling ministry with his preaching.

Washington Gladden (1836-1918). Interested in social reform.

John A. Hutton (1868-1947). Preached counseling from psychology.

Charles Edward Jefferson (1860-1937). Preventive preaching.

Cotton Mather (1663-1728). Preached on social, political, and personal problems of the day.

Robert James McCracken (1904-1973). Preached on contemporary problems; sought Bible answers for personal problems.

Norman Vincent Peale (1898-   ). Most sermons are on personal problems.
Frederick W. Robertson (1816-1853). Preached on the problems of the day and raised
the suspicions of the conservatives.
Ralph Sockman (1889-1970). Preached victory over loss and pain; made religion a daily
concern to his listeners.
Leslie D. Weatherhead (1893-1976). Had a psychological clinic along with his church;
a pioneer in joining psychology and religion.

19. Logic

John Calvin (1509-1564).
Thomas Chalmers (1780-1847).
Augustine of Hippo (354-430). Logical mind.
Newel Dwight Hillis (1858-1929). Reasoned arguments in choice language.
John H. Newman (1801-1890). Influenced people by logic.
T. Dewitt Talmage (1832-1901). Confused assertion with proof.
Tertullian (170-240). Strong logic.

20. Long Pastorate

Alexander Carson (1776-1844). Pastor of one church for 50 years.
Nathaniel Emmons (1745-1840). Pastored one church for 54 years.
J. A. James (1785-1859). Had only one pastorate.
J. D. Jones (1865-1942). Nearly 40 years.
Robert G. Lee (1886-1978). Pastored Bellevue Baptist in Memphis, Tennessee for 35
years.
Alexander MacLaren (1826-1910). At Union Chapel in Manchester for 45 years.
Increase Mather (1639-1723). At Second Church in Boston for 62 years.
Mark A. Matthews (1867-1940). Served 38 years in Seattle.
Paul Rees (1900-   ). Pastor in Minneapolis for 20 years.
Samuel Shoemaker (1893-1963). Calvary Episcopal Church of New York City for 27
years.
Charles Simeon (1759-1836). Pastor of Holy Trinity at Cambridge for 54 years.
Richard Storrs (1821-1900). Pastored one church for 54 years.
George W. Truett (1867-1944). Pastored First Baptist in Dallas, Texas for 41 years.
Alexander Whyte (1836-1921). At Free St. George's in Edinburgh for nearly 50 years.

21. Manuscript Preaching

Phillips Brooks (1835-1893). Read his sermons well.
George A. Buttrick (1892-1980). Full manuscript.
Jonathan Edwards (1703-1758). Read his sermons.
Harry Emerson Fosdick (1878-1969).
Joseph Hall (1574-1656).
H. P. Liddon (1829-1890). Read his sermons.

Peter Marshall (1902-1949). Manuscript preacher.
Paul Scherer (1892-1969).
Alexander Whyte (1836-1921).

22. Martyrs

Balthasar Hübmaier (1480-1528). Burned at the stake because of his views on baptism.
John Huss (1373-1415). Burned at the stake for reforming tendencies.
Ignatius of Antioch (50-110). Wanted to be a martyr.
Hugh Latimer (1485-1555). Burned at the stake during the English Reformation.
Polycarp (68-160). Died at the stake.
Girolamo Savonarola (1452-1498). Martyred because of his political views.

23. Memorized Sermons

Bossuet (1627-1704). Funeral orator.
Thomas Guthrie (1803-1873). Prepared manuscript; memorized it and then delivered it
as if impromptu.
Robert G. Lee (1886-1978).
George C. Lorimer (1838-1904). Memorized his sermons.
Increase Mather (1639-1723). Memorized his sermons.
F. B. Meyer (1847-1929). Later he preached extemporaneously.

24. Missionaries

Adelbert (950-997). Funeral orator.
Anskar (or Ansgar) (801- 865). Missionary to Denmark and Sweden.
Anthony of Padua (1195-1231). Missionary to Africa and Italy.
Augustine of Canterbury (566-607). Missionary to England.
Bernardino of Siena (1380-1444). A missionary reformer.
Boniface (680-755). A bold missionary to ceremony; known by his works, not his
words.
David Brainerd (1718-1747). Missionary to American Indians.
John Eliot (1604-1690). Translator and missionary to the American Indians.
Andrew Fuller (1754-1815). Backed William Carey.
Gregory the Great (540-604). First to send out missionaries since the days of the early
church.
Irenaeus (120-177). Missionary to Gaul.
E. Stanley Jones (1884-1973). Missionary to India.
St. Patrick (372-465). Missionary to Ireland.
A. T. Pierson (1837-1911). Strong missionary interest.
Edwin McNeil Poteat (1892-1955). Missionary teacher in China.
Joseph Sizoo (1884-1966). Missionary in South India.
Robert E. Speer (1867-1947). With Presbyterian Board of Foreign Missions.

James Stewart (1831-1905). Assistant to David Livingstone in Africa
Ulfilas (311-381). Translated the Bible into the language of the Goths.
Francis Wayland (1796-1865). Champion of missions.

25. Mystics

Thomas a Kempis (1380-1471).
Lancelot Andrews (1565-1624).
Bernard of Clairvaux (1090-1153).
Bonaventura (1221-1274). Scholastic method with mystic spirit.
Meister Echardt (1260-1327).
John Geiler (1447-1510). Scholar and mystic.
A. J. Gordon (1836-1895). Philosopher and mystic.
John Tauler (1300-1361).

26. Open Air Preachers

Anthony of Padua (1195-1231).
Bernardino of Siena (1380-1444).
Berthold of Regensberg (1220-1272). Once preached to 60,000 in the open air.
Dominic (1170-1221).
Francis of Assisi (1182-1226).
Peter the Hermit (1050-1115). Leader of the first Crusade
John Wesley (1703-1791).
George Whitefield (1714-1770).
John Wycliffe (1324-1384). Formed a company of open-air preachers.

27. Pastors

Richard Baxter (1615-1691).
Andrew Bonar (1810-1892).
Phillips Brooks (1835-1893). Spent much time with his people.
John Bunyan (1628-1688). Had a pastor's heart.
George A. Buttrick (1892-1980). Strong in pastoral care.
S. Parkes Cadman (1864-1936).
Thomas Chalmers (1780-1847). Well organized visitation program.
Irenaeus (120-177).
Charles Edward Jefferson (1860-1937). Visitation of the sick; stressed pastoral service.
Robert G. Lee (1886-1978). Made ten pastoral calls a day.
Clarence Macartney (1879-1957). Called on congregation three to four afternoons and
  two to three evenings a week.
John Owen (1616-1683). Pastoral quality evident.
William Alfred Quayle (1860-1925).
Alexander Whyte (1836-1921). Good pastor and visitor.

28. Persuasion of Audience

Henry Ward Beecher (1813-1887). Sensitive to his audience.
George A. Buttrick (1892-1980). Always kept audience in mind.
John Cotton (1584-1652). Strong in persuasion.
Dominic (1170-1221). Excelled in persuasion and ethos.
Jonathan Edwards (1745-1801).
Bernard Gilpin (1517-1583). Very persuasive.
R. Leighton (1611-1684). Moved people to tears.
John Owen (1616-1683). Noble persuasiveness.
Matthew Simpson (1811-1884). More interested in persuasion than instruction.
George Whitefield (1714-1770).

29. Prayer

Lancelot Andrewes (1555-1626). His private devotions are spiritual classics.
Alexander Carson (1776-1844).
Francis Fenelon (1651-1715). Great spiritual man.
Francis of Assisi (1182-1226). Man of prayer; example of a godly life.
Bernard Gilpin (1517-1583). Noted for his learning and piety.
N. D. Hillis (1858-1929). Pleaded for richness and fullness of the Christian life.
John Knox (1505-1572). The Queen feared his prayers.
Martin Luther (1483-1546). Often spent as much as three hours per day in prayer.
Robert Murray McCheyne (1813-1843).
Peter Marshall (1902-1949). Noted for the beauty of his prayers.
George W. Truett (1867-1944). Noted for his pastoral prayers.

30. Professors

Albert the Great (1193-1280). Teacher of Thomas Aquinas.
Archibald Alexander (1772-1851). First professor of theology at Princeton.
Anthony of Padua (1195-1231). Professor of theology.
Thomas Aquinas (1227-1274). Lectured on theology.
Isaac Barrows (1630-1677). Professor of mathematics.
Karl Barth (1886-1968). Professor of theology at Basil.
Andrew Blackwood (1882-1968). Professor of English Bible and homiletics.
Louis Bourdaloue (1632-1704). Taught literature, philosophy, and theology.
John A. Broadus (1827-1895). Professor of homiletics at Southern Baptist Theological
   Seminary.
Charles R. Brown (1862-1950). Professor of homiletics; dean of Yale Divinity School.
B. H. Carroll (1843-1914). Professor of Bible at Baylor U.
Thomas Chalmers (1780-1847). Taught theology at U. of Edinburgh.
William Clow (1853-1930). Professor of homiletics and sociology.
Henry Sloane Coffin (1887-1954). Professor of practical theology.

Henry Drummond (1851-1897). Science professor at Free Church College.

William B. Evans (1870-1950). Moody Bible Institute and Biola College.

Theodore Ferris (1908-1972). Taught homiletics at Cambridge, Mass.

Robert Horton (1885-1934). Had been a teacher at Oxford.

Lynn Harold Hough (1877-1971). Professor at Garrett Seminary and President of Northwestern U.

C. Oscar Johnson (1886-1965). Taught homiletics.

Rufus Jones (1863-1948). Professor of philosophy at U. of Southern California.

Gerald Kennedy (1907-1980). Taught homiletics at Claremount Divinity School.

Halford Luccock (1885-1961). Yale professor of homiletics.

David A. MacLennan (1903-   ). Homiletics teacher at Yale.

Robert James McCracken (1904-1973). Theology and philosophy at McMaster Divinity School.

Origen (182-251). Head of a catechetical school at Alexandria.

Garfield B. Oxnam (1891-1963). Social ethics and practical theology at Boston U.

Edwin Poteat (1892-1955). President of Colgate.

Lee R. Scarborough (1870-1945). President of Southwestern Baptist Seminary and professor of evangelism.

Paul Scherer (1892-1969). Professor of homiletics at Union Seminary in New York.

William G. T. Shedd (1820-1894). Professor at Union Seminary in New York.

Fulton J. Sheen (1895-1979). Professor of philosophy.

Joseph Richard Sizoo (1884-1966). Professor of religion at George WashingtonU.; president of New Brunswick Seminary.

Willard L. Sperry (1882-1954). Dean of Harvard Divinity School.

James S. Stewart (1896-   ). Professor of New Testament at New College in Edinburgh.

W. H. Griffith Thomas (1861-1924). Professor of Old Testament at Wycliffe College in Toronto.

Henry Van Dusen (1897-1975). Professor of systematic theology at Union Seminary in New York.

John Wycliffe (1324-1384). Student and teacher of theology.

31. Radio and TV Preachers

Donald G. Barnhouse (1895-1962). Bible-centered radio preacher.

Peter Eldersveld (1911-1965). "Back to God Hour" beginning 1946.

Harry Emerson Fosdick (1878-1969).

Oswald C. J. Hoffmann (1913-   ). Succeeded Walter Maier on the "Lutheran Hour."

Walter A. Maier (1893-1950). Had 15 million radio listeners.

Robert James McCracken (1904-1973). Radio and TV

Paul E. Scherer (1892-1969). NBC's "Sunday Vespers."

Fulton J. Sheen (1895-1979). Radio and TV (400 stations on TV).

Ralph W. Sockman (1889-1970). Radio pastor for 25 years.

Norman Vincent Peale (1898-   ).

32. Speech Training or Teacher

Ambrose (340-397). Well trained in public address.

Augustine of Hippo (354- 430). Teacher of public address.

John Chrysostom (347-407). Teacher of rhetoric.

Cyprian (200-258). Educated as a public speaker.

E. Flechier (1632-1710). Teacher of public speaking.

Gregory of Nyssa (329-394). Teacher of public speaking.

Gregory of Nazianzus (329-390). Student of public address.

Joseph Hall (1574-1656). Teacher of rhetoric. ·

H. P. Liddon (1829-1890). An accomplished rhetorician.

Justin Martyr (100-165). Teacher of rhetoric before conversion.

Joseph Parker (1830-1902). Studied voice training.

William Edwin Sangster (1900-1960). Took private speech lessons and read sermons
   aloud.

Tertullian (170-240). Trained in rhetoric; a born orator.

33. Style and Originality

Thomas Adams (1580-1653). Poetic sermons.

Anthony of Padua (1195-1231). Popular.

Thomas Aquinas (1227-1274). Spoke in language of the people; used short sentences.

Francis Asbury (1745-1816). Plain, simple, and direct.

Augustine of Hippo (354-430). Clear in thought and style.

Donald G. Barnhouse (1895-1962). Direct and simple.

Richard Baxter (1615-1691). No sequence of thought; minute sermon divisions.

Lyman Beecher (1775-1863). Clear, smooth, carefully constructed.

Bernard of Clairvaux (1090-1153). Mastery of words.

Andrew Blackwood (1882-1968). Trained in English literature.

John S. Bonnell (1893-   ). Used rhetoric, questions, and figures of speech.

Bossuet (1627-1704). Clear, vivid style.

Louis Bourdaloue (1632-1704). Forceful and direct.

John A. Broadus (1827-1895). Clear, conversational.

Phillips Brooks (1835-1893). Used many figures of speech.

Charles R. Brown (1862-1950). Simplicity.

John Calvin (1509-1564). Intellectual.

Thomas Chalmers (1780-1847). Used long sentences.

William E. Channing (1780-1842). Beautiful style of presentation.

Jean Claude (1619-1687). Terse style.

Clement of Rome (30-100). Abrupt, simple, flowery style.

William Clow (1853-1930). Simple style.

Russell Conwell (1843-1925). Popular.

John Donne (1573-1631). Used short sentences; poetic.

DuBosc (1623-1692). Written rather than oral.

Theodore P. Ferris (1908-1972). Clarity; depth of thought; used many rhetorical questions.

Peter Taylor Forsyth (1848-1921). Rhetorical questions.

Harry Emerson Fosdick (1878-1969). Polished style.

Francis of Assisi (1182-1226). Simple, practical, effective, tender; noted for gospel paraphrasing.

Washington Gladden (1836-1918). Rhetorical questions.

Thomas Goodwin (1600-1680). Plain style.

Arthur John Gossip (1873-1954).

Roland Hill (1744-1833).

Newell Dwight Hillis (1858-1929). Great word pictures; beauty, force, energy, clarity.

Hippolytus (170-236). Eloquent and suggestive.

Ignatius (50-110). Excellent style and originality.

John Henry Jowett (1864-1923). Fresh, warm style.

Robert G. Lee (1886-1978). Figurative language; many modifiers.

Halford E. Luccock (1885-1961). Vivid and forceful.

Martin Luther (1483-1546). Fresh, natural use of words.

Peter Marshall (1902-1949). Imagery; had a poetic feeling for descriptive words.

Justin Martyr (100-165). Strong, fresh style.

J. B. Massillon (1663-1742). Pure, sincere, persuasive, beauty.

F. B. Meyer (1847-1929). Popular; presented finished and polished material.

D. L. Moody (1837-1899). Simple, faulty grammar.

John H. Newman (1801-1890). Long, beautifully flowing sentences.

Stephen Olford (1918-   ). Alliteration.

John Owen (1616-1683). Sermons were heavy.

Matthew Parker (1504-1575). Popular style of oratory.

Norman Vincent Peale (1898-   ). Simple, free, easy.

Peter the Hermit (1050-1115). Pioneer in preaching in the language of the people.

Paul E. Scherer (1892-1969). Mastery of words.

Samuel M. Shoemaker (1893-1963). Heavy style.

Charles Simeon (1759-1836). Eloquence of style.

Ralph W. Sockman (1889-1970). Mastery of word pictures.

Charles H. Spurgeon (1834-1892). Good style.

Jeremy Taylor (1613-1667). Long sentences; grandiose.

John Tillotson (1630-1694). Simple style.

Ulrich Zwingli (1484-1531). Simplicity of language.

34. Textual

Lancelot Andrewes (1565-1624).

Anthony of Padua (1195-1231). Kept to main divisions of the text.

Francis Asbury (1745-1816).

Isaac Barrows (1630-1677). Exhausted the text.

Henry Ward Beecher (1813-1887). Held to the text.

George A. Buttrick (1892-1980). Expository; exegetical.

Henry Sloane Coffin (1887-1954).

William Jay (1769-1853). Practical textual analysis.

D. Martyn Lloyd-Jones (1895-1981). Exposition verse by verse.
Harold John Ockenga (1905-   ). Expository; biblical topics.
Frederick W. Robertson (1816-1853). Probed a text for doctrine.
Charles H. Spurgeon (1834-1892).

35. Topical

John S. Bonnell (1893-   ).
Peter Cartwright (1785-1872).
Henry Sloane Coffin (1887-1954).
Jonathan Edwards (1703-1758).
Arthur John Gossip (1873-1954).
Newell D. Hillis (1858-1929).
John A. Hutton (1868-1947). An original and stimulating thinker.
Gerald Kennedy (1907-1980).
Robert G. Lee (1886-1978).
Garfield B. Oxnam (1891-1963). Used a text as a point of departure.
William L. Stidger (1885-1949).
John Tauler (1300-1361). A Christian life emphasis; his sermons were like dissertations.
Alexander Vinet (1797-1847). Neglected biblical foundations; used the psychological method.
Leslie D. Weatherhead (1893-1976). Topical and textual; used three-point outline.

36. Unique Features

Isaac Barrows (1630-1677). Sermons were 3½ hours long.
William Beiderwolf (1867-1939). Preached for twenty years without a reference to the second coming of the Lord.
Berthold of Regensberg (1220-1272). Made use of dialogue.
Phillip Brooks (1835-1893). Preaching enhanced by good moral life; read extensively.
John Bunyan (1628-1688). Sermons were long.
George A. Buttrick (1892-1980). Spent one hour in study for every minute in pulpit; spent four hours a day in study.
Samuel Parkes Cadman (1864-1936). Used a chauffeur when calling; constantly visited sick and dying.
John Calvin (1509-1564). Preached 3,000 sermons in 15 years.
B. H. Carroll (1843-1914). Founded Southwestern Baptist Seminary; a member of the Texas Rangers.
Peter Cartwright (1785-1872). Had a strong voice; could be heard by 20,000.
J. Wilbur Chapman (1859-1918). Preached with an open wound in his side; organized a nationwide campaign; conducted 10,597 services in 470 cities; suffered thirteen health breakdowns in fourteen years.
John Chrysostom (342-407). Had 1,000 sermons published; began to preach at age 39.
Clement of Alexandria (150-222). A philosopher and poet; in his writings we find the

first germs of the homily; had a strong influence on Origen.

Thomas Coke (1747-1814). At 70 years of age he volunteered for missionary service: died on the way to the West Indies; first Methodist bishop in the United States.

Theodore Cuyler (1822-1909). Interested in the Temperance Movement; leader of a revival in New York.

Cyprian (200-258). Believed in baptismal regeneration; father of the Roman episcopal system.

Dominic (1170-1221). Founder of the Dominicans.

John Donne (1573-1631). Entered the ministry at age 42.

Henry Drummond (1851-1897). Evolutionist.

DuBosc (1623-1692). Highly educated; logical thinker.

Timothy Dwight (1752-1817). Lyman Beecher was converted under his ministry; president of Yale.

W. A. Criswell (1909-   ). Preached consecutively.

Meister Eckhart (1260-1327). Wrote and taught in Latin; strong influence on Tauler; a Dominican; "Mystical Union with God."

Jonathan Edwards (1703-1758). Intellectual genius; saintly character.

Christmas Evans (1766-1838). Was blind in one eye.

Charles G. Finney (1792-1875). Emphasized preacher's need to be filled with the Holy Spirit.

E. Flechier (1632-1710). Mediator between the Catholics and Protestants.

John Fletcher (1729-1785). Wesley's helper.

Francis of Assisi (1182-1226). Founder of the Franciscans.

Andrew Fuller (1754-1815). Influenced by theological works of John Owen.

Bernard Gilpin (1517-1583). Remembered for his ministry to the poor and the jailed.

Thomas Goodwin (1600-1680). Was a pastor before becoming a Christian.

Arthur John Gossip (1873-1954). Originality of themes.

William (Billy) Graham (1918-   ). By 1955 had spoken to 20 million and with one million making decisions.

Joseph Hall (1574-1656). Spent last years of his life in exile.

John Howe (1630-1705). Prayed and preached most of the day; Chaplain to Oliver Cromwell.

Balthasar Hübmaier (1480-1528). Burned at the stake because of his views on baptism.

Charles Edward Jefferson (1860-1937). Remembered for his nature sermons.

J. H. Jowett (1864-1923). A student of the dictionary, in his study at 6:00 A.M..

John Knox (1505-1572). Combined the statesmanship of Calvin with the eloquence of Savonarola.

Hugh Latimer (1488-1555). Spent 10 years in seminary learning to preach; encouraged Bible reading.

Leo the Great (390-461). Founder of the papacy.

John Livingstone (1603-1672). Had 500 converts to Christ through one sermon; died in exile on the Continent.

D. Martyn Lloyd-Jones (1895-1981). Preached 12 years on Romans verse by verse (from 1:1 to 14:17).

George C. Lorimer (1838-1904). A converted actor.

Martin Luther (1483-1546). Had a warm social affection; wrote thirty-eight hymns and transposed about 600.

Alexander Maclaren (1826-1910). Scholar's mind and preacher's heart; devoted 60 hours in preparation for one message; devotion and discipline. He got his subjects from the text.

Walter A. Maier (1893-1950). Spent an hour in preparation for each minute of sermon.

Peter Marshall (1903-1949). Read Bible to blind grandmother and thereby became excellent Bible reader. "The measure of life is not its duration but its donation."

Justin Martyr (100-165). Felt that Christianity could be explained logically.

J. B. Massillon (1663-1742). Kept his eyes half-closed while preaching.

Cotton Mather (1663-1728). Received his bachelor of arts at age 15; master of arts at age 18. Married three times, had 15 children; set apart regular fasting days to stay humble.

Increase Mather (1639-1723). President of Harvard; studied sixteen hours a day.

Mark A. Matthews (1867-1940). Before he went to pastor a church in Seattle he insisted and that all the elders and deacons of the church resign and be replaced by those of his choice who would support his programs; had 14 assistant pastors at one time; established twenty-nine congregations in and around Seattle.

G. Campbell Morgan (1863-1945). In his study by 6 A.M. and would not be disturbed until noon. Basically a devotional rather than a doctrinal preacher; preached mostly from the four gospels; a student of the dictionary.

Robert Murray McCheyne (1813-1843). Died at age 29; preached for only seven years; he had thirty-nine weekly prayer meetings in his church.

W. Robertson Nicoll (1851-1923). Had a library of 25,000 volumes including 5,000 biographies. Read several books each day.

Harold John Ockenga (1905-   ). President of Gordon-Conwell; great missionary emphasis.

Origen (182-251). Seven shorthand writers were assigned to take down his words; would stop in a sermon and call to prayer.

John Owen (1616-1683). Ready to enter college at 12.

Joseph Parker (1830-1902). Had great Thursday morning meetings; preached through the Bible in seven years.

Norman Vincent Peale (1898-   ). Prefers to be a speaker, not a preacher.

Bishop Quayle (1860-1925). Was a student of the dictionary.

Alan Redpath (1907-   ). Businessman turned preacher at age 30.

Frederick W. Robertson (1816-1853). Died at age 47 of mental illness; memorized all of the New Testament in English and most of it in Greek; got his message subjects from the text.

Samuel Rutherford (1600-1661). Had a great love for Christ but was banished from his pastorate.

Jacques Saurin (1677-1730). Distinguished people reserved places in his church two weeks in advance

Girolamo Savonarola (1452-1498). Failed in first try at preaching and then devoted three years of concentrated study of the Bible before his second try; wanted to be a Christian dictator; had great influence in civil matters.

Samuel Shoemaker (1893-1963). Great midweek services.

Matthew Simpson (1811-1884). Influence on Abraham Lincoln.

Charles H. Spurgeon (1834-1892). Got his message subjects from the text.

T. Dewitt Talmage (1832-1901). Sermons printed in 3,500 newspapers wrote press releases before going abroad to preach.

John Tauler (1300-1361). Great influence on Luther.

Jeremy Taylor (1613-1667). Given a doctorate of philosophy by the king of England.

Tertullian (170-240). Did not become a Christian until age 40.

Thomas a Kempis (1380-1471). Sermons long but powerful.

George W. Truett (1867-1944). Preached to the cowboys; accidentally shot a deacon and nearly never gave up the ministry entirely; wrote letters to the unsaved two mornings each week.

John Wesley (1703-1791). Travelled 250,000 miles on preaching tours; preached more than 40,000 times; averaged fifteen sermons per week.

George Whitefield (1714-1770). Robbed himself of sleep to study the Bible.

Alexander Whyte (1836-1921). After evening services, he would lecture to 400-500 young men.

John Wycliffe (1324-1384). On May 4, 1415 church decreed his books should be burned; twelve years later his body was exhumed and burned.

Ulrich Zwingli (1484-1531). Read widely in the classics; Luther denounced Zwingli because of their differences over the Lord's Supper.

BIOGRAPHICAL
INDEX

Bourdaloue, Louis, 64, 143
Bowie, Walter Russell, 143
Bradford, John, 51, 143
Brainerd, David, 143
Brastow, Lewis O., 86
Bray, William, 143
Breese, Samuel, 143
Brentz, John, 51
Brenz, Johann, 143
Bridaine, Jacques, 143
Broadus, John Albert, 85-86, 86, 87, 92, 119-20, 143
Brock, William, 143
Brokhoff, John R., 122
Brooks, Phillips, 8, 93, 143, 187
Brooks, Thomas, 143
Brown, Charles R., 91, 143
Brown, Hugh S., 143
Brown, J. Baldwin, 143
Brown, John, 143
Browne, Robert, 54
Bruce, Alexander B., 144
Bruce, Robert, 144
Brunner, Emil, 77, 144
Bryan, William Jennings, 74
Bucer, Martin, 144
Bugenhagen, John, 51, 144
Bulkeley, Peter, 144
Bullinger, Johann Heinrich, 50, 52, 144
Bultmann, Rudolf, 77, 144
Bunyan, John, 7, 56, 62, 144
Burchard, Samuel D., 144
Burnet, Gilbert, 144
Burrell, David James, 87
Burton, Nathanael J., 144
Bushnell, Horace, 89, 144
Butler, Joseph, 144
Buttrick, George A., 8
Butzer, Martin, 51

Cadman, Samuel Parkes, 87, 144
Caesarius of Arles, 144
Caird, John, 144
Cairns, John, 144
Calderwood, David, 145
Calvin, John, 6, 43-44, 49-50, 52, 115, 145
Cameron, Richard, 145
Campbell, Alexander, 145
Campbell, George, 59, 118, 132
Campbell, Reginald John, 145
Candlish, R. S., 7, 68, 70, 145
Cant, Andrew, 145
Capella, 127
Caraccioli, Robert, 145
Cardinal Maury, 59
Cargill, Donald Daniel, 145
Carroll, Benajah Harvey, 92, 145

Carson, Alexander, 68, 70, 145
Carstared, William, 145
Carswell, John, 145
Cartwright, Peter, 145
Cartwright, Thomas, 54
Cassiodorus, 127
Cavert, Samuel M., 145
Cazalla, Augustino, 52, 145
Cecil, Richard, 145
Chaderton, Laurence, 145
Chadwick, Samuel, 145
Chalmers, Thomas, 8, 68, 70, 145
Chambers, Oswald, 145, 187-88
Channing, Edward T., 119, 134
Channing, William Ellery, 83, 88, 146
Chapman, John Wilbur, 146, 192
Chapman, Wilbur, 74
Chappell, Clovis Gillham, 9, 146
Charles, Thomas, 146
Charlier, Jean, 51, 146
Charnock, Stephen, 146
Chauncy, Charles, 146
Chillingworth, William, 146
Christopher of Alexandria, 32
Chrysostom, John, 5, 24, 26, 112, 113, 146, 157, 183-84
Cicero, 99, 125, 132
Clarke, Adam, 146
Claude, Jean, 57-58, 63, 146
Clement of Alexandria, 5, 25-26, 146
Clement of Rome, 5, 25, 146
Clifford, John, 67
Clifton, Richard, 146
Clow, William M., 146
Coffin, Henry Sloane, 146
Coke, Thomas, 147
Colet, John, 43, 51, 147
Columba, 32, 147
Connors, Joseph M., 84
Conrad of Waldhausen, 38, 51
Constantine, 20
Conwell, Russell H., 91, 147
Cook, Francis, 93
Cooke, Henry, 147
Cotton, John, 81, 88, 147
Coverdale, Miles, 51, 147
Cox, Leonard, 132
Craddock, Walter, 147
Craig, John, 147
Cranmer, Thomas, 51, 147
Crawford, Dan, 188
Cromwell, Oliver, 54
Crosby, Howard, 147
Cumming, John, 147
Cuyler, Theodore Ledyard, 95, 147
Cyprian, 5, 19, 25, 112, 147

SUBJECT INDEX

Allegory, 24, 36, 115
American preaching, 81-95
  homiletical emphases in, 85-88
American rhetoric, 131-34
Anabaptists, 44, 56
Anglicans, 66
Apostolic period (4 B.C.-A.D. 69), 3-4, 11-16
Arrangement in public speaking, 99, 106-7
Baptists, 56, 82
Biographical illustrations, 179-82
Brownists, 56
Calvinism, 44
Camp meetings, 82-83
Carolingian period, rhetoric in, 128-29
Catholic, *see* Roman Catholic
Central medieval period (1095-1361), 6, 33-40
  homiletical emphases of, 35-38, 114-15
Christianity, in patristic period, 20-21
Church Fathers, 17-21, 112, *see also* patristic period
Classical rhetoric and homiletics, 99-110
Classical rhetoric and homiletical style, 111-23
Congregationalists, 56
Contemporary period (1900-present), homiletical emphases of, 73-77
  homiletics of, 120-22
  preaching of, 8-9, 71-80
Council of Nicea, 19-20
Critical interpretation of Scripture, 76
Crusades, 6, 28
Deism, 83
Delivery in public speaking, 99, 108-10
Diaspora, 18
Early Christianity, 17-19
Early medieval period (430-1095), homiletical emphases of, 30-32, 56-60, 114
  homiletics of, 117-18
  preaching in, 6, 7, 27-32
Early modern period, preaching of, 7, 53-64
Eastern church, 19-20
Ecumenical movement, 67, 72, 76, 83
Epicureans, 18
Evolution, 66, 71
Foreign missions, 67
Fundamentalists, 73, 74, 76
Higher criticism, 72
History of preaching, 3-10
Homiletical emphases, in American preaching, 85-88
  of central medieval period, 35-38
  of contemporary period, 73-77
  of early medieval period, 30-32
  of early modern period, 56-60
  of late modern period, 67-69

of patristic period, 22-25
of reformation, 46-51
of Renaissance, 44-46
Homiletical style, and classical rhetoric, 111-23
Homiletics, 131
  of central medieval period, 114-15
  of contemporary period, 120-22
  defined, 111
  of early medieval period, 114
  of early modern period, 117-18
  of late modern period, 118-20
  of patristic period, 111-13
  of reformatory period, 115-17
  of Renaissance and late medieval period, 115
  of Roman Catholics, 48, 58-59
Homily, 5
Humanism, 42
Idealism, 72
Illustrations in sermons, 179-82
Independents, 56
Indulgences, 35, 43
Invention in public speaking, 99-106
Investiture controversy, 33
Jansenism, 55
Jewish Dispersion, 18
Jewish sermon, 11-12
Kerygma, 15, 23, 30
King James Version, 7, 54
Late modern period (1789-1900), 7-8, 65-70
  homiletics of, 67-69, 118-20
Liberalism, 72, 76
Medieval period, *see* early medieval period and central
  Medieval period
Memory in public speaking, 99, 108, 110
Modern period, *see* early modern period and late modern
  period
Modernists, 73, 74, 76
Moravians, 82
Mystery cults, 19
Neo-orthodoxy, 76
Neo-scholasticism, 117
New Theology, 72
Nicene Creed, 20
Nonconformists, 66, 81
Occasional preaching, 3-4
Patristic period (A.D. 70-430), 4-5, 17-21
  homiletical emphases of, 22-25, 111-13
Pentecostals, 76, 85
Pietism, 55
Pragmatism, 72
Prayer, 14, 106
Preacher, role of, 11

324

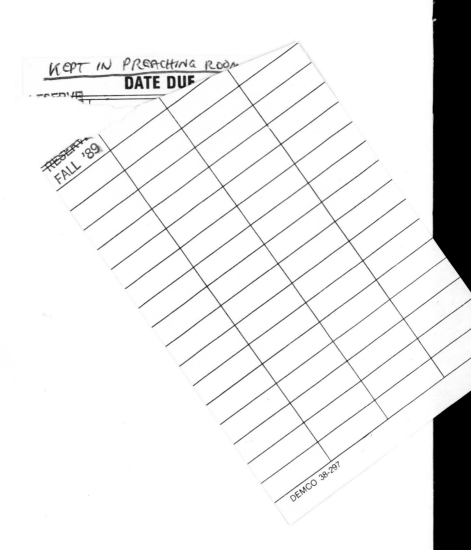